Anatomy of Rebellion

Anatomy of Rebellion

CLAUDE E. WELCH, JR.

State University Press of New York

ALBANY

A grant from the University Awards Program of the State University of New York and the Research Foundation of State University of New York assisted in paying the costs of publishing this book.

Published by
State University of New York Press, Albany

© 1980 State University of New York

For information, address State University of New York
Press, State University Plaza, Albany, N.Y., 12246

Library of Congress Cataloging in Publication Data
Welch, Claude Emerson.
    Anatomy of rebellion.

    Bibliography: p.
    Includes index.
    1. Revolutions--Case studies.   2. Violence--
Case studies.   3. Peasant uprising--Case studies.
I. Title.
HM283.W44   303.6' 2   80-19094
ISBN 0-87395-441-6
ISBN 0-87359-457-2 (pbk.)

Contents

v

Maps

Preface

This book arose from my interest in two forms of collective political violence. One form is the sharp, sudden assumption of power by means of a military coup d'etat. As an instrument of changing government personnel and policies, coups d'etat have far more practitioners than do peaceful alterations effected through the ballot box. The proportion of independent states governed by military juntas has been rising since World War II. I have sought to explain some of the factors in a series of books,[1] in which aspirant colonels come front and center for attention. A chief reason for their intervention, it appears, is domestic group violence. Inadequate means of resolving political issues may lead to frustration and disturbance. The armed forces, called in to suppress public discontent, may seize control, believing themselves better equipped than the incumbents to resolve the salient issues. The study of military intervention in politics thus can lead to examination of political violence as it is mounted against governments, not by the men on horseback, but by the common folk whose smouldering grievances have at last burst into open flame.

The second form of political violence that has drawn my attention is peasant revolution. Rural dwellers — still the vast majority of the populace of the Third World — are usually depicted as politically conservative, tradition-bound individuals, rarely able to unite behind common objectives. Their "amoral familism," in Banfield's phrase,[2] puts inherent limits on peasants' collective action. How, then, can the interested scholar explain the effective organization of widespread violence, supported by rural dwellers, that helped achieve the Chinese or Vietnamese revolutions? I have approached this question in less extensive fashion: partly through brief attention to revolution as a form of political change;[3] partly through an initial exploration of "peasant" warfare in tropical Africa;[4] mostly through teaching at the State University of New York at Buffalo. To the skepticism and interests of Buffalo students, this book owes much. Their interest in "successful" revolutions, however, made apparent a lacuna. The

ix

achievements of some revolutions can be adequately assessed only by examining the obstacles to change. In other words, "success" must be measured against "failure." This concern brought me increasingly to an interest in various "almost-but-not-quite successful" uprisings, whose revolutionary aspirations were far from matched by their achievements.

The confluence of these interests — backing up, as it were, from both military intervention and peasant-based political revolution to rural unrest — brought me to the book in hand. *Anatomy of Rebellion* seeks to illuminate, by a combination of case studies and broader theorizing, the causes and consequences of a certain type of rural uprising. My concern lies with major rebellions of the past 125 years, brought about through a collision of basic values. Some of these changes have been profound. Take, for example, the rural differentiation resulting from the international expansion of capitalism and its concomitant, nineteenth-century imperialism. These brought major changes within Third World societies. "Traditional" ways of life were jarred, indigenous means of decision-making overridden by colonialism. "Modernization" abetted the breakdown of long-standing social ties. Such external forces carried seeds of further transformation with them. Abridgement of existing patterns was certain to arouse protest. Basic values within these societies conflicted with those imposed by the external presence. Reforms often could not be prized out of the authorities by peaceful means. Other means — violent ones — became necessary, and though seemingly inadequate in the short term to bring about reform, succeeded in the long term in bringing basic transformations.

I hope, in this book, to delineate basic features of collective political violence. "Anatomy" means analysis. Just as the physical anatomist works with bodily systems, so the political anatomist works with social systems. In a rough metaphor, one might liken the nervous and muscular systems to communications and coercion within the "body politic." How these systems are linked remains a basic concern of the pages that follow.

Rather than present a single case study, I have chosen (with obvious problems of comparison) four examples. Rather than present each at one time, I have employed a topical division. Analyses of the four rebellions that served as springboards for *Anatomy of Rebellion* have been split among several chapters, these based on different aspects of collective political violence. Admittedly certain values are lost. The holistic nature of a particular uprising may be overshadowed. Some pieces of evidence do not fit well within the schema; others fit all too well, and are repeated perhaps more often than some readers would favor. The framework may suggest an unwarranted degree of conclusiveness. I arrived at the form of presentation after several years' research — but certainly do not consider it the only, or necessarily the best. The selection came from that usual combination inherent in scholarly research: personal interest, informed by general reading and available sources of information. My involvement with Africa south of the Sahara accounts for a great deal of interest. Field work has taken me to tropical Africa on several occasions—though not, regrettably, to Kenya or Zaire. African societies remain predominantly rural, though with an accelerating pace of urbanization. Social and political tensions—some born under colonialism, others resulting from precolonial conflicts, still others the product of post-independence changes— mark them all. The question is whether these tensions can be resolved through peaceful, accepted, institutionalized channels. The multiple coups d'etat in Africa, Chou En-Lai's 1964 suggestion that the continent was "ripe for revolution," the guerrilla struggles of southern Africa, and various civil wars, indicate otherwise. These do not mean, however, that one should foreclose rural rebellion as a major form of collective political violence in Africa. My interest in other parts of the Third World sprang from both desire and need to be comparative. The quest for independence in tropical Africa had been influenced by self-government granted earlier in South and Southeast Asia, and by the guerrilla struggles of China and Vietnam. "Peasant" society characterized much of Asia for a millenium or more and parts of Latin America for centuries; by contrast, the process of "peasantization" south of the Sahara has only recently started. The causes of rural unrest, insofar as they spring from socioeconomic factors, should be examined comparatively. Understanding political phenomena in one continent necessarily required understanding similar phenomena elsewhere.

Some cautions must be noted at this point. The rebels were losers, at least in the short run—and historians rarely are kind to the defeated. Defeat need not preclude reassessment, however. Later political change may seem to justify the original objectives of the uprising; the rebels could in some fashion appear to run ahead of their times. Such reassessment has occurred for two of the four rebellions, accounting in large measure for the profusion of published materials on them. The Taiping rebellion of mid-nineteenth century China may have been the bloodiest civil war of all time, reason enough for attention. Far beyond this, however, Nationalist and Communist historians have drawn—or should one say imposed? —dramatically different conclusions from the uprising. Hundreds of studies in Chinese, plus scores of analyses in other languages, can be consulted by the vigorous scholar. A similar explosion of writings surrounds the Mau Mau rebellion, which rocked the British colony and protectorate of Kenya during the 1950s. The uprising was repressed, seemingly to retain colonial control and the political dominance of a white settler community.

Within months of the termination of the State of Emergency, however, the British withdrew, and murmured no protest when the purported leader of the rebellion was installed as prime minister. Writings on Mau Mau poured forth, during the uprising to justify its suppression, after its crushing to justify its aims. Discerning truth in this welter of material is complex, to say the least. Truth may be even harder to find in those rebellions not yet subject to at least two points of view. The Telengana rebellion, brought to an end by "police action" of the government of India in 1951, has been touted as a Communist-inspired uprising; most of the few studies have been carried out within a Marxist framework not aptly suited to all facets of the problem. Owing to later language agitation in Telengana and incorporation into India, research on the uprising became more difficult. Thus, the documentation available for this rebellion, as for the Kwilu rebellion in Zaire, is but a small fraction of that available for the Taiping and Mau Mau uprisings. The Kwilu rebellion, finally, was directed against a government still in power as this book was being written. The sympathies of the government of Zaire can be discerned from the immediate execution of the uprising's leader, after his return on the basis of a promised amnesty, in 1968.

The four rebellions metaphorically dissected in this book were not "ordinary" uprisings, whatever that adjective may mean. They occurred in societies increasingly touched by "modernization," by the collision of basic values. Multiple sources of discontent existed, tapped by leaders who mixed important ideas of transformation with indigenous ideas of restoration. Motives were mixed, the participants encouraged by a series of factors. The scale of the uprisings was large: perhaps one million Kikuyu gave their acquiescence to Mau Mau; the Telengana rebels controlled 3,000 villages, and the Kwilu rebels an area the size of Belgium; the Taiping armies at their height held sway over more than 100,000,000 people. These were not, in other words, actions by small numbers alone; the uprisings drew on popular wellsprings of frustration. In intention, if not necessarily in execution, the leaders sought certain "modern" objectives. In some respects, accordingly, they aspired to be revolutionary.

Preparation of a book of this scope involved research in many settings. It also required time, unencumbered by the press of other duties. Both the National Endowment for the Humanities and the State University of New York have aided these inquiries, the NEH through a summer research fellowship, SUNY through sabbatical leave. At the risk of anachronism, I used Wade-Giles rather than Pinyin transliteration for Chinese names and terms. My colleagues and students at Buffalo helpfully commented on earlier drafts; I am particularly grateful to Roger Des Forges for his combination of detailed knowledge of China with a general concern for rural rebellion. Those who supported this book financially and who commented critically on various drafts bear, of course, no responsibility for the interpretations that follow. I wish to express special thanks to Anthony Clayton (Royal Military Academy Sandhurst), Thomas Kanza (University of Massachusetts, Boston), Ramon Myers (Stanford University), Elizabeth Perry (University of Washington), Carl G. Rosberg Jr. (University of California, Berkeley), Majjid Siddiqi (Jawaharlal Nehru University, Delhi), Russell Stone (SUNY/Buffalo) and Theodore P. Wright, Jr. (SUNY/Albany), for their observations on my presentation of the complex events recounted below. My appreciation is also great to the Warden and Fellows of St. Antony's college who provided the scholarly milieu where the first draft of this manuscript was written, and to Maureen Stone, Jackie Adamczak, Wilma Pylipow and Phyllis Veitch, who aptly deciphered the scrawls and squiggles I thrust before them. The University of Washington Press gave permission to use a base map with which to depict Taiping military operations.

The last words in this preface belong to my wife Nancy. With her practical mind, she viewed the book as an elaborate pattern woven on the academic loom. The four rebellions provided the warp, the integrative analysis the woof. Those primarily interested in the events of particular uprisings may choose to pursue them uninterruptedly through the book, selecting in each chapter the relevant sections. Those more attracted by comparative analysis may prefer to concentrate on the general remarks that open and conclude each chapter. Naturally, I hope those who peruse the book as a whole find the threads of argument both continuous and connected, as Nancy continually urged me as the first draft took shape. I only wish that she had lived to see the publication of this book, having watched its inception and gestation. To her memory, this book is lovingly dedicated.

Claude E. Welch, Jr.

PART I

THE SETTING
FOR REBELLION

This book focuses on a form of collective political violence. Rebellion seems to testify to the inability of members of a political system to resolve issues peacefully. Directed against those wielding the levers of controls, or against agents of a resented economic or social order, rebellion shows something is not well in the state. Like revolution, it suggests shortcomings in the conduct of political affairs, often intensified by economic pressures or cultural conflicts.

What problems have prompted rebellion? Collective violence has erupted in societies characterized by severely limited opportunities for indigenous political participation. Rebellion often appeared under conditions of sharp ethnic pluralism and exacerbated economic exploitation, where dominant groups resisted reform that would have undercut their preeminence. Where governmental support has been vitiated by corruption, external pressures, or group rivalries, discontent has risen, and has been sparked into violence through inept attempts to repress rather than to resolve. In short, a host of factors lie behind collective political violence. To any single major cause, subsidiary causes and contributing conditions must be added.

Rebellion has traditionally been associated with the discontents of rural dwellers. It is a phenomenon historically far more common than revolution. The presumptively ephemeral results of rebellion, unlike the presumably lasting consequences of revolution, have resulted in far less scholarly attention. The great social revolutions—for example, France, Russia and China—have been recounted, dissected, combed for clues about causes and consequences thousands of times. But major rebellions, four of which are examined in this book, have received scant attention from students of comparative history.

Is there a ready way to explain this seeming lacuna?

The causes of rebellion may appear to lie in the past, in conditions disappearing under the impact of greater global interdependence. What characterized rural settings in earlier periods may hold limited interest for students of the present. I disagree with this assertion. *Anatomy of Rebellion* is based on the premise that rebellion, as a type of collective political violence, remains far from anachronistic. The conditions of the past carry over into the present. Intensified discontent may find few avenues for redress. A turn to violence provides perhaps the sole avenue for change open to a politically and economically weak, yet numerically strong, rural populace.

Transformations wrought by infringements on land, livelihood and local prerogatives have for centuries given birth to agrarian revolts. Few have dramatically improved the conditions that brought their birth. Rebels appear to have lacked extensive political awareness. In reflecting rural grievances, they seemed bound by them, unable to transcend the parochial conditions that sparked collective political violence. Immediate conditions may be rectified; but long-term causes remain unaffected. If there is an orthodoxy in the study of rural uprisings, it is that most rebels are "primitive," unable without assistance from others to challenge the powerholders effectively. As Marx scathingly expressed in *The Eighteenth Brumaire*, peasants standing on their own remain politically impotent in the face of worsening conditions.

Suffusing through this book is, I believe, a greater sensitivity to, and sympathy towards, rural dwellers than Marx and many distinguished contemporary writers have expressed. Rebels not only reflect oppression of the past; they also point the way to future rectification. Collective political violence can contribute to subsequent reform, revolution, or even renewed rebellion; attempts at reordering, though possibly narrow, help set an agenda for later implementation. The political culture of societies marked by rebellion differs from that of societies in which peaceful change has occurred. The consequences are burned deep; historic events influence contemporary politics. Analyzing the past provides an avenue for understanding the present. And, since the "Third World" is overwhelmingly composed of agrarian societies, understanding perhaps the most potent source of domestic political disorder merits close study, not contemptuous dismissal.

Part I of this book explores the setting for rebellion. What conditions prompted, and continue to prompt, the transformation of personal concerns into group awareness and thence into collective political violence? We shall start with brief overviews of four major rebellions: The Taiping rebellion in China, covering roughly the 1850–1864 period; the Telengana uprising in Central India, from 1946 to 1951; the Mau Mau rebellion in Kenya, most active in the 1952–1956 period; and the Kwilu uprising in

Zaire, part of the "Second Independence" political violence that rocked the country between 1963 and 1965. Chapter 1 surveys as well certain background factors that influenced the outbreak of rebellion. Specifically, conditions of geographic marginality, liability to natural disaster compounded by government inefficiencies, and oppressive tenancy exacerbated by collapse of an earlier "subsistence ethic" affect who takes up arms. Chapter 2 examines bases on which indigenous persons are organized for collective political violence; Chapter 3 focuses on the political elite and the strategies they employ to maintain themselves in power and derive further profit from rural sources. All contributed to conditions under which rebellion became possible — though remained far from inevitable. The factors discussed in Part I should accordingly be viewed as long-term causes, as necesary preconditions rather than immediate precipitants.

In Part II, the pace quickens. Specific events such as war intensify the squeeze put on rural dwellers. A quickened sense of relative deprivation, examined in Chapter 4, helps politicize various group and individual grievances. Use of force by the political elite abetted this crystallization. Chapter 5 chronicles the escalation of violence in the four rebellions, in which indigenous resistance to severe economic pressures prompted coercion by the incumbents, and consequent efforts at protection by the (by now) rebels. Leadership, organization and ideology form the basis for Chapters 6 and 7: coordinated resistance required a sense of purpose and a means of translating shared resentment into rectification.

Part III brings the story to the present. Chapter 8 is devoted to the suppression of the four rebellions; accordingly, its focus is the incumbents' actions, and, in particular, the mixes they utilized of repression and pacification. That echoes of the uprisings continue to reverberate forms the underlying message of the concluding chapter. The grievances manifested in rebellions of the scale shown in this book cannot be readily resolved, short of profound societal transformation. Yet, inasmuch as the pressures that prompted collective political violence continue to characterize much of the contemporary world, the ultimate message of this book is that rural violence should not be relegated to the dustbin of history, Rebellion bids fair to be as salient a feature of the twenty-first century as it has of preceding centuries.

CHAPTER 1 /

The Four Rebellions and
Their Physical Settings

The subject matter for this book comes from four large-scale uprisings, separated in space and time, yet apparently based on similar political, economic and social issues. The men and women who participated, often at great personal risk, may have had few alternatives to rebellion. That they were caught up in a cycle of collective political violence reflected unavoidable facts. Rebellion became the recourse of persons caught in intensifying assaults on their ways of life. A heritage of rural violence and denied opportunities for mobility affected the perceptions of the participants. Actors thus in dramas whose denouements they could not readily envisage, they emerged, briefly and tragically, on the stage of history. In many respects, they failed. The collective political violence in which they were involved sprang from causes greater than individuals, with results that (certainly in the short term) brought the protagonists little benefit. Why did they take arms against their troubles? Were there alternatives to rebellion? Under what conditions might collective political violence have brought results other than the seeming failures chronicled in succeeding pages?

To answer these far-ranging questions, we might best, as E. M. Forster suggested, begin at the beginning. Each rebellion coupled idiosyncratic elements with factors widespread in the particular culture, and with aspects seemingly characteristic of major rebellions irrespective of locale or era. Distinguishing among the unique, the culturally specific, and the universal requires facts. Hence, our immediate task is one of description. The four uprisings must first be reviewed, in order to be analyzed.

The Taiping Rebellion—China, 1850–1864

China may have witnessed more rural uprisings than the rest of the world combined. As Chesneaux wrote, "no country has a richer and more continuous tradition of peasant rebellion than China."[1] The fertile, irrigated plains were densely inhabited, their residents liable both to landlord and government extortions, and to the vagaries of flood and famine. Mountain fastnesses and border regions harbored bandit gangs, whose ranks swelled with the displaced and landless at times of social disaster. The coercive and regulative capabilities of the government followed a slow rhythm of waxing and waning. In the ascendancy, peace and prosperity—or, more accurately for the overwhelming majority of the populace, sufficient margin for existence—marked imperial Chinese society. In the decline, disorders became increasingly widespread. Government exactions bore more heavily on a populace less able to pay, as a consequence of local uprisings, crop failures compounded by official blunders, corruption, and the like. Landlord exactions increased as those in Peking lost their ability to regulate local matters. The number and extent of rural uprisings thus followed closely the graph of government administrative capacity. At the nadir of the cycle, the revolts became sufficiently widespread as to help effect a change of ruling houses. This, in brief outline, was the "dynastic cycle," a means of periodizing Chinese history. Successful rebels could claim the "Mandate of Heaven, " and create anew the existing value system. Chesneaux asserted, in an opinion shared by most historians, "Peasant revolts, far from threatening the principle of established order, are finally accepted as functional, as capable of restoring order in troubled times. They acted as safety valves, able to restore to the world the benefits of the Heavenly Mandate."[2]

The Taiping Rebellion bore many similarities to classic Chinese peasant uprisings. Its followers were drawn largely from the dispossessed and socially marginal. The seed of rebellion sprouted and was initially nurtured in an area distant from central government control. Elements of millenarianism were incorporated into the group's appeals. Disappointed or alienated scholars played key roles in the leadership of the rebellion. But these resemblances must be compared with some striking contrasts. It was neither Buddhism or Taoism that furnished religious themes for the Taiping rebels, but an idiosyncratic version of Christianity. The scale of the rebellion dwarfed other rural uprisings historians have examined: the Taiping armies numbered a half-million or more, while the extirpation of the rebels cost no less than twenty million lives. Although slogans for land equalization and heavenly peace had appeared in other uprisings, the Taiping rebels carried out a more thorough-going organization of peasants than had their predecessors, and gave particular attention to the rights of women. Finally, the Taiping rebels seemed to embody a strong racialistic consciousness against the Manchu governors of China.

The humble origins of the Taiping rebellion came in the "God-Worshippers' Society," created in 1846-7 in a remote part of Kwangsi Province.

Kwangsi lay near the southernmost bounds of the Chinese empire. The once tributary society of Vietnam had achieved autonomy under the Ly dynasty early in the eleventh century; lying to the south, Vietnam marked a penumbral zone of Chinese cultural influence. Kwangsi and its neighbor Kwangtung were separated from the Yangtse valley by mountain ranges. Cantonese was the major dialect spoken through the two provinces, although officials and literati could communicate in writing and orally through Mandarin. Boat traffic threaded through the Pearl and West rivers, providing fairly efficient communications in the major irrigated areas; communications outside the two provinces, by contrast, were far more difficult.

Northern Chinese farmers had moved into Kwangsi and Kwangtung in a slow, steady process. Many of them were Hakka or "guest families." Having left the North China plain in several waves, especially in the thirteenth and fourteenth centuries, they retained several features distinguishing them from both the aboriginal residents of South China and other Han. For example, the Hakka spoke a distinct dialect. Foot-binding was not practiced; as a corollary, women were less restricted in their activities. Family loyalty, always strong in the Chinese tradition, was particularly marked among the Hakka. They were further perceived (especially by twentieth century Hakka scholars!) as ambitious and progressive, coupling their longstanding family and group solidarity with the ability to adapt to changed circumstances.

The chief opponents of the Hakka were the Punti, or "original settlers." It was they who furnished land to the Hakka, and witnessed Hakka farmers achieving greater yields. Punti and Hakka found themselves locked in land disputes. Added to the ethnic complexity were the various non-Han ("tribal") people, who "had a latent hostility against the Chinese officials and farmers who had taken land and imposed taxes."[3] As Michael notes, "The rebellion's geographical starting point in the southeast can be explained by the complicated ethnic and social conditions of that area, which sharpened any local conflict."[4]

The local conflicts were paralleled by major tensions resulting from the "opening up" of China. Southern China in the early nineteenth century experienced the disruptive effects of the West far earlier and more intensely than other parts of the Empire. Proximity to the port of Canton made possible the birth of the Taiping rebellion—for it was through Canton that alien ideas and trade surged, disrupting the social balance. Canton was the major entrepot for opium, imported from India. Some 3,210 chests were imported in 1816. The trade grew rapidly, reaching 16,500 chests in 1831 and 40,000 chests in 1840.[5] Imperial edicts notwithstanding, hundreds of thousands of *taels* of silver were spent on opium. It was the peasant who suffered most. Domestic deflation resulted in significant increases in rents without consequent hikes in farmers' revenues. The exchange rate between copper (the specie of most peasant transactions) and silver (the specie in which rents were figured) changed from a 2:1 to 3:1 ratio—in other words, effectively boosting rents 50 percent. A concurrent series of poor harvests over a 20-year period impoverished sections of southern China.

These economic consequences were not unnoticed in Peking. The Ch'ing government objected to the opium trade on financial and moral grounds. Its efforts to halt addiction (as in, for example, prescribing the death penalty for opium users) eventually brought a head-on collision with British interests. The first Opium War (1838-42) was the direct consequence. It seriously disrupted Canton and its immediate hinterland. The victorious British imposed an indemnity and forced the imperial government to accept a mounting tide of opium imports. Scores of boatmen were displaced from their jobs, adding to and intensifying the employment problem that existed prior to the war.

But perhaps the chief consequence of the British triumph was the rise of various local militia and village self-defense units, necessary to control the "bandits" who (according to an 1849 memorial to the emperor) controlled up to 70 per cent of Kwangsi.[6] Militarization of the countryside became a self-perpetuating process. The displacement of various groups and the growth of opium trade encouraged the formation of armed groups, who secreted themselves in mountainous areas and became robbers. The Ch'ing government had not only lost face; it had been shown militarily incapable of resisting alien intrusion. Military inability having thus been demonstrated, and the social fabric considerably disrupted, the growth of violence came as a matter of course. By the late 1840's five major bands roved along the Kwangtung-Hunan border;[7] more than thirty armed groups can be identified.[8] One mid-nineteenth century English observer attributed the Taiping rebellion to the disruptions brought by the Opium Wars:

> Whatever may the final result of the internal troubles which now afflict China, they are, in no small degree, the consequences of that disgrace and defeat which the proud and boastful government of the country sustained in the war with Great Britain....The change was felt in many parts of the country. The people began to oppose the payments of their former exactions, insurrections arose in various quarters, and bands of robbers, always a source of trouble, now began to defy the government....all which arises from that class [i.e. robber and criminal associations] having detected the inefficiency of the imperial troops during the war with the England barbarians. Formerly they feared the troops as tigers; of late they look on them as sheep. Of the multitudes of irregulars who were disbanded on the settlement of the barbarian difficulty, very few returned to their original occupations—most of them became robbers.[9]

Protection against marauders had to come from local resources. Given the ineffectiveness of government troops, village leaders took the initiative in creating *t'uan-lien* companies. Their creation had a decisive effect: as will be elaborated in Chapter 5, these units could not be controlled effectively by the central government—nor, possibly, by anything else. Once the *t'uan-lien* had been created, they had to be maintained, lest they further threaten the social order. Wakeman offers this comment:

> By uprooting the locally unemployed, the militia bureaus thus helped create a group of landless, well-trained and armed *condottieri*, who had to be kept under gentry control. Therefore, when the war ended the militia may have been "officially" disbanded, but probably even more soldiers of fortune were put on *t'uan-lien* payrolls—if only to prevent them from becoming outlaws. In short, once professionals were involved, the militia system became self-perpetuating, since disbandment meant the instant creation of paramilitary gangs of rowdies.[10]

The God-Worshippers' Society sought not only to protect its adherents; under the prodding of its initiators, the Society moved to the offensive, its objective the violent overturn of the Ch'ing dynasty.

By all criteria, the Taiping rebellion was the greatest of the four chronicled in this book. In duration, the uprising spanned fifteen years. Its leader Hung Hsiu-ch'üan was crowned "Heavenly King" 11 January, 1851; his capital at Nanking was recaptured by Ch'ing dynasty troops 19 July, 1864 (seven weeks after Hung's death), and the last Taipings surrendered 9 February, 1866. In geographic scope, as shown on Map 1, the rebellion covered eleven provinces south of the Yangtse, while a series of expeditions took control for varying periods over Kiangsi, Anhwei, Hupeh, and others. In numbers affected, more than 100 million Chinese fell under the sway of the Taipings, whose armies early in 1853 numbered about 500,000. In terms of ideology, Hung elaborated a pastiche of Confucian, Christian and other ideas often radical in the existing context.[11] For example, local officials were supposedly to be elected by the people, or else the most qualified local leaders appointed. Attendance at public worship was proclaimed obligatory. Women and men alike would receive equal shares of land. Concubinage and footbinding were abolished. The Ten Commandments, retitled "Heavenly Rules" (*T'ien-t'ao*), became (according to Jen) "the very foundation of Taiping morality."[12] Some of these reforms remained on paper, others were withdrawn or modified as Taiping ardor cooled and imperial pressure increased, still others led to profound discontent and were to weaken the rebels' support. Nonetheless, these constituted dramatic alterations. The Taiping appealed as well to substantial antipathy to the Ch'ing dynasty, whose rule had become increasingly ineffi-

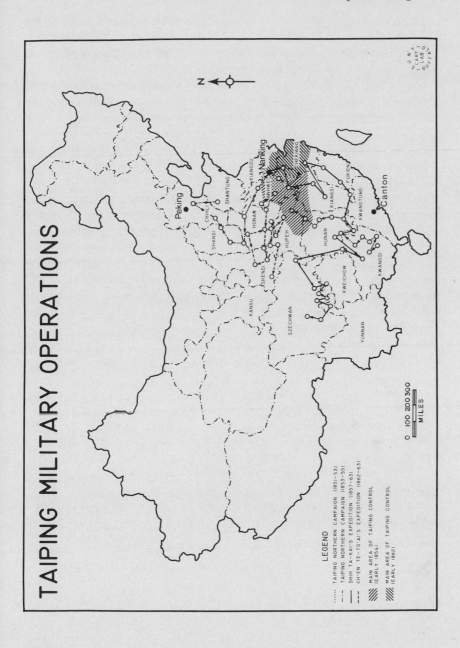

TAIPING MILITARY OPERATIONS

LEGEND

.... TAIPING NORTHERN CAMPAIGN (1851–53)

-·-·- TAIPING NORTHERN CAMPAIGN (1853–55)

——— SHIH TA–KAI'S EXPEDITION (1857–63)

——— CH'EN TE–TS'AI'S EXPEDITION (1862–63)

▨ MAIN AREA OF TAIPING CONTROL (EARLY 1854)

▨ MAIN AREA OF TAIPING CONTROL (EARLY 1862)

0 100 200 300
MILES

Peking · Nanking · Canton

CHIHLI · SHANTUNG · SHANSI · KIANGSU · HONAN · ANHWEI · CHEKIANG · FUKIEN · KIANGSI · KWANGTUNG · HUPEH · HUNAN · SHENSI · KANSU · SZECHWAN · KWEICHOW · KWANGSI · YUNNAN cient and corrupt. A spirit of Chinese solidarity against the Manchu overlords played some part in the movement. Thus sparked by a complex combination of economic, political and social factors, the uprising drew on a wide variety of grievances and aspirations.

Why, then, was the rebellion eventually contained? Taiping leaders committed major strategic errors. Hung and his followers failed to seize the key political prize, the imperial capital of Peking. Taiping forces were divided in 1853 into three groups. One expeditionary force headed west, along the Yangtse valley; a second marched north toward Peking; the remaining troops besieged targets in the central area, around Nanking. The key northern expeditionary force, with about 70,000-80,000 troops,[13] was soon stalled, then forced to retreat. Manchu defensive measures began to bear fruit. Taiping loss of mobility reduced its followers' fervor. Quality of leadership declined, with internal weakening of the insurgents parallel- ed by more effective mobilization of the incumbents. Taiping ideology was too alien, millenarian and racialistic to fit prevailing circumstances. The balance of forces thus shifted toward the imperial government. Drawing to some extent on foreign assistance, the dynasty staved off the Taiping challenge to its own increasingly-numbered days. The Ch'ing rulers rallied both elite and rural sectors, following internal reorganization. The tide gradually turned; the rebels were encircled, confined, and crushed by 1864.

The Telengana Rebellion—India, 1946-51

With a population larger than that of the Americas combined, India counts more peasants than any country save the People's Republic of China. An estimated 80 per cent of India's 600 + million inhabitants dwell in approximately 550,000 villages. India is thus a heavily rural country, and has been for millenia.

Rural uprisings in India have received little attention. This is the result in part of a belief that such a segmented society was practically immune to large-scale, coordinated rural rebellion. The longstanding view of Indian peasants emphasizes their passivity and acquiescence, not their extensive militant involvement. Hinduism and the ubiquitous consequences of caste are often suggested as causes of apparent peasant apathy in the face of dif- ficult living conditions. Take, for example, the following judgment of Bar- rington Moore: "peasant rebellions [in India] in the premodern period were relatively rare and completely ineffective....A highly segmented society that depends on diffuse sanctions for extracting the surplus from the underlying peasantry is nearly immune to peasant rebellion because opposition is likely to take the form of creating another segment."[14]

How accurate is this view? Compared with China, India stands well behind in terms of rural political violence—but it has a far from peaceful history. According to Gough, at least seventy-seven revolts, each involving several thousand peasants, have erupted in India in the past 200 years.[15] None of the Indian uprisings was as dramatic, as violent, as wide-ranging, or as protracted as the Taiping rebellion—but the Taiping rebellion was the most costly civil war in human history. The fact remains that Indian peasants have not been totally passive in the face of perceived oppression.

A survey of rural uprisings in India would stretch this chapter unduly—but owing to their unfamiliarity to most readers, a few words are in order. The greatest revolt was the misnamed "Mutiny" of 1857-8, in fact a series of uprisings that temporarily wrested a half-million square miles from British control. Most rebellions were short in duration. The longest-lasting, in addition to the "Mutiny," was the 1921 Moplah uprising, which lasted six months and probably affected more than one million people.[16] The largest peasant "army," perhaps numbering between 30,000 and 50,000, was raised by the Santhals, an ethnic minority straddling the Bihar-West Bengal border. Not unexpectedly, the region of the heaviest and earliest British impact, namely Bengal, experienced a disproportionate share (nineteen of the seventy-seven revolts listed by Gough) of rural political violence.[17] Bengal suffered from exceptionally high population densities, and was characterized by socioeconomic relationships Zagoria has suggested encouraged radical approaches to change.[18] Nearly one-third of the rural uprisings, however, erupted in geographically marginal areas inhabited by "tribal" peoples. The pattern of rebellion, accordingly, seemed shaped primarily by a combination of high tenancy rates, ethnic diversity and backwardness and/or proximity to centers of British economic and political power.

On the basis of these factors, one would not have expected a major uprising in the Telengana region of Hyderabad state. Population density there was low, certainly by the standards of Bengal, although exhausted soils meant nearly half the garden farms were "sub-basic."[19] The Telengana region was removed from urban centers, and poorly served by communications—as, indeed, was Hyderabad as a whole. (The three central districts of the state had paved roads totalling only 291, 296 and 436 miles.)[20] Daily wages in Hyderabad were lower than any other part of India save Orissa and Madya Pradesh.[21] Telengana lacked a tradition of revolt that could be built upon. In fact, cultivators from the region were reputed to be apathetic and inebriated.[22] On the other hand, a growing cash economy in Telengana, as elsewhere, exacerbated conflict between landlords and tenants, especially between the World Wars. Growing rural indebtedness, falling per capita agricultural yields, and land fragmentation were discerned in various pre-insurrection surveys.[23] But the relevant statistics gave no hint of conditions markedly worse than in other parts of the Indian subcontinent.

Telengana was a political backwater in a state also far removed from the political agitation. Direct British colonial rule did not exist in Hyderabad. It was a "princely state," whose Muslim ruler (Nizam) suffered few restraints from the British in his internal governance. Little encouragement was given politics. Major political organizations developed in twentieth century India, such as Congress and the Muslim League, essentially bypassed Hyderabad. What popular awareness of politics existed came largely through the Andhra Mahasabha, a group fostering cultural awareness among Telugu speakers.

Despite its relative backwardness, the Telengana area was neither apolitical nor isolated from the tensions of Indian partition and independence. The ferment immediately following World War II transformed a situation of latent political, economic and communal conflict into an open confrontation: the political elite (largely Muslim) and large landlords (both Hindu and Muslim) versus Hindu sharecroppers and middle peasants. Events outside Hyderabad interacted with local strains; the result was a rural uprising ended only by the intervention of Indian troops, the forcible displacement of Muslim rulers, and the promise of significant land reforms. The successes the rebels gained thus resulted from military force mounted outside the state, in response to pressures from a restive rural populace.

The rebellion itself erupted in a context of swelling popular political awareness. World War II greatly weakened the power of the British *raj* throughout India. A crescendo of nationalist sentiment confronted the imperial overlords; concern increased, as full self-government approached, for the future of religious communities. Muslim concern had been marshalled and focused through the Muslim League, agitating for division of the subcontinent along religious lines. The Indian National Congress (usually referred to simply as Congress) pressed with equal fervor for independence in a secular, but obviously Hindu-dominated, state. Rising communal violence forced the British administration both to hasten political devolution and to accede to pressures for the creation of Pakistan. Freedom, accompanied by a bloody movement of people between the new states, came to India and Pakistan at midnight, 14-15 August, 1947.

This speedy partition and grant of independence, coming immediately after the War, heightened political and communal awareness even in remote areas. Hindu-Muslim animosities were aroused, as each group sought to entrench itself in areas of control. For the inhabitants of Hyderabad state, communal conflict (though far from as intense as in

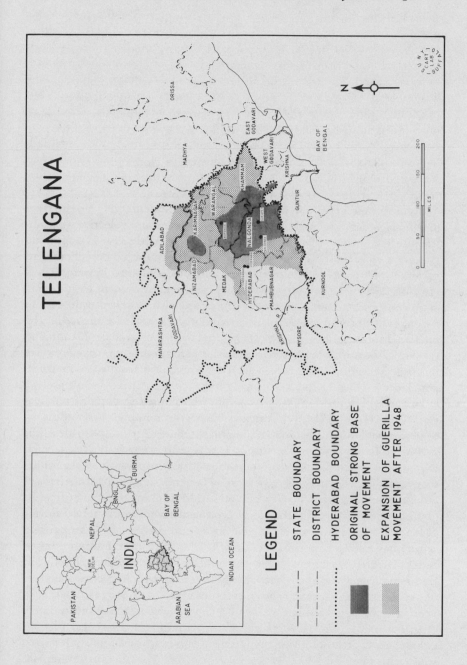

TELENGANA

LEGEND

— · — · — STATE BOUNDARY

— — — — DISTRICT BOUNDARY

· · · · · · · · HYDERABAD BOUNDARY

ORIGINAL STRONG BASE
OF MOVEMENT

EXPANSION OF GUERILLA
MOVEMENT AFTER 1948

Bengal or the Punjab) remained a clear possibility. The Nizam, as noted previously, was a Muslim ruler, Islamic dominance having been established 600 years earlier; the state administration was staffed almost exclusively by Muslims, with Urdu the official language; many major landowners held fiefs (jagirdars), granted by the Nizam to his primarily Muslim followers. The interest of this group lay in separate independence (the goal announced in June 1947 by the Nizam under pressure from militant Muslims) or in affiliation with Pakistan, not in incorporation into India. But such concerns could not touch the economic conflict that racked rural districts. Rural dwellers would have gained no advantage from either separate independence or affiliation with Pakistan, since both arrangements left intact the structure of Muslim and landlord dominance.

Transcending religion and language were economic grievances pitting tenants against landlords. In a seeming paradox, collective political violence was initiated by reforms that satisfied neither the rural elite nor their impoverished sharecroppers. Legislative acts to protect tenants' rights led many landlords to increase their exactions dramatically during and after World War II, and to reduce the informal patron-client ties that had eased the inescapable inequalities of the setting. The ferment of Indian independence and the exacerbation of communal conflict enhanced rural economic tensions. In turn, the strongarm tactics of razakars (Muslim irregular soldiers who combatted Hindu sharecroppers to maintain patterns of local power) escalated violence. The razakars' offensive, in its inept, crude way, fanned further resentment and popular resistance. In a cycle of increased mobilization, some parts of Hyderabad slipped away from central control. In several Telengana districts, notably Nalgonda and Warangal, the populace took affairs into their own hands. The rule of the Nizam, and the power of his supporters, evaporated. Large landowners were expropriated and their properties redistributed. Many of the abuses supposedly ended by new laws were in fact terminated by spontaneous acts of peasants driven to collective political violence.

What the destitute tenants of Nalgonda district had initiated in late 1946 followed paths in 1948 far from the minds of the original participants. Two new actors entered the scene. The Communist party of India declared its support for the rebellion in February, hoping to transform Telengana into a base area from which the bourgeois rulers of India could be overturned. The government of India became concerned about the spillover of violence from Hyderabad and the princely state's unsettled legal status. Hyderabad became, briefly, a focal point of Indian politics. In September 1948, the Nizam was ousted by Indian troops in a swift, efficient operation. Many razakars fled; many others were killed. Peace gradually returned to rural areas as steps toward land reform seemed to satisfy the economic needs of many peasants. The Communists officially abandoned their struggle in late 1951; the Telengana rebellion had proved insufficient basis for the rural revolution they had hoped to carry forward. Far from being a launching pad for an India-wide transformation, the uprising had been contained militarily and defused by economic and political reforms that only marginally improved the lot of the landless.

The Mau Mau Rebellion—Kenya, 1952-1956

The Mau Mau uprising sought by violent means two objectives denied by alien settlement and colonial rule: land and freedom. Choice agricultural lands in Kenya had been garnered by European immigrants; Africans were restricted to increasingly crowded reserves. Political control rested in the hands of British administrators, with the white settlers vigorously demanding a major share; Africans were consigned to a subordinate, local political role. Indigenous pressures for constitutional reform brought scant results. Collective political violence was the means attempted by the numerically-strong but militarily-weak African populace of Kenya. This effort was mounted and conducted almost exclusively by members of a single ethnic group, the Kikuyu. The uprising was confined, as had been the Telengana rebellion, to those defined by ascriptive characteristics.

But far from being an anachronistic return to the past, Mau Mau sought a more rapid move to the future than the British government had been willing to grant. Its partisans attempted to bring military pressure to hasten independence. In these respects, Mau Mau can be perceived as a forward-looking movement. The methods employed by its leaders, however, smacked of the past. Social solidarity behind the rebellion was ensured by oaths, powerful in a "tribal" context, supposedly out of place in a "modern" movement. Oathing ceremonies absorbed the attention of critics, who saw in them an atavistic reversion, rather than a tactical precaution.

To understand Mau Mau, one must grasp the central importance of land. The Kikuyu occupied some of the finest agricultural terrain in tropical Africa. In the eyes of some late nineteenth century European explorers, Kikuyuland was a vast garden. Its fertile red soil, temperate climate and abundant rains were not unique in Kenya; these also characterized the densely-inhabited areas of Nyanza District, adjoining what was known in colonial days as Lake Victoria. What was distinctive about Kikuyuland was its elevation, above the reach of tsetse fly and anopheles mosquito. Free thus from the threats of sleeping sickness and malaria, the so-called highlands provided a base for potential European settlement. This potential, needless to say, did not escape the notice of British administrators. They had arrived as a result of the imperial rivalries with which the nineteenth century was riddled. Her Majesty's Government, privately concerned lest the Nile headwaters be seized by an unfriendly power, and publicly concerned lest Anglican missionaries suffer further indignities at the court of the Kabaka of Buganda, annexed Kenya (then called the East African Protectorate) in 1895. Soon a railway snaked its way inland, covering the 568 miles from the Indian Ocean to Lake Victoria. Midway along its route stood the highlands and the Rift Valley, superlative areas for agriculture and grazing. To provide cargo for the railroad and to move toward economic self-sufficiency for the Protectorate, British administrators encouraged European settlement. This came at the obvious expense of African tribes, the Kikuyu among them.

Kikuyu spokesmen continually underscored their land grievances. Believing themselves unduly and unjustly deprived, they took every occasion to present these concerns to the administration. Yet insofar as the historical record has been opened for scrutiny, there appear to have been only limited attempts, and even less success, in rallying other ethnic groups behind the land issue. Some tribes had been expelled to make way for European settlement, with acreage in excess of Kikuyu losses taken away. The heaviest losers had been the Masai and Nandi. Both pastoral groups, they were removed from hundreds of square miles of prime grazing lands in the Rift Valley and the Mau Plateau, despite a guarantee to the Masai "enduring as long as the Masai as a race shall exist." Neither group protested strongly. Ignoring the European presence, the Masai and Nandi retained a nomadic way of life minimizing contact with settlers.

For the Kikuyu, withdrawal from the European presence was impossible. Their geographic centrality maximized the settler impact. Between 1903 and 1906, approximately 60,000 acres were alienated, with approximately 8,000 Kikuyu receiving payment (derisively low) of Rs.3848[24] (at the prevailing rate of exchange, approximately $513). Pressure was also exerted against "squatters," Kikuyu who continued to cultivate their *shambas* on lands claimed by Europeans. By mid-1910, some 11,647 Kikuyu were cultivating approximately 11,300 acres of settler-controlled terrain.[25] European agriculture rested on African labor. Settlers could prosper only with an abundance of cheap labor and with restrictions on African cultivation of cash crops. The colonial impact on the Kikuyu was accordingly intense, due to their placement adjacent to "white man's country," their involvement as "squatters" and laborers, and their growing resentment of a colonial administration that gave little heed to their economic, social and political grievances. An adaptable social structure encouraged Kikuyu, unlike their pastoral colleagues, to adopt selected aspects of European

civilization. The combination of an intrusive alien presence with individual mobility resulted in widespread feelings of relative deprivation,
described in the chapters that follow. Grievances became focused on land.
Since claims for rectification of what the settlers had grabbed were, in effect, claims against the entire superstructure of colonial rule, they could
not be granted by the imperial power until it was ready to concede African
self-government.

In traditional Kikuyu society, landlessness was unknown. Each *mbari*
(sub-clan or lineage) held land for its members, with individual cultivation
permitted, and with migration to new lands sustaining the young and ambitious. Many Kikuyu, however, did not farm within their own *mbari*
lands, but squatted elsewhere. Their status—*ahoi*—was recognized. As
long as the frontier, as it were, was not closed, the *ahoi* had recourse.

The delineation of reserves on which many Kikuyu were forced to live
and the intensification of segregation within the "white" highlands closed
this safety valve. The reserves were unsatisfactory to Africans, for a variety
of reasons. Formal title was vested in the Crown; the reserves could be, and
in fact were, altered—to Kikuyu detriment, although land in the reserves
was not supposed to be alienated save for public works and temporary
trading.[26] Severe blows were dealt to the traditional *githaka* system of land
tenure, details of which appear in the following chapter. Administration
within the reserves was carried out by chiefs perceived often as self-seekers:
by currying favor with the British, a handful of Kikuyu rose to positions of
power and prestige. (The leading example, senior chief Kinyanjui, started
as a donkey boy for an early British administrator). Population growth and
certain agricultural practices pushed the reserves to dangerously high den-
cities by the late 1940s. Most important, the crowding of the reserves could
not be eased by expansion, as had marked the Kikuyu for centuries prior to
the European intrusion: areas set aside for alien settlement and forest
preserves hemmed them in.

The Mau Mau rebellion was preeminently a Kikuyu movement. It was
an uprising born of land grievances—themselves a reflection of the inequality imposed by colonialism. Even among the Kikuyu, however, the intensity of support for collective political violence differed markedly. In
seeking land and freedom, the rebels looked forward to dramatic revisions
in the existing economic and political order. They drew support dispropor-
tionally from the squatters, the young, the landless, and the urban proletariat—groups that stood to gain from change in the system. The main
opponents of the rebels in the reserves, the "Loyalists" encouraged by the
British, came from the older, better off, rural and Christian sectors of the
Kikuyu populace.

In the course of the uprising, geographic factors played a not insignifi-

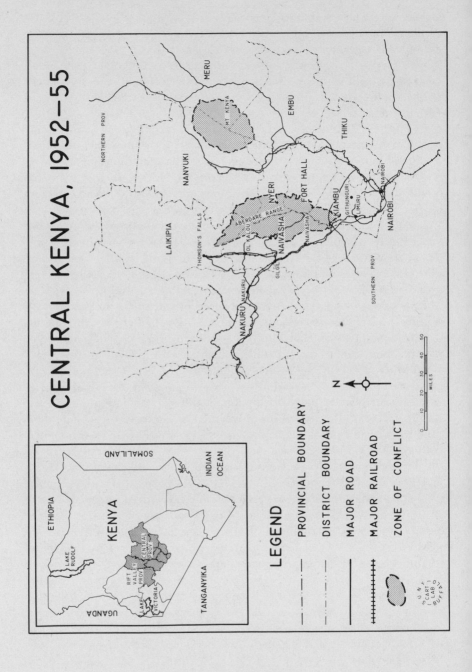

CENTRAL KENYA, 1952–55

LEGEND

———	PROVINCIAL BOUNDARY
———	DISTRICT BOUNDARY
———	MAJOR ROAD
++++	MAJOR RAILROAD
	ZONE OF CONFLICT

cant role. Note has already been made of the white highlands and forest reserves that halted Kikuyu expansion in response to demographic pressures. North of the Kikuyu towered Mount Kenya; to the west, the Aberdare range rose steeply. The eastern slopes of the Aberdares were cut by rivers into a series of parallel ridges. These were important sociologically and militarily. Each ridge tended to be settled by a single *mbari*; the British conquest of the Kikuyu proceeded piecemeal, almost ridge-by-ridge, with centrally organized resistance not being mounted. The forests rising above the 8,000 foot contour provided refuge for fighters, as well as for bandits (*komerera*). This factor is shown on Map 3. From hidden centers in the forest, guerrillas could sally forth on raids. The advantage of concealment was balanced by the disadvantage of communications: between Mount Kenya and the Aberdares stretched open country, making coordination between the two difficult under military pressure; the dense growth of the forests and the dissected terrain impeded movement. Mau Mau fighters were increasingly confined to the mountain slopes. They never gained the military strength and initiative sufficient to engage in large-scale, open combat with the far better armed British. The coercive might of the incumbents turned the guerillas' refuge into a trap from which escape was difficult.

Conversely, however, the British confronted major problems in reducing the land crowding that encouraged Mau Mau. Kikuyu traditionally dwelled in scattered homesteads, rather than in compact villages. Individual farmers did not till compact areas, but devoted their efforts to scattered fragments. Such diffusion, understandable within the context of decentralization that characterized Kikuyu society, immensely complicated the suppression of the rebellion. Surveillance was next to impossible. Agricultural improvements could not be easily effected. Rewards, in the form of land, required careful surveys, complex given the fragmentation. Hence, two of the most significant steps taken by the British were "villagization" and the consolidation of individual landholdings. By these steps, detailed in Chapter 8, the colonial administration carried out a profound transformation of land practices that directly countered Mau Mau, and brought the uprising—though not the desire for independence—to a temporary halt.

The Kwilu Rebellion—Zaire, 1963-1965

The Kwilu district, comprising just over 30,000 square miles in west central Zaire, cannot be readily distinguished physically from many other parts of Africa. Savannah vegetation (open grassy plains) interspersed with occasional stands of forest characterizes the area. Though sliced by rivers, like Kikuyuland, into a series of parallel valleys, Kwilu lacks the sharp relief, fertile soil, and salubrious climate of the Kenya highlands. The intense population pressures that marked the sections of China, India and Kenya we have been surveying did not apply to Kwilu; although its population density—14.9 persons per square kilometer in 1956[27]—was relatively high for Zaire as a whole, it was less than one-seventh that of the least dense Kikuyu reserve.[28] The effects of human occupation struck all observers of Kwilu. Family needs for cultivation and cooking had, by the early 1960s, stripped away the forest cover of much of the district. A family of six, following the typical African pattern of shifting bush fallow farming, cleared a hectare (2.471 acres) every two years,[29] whose sandy soil quickly became desiccated and liable to erosion.

It was economic geography, and in particular the ubiquity of oil palms, that marked Kwilu. Profound change had affected the indigenous economy during the colonial period. In 1911, Huileries du Congo Belge (HCB), an offshoot of the Unilever conglomerate, received 750,000 hectares as a concession.[30] The HCB sought palm oil, either from natural stands or from plantations. Nature favored Kwilu for palm production. The *Elaeis* variety grew widely and readily in river valleys. In 1956, Kwilu produced 31.2 percent of all palm oil from the Belgian Congo, this constituting 10.4 percent of the plantation production and 43.2 percent of the natural production.[31] Whatever the form, African labor was essential. Palm nut harvesters (*coupeurs de fruit*) made possible the rural industry of Kwilu. Some 40,000 of them—18.7 percent of the adult male population[32]—constituted a nascent rural proletariat.

The economic foundations of collective action in Kwilu differed in some respects, accordingly, from those examined thus far. Abuses of tenancy and intensified economic exploitation by landowners contributed heavily to the Taiping, Telengana and Mau Mau rebellions. Land redistribution figured among the chief goals of the uprisings. In general outline, these outbursts of collective political violence took place in settings marked by rural indebtedness, concentrated land ownership often in the hands of a minority, and the emergence of a landless populace. A squeeze on rural dwellers, suddenly and sharply exacerbated by external events (the Opium War for the Taiping rebellion; the tensions of independence and partition for the Telengana uprising; the sharp drop in Kikuyu squatter income after World War II and the return of veterans for the Mau Mau revolt), led to civil disturbance. Different sorts of economic shocks marked Kwilu. Its residents experienced tightening rural squeezes due both to international events, such as recession in palm oil prices, and to local events affecting production, such as breakdowns in transportation. The external market, and internal conditions affecting marketing, had direct and immediate impacts on the *coupeurs de fruit*.

The rebellion in Kwilu developed from roots of collective action laid down decades earlier. Previous instances of economic strain had encouraged joint action. The most severe blow to rural livelihood had come in the Depression when palm prices plummeted with the international decline of trade. Harvesters who had received 0.25 francs per kilo received .05 francs instead[33] — while head taxes and other fixed charges had to be paid. A series of strikes in 1932, examined subsequently in more detail, represented the *coupeurs'* response to events beyond their control. Religious movements provided a further avenue for collective protest. The growth of cults represented, in effect, a sublimation of political discontent. Various forms of the "religion of the oppressed," in Lanternari's phrase, substituted for political action. The bases for collective action, derived from labor solidarity and messianism in the 1930s, and reinforced by feelings of ethnicity, were strengthened in 1959-60 in the form of party politics. Kwilu became the focus for the Parti Solidaire Africain (PSA), some of whose leaders, excluded from national government coalitions, turned in 1963-4 to violence. The area that fell under rebel control appears on Map 4.

The Kwilu uprising was one of a series of rural rebellions in Zaire (then called the Democratic Republic of the Congo) in the 1963-5 period. In many respects, the revolts were parallel, independent events, rather than tightly coordinated attempts to overthrow the central government. Their simultaneity, I believe, testified to the combination of weak, ineffectual incumbents with disappointed popular and elite expectations. A general theme, a "second independence," linked the rebellions. The grant of self-government in mid-1960, as we shall see, was perceived by Congolese as an immediate opening of a cornucopia of riches. The departure of Belgian colonists, it was popularly believed, would result in far better standards of living for all. Expectations outpaced reality, however. The fruits of independence were quickly garnered by a few privileged Congolese who were in no position, given the precarious foundations on which the government rested, either to satisfy or to suppress these widespread conceptions. The armed forces were ineffectual and poorly trained — with the result that almost any determined group could establish a territorial beachhead without resistance. The success of one revolt led to other attempts. A chain reaction of collective political violence, in other words, was unleashed by the interaction between disappointed popular expectations and insufficient government response. Little risk was attached to rebellion; anything short of an uprising seemed to evoke no response.

In the discussion of the Telengana rebellion a few pages earlier, I made note of the Johnny-come-lately attempt of the Communist party to convert this essentially spontaneous uprising into a mass popular struggle against the government of India. The CPI tried to graft a Maoist concep-

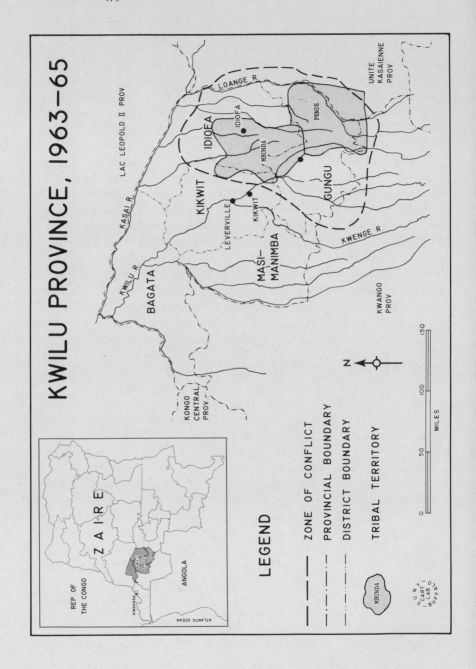

KWILU PROVINCE, 1963–65

LOANGE R.

LAC LEOPOLD II PROV.

UNITE
KASAIENNE
PROV.

KASAI R.

IDIOFA

IDIOFA

PENDE

MBUNDA

KIKWIT

GUNGU

KWILU R.

LÉVERVILLE

KIKWIT

BAGATA

MASI-
MANIMBA

KWENGE R.

KWANGO
PROV

KONGO
CENTRAL
PROV.

N

ZAIRE

REP. OF
THE CONGO

KINSHASA

KWILU
PROV.

ANGOLA

ATLANTIC OCEAN

LEGEND

ZONE OF CONFLICT

PROVINCIAL BOUNDARY

DISTRICT BOUNDARY

TRIBAL TERRITORY

MBUNDA

S U N Y
S.CART.
LAB.
BUFFALO

0   50   100   150

MILES

tion atop a rural insurrection that had (by the expulsion of the razakars and large landlords from the countryside) already achieved its relatively limited goals. The Communists' effort failed; the Telengana peasants were not disposed to act in accordance with the directives of essentially urban-oriented leaders. A related phenomenon occurred in the Kwilu rebellion. Pierre Mulele, whose background and ideas will be fleshed out in succeeding chapters, brought to Kwilu a set of Maoist principles for guerrilla warfare. He tried to infuse political consciousness based on class awareness into a setting of general rural discontent. The ideas that motivated the uprising thus existed on two different planes: the popular concept of a "second independence," perceived as an opportunity for enrichment; the Mulelist concept of a rural-based revolution, sweeping away a bourgeois political elite. These concepts were neither identical nor fully compatible.

The immediate successes of Mulele and his supporters may have surprised even themselves. An area of the size of Belgium passed quickly under rebel control. Government forces seemed to melt away, as word spread of the superior magic (*dawa*) with which Mulele was said to be endowed. The discontented populace quickly identified with this effort mounted by a local son. The foundation for collective action earlier established by strikes, messianism, and electoral campaigning by the Parti Solidaire Africain (PSA) was activated. A shortcoming apparent in the Mau Mau rebellion surfaced in the Kwilu rebellion as well. Ethnic factors—as much a foundation for collective action as the means just mentioned—circumscribed Mulele's appeal. The class solidarity he proclaimed was in reality tribal solidarity. With close to unanimous support among the Bapende and Mbunda, Mulele's lightly-armed partisans had no initial difficulty taking control. When the troops of the central government no longer broke and fled at the partisans' approach, however, Mulele's *dawa* was proven wanting. Control by the Zaire government was reestablished by stiffening its coercive forces and by exploiting the movement's narrowness. Those who gave their fervent support to the rebels early in the uprising returned to sullen acquiescence as the incumbents reasserted their power.

These brief descriptions of the four rebellions have but scratched the surface of these important, complex phenomena. More details must be added—and will be in succeeding chapters. At this point however, we should start to unite descripton with analysis, to move from juxtaposed case studies to comparison, to complement factual information with concern for theory. The remainder of this chapter is, accordingly, devoted to general observations on a specific problem: Why do rebellions erupt where they do?

Those driven to collective political violence in the Taiping, Telengana,

Mau Mau and Kwilu uprisings were overwhelmingly men of the country-side, who seem to have kept their distance from urban centers. The rebellions were born and died in rural settings. Despite proximity to major cities — to Canton, Hyderabad, and Nairobi — the partisans recruited their followings among other rural folk, and seemed to shy away from direct attacks on urban areas. (The obvious exception, the Taiping capture of Nanking, reflected not only the weakness of the distant Ch'ing government, but also the determination of Taiping leaders at the crest of their movement to establish themselves as rivals to the Peking government and claim the "Mandate of Heaven.") Since conditions in certain parts of the countryside appeared to prompt and facilitate rebellion, we should see what factors distinguished the various cradles of collective political violence.

It is possible to identify three schools of thought on the broad question posed above. Rebellions erupt where they do, it has been argued, because geographic conditions foster a widespread sense of separation, indeed of alienation, from the central government, a sentiment that both reflects and promotes hostility in those areas. Opposition to those who govern, in other words, may be inherent in certain settings and likely to promote violence. More specifically, areas under the hammerblows of multiple and unexpected disasters may witness the emergence and rapid growth of collective movements — including rebellions — seeking major transformations. Thirdly, regions of intensive and extensive agricultural commercialization may be particularly susceptible to rural unrest, including rebellion. Each of these broad approaches finds some support in the cases we are examining; each accordingly merits fuller attention as part of our assessment.

Geographic Marginality

Certain types of physical setting facilitate rebellion, in part for the simple reason such settings make governmental control difficult.

Geographic marginality is a broad term. It incorporates several distinct characteristics, such as remoteness from centers of political control, broken terrain in which a melange of groups may historically have taken refuge, and a historic fluidity of recognized boundary lines, whose enforcement may occasion resentment. In such marginal areas, the writ of government receives little attention. Inhabitants prize their distinctive way of life, and resent infringements of it. Able to take refuge in readily-defended redoubts, they resist the intrusion of "outside" ways — including, naturally enough, the taxes, conscription, and legal codes of the central government. In short, these settings encourage a sense of psychological separation from the national political system that parallels, and to a large extent is reinforced by, the physical separateness of the regions themselves. They become reservoirs for potential rebellion.

The fact remains, however, that such reservoirs rarely give rise to movements that effectively challenge the central government. Discontent may simmer, periodically giving rise to localized upheavals of little consequence to the regime. Such bleeding off in isolated areas may even serve the incumbents as safety valves. Endemic discontent, if concentrated geographically, can be contained. Distance from the center of political control reduces the chances for successful governmental overturn.

An obvious area of geographic marginality is a frontier—in Webster's definition, "a region that forms the margin of settled or developed territory." An open area of this sort encourages certain patterns of life—especially those patterns flourishing in the absence of extensive governmental control. Frontier zones thus attract, and in turn encourage, a particular modus vivendi. Individuals who prefer to administer themselves; a way of life emphasizing mobility, independence and control of weapons; a chance for individuals to start anew: such are the attractions of the frontier. The combination of social values such as independence, mobility and resistance to outside control with efforts at government enforcement would readily produce discontent, and potentially lead to rebellion.

Mao Tse-tung took account of such factors in describing suitable "base areas" for guerrilla activity.[34] Zones of weak or confused political control provided ideal havens; the confluence of several provincial or national boundaries often meant limited opportunities for governmental observation. These common-sense suggestions had clearly crossed the minds of some of the leaders described in this book. Hung Hsiu-ch'üan, for example, chose an isolated mountain fastness near the Kwangsi-Hunan border for the God-Worshippers' Society. Mao's desiderata went further, however. Potential base areas required, in his view, a fair degree of economic self-sufficiency, a history of previous political or revolutionary activity, and access to major political targets. Kikuyuland and Kwilu had each witnessed earlier outbursts of popular discontent; the Telengana districts, by contrast, appeared politically backward. Of the four rebellions, only Mau Mau partisans and Telengana sharecroppers started close to the capital—and, excepting the Taiping capture of Nanking, no major city fell to the rebel bands. Admittedly, an active urban underground in Nairobi supported Mau Mau fighters with funds, information, and some material—at least until Operation Anvil in April 1954 rooted out the rebellion's supporters, but the base was narrow. The followers of Hung Hsiu-ch'üan attempted to storm major political targets. Members of the Telengana, Mau Mau and Kwilu uprisings, by contrast, did not expand beyond the rural areas in which immediate grievances provided a ready basis for collective action. The "base areas" in the four rebellions gave birth to rebellion, not to immediate political change at the national level.

In summary: geographic marginality does not a successful uprising make. Areas outside ready government control may harbor traditions of resistance. Discontent takes root readily. Inaccessibility limits the regime's ability to repress—but similarly complicates the would-be rebels' ability to effect major change by capturing the capital or key cities. Insurgency may indeed be correlated with certain types of mountainous or swampy terrain[35]—but correlation is not causation. Geographic marginality facilitates collective political violence; it does not cause it. We must search further for preconditions and precipitants. A suggestive clue comes in the relationship between disaster-prone environments and mass movements.

Natural Disaster and Collective Political Violence

Disaster-prone environments, in the simplest terms, are physical and cultural areas whose inhabitants are liable to periodic large-scale loss of life and destruction of property as a result of climatic variations or unexpected invasions of disease. Areas of uncertain rainfall and high population density may suffer from drought and consequent famine; monoculture economies may be devastated by blight or disease. Low-lying lands subject to floods are obviously risky, though perhaps highly fertile. Unexpected frosts or heat waves can ruin crops. Contemporary urban areas can be subjected to significant problems—witness the agonies of Eastern seaboard American cities when buried by snow or immobilized by electrical failure—but these are disaster situations in which the perceived primary environment remains largely intact, or where damage can be quickly repaired.[36] The same observations can be applied to rural areas; yet it has been in these settings that millenarian movements have been most prominent. In such movements, participants expect widespread change: the imperfections of the here-and-now will be totally destroyed and a new order brought into being. Adherents expect salvation that is collective (enjoyed by the faithful), terrestrial (not to be realized in some other-worldly heaven), imminent, total, and miraculous.[37] In Barkun's judgment, the origins of such millenarian movements should be sought in multiple disasters. Unique events can be shrugged off, perceived as temporary aberrations. Repeated events, however, require different forms of explanations and adjustment.

One possible adjustment comes through apathy, resignation, or withdrawal. Multiple disasters can be construed as divine acts, over which no human control is possible. Fatalistic acceptance, especially if inculcated over several generations, is a frequent response. Long-term decline can be taken in stride, with a gradual, downward adjustment of social expectations. Individual frustration in such an environment can be mitigated by personal actions, notably emigration. Large-scale stress may be met as well by defensive structuring,[38] in which external stresses are countered by new social mechanisms. In short, millenarian movements represent one of at least three collective responses to multiple disasters.

It would be inaccurate to describe disaster as a totally natural phenomenon. To the extent that humans are aware of, and partly in control of, their environments, natural occurrences can be amplified or mitigated by human action. The likelihood of flood can be enhanced by failure to maintain levees or to dredge channels; the consequences of drought can be accentuated by inadequate food reserves, government inattention, or misappropriation of relief funds and supplies. Turn these shortcomings around, and it becomes apparent that foresight and concern can significantly reduce the toll of disaster. There is a political lesson here as well. The more the negative consequences of natural events are ascribed to government than to God, the greater their potential political effects. The regime of Haile Selassie, for example, was unthroned in large part from drought, magnified into famine by government mishandling.[39] Political ineptness certainly appeared in the four rebellions, accelerating (as will be illustrated in Part II) a sense of relative deprivation and, more important, a belief the incumbents were inherently hostile to the needs of the aggrieved rural populace. The point is that natural occurrences can show a government in its worst light, as the perpetrator of further grievances.

Disasters do not, by themselves, lead directly to rebellion. By focusing popular awareness on regime shortcomings, however, they open the way (in the presence of other conditions) for broader attempts at collective action. Multiple or repeated disasters compound the strain on government units. Creaking under the unexpected obligations, inefficient incumbents find their abilities and resources pushed to the breaking point. Where populations are dense and disaffected, political shortcomings become especially palpable. If these are coupled with changes in rural social values, notably the commercialization of land and commodities, discontent is bound to rise. The question remains, however, whether any collective expression of widespread disaffection will take the form of collective political violence.

Land Scarcity, Ownership, and the Subsistence Ethic

When more people live in a rural area than can be supported by indigenous agriculture, adaptation is necessary—particularly should there be too little food for too many people.

Peasant sensibility, over hundreds of years, developed several means of coping with land and food scarcity. The quickest solution to land shortages in a given area is migration; the quickest solution to food shortages, a reduction of consumption to, or below, the caloric minimum. As long as sufficient adequate agricultural land can be obtained by pulling up stakes, rural dwellers will drift toward less-populated areas. The long-term expansion of African peoples, for example, represented a natural response of moving out of high population areas, where soil had been depleted. Agricultural techniques can be changed to increase food production. More intense cultivation can palliate the consumption production inequality Introduction of new crops may also make possible denser rural populations. But these alterations do not occur automatically; they may require significant adaptation of existing practices.

A dense rural population, even one assaulted by multiple disasters, does not turn inherently to collective political violence. Irish peasants during the 1846-9 famine remained passive, for example: the *fellahin* of the Nile valley, whose increase in numbers has outstripped almost all technological improvements this century, appear politically inert as well. Crowding does not suffice as an explanation of rural political movements, but it does constitute an important factor in the situation.

The relationship between population density and collective political violence depends on concentration of land ownership and the reduction (concurrent with the growth of a rural cash economy) of landlord-client links. This is a basic characteristic of rural rebellions. The fact of concentrated ownership does not *ipso facto* result in rebellion. Peasants may remain mute, attributing their lot to Fate. Inequality might not be perceived as inequity. Powerful social sanctions can be invoked against those who question the system. Rural dwellers in fact may acquiesce in what the outside observers would term significant inequalities in ownership, *as long as the participants share a set of values that respects mutual rights and ensures adequate bases for survival.* Information about land ownership is a starting point; it must be supplemented by information about social structure and values.

Measurement of the concentration of ownership presents formidable problems. The phenomeon itself is complex. In most societies, so-called tenants may in fact possess land of their own, with sharecropping a supplement. The concept of individual title, common in the West and in East Asia, is historically far less important in certain areas. In sub-Saharan Africa, land was commonly vested in the entire clan or community. The *tsu* (clan) lands of China existed alongside private plots. It would have been socially and historically incorrect to speak of individual ownership in the Russian *mir* or Mexican *ejido*. Historical reconstruction of land distribution requires archives and patience possessed by few countries, and by equally few scholars. The *World Handbook of Political and Social Indicators* suggests, by omission, the problems of definition and measurement, and the political sensitivity, of land distribution statistics: the *Hand-*

book included data from 54 countries, and omitted data from 82.[40] (All of Africa, Socialist bloc states, and much of the Middle East does not appear in the relevant table.)

Even if ownership is skewed, in the sense of both a high concentration of agricultural property in the hands of a minority, and a high incidence of tenancy and sharecropping, the society may appear relatively stable. Five factors must be introduced in order to create a situation of concentrated ownership hospitable to collective violence directed against the owners, and collective political violence directed against members of the ruling elite.

The first factor involves open frontiers, to which reference was made earlier. As long as abundant agricultural land is available, and individual peasants enjoy the opportunity to seek it out, the pressures that bubble up into political violence cannot accumulate. Take, as one example, Thailand. For most of the country, agricultural resources are abundant. Hindley notes that a relatively low ratio of men to land resources is coupled with a relatively equal distribution of land ownership; in combination with other factors, this results in low levels of Thai political awareness. Only in northeastern provinces marked by "land-hunger" is there a hint of political unrest and insurrectional activity.[41] When peasants perceive they cannot readily escape from traps of debt or landlord exactions, they may find themselves pushed toward violent solutions. A realistic possiblity of setting up a new homestead functions as a safety valve. The absence of opportunities for the Kikuyu to acquire land outside the crowded reserves, by contrast, bottled up resentment, as did the endemic conflict in Kwangsi between Hakka and Punti. Evidence thus suggests that lack of land outside the control of the dominant elite facilitates widespread disaffection.

Secondly, legal sanctions for a landowning system must exist. Grievances based on maldistribution do not surface in societies where lands are held in common, individual cultivators are entitled to usufruct, and checks and balances inhibit the accumulation of property in the hands of a few. Other types of grievances certainly do come to the fore: a chief in African society, responsible for land allocation, may abuse his position and reward his followers with the richest terrain; the immigration of another group can result in frictions and tension. But the essential foundation for collective political violence erupting from land does not exist in systems of land tenure marked by recognized, respected, mutual obligations. Should the checks and balances disappear, however, the result may be profound friction. As will be shown later in the Telengana rebellion, the "cooking" of contracts reflected the transition from a customary system of responsibility joining proprietor and peasant to a legal framework in which clear advantage lay with the better off.

The penetration of the cash economy, capitalism and rents in the countryside constitutes the third essential factor. Perhaps the two most influential recent works on peasant political involvement emphasize how capitalist economic relationships eroded the social foundations on which rural communities had been built. Land, previously part of one's patrimony rather than a commodity, became subject to the cash nexus rather than a part of a system of mutual obligations. For Barrington Moore, the collapse of feudalism as a result of cash penetration profoundly influenced social relationships:

> They began to treat land more and more as something that could be bought and sold, used and abused, in a word like modern capitalist private property. Under feudalism too there had been, of course, private property in land. But ownership of land was always burdened and hedged with a great variety of obligations to other persons. The way in which these obligations disappeared, and who was to win or lose by the change, became crucial political issues in every country that knew feudalism.[42]

Eric Wolf speaks in terms of a "revolution" stemming from capitalism:

> This revolution from the beginning, however, takes the form of an unequal encounter between the societies which first incubated it and societies which were engulfed by it in the course of its spread. The contact between the capitalist center, the metropolis, and the pre-capitalist or non-capitalist periphery is a large-scale cultural encounter, not merely an economic one ....What is significant is that capitalism cut through the integument of custom, severing people from their accustomed social matrix in order to transform them into economic actors, independent of prior social commitments to kin and neighbors.[43]

The cash economy has numerous repercussions. Families may lose their land through events largely beyond their control. The cost of social ceremonies, or the crushing impact of a disastrous harvest, may trap them in debt thrall. The requirement that taxes be paid in cash rather than kind—or, for that matter, the imposition of levies where none have previously existed—results in further social shocks. Little imagination is necessary to envision other consequences. Thus, the fourth factor is the collapse, usually under the pressure of increasing use of cash, and often under the impetus of external colonial rule, of mutual obligations between landlord and tenant. This erosion changed the nature of indigenous social relations, leading to a profound sense of relative discontent. The "subsistence ethic"[44] collapsed; resources were extracted from peasants who increasingly lost their leverage to reduce inequities.

Finally, collective political violence requires links among rural dwellers, a sense of shared grievance that both transcends and incorporates the discontent individuals feel. Without a foundation for collective action, a society marked by concentrated land ownership and egregious landlord-tenant relationships may escape rebellion. Individual concerns must be linked in some fashion. Collective action may stem, for example, from the givens of real or presumed kinship — more broadly, from ethnic or national awareness. It may stem, secondly, from economic circumstance, with class awareness motivating participants. Religious beliefs provide a third foundation for collective action: peoples of otherwise diverse backgrounds may share expectations that (as in some millenarian movements) bring them together in joint opposition to those in control. These foundations for collective action will be examined subsequently.

To summarize our initial ideas, we would expect to discover rebellion — collective political violence involving large numbers of people and evoking coercive responses from the central government — under conditions of high population density, of social rootlessness resulting from tenancy and violation of the subsistence ethic, of traditions of resistance to government exactions, and of means of communicating grievances on the basis of shared values. A rapid shift in the conditions of life is more likely to spark resistance than is a gradual decline in them. Political violence would more readily spread in regions that have been lightly administered by the central government, in which traditionally mobile peoples have sought refuge, and which they can readily protect against military and administrative pressures. Traditions of resistance can be harbored and perpetuated most easily among peoples who, for varying historic and social reasons, lack ties of loyalty to the central government. Acts of resistance may most readily break out within groups whose status has been subjected to significant and sudden decline, especially if exacerbated by the government.

Far more than geographic marginality, natural disasters, rural overpopulation, and land tenancy are thus involved in rebellion. One must add other arguments: perceptions of discontent and relative deprivation; social structure and values; government actions spurring violence; the rise and recognition of leaders. These pieces of the mosaic will be added and elaborated upon in later chapters.

CHAPTER 2 /

The Bases for Collective
Political Violence

Rebellions on the scale just described did not spring full-grown from a leader's brow. They took shape within a social context that encouraged collective action. As group actions — attempts by the militarily weak but numerically strong to enhance their positions — these spread from a restricted nucleus of initiators to a far broader circle of followers. A qualitative change was necessary in the scale and rationalization of action: they indulge in personal acts that, *in the presence of facilitating conditions*, may led to collective action. Advocates of change may be numerous. Unless the potential field of action has been cultivated, fertilized and watered, however, the seeds they sow will not bear fruit. Would-be insurgent leaders can storm the bastions of power only with cadres of supporters.

Reciprocal relationships exist between settings for collective action and initiatives by individuals. Yes, there can be — and have been; and will continue to be — prophets of political change whose seeds of protest appear to bring into being widespread political change. Their contributions are essential, for collective action remains latent without some degree of personal encouragement. Individuals articulate grievances, promote a sense of identification among potential insurgents, and attract further support through personal qualities. To ascribe the paramount role in inciting rebellion to a handful of people — to Hung Hsiu-ch'üan, Jomo Kenyatta, or Pierre Mulele — overlooks a fundamental fact, however. These men gained influence, in large measure, by utilizing indigenous building blocks, by making manifest latent bonds of solidarity among the challengers of the regime. In other social settings, their influence might have been nonexistent.

As may geographic marginality, social structure can harbor the basis for collective political violence. Certain types of social arrangements nurture rebellion. The four cases to which we are giving detailed attention shared several characteristics that, in combination, provided a foundation from which collective political violence erupted. The overwhelming majority of the population lived in rural areas, in conditions in which their ideal of relative autonomy in dealing with others was regularly and rudely interrupted by the fact of their social, economic and political subordination. Power was concentrated in the hands of a few who, at the time of the uprisings, were differentiated from the rustic majority by race, religion, language, and style of life. Inequality was endemic, a potential source of conflict. The unavoidable frictions between individual or local aspirations, and the demands made by the central government and its indigenous allies, could be politicized. The continued salience of communal or ethnic ties—perhaps even their reinforcement—within a changing context of political and economic relationships permitted the collective organization of protest. Permitted, not necessitated, one must note. Social structure facilitates collective political violence, but does not, I believe, serve as the *fons et origo* of all rebellion. To justify this assertion, let us turn, in greater detail, to various strains and disequilibria prominent in societies liable to rebellion.

Inequity and Social Strain

No social system exists in total harmony or equilibrium. Such a condition may serve scholars heuristically, as models or ideal types against which actual conditions could be contrasted. But, as a moment's reflection will sustain, individual societies can tolerate wide ranges of internal strain or even overt conflict without serious weakening of the social fabric. Conflict may be endemic, but ritualized; safety valves can prevent the accumulation of resentment through periodic binges, role reversals, ceremonies, and the like.[1]

Equally, no social system exists without inequalities. Since Aristotle—and no doubt long before notes taken by Aristotle's students were collected into *Politics*—students of political violence have heeded his generalization, "The cause of sedition is always to be found in inequality."[2] But what, precisely, is the inequality that results in "sedition"? Individuals differ in power, status, wealth, physical attractiveness and coordination, forcefulness, and in a multitude of other ways. Not all inequalities among persons are politically significant, however, in the sense of giving rise to "sedition." It is *inequality perceived as inequity*, I suggest, that gives rise to collective action, including collective political violence. Inequality (real or imagined; individual or group) becomes the basis for resentment when differences are perceived as unjust. Contrasts in power, status, or wealth (class) can be politicized. Whatever degree of earlier acceptance may have existed fades away. Justifications for such differences, as we shall see in the following chapter, lose their validity as indigenous persons challenge justifications for minority control. Inequalities in power, status, and wealth must be presented as inequities to lead to collective political violence.

Truism number one of Political Science 101 is that persons differ dramatically in terms of participation and power. The reins of government are held by few. Those who become political "gladiators," in Milbrath's term, constitute a small proportion of any society.[3] Admittedly, some conditions facilitate intensive and extensive consultation over political decisions—village palavers provide avenues for discussion and expression of diverse perspectives before consensus is reached; referenda or plebiscites carried out on the basis of prolonged, widespread prior discussions have occurred. But the majority participate in politics episodically at best. Disparities in political power flow inherently from the fact that political resources are never distributed equally.[4] Under normal conditions, as it were, this state of affairs passes without comment. The existence of a "ruling class" may be accepted, seemingly without murmur, by the governed. What the outside observer perceives as unjustifiable inequity may be rationalized, within the particular society, as justified inequality.

Not only do individuals bring different political resources, in terms of power; they also enjoy different economic resources. What differences exist can be left relatively untouched by government action; considerably reduced by government action; or considerably enhanced by government action. In the rebellions to which I shall continue to draw your attention, concentration of economic resources in the hands of an identifiable minority had occurred, with the direct support of the government. Active encouragement of income inequalities, in a nutshell, constituted the incumbents' basic policy. In Imperial China, gentry and their bureaucratic allies mulcted the peasants of a share of their production sufficiently resented to result in rural revolt. The *jagirdars* and *deshmukhs* of Hyderabad exerted a similar squeeze on the Telengana peasants. Pronounced income inequalities marked Kenya and Zaire as well, with white skin an almost certain passport to both relative affluence and political power. In all these societies, in other words, a transfer of resources took place, from the rural, indigenous sector towards better-off landlords or the urban or cash crop minority sector.

Taken over time, these inequalities in economic resources (especially as reinforced by government actions) would have led to clear-cut class differentiation. It is arguably possible that the rural majorities in the four rebellions constituted classes "in themselves." Truism number two of Political Science 101 is that a class in itself is not necessarily a class *for* itself. Collective political violence stems from inequity, but the violence may not rectify the particular conditions. Our chosen subjects seem to illustrate the validity of truism number two, if it is not pushed too far. Desire for material improvement — for reducing inequities in resource distribution — helped fuel the four rebellions. Economic inequality became perceived as economic inequity correctable through collective political violence limited to redistribution. A fundamental revolution in power relationships required steps beyond those the participants could take.

Differences in political power and in economic resources correspond to a considerable degree with differences in social status. In the rebellions with which we are concerned, the coincidence of power, resources and status helped account for the speed with which an attack on one led to an assault on the others. The top of the social pyramid was occupied by those who held political power, who controlled key resources, and who monopolized the prestigious positions. Prestige, power, affluence: all these qualities were congruent, and seemingly vested in the same restricted group. An elite existed within each system: the gentry, literati and officials of Imperial China; the Nizam, *deshmukhs* and Muslim officials in Hyderabad; the colonial officers, European farmers, and businessmen in Kenya; the *nouveau riche* Congolese elite who stepped into the positions vacated after independence by Belgians. Such clear indications of inequality led soon to perceptions of inequity.

The elite considered inequality justified, indeed perhaps the cornerstone of the entire social structure. Those in control, I shall seek to document in the following chapter, had little inkling of the resentment aroused by their hammerlock on power, status and wealth. They approached reform with caution, believing it might undercut their control. They tightened the screws of economic exaction, believing their coercive might and moral superiority would carry the day. They found it difficult to sympathize with rural dwellers mired in a position of permanent inferiority. The price of progress, their rationalization ran, was suffering and shortage in the countryside. Inequality, to the elite, was not inequity. Continued extraction of resources from the peasants, or quick punishment if they proved recalcitrant, composed their chosen course. In short, elite intransigence added rigidity to social structures not known for their flexibility or adaptability.

Such intransigence was compounded by the unusual stresses imposed by pre-rebellion conditions. As noted in the preceding chapter, the outbreak of collective political violence was preceded by major changes in local conditions. British pressure in the Opium Wars compounded the dynastic decline the Ch'ing government was experiencing; the turbulent events of independence and partition analogously undermined the position of the

Nizam. Although World War II had hastened independence for India, its effects on indigenous political awareness went unnoticed by the colonial administration of Kenya, which became far more interventionist in African rural affairs and continued to support white settler interests. The grant of self-government to the Congo, finally, aroused unfulfillable expectations, as relatively few Africans could move into the administrative and commercial positions abandoned by the Belgians. There was little incentive, given these conditions, to adopt new approaches. The barriers of power, status, and wealth were in many respects strengthened in the face of challenge. To the governed, inequality became more pronounced; the crises underscored their inferior status. Some form of organized resistance appeared necessary, the issue being the social foundation on which it could be created.

Collective Action and Social Structure

Dynamic analysis of rebellion requires attention to the bases on which collective action can be undertaken. Individuals' perceptions of inequality and inequity must be generalized in some fashion for collective action to result. A group rather than a person must be presented as the victim of inequity. Facets of the existing social structure furnish several potential foundations. Four major means of building a sense of community can be employed: 1) ascriptive and cultural ties, based on ethnicity or language; 2) religious beliefs, as in the development of millenarianism; 3) economic links, notably through class awareness and action; and 4) political bases, such as region or nation, in which boundaries affect the scope of action.

Ascriptive bases for collective action existed in the four cases that were strengthened by antagonisms. Land conflict between the Hakka and Punti had sharpened the Hakka sense of identity in Kwangsi Province. Hung Hsiu-ch'üan started the *T'ai-p'ing t'ien-kuo* with a handful of Hakka followers, in response to needs they felt acutely. The peasants of the Telengana districts also drew on particularism. As Hindus, and as speakers of a language different from that of the Nizam's court, they developed a basis for collective action based, in large part, on their village culture. That the Kikuyu felt an acute sense of grievance against British settlers need not be reiterated; the point is that this resentment was propagated along lines of ethnic solidarity. Finally, the Kwilu rebellion enjoyed support that was universal within limited bounds: Mulele and his followers could count on the assistance of almost all Pende and Mbunda, but received little aid beyond these ethnic groups. Rebellion developed on the basis of an underpinning of cultural similarity, this having been sharpened rather than muted by social change.

Ascriptive ties do not differentiate within the group on the basis of power, status or wealth. In eyes of the beholder, all sons and daughters of X are equal — by the fact of belonging to the particular culture. An ethnic or cultural community can contain within itself a whole range of contrasts of power, status and wealth. What matters is their salience *relative to* other contrasts within the society as a whole. As we have seen, and will consider in detail in the chapter that follows, the perceived differences inside the group shrank by comparison with the differences between all its members and those of the dominant minority. Let us take one example. Vis-a-vis European settlers, all Kikuyu, irrespective of personal attainment, were deemed inferior. Race or culture in colonial Kenya defined almost all aspects of subordination and superordination: whites enjoyed power, status and wealth; blacks did not; Asians occupied an ambiguous intermediate position. Collective action cut across differentiations among the Kikuyu to a substantial extent in the early phase of Mau Mau; ethnicity had consigned them all to a second-class citizenship. Although this example is the most striking, it had parallels in the other rebellions.

In at least three of the four uprisings, significant adaptations made in indigenous belief systems abetted popular mobilization. By far the most striking was Hung's adaptation of Christian beliefs — though clearly not to the exclusion of traditional Chinese values. This melange, to which I shall return in Chapter 7, injected millenarian elements into the rebel ideology in a form more pronounced than in previous Chinese peasant uprisings. Hung himself was profoundly affected by his personal religious experiences. The early history of the God-Worshippers Society was marked by a deep sense of revelation, and a consequent sense of mission to be accomplished. The later dilution of Taiping ideals notwithstanding, religious ideals provided a significant basis for creating and motivating a community of believers. Although no profound changes in either Hindu or Muslim beliefs resulted from the Telengana rebellion, religious/communal perceptions of differences were sharpened. The use of belief systems in the Mau Mau and Kwilu rebellions remained limited, but represented adaptations of previous practices. Existing beliefs in magic were employed and extended to insure solidarity. Various Mau Mau oaths threatened sanctions for those who betrayed the movement — a threat made real during the 1953-4 civil war that racked Kikuyu society. The Kikuyu presented a united front in the early stages of the uprising, testimony to the efficacy of oathing (among others) in countering fission, and tried to reinforce solidarity by increasingly strong oaths as time passed. Finally, Mulele consciously used *dawa* to motivate his followers. Belief in their physical invincibility proved far more important to the rebels in their early encounters with government troops than did their limited armaments. Magic thus provided an *esprit de corps* not dissimilar to the religious fervor induced in the Taiping rebellion.

Interpretations of collective action based on class origins and outlooks have gained increasing prominence in contemporary social science. Marxist interpretations of all four rebellions have been published,[5] and scores of scholars have mined the suggestive hints with which Marx's copious writings are studded for application to collective political violence. In their view, class conflicts provide the motive forces of history; rural rebellions should be approached as evidence of *prises de conscience* by economically subordinated groups.

Marx distinguished, as is well known, between a class in itself and a class for itself. He consigned the peasantry to the former category, incapable of pursuing its own real interests without outside assistance. His often-quoted words from *The Eighteenth Brumaire* bear quotation one more time:

> The small peasants form a vast mass, the members of which live in similar conditions, but without entering into manifold relations with one another. Their mode of production isolates them from one another, instead of bringing them into mutual intercourse...the great mass of the French nation is formed by simple addition of homologous magnitudes, much as potatoes in a sack form a sackful of potatoes. In so far as millions of families live under economic conditions that divide their mode of life, their interests and their culture from those of other classes, and put them into hostile opposition to the latter, they form a class. Insofar as there is merely a local interconnection among these small peasants, and the identity of their interests begets no unity, no national union, and no political organization, they do not form a class. They are consequently incapable of enforcing their class interest in their own name, whether through a parliament or through a convention. They cannot represent themselves; they must be represented.[6]

These noted judgments did not represent Marx's last or only word on the subject. A writer as prolific was bound to have variations on any theme. In general, however, Marx viewed peasants as members of a doomed class, whose revolts were in part the dying gasps of a moribund feudal system. Despite the opposition peasants might have mounted, Marx dismissed their effects on social change out-of-hand. His offhand condemnation of the "idiocy of rural life" betokened his seeming insensitivity to the possibility of change emanating from the countryside. Another example comes in *The German Ideology*: "The great risings of the Middle Ages all radiated from the country, but equally remained totally ineffective because of the isolation and consequent crudity of the peasants."[7] Only late in his life, under the influence of Lewis Morgan, and with increasing interest in Russia, did Marx modify his judgment slightly. The various drafts of his noted letter to Vera Zasulich hinted that the peasant commune (*mir*) could facilitate a leapfrogging of historical stages.[8] This idea, however, seems more a cross-current than the main stream of Marx's thought; he and later Marxian analysts stressed the importance of consciousness, assistance, and representation brought rural dwellers from outside their narrow milieu. To the extent that peasants constitute a "class of low classness," in Shanin's terms,[9] their collective action would be subject to splintering and would require supplementation by other factors, such as ethnicity or religion, and by other participants, such as workers or intellectuals.

It is easy — perhaps far too easy — to dismiss the seeming failure of rebels such as those considered in this book as the consequence of their fragmentation and isolation. What allies, in fact, might have been sought? "Low classness" characterized groups other than peasants. Workers provide a case in point. China in the mid-nineteenth century, and India, Kenya and Zaire a century later, had been touched — but not been totally transformed — by capitalism. The proletariat (certainly by comparison with that of industrialized societies) was small, isolated, relatively unorganized, and at an incipient stage of class awareness. The problems confronting the proletariat may have differed substantially from those confronting the peasantry: alliance, even were consciousness present, might not have brought the desired results. Alliance with educated spokesmen was also liable to difficulty. Intellectuals in the four societies had not been pressured, I would suggest, into an intelligentsia marked by strong opposition to the government. Many may have been co-opted into the structure of power and privilege, serving their political masters as subalterns, and reluctant to sully themselves with peasant matters. Defection from the governing stratum on behalf of rural causes faced similar obstacles. The homogeneity and minority position of the ruling group meant potentially disaffected members experienced strong peer pressure to remain "loyal." In short, there was no ready or obvious road to bring together classes of "low classness" in collective action, nor to incorporate assistance from better educated groups.

The ultimate demonstration of ascriptive, religious, class or national solidarity came in the correspondence between proclaimed reasons for the rebellion and the accomplishments of the insurgents. Here, the scholar confronts a serious problem: to what extent can he rightfully impute motives of any sort to the participants? As evidence presented in later pages will show, many of the rebels' proclaimed economic and political objectives were primarily hortatory. Intended as ideological rallying points, they were widely supported among the disaffected populace — but went beyond what could have been achieved by even the most drastic redistribution. Let me provide an example from Kwilu: "A beautiful house, complete with furniture, will be built for each person by the new government."[10] I have no doubt that this desire—in conjunction with other factors—impelled many followers of Mulele to engage in collective political violence. Such ideological pronouncements, to which we shall return in Chapter 7, point to some degree to external support for rebellions. Appeals may be directed as much to the outside world as to the domestic participants, to rally international support and recognition. That the four rebellions (with the possible exception of Kwilu) passed up opportunities to influence outside audiences figures among the reasons they remained short of rural revolutions.

To castigate the claims on which collective action was built is, of course, ridiculous without examining the extent to which the rebels made good their promises. Economic redistribution was attempted in all four rebellions, and was especially marked in the Taiping and Telengana uprisings. Is it accurate to regard this redistribution as a response to insurgent solidarity based on class? The answer, I believe, must be mixed. The transfer of property from a culturally differentiated minority to a deprived indigenous majority—as occurred to a substantial extent in Hyderabad—cannot be construed simply as a reflection of economic facts of life. Ascriptive factors, in the form of hostility between the Muslim court and Hindu tenants, played as significant a role. The extent to which class supplanted ethnicity as a basis for collective action might be perceived in resource redistribution *within* the numerically preponderant populace. On this basis, it would seem that the Taiping rebels, whose basis for collective action had grown rapidly from the original Hakka roots, manifested a higher degree of class solidarity than the Telengana rebels—though the difference may be one of degree. Clearly, however, class analysis by itself requires supplementation by reference to the other forms—cultural, religious, and national—of achieving social solidarity.

Rebel appeals on behalf of Kenya and Zaire as entities illustrate the broadening of political arenas that, in many respects, marked the deathknell of European rule in tropical Africa. The two states were artifacts of the colonial era. In the pre-colonial period, several political systems rose and fell in various parts of both. None, to my knowledge, covered an expanse comparable to the size and diversity of either Kenya or Zaire. Many historical connections existed among the various societies of both, in trade, intermarriage, and conflict. Similar conditions of life, particularly for agricultural groups, engendered similar social structures: communal land tenure, shifting bush fallow cultivation, and far-flung trade networks for essential commodities such as salt marked the basic agricultural or pastoral economy; respect for elders and/or chiefs characterized political organization; clans helped order social relationships, as often did age-sets marked by initiation ceremonies, clear-cut divisions of labor, and social obligations based on kinship. Such similarities helped pave the way for wider political awareness. The key impetus to nationalist sentiment came through European impact, however. Nationalism in tropical Africa may be described as indigenous responses to the inequalities and inequities of colonial rule.[11] Its roots were thus somewhat more political than cultural; it sought the creation of nations within boundaries drawn largely for imperial convenience; anti-colonialism continued a process of nation-building unwittingly initiated by the actions of Europeans.

The sense of nationalism evoked in the Taiping rebellion drew upon deep cultural and political roots that preceded resentment of the Manchu rulers. The sense of nationalism evoked in the Mau Mau and Kwilu rebellions, by contrast, depended far more upon resentment of the alien presence, with social and political similarities contributory. By the mid-nineteeth century, China as a unified imperial state had a history spanning two millennia.[12] Kenya and Zaire, by contrast, had been carved out late in the nineteenth century. The impact of alien rule and colonial adminstration varied radically: the Ch'ing dynasty drew on the scholar-gentry group of ethnic Chinese that had served earlier rulers; the British and Belgians entrusted few responsibilities, above the village level, to indigenous persons. Such differences in the extent to which outsiders dominated political power (plus, to reiterate, status and wealth) were to affect the course of rebellion. Further, perceptions of ethnic differences lay closer to the surface in the two African rebellions than in the Taiping uprising — and these differences, utilized by the incumbents, help explain the insurgents' defeat.

Let me conclude these introductory remarks by stressing what should be obvious already. Reinforcement among these four strands of collective action eased the emergence of collective political violence. The manifold sources of strain could simplify the socio-economic-political context, creating polarization rather than pluralism, transforming perceptions of inequality into rejections of inequity. The way was opened thereby for widespread collective political violence. Against its possible eruption, however, powerful factors maintaining the status quo remained. By examining the strains inherent in the four societies, we can fully grasp the obstacles to rebellion that aspirant rebels confronted.

Bases of Inequality in Late Ch'ing China

Inequality pervaded the basic social fabric of China under the Ch'ing and preceding dynasties. A number of strains existed that, under varying circumstances, resulted in collective action. Yet challenges to the basic assumption of inequality remained rare. The leading philosophies, with the exception of Taoism and some millenial beliefs, presumed fundamental differences among individuals.[13] It was not a closed system, however. Opportunities for personal mobility existed. Although the "scholar-gentry" group dominated power, status, and wealth, its membership was not exclusive or closed. Lacking were the separations brought by caste in India, and the segregation resulting from race in colonial Africa. The fact of inequality was mitigated by instances of upward movement, by peasants who broke away from the physical labor and low income that had been their lot to the greater prestige and affluence of officialdom.

Deeply ingrained acceptance of inequality, coupled with opportunities for individual and family advancement, and further coupled with the heavy demands of survival, produced (under most conditions) a relatively stable, self-regulating system. Administrative techniques developed over centuries left villagers a reasonable degree of autonomy from governmental demands — apart, of course, from the inevitable taxes. Chinese villagers could, in times of peace and prosperity, remain far removed from affairs of the *yamen*, the office of the district magistrate appointed by the Imperial government. Dynasties might rise and fall in Peking; the rhythm of rural life followed time-honored patterns. Under most circumstances, inequality did not result in sedition that engulfed areas removed from the traditional foci of restiveness.

On the other hand, Chinese history is replete with rebellions, in which unrest spread beyond its usual haunts. Inequities clearly existed, and led to collective political violence. These uprisings generally sought to rectify local, immediate grievances that had intensified for various reasons. Their eruption testified to increased governmental inefficiency; to inability to counter exactions of landlords and excessively corrupt officials; to military ineptitude in the face of domestic and external challenges; to failure in countering natural calamities. The dynastic cycle rolled onwards, a ruling line eventually losing the "Mandate of Heaven" that supported its claim to control. Rebel pressures thus played a central part in the renewal of the "mandate." The system was, in effect, reinvigorated rather than transformed. Resentment and strain, translated into collective political violence, led to reaffirmation and revitalization. In Moore's judgment, energy that might have been directed toward modernization "mainly dissipated itself in fruitless revolt and insurrection within the prevailing framework."[14]

It seems clear from the historic record that several factors contributed to rural uprisings in China. These causes interacted in a variety of ways, with the understandable result that no single factor can be isolated as The Cause of a particular uprising. This does not obviate the importance of delineating various disequilibria. They can be divided among economic, social and political factors—with the immediate caveat that these categories are by no means mutually exclusive. Among economic factors, one should note:

the legal framework for individual land title;
the increased prevalence of sharecropping, especially under conditions of high soil fertility and population pressure; and
the latitude landlords enjoyed, at times of administrative weakness and heavy land demands, of increasing their exactions.

Equally complex and important are sociological factors, such as the following:
blocks to individual mobility, especially with the crystallization and perpetuation of status differences;
weakening of the information links between village leaders and administrative officers carried through the "lower gentry";
frustration of opportunities for upward mobility, as in preference based on ascription rather than achievement, or in sale of degrees rather than effective utilization of examinations; and
natural disaster that affected the subsistence ethic on the basis of which peasants judged relationships with landlords.

Finally, there remain several political strains, exacerbated in crisis periods:
widespread rural distrust of government intentions and activities;
general inability of the Imperial government to affect substantial parts of village life;
a belief, linked to the nadir of the dynastic cycle, in the popular right to revolt against unjust or tyrannical princes;
under the Ch'ing dynasty, Manchu control of the court, with the support of an overwhelmingly Han bureaucracy;
the difficulty of communications, given distance;
fragmentation of political power and duplication of administrative responsibilities, reducing the initiative members of the government could exercise.

Let us give brief attention to these.

Economic strains. Affluence in Imperial China—as in almost all agrarian societies—stemmed ultimately from control over land. Peasant production formed the cornerstone of society. Expressed in a different and perhaps more apt metaphor, the sweat of rural dwellers made possible the luxury of the ruling class. As should be expected, possession of land was prized. Possession is the correct term — for, unlike many other so-called "traditional" societies, Imperial China was marked by individual titles. Land had been a commodity since the Sung dynasty, and thus had been freely bought and sold for close to a thousand years prior to the Taiping rebellion. The way was open, at least in theory, for rapid polarization between haves and have-nots, for the crystallization of conflict between landed and landless on the basis of property falling into the hands of the wealthy.

Under "normal" circumstances, such pronounced polarization did not emerge. The land patiently accumulated by an individual was divided among his sons; the absence of primogeniture meant that offspring of a wealthy but prolific person would have to scramble on their own. A gradual drift of families into and out of the bureaucracy opened up opportunities for land acquisition. The landless could, in theory and occasionally in fact, receive official positions through success in examinations — and gain thereby the chance to accumulate property on their own. The overwhelming majority of titles were achieved rather than inherited. Reward of individual merit meant a modicum of economic redistribution, or at least difficulty in maintaining preeminence over several generations.

Such "normal" circumstances were interrupted, however, by circumstances in which landlords could accumulate additional property and/or extract higher rents from their tenants. The subsistence ethic could be, and was, violated under conditions of land scarcity. Arable land, on a per capita basis, dropped by more than half, from 3.86 *mow* in the mid-eighteenth century to 1.86 *mow* in 1833.[15] Admittedly, more intensive cultivation mitigated part of the negative effects. But the economic and social consequences were profound. Subdivision among heirs meant plots too small to sustain families; sharecropping became necessary. Litigation over mortgages increased as unpaid back rents mounted. Crop failures meant land had to be mortgaged to meet taxes and purchase food — and those with cash to lend could thereby accumulate property. A surplus of potential sharecroppers meant landlords could raise rents.

It should be noted that wealth did not lead directly to either status or power. The route, rather, was indirect. Ho puts the matter thus: ". . .money in Ming-Ch'ing China was not in itself an ultimate source of power. It had to be translated into official status to make its power fully felt."[16] Wealth generally derived from control over land. Land inequalities could be interpreted as inequities from which rebellion could spring. To such economic differences, however, social strains had to be added to facilitate collective action.

Social strains. The premise of inequality affected relations among social strata. In broad terms, Chinese society was viewed as being composed of six layers. At the apex stood a small number of hereditary officials, nobles and bureaucrats. In this group alone, position was determined ascriptively. Immediately below this group stood the scholars, whose success in official examinations granted them great prestige — and opportunity for government appointment. The third and by far the largest stratum included those engaged in agriculture (a broad category ranging from wealthy landlords to impecunious tenants). Artisans and craftsmen stood next in the hierarchy, then merchants and tradesmen. Finally, the bottom layer was filled by members of undesirable callings — by actors, prostitutes, tanners, and the like.

From a sociological perspective, this division obscures far more than it clarifies. The traditional differentiations among the four main functional orders (scholars; tillers of the soil; artisans; and merchants) do not adequately describe the stratification of Imperial Chinese society.[17] The sharpest, clearest distinction lay between ruler and ruled, this based on mental rather than menial work. As stated by Mencius, "Some labor with their minds and some labor with their physical strength. Those who labor with their minds rule others, and those who labor with physical strength are ruled by others. Those who are ruled sustain others, and those who rule are sustained by others."[18] Access to official status (apart from the hereditary ranks) depended on success in a series of competitive examinations. Such examinations became a feature of Chinese society early in the seventh century A.D. The degree earned determined the level at which officials could enter and rise in official circles, within the nine ranks into which the bureaucracy was divided. Holders of the highest degree, the *chin-shih*, could look forward to direct placement in a government position. Holders of the *chu-jen* degree (earned through Provincial-rather than national-level examinations) might achieve minor posts. Those more blessed by cash than by intellect or determination could purchase the *chien-sheng* degree, becoming privileged thereby to wear the scholar's gown and cap but not to enter government service.[19] Finally, holders of the *sheng-yuan* degree enjoyed pre-eminence in village settings, as scholar-commoners rather than scholars. Their attainments made them respected intermediaries between their illiterate brethren and government officers, and admired local leaders. They formed a vital connecting link in Imperial Chinese society.

In theory, anyone could sit for the examinations; in reality, access was restricted. Formal training required years of concentrated effort. Educational opportunities supposedly available to all were in fact usually limited by economic circumstances: few could afford the time and tutoring expenses incurred in study. Some commoners succeeded, their attainments trumpeted as proofs of mobility; most did not. So long as this safety valve was not clogged, upward mobility remained a possibility. Horatio Alger's heroes had many forerunners in Imperial China.

Even within this privileged group, problems arose. The chief social strain for scholars came in the fact that far more succeeded in examinations than could be accommodated in officialdom. Imperial China was a lightly administered state. In 1749, there was roughly one magistrate per 100,000 inhabitants; 70 years later, one per 250,000 inhabitants.[20] Taking the government as a whole, about 40,000 positions had to be filled with (by the early nineteenth century) more than three times that number of available or expectant officeholders.[21] Those who achieved the *chin-shih* degree could look forward to a life of relative comfort and social prestige. Those who failed in the examinations, or had to content themselves with a minor degree, could not bask in such glory. Their position was ambiguous. On the one hand, they shared the basic values and outlooks of the governing group; on the other hand, they remained outside the *yamen* from which power was exercised. Unsuccessful degree candidates knocked on the door of success, but were turned away. Under most conditions, they remained supporters of the system. However, they could, and did, mount resistance to the system. Wolf provides this assessment: "Thus there existed, under any dynasty, a sizable population of scholar-gentry who were personally antagonistic to a government that refused to grant them their due and would, under given circumstances, support a local or regional reaction against the central power."[22]

An even wider range in wealth and power marked members of the *kung* or agricultural group. The vast majority of Chinese lived on the land. A whole gamut of contrasts existed. Some were well-off landlords, a rural gentry though without heritable titles. Others were, in terms important subsequently in the Chinese revolution, rich, middle and poor peasants. Landless sharecroppers clearly lacked the resources (economic, social and political) of the landed gentry — yet both groups were assigned by tradition to the same category. Social strain, as should be expected, pitted propertied against propertyless. To assume a simple polarization, however, would be to commit an historical error. The differences in power, status and wealth ranged along a continuum. Families rose and declined, over time, in their social position. Kinship ties (including, particularly in South China, clan links) meant the better off were never totally isolated from the poorer off. Absentee landlords, however, were less likely to be aware of problems their tenants confronted than were those who remained in rural areas.

The other major groups in the traditional social hierarchy, the artisans/craftsmen and the tradesmen/merchants, included analogous ranges of wealth and power. They could accumulate wealth — yet, unless they translated this into land and into educational success marked by degrees, their status remained low. Not being tillers, they were somewhat more mobile, perhaps more vulnerable to economic changes, and potentially better able to engage in collective political violence. The Taipings drew strong support from unemployed boatmen, charcoal burners, and other groups affected by the social disruption of the 1840s. It stands to reason that they, and members of the lowest stratum of all in the hierarchy, might have rallied to the Taiping cause because of its verbal commitment to equality. Low in terms of power, status and wealth, they stood to benefit from any significant social restratification.

All these comments, however, must be weighed against both the theory and the fact of upward mobility. Individuals were not locked in from birth into a set of roles from which escape was impossible. The caste system that affected Telengana villagers, and the racial blocks that marked colonial Africa, imposed barriers more difficult than in Imperial China. Power, status and wealth were not frozen, but somewhat changeable in their distribution — with the obvious caution that a gulf lay between officials and all others.

Social strain in Imperial China was intensified when avenues of entry into the official class became choked. Sale of degreees to bolster government revenues eroded the meritocratic basis of examinations. Reservation of positions on a ethnic basis weakened the system as a whole. Beyond these obvious weaknesses, the whole concept (some have argued) may have been at fault.

Under the "normal" conditions of pre-twentieth century China, however, one should not dismiss the *chin-shih* degree. Admittedly, success was based in large measure on knowledge of the classics and elegant writing rather than on administrative or technical training — inappropriate foundations for governing it would seem. If I may argue by analogy, however, the British Empire at its height was administered by persons whose practical education had not strayed far from Sallust, Xenophon, or Lucretius. "Greats" as taught at Oxford and Cambridge provided a similar basis to that absorbed by *chin-shih* recipients. As Ho notes, "the sufficiently liberal education preparatory to taking the examinations not infrequently equipped candidates with common sense and sound judgment, qualities which were essential to the making of good administrators, especially in an age when comparatively simple administrative problems required no great amount of compartmentalized knowledge."[23] The examination system recruited talented individuals who provided continuity for nearly 1,300 years. Although abused on occasion, as in the sale of degrees, the system reduced the strain that would have resulted had officials been recruited on narrower bases. The mid-nineteenth century, with extensive corruption, sale of degrees, and reservation of positions for Manchus, was a period of restricted entrance to the bureaucracy, and thus was a time of declining administrative effectiveness and widespread social strain.

Social strain existed as well in the relations between rural dwellers and the *yamen*. For the overwhelming majority of the Chinese rural populace, that government was best that interfered and exploited least. The imperial administration was to be held at arm's length, or further if possible. Individuals' responsibilities lay foremost to their families; the district magistrate and all he represented were often unwanted superimpositions. Thus, in Hsiao's careful judgment, "villagers came to regard the yamen not as a place where they could apply for justice or protection but a ruinous pit to be avoided as best they could."[24] Strain thus was inherent in the relationship between the central government and the ordinary peasants, and increased markedly with inept administration.

To help keep the government at arm's length, preserving thereby as much local autonomy as possible, rural dwellers relied on several stratagems. Withdrawal, passivity, and surface acquiescence marked the most common steps. In cases of dispute, villagers drew support from the "lower gentry," who bridged the literate-illiterate, official-peasant gap. The Ch'ing administration sought to restrict rural initiative through this group. Official Confucianism, inculcated through periodic lectures, various ceremonies, and most important through the examination system, encouraged conformity. Peasants were exhorted, for example, to "work diligently at your proper calling in order to give settlement to the aims of the people" or to "pay your taxes fully in order to dispense with official urging."[25] Such maxims collided with an ineluctable fact: the difficult circumstances under which peasants survived. In Hsiao's judgment,

> The dire want and glaring inequities that were the lot of many villagers silently but indisputably controverted almost every one of the injunctions of imperial Confucianism ...in a country where economic production was seldom sufficient to sustain all its inhabitants, where privileged families enjoyed prosperity at the expense of the unprivileged (even though it was only a limited prosperity), and where calamities often brought misery to many of the people, the practice of "virtue" and performance of duty became a luxury which not many could afford.[26]

Thus, the unavoidable disparities between official doctrine and rural actualities produced strain. Under conditions of reasonable weather and basic administrative competence, the disjunctures could be avoided by passivity. Under conditions of natural disaster and official incompetence, strain increased to the breaking point and other resolutions had to be sought — including collective political violence.

Note has already been taken of the interrelationship between natural disaster and human failing. Calamities could be avoided by administrative foresight, exacerbated by administrative ineptitude. Villagers were well aware when "ever normal" granaries were emptied by official defalcation. or dikes not maintained as a result of corruption. Unusual weather conditions threw a strong spotlight on the government, illuminating its relative ability, or inability, to aid the rural populace. In peasants' eyes, officials and landlords who neglected to adjust taxes and rents after natural disasters obviously did not sympathize with the peasants' plight. The subsistence ethic had been violated. Once again, the strains unavoidable in official-peasant and landlord-peasant relationships would become more serious — potential incentives to collective action.

In broadest terms, the inequalities inherent in widespread tenancy and sharecropping were widely perceived as basic inequities. Imperial Confucianism, as we shall describe in greater detail in the following chapter, sought to smooth these over by emphasizing duty, obedience, and "virtue." For each tenet of the official belief, however, a corresponding "false doctrine" existed. Confucianism might rationalize the condition of poor peasants; it could not explain away the fact of exploitation. The numerous peasant rebellions with which Chinese history is studded testify to the ultimate explosions resulting from social, economic and political strains. At some point, collective political violence became the weapon of the weak, seeking relief from the exactions they faced.

Political Strains. The broad observations already made point to several inadequacies in rural administration. Political strains criss-crossed Imperial China. The government sought to quiet opposition by severely constraining the ways in which local dwellers could exercise initiative. The controls were directed primarily toward the literati, whose influence over the peasantry derived from the high status accorded scholars. Stress on official Confucianism meant ideological control — at least in theory — given the paramountcy of obedience ("Honor and respect your elders and superiors," in the 1652 instructions issued by the Shun-chih emperor.)[27] Theory did not conform with reality, however. Attempts to render scholar-officials innocuous to the regime undercut their ability to cope effectively with severe problems. Hsiao — highly critical of late Ch'ing practices — reached the following conclusion:

> After generations of indoctrination and seeking "merits and fame" in the examinations, [scholar-officials] finally became resigned to a philosophy of life that attached little significance to anything beyond personal advancement and gains. Many of the scholars emerged as obedient officials, but few of them became loyal servants of the imperial cause or faithful defenders of imperial Confucianism. They were harmless in ordinary times, but in times of emergency few of them were prepared to help their sovereigns to face the crises.[28]

The reluctance of those atop the political ladder, it may be assumed, betokened an even greater reluctance of those lower in the hierarchy to support the regime actively. Their desire, already noted, was to be left alone. Obviously, government sponsorship of widely beneficial public works (levees, irrigation channels, ever-normal granaries) won support — for taxes should serve purposes other than officials' enrichment. Increased tax levies, a leading feature of nineteenth century China, aroused antipathy; protests, riots, and support for rebels like the Taipings testified to distaste for these exactions.[29] There is ample evidence in Hsiao's book to justify the assertion that peasants regarded official initiatives with the usual pinch of salt. Government steps usually meant greater impositions on already hard-pressed rural dwellers; the common reaction thus was distrust.

The fact of the matter was that the Ch'ing dynasty had little direct power over rural dwellers. China as a whole was large, complex, and fragmented. In pre-telegraph days, even the most urgent exchange of communications between the capital and a remote area consumed several weeks. Provincial officials were circumscribed in the initiative they could exercise, as a result both of the deadening indoctrination noted above, and of the government's tendency to assign officials overlapping responsibilities. Imperial bureaucrats were distrusted, despite their purported fealty to Confucian ethics. The rulers were "consistently more interested in making officials obedient and subservient than in evolving an efficient administration ....Almost every regulation adopted by the emperors to govern officialdom aimed at rendering it innocuous — just as practically every measure of rural control was calculated to make the peasantry peaceful and harmless."[30]

Under ordinary circumstances, as previously stressed, these various political strains could be borne. The devices of Imperial control helped maintain a general equilibrium in earlier but not later parts of the dynastic cycle. The rising challenges to the Ch'ing administration during the nineteenth century compounded existing strains. A vicious circle took shape, external pressures exacerbating internal pressures. Existing channels for problem resolution could not cope with the demands placed on them. Rural discontent swelled. The signs of dynastic decline multiplied. In these circumstances, the question became the basis on which collective action could be mounted. What opportunities lay open to potential rebels against the Imperial government to rally support? To what extent might ethnicity, religion, class, or nationalism undergird collective political violence?

The roots of the Taiping rebellion were embedded in Hakka distinctiveness. The "guest settlers" maintained their ethnic identity in several ways, as noted in the preceding chapter. In outward appearance, Hakka wore hats and clothes of distinctive cut; women's feet were not bound. Marriage outside the group was strongly discouraged. The Hakka clung to their own language, regarding it as superior to other dialects. Their industry and application enabled them to prosper where others had failed—for they could find space only in mountains or less fertile areas.

These contrasts were especially accentuated in Kwangsi and Kwangtung, provinces of seemingly endemic anarchy. Conflict over land hardened communal lines. Ethnic pluralism and powerful lineages produced both social cleavages and considerable local violence. Disputes between the Punti (natives) and the "guest settlers" left a residue of distrust, and pushed both groups vigorously to defend themselves. Hung Hsiu-ch'üan drew upon such a sense on commonality, "a spirit of unity based on language, tradition, and the need for common defense which made every Hakka feel a fraternal loyalty to every other Hakka."[31]

Yet the beliefs encouraged by Hung were more religious than ethnic in content. The God-Worshippers Society won its initial coverts among the Hakka, the group to which Hung and his close associate Feng Yun-shan could most readily preach. The beliefs espoused were universalist, not ethnically particularistic. A restricted initial appeal to one ethnic group did not foreclose its widening to other audiences. As we shall see in examining the Taiping ideology, its claims gave no special place to the Hakka. Appeals were directed to those from many ethnic and economic backgrounds—although the most obvious gainers were those lower in the economic hierarchy.

Given the Taiping concern for diminishing inequalities in landowning, should the rebellion be deemed a class-based uprising? The overwhelming bulk of Taiping followers came from the poor. Farmers and lower class workmen made up the great majority in the beginning; gangs of river pirates joined, as did other floaters for whom the rebels seemed to offer a better future. Such support from the destitute was countered by opposition from the gentry. Note should be taken here of the reasons for their stand:

> The scholars and retired officials who made up this class provided the most consistently anti-Taiping throughout the movement's history...(since), as doctrinaire Confucianists, the gentry placed loyalty to the emperor above all other virtues and ipso facto opposed revolutionaries. Second, the gentry felt a special responsibility for the perpetuation of China's Confucian heritage. To this end the members of the gentry class scrupulously rejected all unorthodox doctrines...Third, the gentry had become virtual captives of the Manchu regime, dependent on Peking for their whole way of life....Any threat to the status quo was a threat to their personal and class interest.[32]

Perceptions of class clearly accounted for a substantial measure of Taiping support. The basic split came between officials and almost all others—in other words, along the basic line of cleavage within Imperial Chinese society. The conflict was not one between classes defined in a strict Western sense, in terms of control over the means of production. What drew most of the rebels together was their sense of economic, political, and social subordination. They were disadvantaged in almost every respect by comparison with the gentry. In seeking rectification, the Taipings made demands for redistribution, Thus, what started from ethnic roots and grew as a result of religious conviction was further encouraged by economic disparities.

Finally, the rebels never hid their desire to unseat the Ch'ing dynasty. Han nationalism played a not insignificant part in the support the Taipings won. Not only was the government inefficient; it was dominated by Manchus, even if they were surrounded by Chinese servitors. In other words, Hung united under the Taiping banner four major bases for collective action. This multiple appeal, one can surmise, accounted in large part for the rapidity with which the movement spread from the mountain fastnesses of Kwangsi into the thickly-populated Yangtse valley.

Yet one must not ascribe initial Taiping success solely to the multiple sources of resentment its leaders tapped. Equally in the picture were the shortcomings of the Ch'ing administration. These will require attention—but only after the bases of collective political violence in the Telengana, Mau Mau and Kwilu rebellions have been considered.

Telengana: Communal and class perceptions of conflict

The Telengana area in 1946 was politically and socially peripheral to India as a whole. Peasants eked out a barely adequate subsistence. The rhythm of rural life seemed to conform to time-honored patterns. Progress, even the idea of change, seemed to have bypassed the region. Narrow concerns of village or caste absorbed the inhabitants' energies and interests. To the outside observer, Telengana appeared to be a relatively passive, forgotten backwater, far removed from the primary concerns of Indian politics. It would have been difficult to imagine such rural dwellers capable of mounting an attack on one of the longest-established ruling houses of the world.

That there were inequalities and perceived inequities in pre-rebellion Hyderabad cannot be denied. The Nizam counted among the world's richest men—and his wealth came only from peasant toil and taxes. His entourage of *jagirdars* and *deshmukhs* squeezed rural producers for half or more of their crops. Within Telengana villages, hereditary landlords and headmen lorded over their subordinates in ways seemingly calculated to arouse resentment. Yet for most of its history, rural Telengana appears to have slumbered, its residents accepting what outsiders often perceived as injustices as the product of fate. Better, it seemed, to conform to present inequalities in the hope the next incarnation of one's soul would be less toilsome. The belief in *karma* justified conformity to one's situation, despite its vicissitudes, as part of the cosmic order. In Hutton's words, *karma* rendered "the superficially inequitable distribution of functions acceptable as being part of a divine order of the universe and a transient episode in the prolonged existence of the individual soul, which by acquiring merit in one existence may rise in the scale in the next, or which may be suffering from a degradation in caste merely by reason of its transgressions in a previous life."[33]

Religious injunctions for conformity and acceptance reinforced the engrained conservatism of rural dwellers in several respects. Peasants in Telengana, as in most of the world, were cautious skeptics when it came to change, reluctant to embark on new steps until their efficacy was clearly shown. The surface inertness of peasants did not entail automatic rejection of collective action—but often made it extremely difficult. Individuals might rationalize their plight as a result of *karma*, as the consequence of dereliction in a previous embodiment rather than as the consequence of human exploitation. Only if they believed that something (or, more accurately, someone) accounted for their tribulations might they potentially be mobilized. Further, the resentments felt individually would have to be generalized in some fashion; coordination of effort lies at the core of collective action. Finally, the potential participants would have to be convinced that their hoped-for gains outweighed the risks they would run. No one of these steps was easy.

On the eve of the rebellion, Hyderabad marked 200 plus years under the Asaf Jahi dynasty. The ruling class was a landed class: power, status and wealth flowed from control over agricultural terrain. The Nizam and his immediate retainers enjoyed the lion's share. A little more than one-third of Hyderabad villages were directly administered by him in the *Sarf-e-Khas* lands. This was not an insignificant resource: a population of six million in an area of 33,700 square miles, about the size of Hungary.[34] The system smacked of feudal patrimonialism with a high degree of personal authoritarianism. Jagirdars enjoyed fiefs granted in return for services to the court. An observer in 1923 castigated the Nizam's administration as "a jumble of varied eccentricities."[35] The court asserted wide-ranging power to allocate land that could profitably be tax-farmed—yet appeared to do little to halt the extractions that weakened the legitimacy of the ruling class as a whole. As we shall see in Chapter 4, the subsistence ethic was increasingly violated in the princely state as a whole.

Economic deprivation was severe. The Telengana area was arid, infertile, overcrowded and liable to declining yields. A substantial portion of the farms were "sub-basic" for a family of five: 32 percent of dry farms, 43.6 percent of wet (irrigated) farms, and nearly 50 percent of garden farms fell below the minimum.[36] Continued subdivision of lands meant scarcity and risk, as did the increasing conversion of subsistence farming areas to the production of commercial crops such as castor seeds and peanuts. Land concentration accelerated during the twentieth century. The consequence can be readily foreseen. Peasants lived close to the margins of existence. Tawney's famous remark about cultivators in China applied equally well to those in Telengana: "There are districts in which the position of the rural population is that of a man standing permanently up to the neck in water, so that even a ripple is sufficient to drown him."[37]

A substantial portion of the Telengana populace had been pushed into tenancy and sharecropping prior to the rebellion. By 1947, about two-fifths of the rural dwellers in Hyderabad as a whole were engaged in agricultural labor, with perhaps two-thirds of these laborers owning no land of their own.[38] But in Warangal district itself, the focus of the rebellion, the insecurity was even greater. A 1931 survey, to which fuller attention will be given in Chapter 4, showed Warangal had the highest percentage of landless tenants and the highest percentage of tenants holding one-year contracts of all districts in Hyderabad.[39]

Indebtedness added to the other burdens peasants experienced. Funds had to be borrowed on occasion: for seed and tools; for ceremonial occasions, such as marriages; for tax payments; for the various unexpected, or certainly undesired, contingent expenses that afflicted the rural populace. Little escape from debt thralldom was possible, given both the marginal nature of many farms and the increasing tendency of money lenders to demand repayment in cash. The suppliers of credit, who had in earlier days conformed more fully to the expectations of the subsistence ethic, turned into loan pirates. Small landowners were increasingly pushed downwards into tenancy, or into a form of perpetual indebtedness known as *bhagela*. Increased use of money thus reduced the autonomy many village dwellers had enjoyed. The barter economy became more and more monetized, with (by 1929) three-quarters of rents being paid in cash.[40] As might be surmised, peasants felt themselves victimized by individuals outside their control, although the increasingly disliked landlords lived in rural areas.

Further squeezes on small-scale cultivators were made by village headmen and record keepers—who, it should be noted, were overwhelmingly Hindu. Such positions of local significance opened the way to exactions for personal benefit. The headmen enjoyed hereditary positions. No organs of local government responsible to the inhabitants existed. (Even at the district and *taluqa* levels, members of various boards were appointed by the court.) Record keepers (*patwaris*) wer literate in an almost totally illiterate society: the 1931 census showed only 4.1 percent of Warangal district residents to be literate.[41] The headmen and record keepers could readily take advantage of their positions to mulct a little bit more from their fellow villagers.

All I have written thus far should make abundantly clear that Telengana peasants did not enjoy a carefree existence. The overwhelming majority suffered economic woes of some sort. Though these might have been ascribed to *karma*, the various vicissitudes in fact reflected abuses of a system based on a scarce commodity—land—increasingly subjected to the use of cash. Apart from extending irrigation, little new area could be opened for cultivation; population growth brought further subdivision; cash crops occupied evergreater amounts of cultivable land; there were few opportunities for industrial employment, and scant desire for emigration, even were there somewhere to go.

As one should expect, these various economic inequalities were closely linked to social differentiations. The overwhelming contrast was that between Hindu sharecroppers on the one hand and the privileged—Muslim officials, *jagirdars*, and large Hindu proprietors—on the other hand.

The top rungs of the social ladder were occupied by Muslim officials, and major Hindu landlords who associated themselves with the Nizam. It will be recalled that Hindus constituted nearly 90 percent of the population of Hyderabad; yet the government and repressive forces were almost totally Muslim. To be specific, Muslims constituted 75 percent of the state officials and 95 percent of the police and military services.[42] The power of Hindu landlords stemmed from the fact the court drew on allies linked to it by mutual interest in maintaining a socioeconomic order of obvious profit to them.

A reform of the late nineteenth century, as Chapter 3 will illustrate, eliminated auctioning off revenue collection in government administered areas in favor of direct collection by the state. The result was a mutually profitable alliance between the Court and major landlords, most of them Hindu. Their involvement in money-lending made *deshmukhs* purveyors of the detested *bhagela* indebtedness. The Muslim-Hindu gulf was thus joined by strain between Hindu sharecroppers and Hindu *deshmukhs*.

These income and status differentiations were not the only lines of demarcation within the majority populace. The Hindu community was fragmented by that distinctly Indian phenomenon, caste. The social divisions inherent in caste provided social strain and complicated collective action; although individual castes (*jati*) might be mobilized in favor of joint objectives, cooperation across *jati* lines was often difficult.

The essentially feudal society of Hyderabad was pervaded by caste.

Caste customs and regulations provided the Hindu majority the basis for social interactions, maintained a compartmentalized and essentially homeostatic society, and crippled any attempts at joint action. An individual's birth determined his or her position in society, and heavily influenced career choice and marriage partner. Marriage outside the caste was rare; an occupation was often monopolized by members of one caste; subordinate and superordinate relationships among *jati* existed in all areas. Although it would have been impossible, and probably fruitless, to rank in social prestige the 3,000 or so castes that marked India at her independence, their importance for social stratification cannot be underestimated.

By far the largest caste in Hyderabad—indeed, in south India as a whole—was the Reddi caste. Hutton estimated 2 to 3 million Reddis in the area, most of whom were farmers or landowners[43]—obviously occupations important for any rural rebellion. As might be expected, many *deshmukhs* were themselves Reddis, leading to social strain within the caste itself. Although social strain among groups was mitigated to a substantial degree by the caste system as a whole, with its elaborate prescriptions for avoidances and interactions, economic inequality within a single caste posed complex social issues. The dominant communal cleavage in Hyderabad remained that between Muslims and Hindus, yet the latter were thus subject to a multitude of tensions, rooted in caste and economic differentiation.

Political tensions remain to be treated. As noted in the preceding chapter, the events of Indian independence and partition disturbed even the placidity of Hyderabad. The princely state could not be isolated from the rest of India, nor had it been isolated in the period of the British *raj;* yet the pace of change differed from neighboring areas. Not having been incorporated into British India, Hyderabad retained many aspects of its essentially feudal structure. Political change was both partial and belated. The Nizam remained intent on exercising power. Although British pressure and an enterprising leader, Sir Salar Jung, encouraged administrative reform, including the establishment of a Hyderabad consultative legislative council and cabinet late in the nineteenth century, these institutions remained powerless. A series of reforms in British India from 1919 to 1937, in which undivided imperial control yielded to dyarchy and this in turn to provincial self-government, had no real parallels in Hyderabad. Essentially hereditary positions in the princely state (including the *deshmukhs* and *jagirdars*) contrasted sharply with the elective positions outside its borders. Thus, I suggest, an unavoidable political and economic strain affected Hyderabad politics as India edged towards self-government. Despite its special status, Hyderabad and its residents were linked to the larger context of political change in India.

Members of the Nizam's administration were fully aware of their minority status. Ideally, many wanted full independence; failing that, loose ties with Pakistan. Their interest in links with Pakistan rather than India resulted more from political considerations than from religious scruples. Had Hyderabad been linked to Pakistan in some fashion, the status quo—in other words, Muslim dominance—might have been solidified. Any form of strain that became inflamed along communal lines risked upsetting the delicate balance between minority control and majority acquiescence. The more marked the religious tensions throughout the subcontinent as a whole, accordingly, the more likely there would be stress in Hyderabad.

Muslims dominated the few political institutions that existed in Hyderabad, although the new legislature established in 1946 contained twice as many Hindu as Muslim seats. Frankly, there were almost no political avenues by which the majority populace of Hyderabad—including the villagers of Telengana—could advocate and pursue change. Perhaps the only indigenous institution attuned to Hindu concerns was the *panchayat*, or caste council. As the title suggests, however, *panchayats* confined their attention to relatively parochial matters; they could not resolve the fundamental economic, social and political inequalities that were firmly grounded in the pre-1948 structure of Hyderabad. District boards were not only nominated, as already noted; they were essentially impotent. The government was zealous in banning any political organization suspected of pressing Hindu rights. Landlords and village heads tended to respond more in terms of self-interest than in terms of service to their "constituents." The residents of Telengana were perforce mute observers of the political pressures swirling about them. Such strains, seemingly without channels for peaceful resolution, could provide impetus for collective political violence—if an appropriate basis for collective action existed.

The strains briefly considered thus far do not constitute an exhaustive catalogue. They are intended to illustrate a setting in which inequality was marked, and increasing. The conditions in Hyderabad were not unique; other parts of India witnessed similar disjunctures. The Telengana villagers were not the only ones to turn to rebellion, in the seeming absence of means for reform. Their violence, however, required a foundation on which individual discontent could become a generalized grievance—in short, a basis for collective action. What types of identification could the rebels draw upon in their struggle against the Nizam and his allies?

The Telengana rebellion, it should be apparent, was not a simple Hindu-Muslim confrontation writ large. The uprising started as a classic landlord-tenant confrontation, to which communal tension contributed by creating an atmosphere of general political tension. Hindu *deshmukhs* allied with the court and the values for which it stood aroused grievances from which collective political violence sprang. The interests of the rural disadvantaged required land redistribution, not necessarily total destruction of minority political control. Nonetheless, the power of Muslims, especially many *jagirdars*, was liable to challenge by rival dwellers.

In looking thus at sources of strain, we must remain aware of the complex social structure that existed in Hyderabad, divided along ascriptive, religious, and economic lines. Depressed groups—the "Hill" Reddis, the Telagas—stood on the bottom rung of the social ladder. A relatively high correspondence existed between Islam and power, status and wealth. On the other hand, the richest landlords were Hindus, notably members of the Kapu group of the Reddis. The princely state was, immediately following World War II, more a pluralized than a polarized society. It was a setting rife with tensions, not necessarily a setting propitous to largescale collective political violence.

Finally, strain existed in Hyderabad as a simple consequence of its geographic placement. Without the pressures of Indian independence, the Telengana rebellion might never have taken place. The Hyderabad borders were permeable to various pressures. Ideas and aspirations could cross them readily, given the ties of language, *jati*, and religion that extended into Hyderabad from neighboring regions. The idea of a state in which Telugu would be the official language arose in India, and gained support in Hyderabad. The communal coloration of the Nizam's government was reinforced after 1947 by actions of Muslim razakars, many of whom entered Hyderabad from the now-partitioned India. Hindu villagers in Telengana, with encouragement from the Andhra Mahasabha and later the Communist party of India, took village power in their own hands. They responded, even if indirectly, to the currents of *swaraj*—self-government—that were sweeping through the subcontinent. The international context thus directly affected various bases of social strain.

It is thus not possible to give a simple answer to the question posed a few paragraphs ago. Potential rebels could draw upon several foundations for collective action. Since Hindus tended to rank low in power, status and wealth, it could be argued that collective violence should be mounted communally, by the numerically strong but economically and politically weak. It could also be argued that class rather than communalism would constitute the crucial glue, since Hindu *deshmukhs* were as much the targets of the uprising as the Nizam and his court retainers. In fact, given the more immediate impact *deshmukhs* had on village affairs compared with the distant court, land and economic grievances shorn of religious identification might appear to be greater contributors to rebellion than communal identifiction. And, finally, it might be argued that the ultimate basis for collective political violence was competing nationalisms, embodied in Congress and the Moslem League. Their incompatible claims led to the partition of the former British territory. Major changes engulfed all princely states, whose inhabitants could not be isolated from growing political consciousness. This mixture of motives, this overlaping of bases for collective action, characterized the Telengana rebellion. Its participants responded to a variety of economic, social and political strains — as had the Taiping rebels before them, and as would the Mau Mau and Kwilu rebels in following decades.

Kikuyu Clans and Communal Land Tenure

Communal land tenure stood at the heart of the Kikuyu social structure. In this respect, a profound difference existed from "traditional" Chinese and Indian societies. In the former, individual proprietorship, including the sale of land, had been known for a millenium when the Taiping rebellion erupted. In the latter, *zamindars* (a more inclusive term for India than *deshmukhs*) had for centuries reaped the economic benefits of their control over sharecroppers. Landlords, in short, characterized both societies. Their counterparts, however, were largely unknown in precolonial Africa. Although the label of "feudalism" has been attached to certain African societies,[44] it does not limn historical reality.

In broadest terms, the persistence of communal land patterns south of the Sahara testified to a relative abundance of tillable soil. Shifting bush fallow agriculture represented the dominant pattern: an area would be cleared for cultivation, farmed for 25 years depending on soil fertility, then allowed to return to bush for ecological regeneration.[45] Intense population pressures would be met through a variety of means, stopping short of formal recognition of individual land title. Rights to land existed in the name of the group, whose members were entitled to what they grew. Usufruct was granted, and permanent improvements recognized. Neither incorporated the Asian — or European — conception of individual proprietorship. The "Asiatic mode of production" (to note one of Marx's murkier concepts) had little applicability in tropical Africa.

It follows, accordingly, that peasantries as known in Asia and Europe did not exist in pre-colonial tropical Africa. Availability of land and opportunities for migration; the paucity of cities; the "absence," in Fallers' words, of "literary religious traditions"[46] that emphasized rural dwellers' rustic nature; the relatively limited power of the traditional state: these figure among the arguments advanced. The most important, however, was the absence of landlordism. Only with the advent of colonial rule were severe restrictions, both legal and sociological, put on communal land tenure, and rural cultivators reduced to subordinate economic and political roles. The transformations were great in extent, profound in their impact. In order to grasp the magnitude of alterations, it is appropriate to survey pre-colonial social structure, leaving to the two following chapters information about the consequences of European colonial rule.

Social structure among the Kikuyu was far more diffuse than hierarchical. Based in large measure on the *mbari* or clan, solidarity depended on ancestral ties. Considerable geographic diffusion came about as the result of both population growth and fissiparous tendencies generally. Initiation ceremonies marked important transitions in life for individuals, and emphasized commonality (through age-sets) among the Kikuyu clans. Status differentials within the society as a whole existed, with elders and family heads recognized as preeminent. Political power was split among several centers rather than concentrated. Kikuyu society lacked a paramount chief or analogous single, living focus of the political system. It was, in short, acephalous and uncentralized.[47] Since these characteristics directly impinged on the Mau Mau rebellion, careful note must be taken of each.

Geographic movement deserves initial attention. There is no place or date that marks the founding of the Kikuyu people. The most thorough recent study places the origin of the Kikuyu from an amalgam of several peoples late in the sixteenth century.[48] Moving generally to the south and west in areas of high agricultural potential, the Kikuyu developed both a highly successful farming way of life and a set of beliefs that, in Muriuki's judgment, "acted as a focus, or symbol, of unity, thereby welding together the various disparate elements into one people...and...legitimized Kikuyu claims to the ownership of land, since their present homeland was bestowed upon their mythical ancestors by Providence."[49] Diffusion was encouraged by population growth (itself a reflection of the fertility and salubrious nature of their areas of settlement), the coexistence with and eventual absorption of hunting-based peoples, and the maintenance of ceremonies reaffirming solidarity.

Migration was a gradual process. The absence of written documentation makes it necessary to rely on oral traditions, in which the *mbari* (lineages or sub-clans) and *mariika* (age-sets) played key roles. Each lineage identified itself in terms of common descent from its founder. This tie of kinship, however, was buttressed by land. Each *mbari* possessed lands, whose utilization was affected by group norms. In Muriuki's words,

> all the land belonged to the *mbari* as a whole, and...any member of the *mbari* had the right to utilize any part of it so long as no one else had made prior claim to it and, more important, provided that the head of the *mbari*, the *muramati* (guardian) was informed.[50]

A clear identification of land with a family existed, however. As Kenyatta expressed the matter, differing in emphasis from Muriuki,

> The sense of private property vested in the family was so highly developed among the Gikuyu, but the form of private ownership in the Kikuyu community did not necessarily mean the exclusive use of the land by the owner, or the extorting of rents from those who wanted to have cultivation or building rights...the land did not belong to the community as such, but to some individual founders of various families who had the full rights of ownership and the control of the land.[51]

The contrast between these statements is more apparent than real. As long as land remained available, free scope for settlement existed. The general principle of communal land tenure could coexist with recognized family claims to land. It was the combined effect of restriction on migration imposed by British rule, colonial efforts to foster Kikuyu movements into wage labor or sharecropping on European farms, and growing abuses of power by the *muramati* that afflicted the self-equilibrating nature of the system. In the past, migration to new lands, and the opportunity of founding new *mbari*, provided safety valves; after 1903, these avenues became increasingly blocked by the British administration.

Note should be taken of the nature of settlement. The topography of Kikuyuland imposed certain geographical givens on the *mbari*. The eastern escarpment of the Nyandura (Aberdare) range is cut into a series of parallel ridges by rivers. Communication between ridges even today remains difficult.[52] Thus, it was not surprising that social solidarity was strongest within an individual ridge, for such constituted the foundation of an *mbari*. Again to quote Muriuki,

> The settlements were invariably acquired on a ridge basis, each clan settling in its own ridge. It is clear, therefore, that the nature of the terrain, in conjunction with the nature of immigration, were of vital importance in influencing the pattern of land tenure that emerged. Land acquisition was on the basis of first come first served....Land initially belonged to an individual or a small group of closely related people. But with the increase in population, this circle grew wider through the generations to include the descendants of the original pioneers . . .such a group had a strong community interest...This, then, saw the birth of the ancestral land, to which in the course of time the descendants became deeply attached for economic and religious purposes.[53]

It should not be assumed that each ridge was socially homogeneous, populated by members of a single *mbari*. The point is rather that settlement of the lineage was traditionally located in a particular site. None of the land under the control of the *mbari* could be alienated without concurrence of all adult males. However, opportunities for cultivation could be offered to *ahoi* (tenants) or *anthoni* (in-laws) "so long as they were of good behaviour and provided the consent of the whole *mbari* had been sought beforehand."[54] The *ahoi* played a useful part in opening land for cultivation, and were welcome to work available areas. Tenants formed an essential part of the social structure yet were qualitatively different from the sharecroppers of China and India. It was only with the imposition of colonial rule that *ahoi* were pushed into clearly inferior positions.

The geographic constraints and the descent-based nature of the *mbari* obviously complicated the establishment of a sense of unity on the basis of the Kikuyu as a whole. The relatively egalitarian social structure militated against the establishment of a system of political paramountcy. Acephalous Kikuyu society, in other words, by definition lacked a hierarchy in political power, although elders, as members of the *kiama* (council) enjoyed high status. A sense of corporate identity of standing above the *mbari* rested on institutions such as the *mariika* (age-sets). As was noted above, initiation ceremonies marked transitions in personal status (e.g. circumcision, after which marriage could be embarked upon) on a group as well as an individual basis. The ceremonies also emphasized the cultural unity of the Kikuyu, developing among those initiated concurrently a sense of solidarity—of sisterhood or brotherhood—transcending clan or territorial differences. Muriuki notes the following consequences:

> Among themselves, the members of an age set demanded and encouraged cooperation, solidarity and mutual help as a result of which an age group exhibited a strong sense of comradeship and fraternal egalitarianism.[55]

The highest status in Kikuyu society was enjoyed by elders. Given the presumed equation of age and experience with wisdom, the senior elders occupied a position of respect—as was indeed typical of "traditional" societies. This did not result, however, in a gerontocracy. Although councils of elders (*kiama*) existed, this was a mark of social status. Leadership, though correlated with age to some extent, depended far more on personal qualities. Ability to represent effectively the wishes of his peers seems to have been the chief criterion for selection:

> the *muthamaki* (spokesman) was no more than the chairman of a territorial unit or leader of his riika [age set]. His powers were very circumscribed and he could only act in accordance with the wishes of his peers who delegated power to him. He was not a chief; the idea of chiefs had no basis in the political institutions of the Kikuyu....[56]

In summary, pre-colonial Kikuyu society manifested seven major characteristics.

1. The openness of Kikuyu society reflected its relatively pacific expansion, which occurred by purchase of land from or absorption of hunting groups.

2. Although the ethnic group as a whole was subject to periodic natural calamities, such as plagues of locusts or disease, the general fertility and salubrity of the Kenya highlands permitted considerable population growth through opening additional land to cultivation.

3. This expansion came about in large measure through clans (*mbari*), based on lines of descent, areas of settlement, and maintenance of *mbari* land on which clan members had right of settlement.

4. *Mbari* terrains could not be permanently sold, save under unusual circumstances, and provided a foundation for continued lineage identification.

5. Recognized difference of status existed, based to some extent on age. Considerable scope existed for individual leaders, who derived their power from consensual support. Leadership was neither hereditary nor based on a formal examination system, but depended on a gradual process of recognition and experience.

6. Although central political institutions were lacking, the age set (*mariika*) system instilled a sense of Kikuyu cultural identity.

7. Squatters (*ahoi*) played important roles in the opening of new lands, receiving cultivation rights in return for labor. As long as new areas continued to come under cultivation, squatters enjoyed relative security; with checks put on expansion, they were liable to eviction.

The picture presented thus far of the Kikuyu prior to colonial rule suggests a relatively egalitarian society. Admittedlly, differences in power, status and wealth existed. A respected *mbari* elder clearly enjoyed greater prestige than a younger, untested individual; through his *kiama* membership, he exercised a degree of power consonant with his status. Wealth could be accumulated to some degree, depending on the amount of land under cultivation. The limiting factor was labor. Hence, the more wives (for Kikuyu society recognized and encouraged polygyny), offspring, and *ahoi* clients a head of household counted, the larger the terrain that could be tilled and the greater the concomitant status and wealth. On the other hand, a ceiling of sorts existed on accumulation, owing to duties to members of the same age set and sub-clan. Even squatters enjoyed some degree of social security, for they could return to clan lands or move on to different areas if evicted by their patrons.

Such dynamic equilibrium—of growth accommodated over time by the founding of new clans and the settling of new lands—required regions for expansion. Any major interruption could induce strains potentially unaccommodatable within traditional means of problem resolution. The British invasion of Kikuyuland obviously had such an impact. Movement beyond lines drawn by the colonial administration was blocked. The Kikuyu were confined to increasingly crowded reserves, or made liable to eviction from the whiteowned lands on which they squatted. To foreshadow the consequences of British rule, differences of power, status and wealth were dramatically sharpened among the Kikuyu. Some were selected as imperial adjuncts: imposed as chiefs in a society where leaders had emerged through process of internal consultation and selection, they could abuse their new powers to grab land for themselves and their families. The imposition of taxes payable in cash pushed individuals into wage employment, meaning a partial surrender of the autonomy they had enjoyed. The arrival of white farmers, administrators and businessmen, and of Asian entrepreneurs and clerks, encouraged commercial and industrial expansion with its concomitant, greater income inequalities. Administrative need for educated Africans in lower civil service positions opened new avenues to employment and status—a water meter reader, as Jomo Kenyatta became, gained a fair amount of prestige, in addition to salary of 250 shillings per month. Education—and especially literacy in English—became prized. An alternative avenue to status opened, this based on formal educational attainments rather than *riika* or *mbari* leadership. These alterations—all of which affected bases for collective action among the Kikuyu—resulted from the imposition of colonial rule.

Within the Kikuyu *qua* ethnic group, two contrasting routes for collective action existed. An *mbari* drew together men, their wives, and offspring from several geographic settings and economic circumstances. (Upon marriage, wives were adopted into their husband's sub-clan; the Kikuyu did not practice endogamy.) On the other hand, *mariika* were separated by sex and age. Members of each group, as they were initiated, developed a strong sense of group esprit. Neither basis for collective action detracted from a sense of commonality among the Kikuyu as a whole. *Mbari* were drawn from the various clans descended from the nine daughters of Gikuyu and Mumbi, legendary founders of the Kikuyu people. Under most conditions, *mbari* ties were far more salient than identification with all the descendants of Mumbi. Some conditions were unusual. In the Mau Mau rebellion, as in other times when it was necessary to foster solidarity and unity within the Kikuyu community, the myth of common ancestry became important.[57] The belief was there, activatable as circumstance demanded. The initiation ceremony for each *riiki* "binds together those of the same status in ties of closest loyalty and devotion," in Kenyatta's words. The age-group thus served as a "powerful instrument for securing conformity with tribal usage."[58] The rite of circumcision, which prepared Kikuyu for marriage, was an occasion on which responsibilities to others and a sense of ethnic identity could be inculcated.

It was the shock of colonial occupation that encouraged collective expression of grievances along ethnic lines. The Kikuyu felt the impact of British rule more markedly than other groups in Kenya. The fact that collective political violence in the Mau Mau rebellion followed essentially ethnic lines did not mean, however, that other foundations for collective action did not exist or contribute to the uprising. Let us take brief note of these, for they provide an instructive contrast with other cases.

Religious movements provided many African societies means of coping with the strains imposed by colonial rule, [59] as a surrogate for political protests banned by the administration. Adaptation of Christian messages—especially those dealing with equality of believers—cloaked criticism of British rule. Religious protest was a step toward political action. Several Mau Mau participants have suggested in their memoirs that indigenous sects derived from Chrisitian teachings—and not dissimilar to the God-Worshippers Society of Hung Hsiu-ch'üan—marked a stage of their pilgrimage toward rebellion.[60]

Several aspects of Christianity, as brought to Kenya by European missionaries, collided with basic Kikuyu values. Female circumcision and polygyny were two chief areas of contention. Perhaps somewhat surprisingly, as will be shown subsequently, the effects of this controversy were felt more in education (over which the missionaries exercised near-total control) than in religious schism. Independent churches were rare among the Kikuyu, and few significant links seem to have been established by Mau Mau leaders with independent churches among other ethnic groups.

Religious elements did enter into the Mau Mau rebellion through the oathing ceremony, also a subject for later attention. The symbols used, however, had an impact primarily on Kikuyu participants. Rather than broaden participation, the religious background to Mau Mau was one that reinforced ethnic identification. There was no parallel in colonial Kenya to Hung, who transcended initial Hakka particularism through his adaptation of both Christian teachings and themes of rebellion common in Chinese history.

Relative to the privileged Europeans, all Africans in Kenya were downtrodden. The degree of perception of subordination varied markedly, however, based on proximity to foci of colonial impact and adaptability of indigenous values as the constraining variables. The Kikuyu felt the British impact sharply, other groups far less so. The degree of "classness" cutting across the Kenyan African population was low relative (in situations of conflict) to ethnic identification. I do not wish to imply that economic deprivation was unimportant in the Mau Mau rebellion; it was, in fact, a basic cause. It tended to result more in grievances expressed on a tribal than on a class basis, however. By comparison with the intensity of feeling on ethnic lines, class was a secondary basis for collective action. Whether an individual supported or opposed Mau Mau depended to a large extent on his power, status or wealth: those who had gained as a result of the British presence hesitated to give full support to the rebels, whose call for changed economic and political relationships indirectly threatened their positions. Even among the Kikuyu, accordingly, the extent of support varied to some degree with personal circumstance, as defined economically.

Finally, political change that would benefit the Kikuyu meant some type of alteration for Kenya as a whole. The multi-ethnic character of the colony had a clear effect on the Mau Mau rebellion. The chief protagonist of constitutional change benefiting Africans was the Kenya African Union (usually known by its acronym, KAU), whose membership, though heavily Kikuyu, drew from many African ethnic groups. The differential impact of colonial rule in various parts of Kenya entailed an equally uneven support for KAU. Further, the antipathy felt toward the British by the Kikuyu far outstripped that of other Africans. The well-known process of divide-and-rule meant the Kikuyu could be isolated from other ethnic groups to some extent. Yet one must not underestimate nationalism, in the sense of a desire for Kenyan independence, as a basis for collective action. Though muted relative to the intensity of Kikuyu feeling, it nonetheless influened the accomodations the British soon had to make. Even though the colonial administration crushed Mau Mau militarily, it soon had to concede political independence, open the white highlands to African settlement, and welcome the supposed leader of the rebellion to the heights of power. The rebellion hastened change that affected the entire colony.

Kwilu: Economic Impetus to Ethnic Rebellion

The Mau Mau rebellion surged along "traditional" lines of collective action. Its initiation testified to grievances experienced most heavily by the Kikuyu; its suppression became synonymous to the British with cauterizing the Kikuyu of their political militance. The more marked the impact of the colonizing power, the greater the resentment accumulated by the colonized and the greater the desire of the incumbents to reassert control. Far more than ethnic exclusiveness entered into the rebellion. Although cultural ties served as the basis for collective political violence, precipitating grievances stemmed from a variety of sources.

Similar phenomena affected the 1963-4 uprising in Kwilu. It, too, sprang from groups profoundly touched by the economic, political and social consequences of colonial rule. It erupted, as noted earlier, in an area marked by religious syncretism, labor unrest, and political party solidarity.

A rich foundation for collective action existed in Kwilu. Support for rebellion extended throughout the countryside. In the judgment of the most thorough Western observer of Kwilu politics, "rural radicalism"[61] pushed leaders to stands more extreme than they might otherwise have taken. The desire for dramatic change was not brought from outside the local setting; on more than one occasion, residents of Kwilu had risked imprisonment or death for their views, without prompting from others. Collective political violence in Kwilu long antedated the "second independence" uprising of 1963-4, and drew on strains inherent in the local setting.

The question — Why did the rural populace of Kwilu seem to accept Pierre Mulele's Maoist message with such enthusiasm? — thus can be answered by history: a history of many forms of protest, often based on ethnic solidarity, but drawing on religious, economic and political sources as well. Protest took root in a setting marked by substantial transformation of the former subsistence agricultural basis. One should not assume that residents of Kwilu were economically disadvantaged as a result of this transformation. For the great majority of the colonial period, they enjoyed a relatively privileged position. Harvesting palm products brought them economic benefits and (more speculatively) political awareness few other rural dwellers could match. The rewards of full-scale participation in the cash economy carried corresponding risks, however. Collapse in world market prices, or interruption of marketing or distribution, placed the cash-dependent *coupeurs de fruit* in an immediate bind.

The *coupeurs de fruit* (heavily but exclusively drawn from the Pende group) had abandoned the surety — as well as the relative poverty — of subsistence agriculture from the 1920s. They enjoyed no influence over the prices they received for the palm nuts so arduously gathered throughout the year. Compared individually with the gigantic plantations of Huileries du Congo Belge, harvesters were impotent. Their participation was limited to collection; oil presses remained in European hands, with there being, in the mid-1950s, but one African owned mill among the 100.[62] The absence of indigenous influence over palm prices paralleled African impotence vis-a-vis government economic policies. Impressed labor, which marked Kwilu until the 1931 Pende revolt, seemed necessary to the administration to make plantations economically viable. Government revenues had to be maintained despite economic vicissitudes. The sudden drop in world prices during the Depression affected the *coupeurs'* income, not the taxes they owed. Their earnings dropped 50 to 60 percent; the head tax remained unchanged. This levy (45 francs for an unmarried laborer, up to 80 francs for one with several wives) required a minimum of one-fifth to one-quarter of annual earnings. (The average amount collected annually was 180-200 cases of palm nuts: the minimum tax required 43 cases, about 1,500 kilograms.)[63] By August 1934, prices paid for palm products plummeted to one fifth their 1928 levels.[64] Disjunctures among earnings, expenses, and expectations gaped widely. In the eyes of the harvesters, colonial insensitivity to their plight violated the basic norms.

As regular participants in the cash economy, the *coupeurs* were sensitive as well to shortages of necessary imported goods. World War II, as might be expected, severely restricted consumer products, even while palm production soared. Shortages continued even after the arrival of peace. Elsewhere in Africa, and perhaps most notably in the Gold Coast, such scarcity led to major political consequences. Organized boycotts and protests led to the unexpected police killing of six marchers in February 1948; the subsequent Royal Commission recommended substantial constitutional advances leading to early self-government for the Gold Coast.[65] This decision set Great Britain firmly on the path to African decolonization — even though the resolve was by no means as clear or strong when applied to settler-dominated Kenya. Belgium heeded warning signals in a different fashion. Political advance would be discouraged and delayed. Instead, economic and social transformations would be encouraged, creating thereby, at some distant time, a foundation on which political progress might occur. Explicitly political groups for Africans could not legally exist in the Belgian Congo; surrogate forms had to be used. As a result, ethnic associations and syncretistic religious movements followed in the wake of economic deprivation and political stagnation; parties could organize openly only in 1959-1960, and thus had scant opportunity to gain experience in governing before self-government was granted 30 June, 1960.

Economic discontent crested with the post-independence collapse of many services throughout Kwilu. The flight of most Europeans in 1960 immobilized large parts of the commercial sector. The *coupeurs* could harvest palm nuts — but these could neither be sold, transported, nor processed. This abrupt collapse coincided with an equally abrupt deflation of popular expectations. As we shall see in Chapter 4, the sense of relative deprivation grew to major proportions. The hopes nurtured by independence were punctured; the process had been sabotaged in some fashion. Economic, social and political grievances interacted to make the dream of a "second independence" all the more appealing. Not unsurprisingly, the disaffected palm nut harvesters played a prominent part in the resulting collective political violence. Their discontent may well have been higher than that of other rural dwellers, given the severe consequences of economic collapse on their expectations and style of life.

In comparison with the Kikuyu, the economic-cum-social discontent inherent in land alienation remained muted among the major ethnic groups of Kwilu. Ample land existed for cultivation. Even given the establishment of plantations, residents had little difficulty finding new plots to till. Only 1.8 percent of the entire area was under cultivation.[66] In his detailed study of Kwilu, Nicolai examined a Pende village, whose land chief controlled 185 square kilometers; only 40 square kilometers, almost entirely covered by oil palms, were exploited by residents. [67] The unsupportable population densities of Kikuyuland had no parallel in Kwilu. Land chiefs among the Pende did not become centers of controversy, nor did they appear (unlike many Kikuyu chiefs recognized by the British) to abuse their positions to grab terrain for their own exploitation.

To be certain, colonial administration led to substantial modifications in the traditional social structure. Village influentials were incorporated into lower government echelons. Their responsibilities in labor recruitment, tax collection, and other unpleasant tasks significantly reduced what indigenous legitimacy they may have enjoyed. The Pende social structure included clan notables and land chiefs, not village chiefs per se. Belgian creation of such individuals—giving them powers and duties outside the usual sphere of corporate responsibility—induced social strain.

The effects of Western education deserve brief note. Those employed by the colonial administration enjoyed relative power and affluence; yet the Belgians preferred, for obvious reasons, to employ those literate in French. (Despite the concern of Flemish speakers, French was the official administrative language in the Congo—perhaps surprising in view of the fact that, by 1958, those of Flemish extraction accounted for 53 percent of the colonial civil servants and 83 percent of the missionaries.)[68] The educated *evolués* both gained prestige and aroused some antipathy among their less trained brethren; as we shall see subsequently, *evolués* occupied most leadership positions in the rebellion, yet the uprising itself was directed in large part against the abuses of members of this group. This seeming paradox of the educated leading collective political violence against other educated persons, I hasten to add, is not unusual in rebellion: in the Taiping and Mau Mau rebellions, the strongest indigenous opposition came from those whose educational achievements had placed them among the socially privileged.

Kwilu as a whole was, and remains, a multiethnic region with clear zones dominated by single groups. The relative homogeneity of individual villages contrasts sharply with the polyglot nature of the whole region. An ethnic map[69] shows a patchwork of groups: Mbala, Ngongo, Sonde, Pende, Singa, Tschokwe, Lunda, Yansi, Pindi, Mputu, Ngoli and even more, are displayed. Kwilu was in many respects a zone of refuge: from agents of European and Arab slavers; from the expansive Bakongo, Lunda, or Tschokwe; from the demands of imperial rule. It was also a zone of opportunity, with palm nut harvesting attracting immigrants. Huileries du Congo Belge and other large employers encouraged the settlement of dependable workers, not necessarily indigenous to the locale. Towns such as Idiofa, Kikwit, and Leverville were centers of economic change in the colonial period. Collisions among members of different groups represented a social strain that could fracture the common goals of Kwilu residents. The problems of the Parti Solidaire Africain in the face of ethnic fragmentation, we shall see in Chapter 6, hinted at problems of unity later encountered during the rebellion.

These social and economic strains were matched by a series of political strains. These cannot be disentangled from the facts of colonial administration. Kwilu was an artifact of Belgian rule. An appendage of the Bakongo-dominated lower Congo through most of the preindependence period, Kwilu was politically submerged, though economically central. In the Free State period and early years of Belgian administration, Kwilu formed part of the Kwango district. The creation of provinces (four in 1926, enlarged to six in 1933) maintained this subordination: Kwango was one of six districts in Congo-Kasai Province 1926-33; one of four districts in Leopoldville Province after 1933; not until 1954 was Kwilu administratively defined.[70]

Incorporation in Leopoldville Province meant an important boost to political awareness in Kwilu, beyond that stemming from economic development. Residents of Kwilu constituted a permanent minority in relationship to the Bakongo, whose quest for unification with fellow Bakongo in the Portuguese colony of Angola and the French colony of Moyen-Congo stirred the political waters for many years. In the terminal years of Belgian rule, the Bakongo party ABAKO—Alliance des Bakongo—mounted the most potent challenge to the colonial administration. ABAKO desire for an ethnically homogeneous state separated from the remainder of the Belgian Congo, or at best linked to it by weak federal bonds, imperiled the commitment of Kwilu leaders to a unified state within the colony's existing boundaries. The Parti Solidaire Africain thus developed in an intense, complex political atmosphere replete with strain.

Political leaders had to take cognizance as well of "rural radicalism" that affected popular perceptions. As I shall seek to illustrate in later chapters, the initiation of party activity opened the floodgates of public pressure. In many respects, the leaders were themselves led; their efforts often were expended in reining back seemingly insatiable rural demands for material and political benefits. Of the four rebellions analyzed in this book, that in Kwilu seems to have manifested the farthest-reaching indigenous concern for change.

Let us turn now to the foundations for collective action. These will be analyzed, following the pattern of previous sections, in terms of ethnic, religious, economic, and regional/nationalist bases.

Most ethnic groups in Kwilu were decentralized in structure. They were acephalous societies, lacking powerful chiefs who could have served as symbols of resistance to imperial pressures, or been incorporated into the colonial superstructure. As among the Kikuyu, clans served as regulators of social relationships. Marriage was exogamous: a new bride moved to her husband's village, but their children belonged to her clan and often, at adolescence, left to join their maternal uncles. Land helped sustain clan solidarity. It was the property of the ancestors. Allocation for use rested on land chiefs. Serving in effect as intermediaries between the ancestors and current inhabitants, the land chiefs functioned as trustees, able to grant rights ranging from simple usufruct up to full cession. Pende villages historically started as single-clan settlements; Nicolai observed a continuing tendency for each clan to occupy a distinct part of a village.[71] This may account for the absence of village chiefs within the traditional Pende social structure; Belgian rule brought them into being as administrative adjuncts. Age-sets seem to have limited importance—the Pende lacked counterparts to the Kikuyu *mariika*.

That this decentralized system could serve as a focus for collective political violence was amply demonstrated in 1931. The Pende revolt of that year represented perhaps the most significant challenge the Belgian administration confronted between the termination of the Free State in 1908 and the Leopoldville riots of January 1959. I have already taken note of the abrupt descent of palm prices in the face of steady or even rising tax burdens. This grievance was reinforced by covert continuation of labor impressment, by obligatory relocation of villages close to roads (this step being taken to combat sleeping sickness, enhance commercial development, and increase administrative surveillance), and by mandatory participation in road building. Resentment among the *coupeurs* burst into the open in May 1931, with the decapitation of a European territorial agent. Repression was rapid and brutal after negotiations collapsed. Some 550 Pende were killed by the Force Publique, none of whose members died. The rebels believed that magic guaranteed their invulnerability against the rifles of the Force Publique.[72] This sharp outburst—clearly more than a "primary rebellion" against the initial imposition of European rule—betokened the willingness of the Pende to engage in collective political violence, and of the Belgian administration to meet local challenge with overwhelming force. The revolt both revealed and encouraged a foundation for action that could subsequently be drawn upon. Pende solidarity was forged in collective resistance.

A second manifestation of discontent translated into collective action came through religious syncretism, and in particular through the Mpeve sect and Kimbanguist beliefs.

Not unsurprisingly, the Mpeve sect surfaced in 1932, expressing in other ways the grievances that had erupted in revolt the previous year. A "talking serpent" would bring forth prophets and messiahs to combat the white master, chasing them from the land. A new era of happiness and prosperity would open. Followers of the movement would gain invincible power by drinking a magic potion from special cups.[73] Some adherents refused to pay taxes or meet other colonial obligations.

Even more widespread was the influence of Kimbanguism, a syncretic religious movement that spread into Kwilu after World War II. The implications of Kimbanguism were profound and millenarian: foreign rulers would be ousted and a golden age ushered in, in which Africans would enjoy a new way of life. Administrative efforts to stamp out this challenge to Belgian rule started shortly after Simon Kimbangu began proclaiming his message in 1921. As had Hung Hsiu-ch'üan, Kimbangu responded to personal dreams and visions. He adapted the teaching he had received through the Baptist Missionary Society to the politically repressed conditions of the lower Congo. He mixed appeals for ethnic solidarity (the proposed regrouping of the divided Bakongo people within a single "Kingdom of the Kongo" received powerful impetus from his teachings) with claims to magical healing powers, and pride in African accomplishments.[74] All followers of Kimbanguism could look forward to a bright future, once the colonial presence had been expunged. Despite the ascriptive overtones of Kimbangu's teachings, his ideas nonetheless seeped into non-Bakongo areas, including Kwilu. Acceptance of these ideas constituted a potential foundation for collective action broader than that manifested in the 1931 Pende revolt.

That the ethnic protest embodied in the 1931 uprising, and the religious separatism manifested in Mpeve and Kimbanguism, had economic roots needs no elaboration. The Depression and World War II stimulated a variety of responses throughout all colonial Africa. One of these, I believe, was the beginning of a sense of nationalist awareness. This was closely linked in Kwilu to ethnicity, given the prominence of the Pende among the *coupeurs de fruit*. More broadly, however, the entire colonized populace suffered from inferior economic, social and political positions. Separate salary schedules existed for blacks and whites, the latter also receiving ten times the annual paid vacation given the former. Africans could not purchase and consume alcoholic beverages until 1955; only in February 1953 could Africans own land in rural and urban areas,[75] earlier decrees having removed from them all legal controls over land. Only in August 1959, less than a year before independence, were civil liberties formally extended to Congolese by the Belgian government.[76] Such overwhelming evidence of discrimination based on race, of unjustifiable inequity in a society over-whelmingly composed of indigenes, provided grist for the millers of African nationalism.

Anti-colonial sentiments, as these took shape in the Belgian Congo, tended to coalesce along lines already demarcated: along ethnic lines, reflecting (inter alia) the spectacular success of ABAKO and the effects of escalating tribal awareness; along religious lines, especially with the in-direct contribution of Kimbanguism to political militance; along lines of economic differentiation, with Africans aspring to gain the positions and privileges of Europeans; and along political boundaries, as these affected the elections belatedly organized by the colonial administration. All pro-vided foundations for collective action. Paramount among them seems to have been ethnic sentiments. What Zolberg called the "politicization of residual cleavages"[77] afflicted Zaire in its belated and short-lived spurt of indigenous nationalism. Once the brakes of the colonial administration had been released, a political free-for-all erupted. The groups best able to respond rapidly to rural demands for change enjoyed an inside track to the positions of power, status and wealth opening as a result of the Belgian departure. Many rural areas, far from being placid backwaters, proved themselves roiling streams of political turbulence. "Rural radicalism" en-couraged aspirant politicians to make fantastic, unfulfillable promises that they (but not their constituents) quickly forgot. The most effective ways to tap the wellsprings of discontent involved castigating the colonial ad-ministration, promising a prosperous future freed from compulsion, and appealing to ethnic solidarity behind the favorite son. Religious, economic and political protest became increasingly channeled along tribal lines. The other bases for collective action thus were joined to, and in the process reinforced, the parochialisms inherent in ethnic awareness.

I should not conclude on a note of particularism, however. A rebellion that is propagated along lines of tribal identification need not be *ipso facto* any less "modern" in its origins and objectives than a rebellion based on religious, economic or political lines of collective action. In most cases, ad-mittedly, a parochial basis for recruiting support establishes an outer limit of cultural affinity beyond which the uprising cannot reach; such a rebellion can be contained within its particularistic confines. Yet what drives individuals to collective political violence in plural societies may not differ in any substantial measure from what drives individuals to collective political violence in more homogeneous societies. Pende and Kikuyu grievances, after all, were not all that unusual. The fact that they surfaced in heterogeneous social settings meant that they could be combatted by tactics of divide and rule rather than be resolved by peaceful means.

Rebellion, as a form of collective political violence, does not erupt spontaneously. If there is one central message of this chapter, it is that the spread of support for violence probably follows previously established patterns of collective action. Some previous endeavor, even if crushed with the loss of hundreds of lives as was the 1931 Pende revolt, eases the task of organizing. A building block ready at hand can be utilized far more quickly than a new foundation can be constructed.

The building block for collective action to which this chapter has given greatest attention is ethnicity. Its roots lie deep in popular awareness; periodic reaffirmations of group identity remind individuals of their heritage; economic and social transformation may well increase the salience of ethnic identification. Under the circumstances that prevailed in the four societies we are examining, ethnicity provided a somewhat more convenient, compelling basis for collective action than did religious, economic or political bases. Yet to trumpet ascriptive awareness as The Cause of rural rebellions seriously underestimates the contributions made by other factors. Although they may reinforce rather than transcend ethnicity, they must be given attention in their own right. Economic deprivation, millenarian visions of social transformation, political slights inescapable in a colonial context: all contributed, and will continue to contribute heavily, to the generalized sense of inequity from which collective political violence springs.

There is little need to underscore the weakness inherent in rebellion that remains ethnically exclusive. It exchanges intensity of commitment for narrowness of appeal. Unless alliances with other disaffected groups can be formed, the incumbents can hone the time-honored weapon of divide and rule. In all four rebellions, such attempts were made. Hung Hsiu-ch'üan succeeded in appealing to Han nationalism far broader than the Hakka roots of the God-Worshippers' Society; Pierre Mulele tried to coordinate the Kwilu uprising with other "second independence" manifestations, but time was against him; leaders of the Kenyan African Union sought to bring peaceful political advance to all blacks in the colony, but were upstaged by Kikuyu militants who could not carry their violent message beyond the Kikuyu, Embu and Meru; the Communist party of India sought to use the Telengana rebellion as a springboard for deposing the newly-installed Congress government of the newly independent nation, but found the base too narrow. Perhaps the temptation of rapid action, or the intolerable nature of existing inequities, prompted violence before the most inclusive foundation could have been achieved. But this is second-guessing, not analyzing.

Obviously, the strains that prompted insurgent action did not entirely escape the incumbents' awareness. Many were the direct result of government policies; others were unintended consequences. Why did the regime fail to deal with the various grievances in a peaceful, effective manner? Could it in fact have done so? Or were the inequities that helped give rise to collective political violence so closely intertwined with the incumbents' *modus operandi* that reform was impossible, confrontation inevitable? Collective political violence testifies to more than foundations for joint action; it illustrates the failure of strategems through which control might have been retained. These form the subject of the next chapter.

CHAPTER 3 /

Alien Rule and the
Potential for Discontent

Maxims for Minority Control

In much of the Third World, alien rule reshaped social, economic and political relationships between city and countryside. Colonization altered existing balances. New values were introduced; economic transformation entailed far greater use of cash and involvement in the vagaries of international trade; a variety of new groups contested with the traditional elite for power, status and wealth. All these changes occurred in a context in which ultimate political control had been removed from indigenous leaders. Alien minorities controlled the levers of power. Separated from the great majority of the populace by culture and outlook, the ruling groups differed from their subjects by gaps greater than the usual gaps between governing and governed. The two sides appeared to hold little in common. These contrasts could be readily politicized, guiding the hostility that arose from differences in power, status and wealth into collective political violence. Control by an alien minority contained the seeds of collective action.

To ascribe rebellion to the imposition of minority rule is a simple, attractive hypothesis. Arrogation of political control by a culturally distinctive minority seems bound to arouse resentment. Monopolization of key positions by "strangers," particularly if accompanied by economic exploitation, has often given birth to efforts at redress. The upwelling of nationalist sentiment after World War II appears to confirm the hypothesis. A twenty-year wave of decolonization transformed the political maps of Africa and Asia, and almost tripled membership in the United Nations. Nonetheless, colonization by alien groups has been historically common—and, in some cases, uncommonly persistent. A small number, relative to the population over which they lord, can exercise longstanding power. Their success must be attributed to several means, among them co-optation of indigenous leaders, propagation of beliefs in the rulers' cultural and political superiority, a sense of certainty among the rulers as to the rightness of their control, and (not least) coercive might. It is the purpose of this chapter to probe these means. Aptly employed, they can stave off collective political violence; for at maximal efficiency, such devices not only justify alien control, but also provide governance that is generally accepted. Ineptly employed, or challenged from below by accumulated resentments, such devices only increase the sense of resentment felt by members of the majority.

It is no simple task to examine the perceptions of rulers and rebels. The analyst must avoid transplanting or imposing ideas drawn from other cultures — yet simultaneously must seek the impossible, by putting himself in the frames of mind of both protagonist and antagonist, in environments markedly different from his own. Ethnocentrism constitutes the major barrier to comprehension. It is a trap difficult to avoid. For the scholar, accustomed to dealing with written accounts, adequate understanding of rural dwellers proves especially difficult. Nonliterate people leave few, if any, records. What survives as documentation tends to come either from the dominant minority, ready to depict its opponents as "bandits," ne'er-do-wells, or misled primitives, or from an educated fringe of the rebels, anxious to justify their uprisings through lurid recitals of grievances. It is necessary to infer, perhaps more accurately, to guess, the responses to the following crucial questions:

How did rural dwellers perceive alien rule at various times?
To what extent did they attribute grievances to the acts of the government, rather than to an inexorable hand of fate?
If collective action occurred, did the roots lie mainly in cultural discrimination? economic inequality? denial of political rights? violation of the subsistence ethic?
Was the participation of rural dwellers in rebellion enthusiastic, reluctant, or coerced?

Maintenance of minority domination, it would seem at the outset, was all the easier when the majority remained politically untutored, seemingly unable to envisage alternative formats of social, economic and political organization. Fatalistic outlooks about the possibility of alteration could nip in the bud any widespread efforts to mobilize rural support for change. The greatest weapon in the hands of the government might have been not a machine gun, but widespread public reluctance to challenge the status quo. It was thus obviously in the interest of the government to maintain the nonmobilized status of the population.

The advocates of rebellion had to arouse the majority to contest for the rights denied them. As might be expected, there were many means at hand. A likely consequence of the minority monopoly of power, status and wealth was a sense of relative deprivation among the majority. This could be politicized, used as a basis for collective political violence. Violence used to maintain the status quo may incite more than suppress. Even more fundamentally, an alien minority perceived as unable to defend their interests may slide quickly down the slippery slope: the myth of their might having been shown hollow, any remaining power is soon deflated. Actions of a strong, determined leader can help convince waverers of his cause, while an ideology of change can set forth both a critique of the existing inequalities and a rosy picture of what can be attained. To these concerns, we shall turn in the chapters that follow. Our interest for the moment must be focused on the incumbents and the means they employed to protect their interests.

The "ruler's imperative," to borrow Wriggins' term,[1] can be encapsulated in four maxims. These refer to the political awareness of the populace, values stressing hierarchy and conformity, discouragement of challenges to the existing order, co-optation of indigenes, and (in the last resort) recourse to coercion. Each deserves further discussion, both in general terms and in terms of specific adaptations within each of the societies being closely scrutinized.

The first maxim refers to popular perceptions of politics. In brief, the ruler should:

> Keep the populace, as far as possible, politically untutored and socially divided, with the direct impact of the government on rural life and the extraction of taxes as minimal as possible consistent with the needs for public order and government revenues.

The strategy of divide and rule long has attracted the rulers of empires. The point is to avoid a direct confrontation between the minority governors and the majority governed. Governing society polarized on these lines is nearly impossible. The rulers must avoid becoming the target of resentment. If grievances can be steered away from the government and projected instead on rival internal groups, those atop the political pyramid enjoy greater security. Pitting groups against one another risks internal disruption — but need not directly challenge the ruling minority.

A perhaps less practiced concomitant to divide and rule is minimization of change. Should inhabitants directly experience few effects of alien minority control, they can cling more fully to their time-honored life styles. Forced change arouses both resentment and high expectations for fulfillment. Conscious introduction of new practices in the countryside — as came about in Kenya and Zaire under European colonial rule — made abundantly clear the subordinate position of the majority. The intense relative deprivation in both societies, I shall suggest in later pages, bore witness to the profundity of the colonial impact. Great Britain and Belgium justified rural intervention abetting European agriculture and commerce as best serving African interests. The result reversed the colonists' intentions. The greater the direct involvement of the alien minority in rural change, the greater the discontent that may be aroused, and the greater the ultimate difficulty in maintaining imperial control. European colonists might have taken a lesson from the Manchu rulers of Imperial China, or the Muslim rulers of Hyderabad. Despite their minority status, both persisted for centuries rather than decades, a reflection in large part of their general inclination to *control* rather than *develop* rural areas. The former practice minimized alterations and stressed conformity with established practices; the latter practice maximized changes, especially those linked to market agriculture, and required significant adaptation of established values and social structures. More of these concerns anon.

Obviously, no government could totally have avoided an impact on rural dwellers. Without revenues, it could not have long continued. Villagers felt the imperial hand most through tax collections, and in particular through head taxes assessed directly on the populace. When an unsympathetic administration demanded these in times of natural disaster, resentment multiplied. We need not turn to the Bible or Jean Bodin[2] to imagine the disgruntlement, or even fear, with which these levies were paid. Rural rebellion often erupted with the imposition of new or higher taxes, or the collection of existing taxes in circumstances of sudden impoverishment.[3] Recognizing this fact, many administrations imposed indirect levies, a salt tax being a notoriously good producer of revenue; hikes in taxes would be passed on to consumers, but blame for higher prices could be pinned on merchants. The rural impact could also be kept low by avoiding military conscription, relying instead on volunteers. As we shall see in the final maxim, each government had ultimately to raise, train, and support an army; despite this necessity, imperial rule was best served by keeping a low military profile. Minority control did not rest alone on cooptation and manipulation of values; it had an underpinning of coercive might. But the less the need to use the armed forces to prop up the government, the fewer the negative impacts on rural tranquility.

It is cheaper, if not necessarily easier, to govern by right rather than might. Successful translation of coerced obedience into recognized virtue eases the tasks of any administration. The second maxim starts from recognition of this fact:

Sustain a system of values rationalizing the stratification of power, status and wealth, both justifying thereby the unequal distribution of resources and encouraging acceptance of government decisions.

A useful approach has been suggested by Dahl and Lindblom. They define three strategies by means of which social controls can be exercised: control by means of command; direct field control; and spontaneous field control. The most obvious, perhaps, is the first: fear leads to obedience; compliance results "exclusively by virtue of a penalty prescribed by the controller for non-performance...."[4] Control by means of command can most effectively be exercised in relatively constrained settings. The superior requires rapid access to means of punishment and close surveillance of his charges—plus, of course, coercive might on his side. Military boot camps provide an example; "punitive raids" of colonial history another. Both taught the raw recruit or the untutored "native" that the power of the superior was overwhelmingly strong, that resistance was futile, that acquiescence would be far less costly than opposition. Control by means of command requires marked disparities in power between controller and controlled, and perhaps also results from limited knowledge about the controlled. Both these points marked the scramble for Africa. Significant, and at times enormous, differences in fire power separated European-led imperial troops and indigenous armies. As Hilaire Belloc put it, "Whatever happens we have got/ The Maxim gun and they have not." Such contrasts in military might were buttressed by Europeans' belief in their inherent cultural superiority. In the late nineteenth century blossoming of social Darwinism and hierarchies of cultures, control by command could be rationalized as serving indigenous interests. Colonists and administrators considered it fully appropriate to "dominate in order to serve"—even if this entailed occasional brutal lessons regarding who governed.

The second strategy of Dahl and Lindblom moves from repression toward reward. In direct field control, superiors reinforce their position by conscious manipulation of wants, desires, gratification and deprivation. The iron fist is encased in a velvet glove; coercive might is supplanted by psychological inducement, although power differentials remain in the background. Direct field control would seem to require greater knowledge of, and perhaps somewhat greater sympathy for, the outlooks of the subordinated group than does control by command. Direct field control may also reflect a sober assessment by the superiors that the costs of coercion necessary to effect change far outstrip the costs of psychological manipulation. The way opens to persuasion rather than command. Control by command seems related to direct field control in the way rape is related to seduction: the victim is affected in either case, but the means differ psychologically and in terms of force (real or implied). In short, direct field control is a type of interaction between superiors and subordinates intended to bring change in the latter without overt employment of force, but with conscious employment of psychological means.

Spontaneous field control refers to unintended manipulation of wants, desires, et cetera. Its goal, of course, is the internalization by the subordinate group of the various goals, outlooks, and values of the superior group. Such a process is never easy, almost always protracted. Values cannot readily be transplanted from one culture to another, unless there exists some affinity between the two. The process to which I have been alluding is that of legitimation, the translation of might into right. In the long run, no group can maintain hegemony over another unless it enjoys a foundation of legitimacy. As long as this foundation remains strong, inequalities may not be perceived as inequities giving rise to the "sedition" of which Aristotle spoke.

Several obstacles lie in the path of those attempting to legitimate alien domination. Memories of its imposition may embitter relationships; knowledge of its maintenance may open continuing wounds. Few ties may join dominating to dominated. The rulers may maintain a distinct style of life — necessary if they are not to be assimilated into the far more numerous subordinate groups — at the risk of "us versus them" distinctions. Administrative attempts to bring change can arouse further discontent, while inflaming the sense of group identification. That rebellion broke out in the four societies seems to indicate that legitimation remained incomplete. Collective political violence was turned against the alien control itself established and maintained by force. Yet for many years, even centuries, the patterns had gone without strong internal challenge. In what ways was the stratification of power, status and wealth rationalized?

To the victors, rationalization was simple: greater control came from their superiority, for their benefit. Wealth and power seemed, simplistically, their own reward. The Manchu and Muslim conquerors of Ming China and Hyderabad found agricultural riches unparalleled on the steppes whence they came. European imperialists proclaimed the importance of African colonies as sources of raw materials and markets for manufactured goods.

To the subordinated, however, their long-term subduing did not flow from the barrel of a gun alone. In China and Hyderabad, political subordination and economic transfer long antedated the advent of the dynasties against which rebellion later was mounted. Both governing houses established a new top layer over a population inured to political impotence and extraction of taxes. Many acephalous societies of tropical Africa, by contrast, lacked such heritages: without centralized organs of government much above the clan or age-set levels, these societies suffered profound shocks from the imposition of colonial rule and taxes. The transfer of resources from indigenous persons to the new colonial administration frequently required use of force — an early indication that "development" European-style did not suit the taste of all Africans. Economic inequalities in China and Hyderabad were *continued*, not implanted. As long as extractions remained within bounds—in other words, not to the extent of abusing the subsistence ethic—rural dwellers could generally be expected to hand over requisite rents and taxes, since they had become accustomed to both over several centuries. In tropical Africa, economic and political inequalities had been relatively uncommon, certainly in decentralized societies such as the Kikuyu and Pende. Taxes were detested innovations, not long-recognized burdens from which escape was impossible. The imposition of inequality in tropical Africa thus demanded a fuller rationalization and greater use of force by the colonial powers than did the continuation of inequality in China or Hyderabad. Ruling groups in the latter did what came naturally to dynasties. There were no canards about development; wholesale transfers of resources from the peasantry were made without their being rationalized as promoting beneficial change. Compulsion was used to collect taxes from the reluctant; rarely, if at all, was compulsion used to introduce new crops.

The colonial adminstrations of Kenya and the Belgian Congo believed in the trickle-down idea of economic and social change. What abetted European enterprise would eventually benefit African indigenes. To the British and Belgians, better transportation, the opportunity to participate in the world market, and the use of physical punishment or other penalties against Africans who resisted schemes of economic betterment, were appropriate in and of themselves. Coercion entered the picture since many colonial possessions were far from being major sources of wealth. The economic rationale for colonial expansion was hoist with its own petard. The scramble for Africa had been justified to Europeans in large measure from the financial and commercial benefits that supposedly would result. Colonial rule was imposed on areas lacking much of the infrastructure for rapid development; the home governments were reluctant to invest large sums from metropolitan sources in the colonies; the burden, as usual, had to be borne by indigenous producers. They obviously had little reason to expect that the gradual trickle down of resources to their origins would occur. Unaccustomed to having revenues extracted from them, many peoples of Africa rejected, through sporadic violence, the demands placed on them. Only where taxes had a pre-colonial analog (such as the *jangali* cattle tax of Northern Nigeria) did their levying occur without protest.

The rationalization for different income levels rested, in the final analysis, on indigenous acceptance of the idea such contrasts flowed justifiably from differences in political power. Those who ruled were (somewhat more than metaphorically) a race apart. The conquering groups stressed their distinctiveness, economically, culturally, and politically. They retained the top positions in administration and the choicest lands for exploitation. The dominant minority, to reiterate, believed stratification flowed from the combined result of conquest, greater coercive power, superior civilization, et cetera. The dominated majority eventually had to conform, acquiescing in (though continuing to resent) their subordination. To these rural dwellers, proverbs counselling conformity had long existed in folk wisdom. The ruler's imperative, accordingly, led him to build on these indigenous values. Peasants' places were on the land, not in the corridors of government. Those who toiled with their hands reaped lesser rewards than those who toiled with their minds. Low economic wealth thus correlated with low social status and limited political power.

The governing minorities attempted, with differing successes, to build upon existing hierarchies of political power and social status. To them belonged the top rungs. The Ch'ing dynasty, for example, filled the small stratum of hereditary nobles with Manchus and reserved a portion of official positions filled by examination for qualified Manchus. However, co-opted Han filled almost all the prestigious, lucrative posts. The Chinese imperial bureaucracy and the respect due to scholar-officials had preceded the Ch'ing dynasty by a millenium or more. Early Manchu rulers wisely revived the examination system, which had lapsed briefly, and espoused Confucian values justifying social gradations. Similar steps accompanied the Muslim takeover of Hyderabad. The invaders became the top layer in an incredibly pluralistic setting. They emphasized *karma*, which elevated conformity and passive acceptance of one's status into cardinal virtues. Such values — Confucian acceptance or *karma* — had long justified social inequalities. They lacked counterparts in many non-hierarchical settings, including acephalous societies of tropical Africa. I do not mean to suggest that these societies were fully egalitarian: they were not. The Kikuyu and Pende recognized gradations of social status and prestige. These differentiations, however, were internal to both societies: there was little comparable to the baroque complexities of caste, or the longstanding Confucian order, that eased the imposition of a new stratum and its recognition within the existing order. The prior existence of social differentiations simplified the ruler's imperative in China and Hyderabad; the more limited nature of social differentiations complicated the ruler's imperative in much of tropical Africa.

A related status and power phenomenon should be noted here. The "cultural distance" between conqueror and conquered may well have influenced government actions more in tropical Africa than in our Asian examples. The Manchu and Muslim overlords came from nomadic steppe backgrounds. They stemmed from essentially nonurban civilizations untouched by the industrial revolution. Their roots were close to the soil. By contrast, European administrators and settlers installed in Africa came from societies whose outward thrusts owed much to industrialization. They came to a continent where pastoralism and subsistence agriculture occupied the overwhelming bulk of the populace; they came convinced of their cultural superiority; they rested confident in their coercive might. Beliefs that were racialist, and in many respects racist, sprang from and were reinforced by, this sense of cultural distance. Indigenous patterns of social stratification could accommodate invaders of the Manchu and Muslim stripe far more readily than invaders of the late nineteenth century, imperialist European variety: the latter were exotic interlopers, far removed by background from their subjects.

Contrasts in power seem also to divide along Asian and African lines. Both coercive strength and political intentions differed in the alien governments against which collective political action erupted. Manchu and Muslim conquerors used superior horsemanship, but otherwise drew on weapons generally available to those they defeated. Europeans by comparison used Maxim guns against *assegais* and arrows. The distinction should not be pressed too far; to foot soldiers, a cavalry is an overwhelming opponent; far more than differences in firepower led to European victories in colonial wars. A more marked disparity emerged after conquest, however. The Asian dynasties were ruling houses that extracted. They did not essay any profound alteration of rural structures of power. They installed a new government in the capital, and selected lieutenants for provincial and district duties. Village leadership was not altered markedly by the alien rulers. The existing social structure remained intact; the new layer of rulers atop the hierarchy had little impact on the key concerns of the indigenes. *Plus ça change* . . . .The Asian rulers lacked both inclination and power to effect profound change. Not so, it seems, with the European colonial examples. The British and Belgians justified their dominance in large measure by the effects wrought in rural areas. They encouraged elements of what may be termed a rural social revolution. Part sprang from religious fervor, from the missionary zeal that abetted the expansion of colonial rule: a new message had to be brought to the unconverted. Part sprang, as suggested earlier, from the desire for economic development, especially through cash crops that might entail land alienation for settler or plantation agriculture. Part sprang, most broadly, from the belief of the colonizing powers that they had both right and obligation to make changes in indigenous culture patterns. In this process, recognized indigenous leaders were often the victims. As will be shown below, neither the Belgians nor the British entrusted significant power to African chiefs: "indirect rule" had little relevance in the Belgian Congo or in Kenya.

Let us now join these observations about wealth, status and power to the forms of control suggested earlier.

Contrasts between invader and indigene were drawn far more sharply in colonial Africa than in imperial China or Hyderabad. European administrators, missionaries and settlers sought economic change and religious conversion, both impinging directly on the structure of the subject societies. Disparities in power were marked, a sense of racial separateness sharp, and Europeans convinced that their domination was fully justified. Control by command came readily, particularly in the early years of colonialism. Direct field control required fuller knowledge of African outlooks, and perhaps greater humility about their own judgments, than many early Europeans in Africa possessed. Spontaneous field control was almost out of the question. It required the prior development of a cadre of Africans sharing the values of colonial administrators and settlers — no easy task, given the impositions and indignities the Africans suffered, and given the racist attitudes that marked many Europeans. Only with religious conversion, the spread of education, and the co-optation of indigenous leaders, did a group of intermediaries come into being, on whose shoulders some of the burdens of empire could rest. Many of these factors did not apply, or were of far less significance, in Ch'ing China or Hyderabad. Despite the distinct cultural origins of the governing elite, their values seemed significantly to overlap those of the indigenous subjects. Each dynasty enjoyed greater time to reach cultural symbiosis, as it were. History was on their side in another way. The histories of China and India were replete with waves of invaders installed atop the political hierarchy; external domination of a not too onerous sort could be borne. The invaders did not disturb the relative autonomy villagers enjoyed by decreeing profound changes; as with the revival of the examination system, the new rulers reinforced elements of the traditional culture. All these seem to point to the likelihood that direct field control, and even an element of spontaneous field control, sufficed. There was perhaps both less temptation and less opportunity for control by command. Legitimation may have come more readily to the relatively passive Asian dynasties and the unchanging societies over which they presided, than to the more interventionist European administrations and the varied societies they sought to transform.

No one of these governments could have survived without indigenous political adjuncts. Relative to the total population, the alien invaders were few in number. The most numerous proportionally were the Muslims of Hyderabad, who by 1948 comprised more than eleven percent of the populace. The non-African population of Kenya in 1952 was estimated at 200,000 (42,000 Europeans, the rest almost exclusively Asians); the dominant whites were a scant three-quarters of one percent of the African population of more than 5.5 million.[5] In the Belgian Congo, the European population of 114,341 early in 1959[6] remained a minute fraction of the estimated 13 million Africans. The Manchu court, administrators and bannermen paled in numbers against their Han subjects as well. Indigenous persons were thus essential props for alien minority rule; their selection required the rulers' attention to the following maxim:

Ensure the existence of channels through which appropriately qualified individuals from the subject populace could participate in governance, helping thereby to legitimate the system.

Two questions require assessment: who participated? with what responsibilities and resources? These are, of course, classic questions for politicians and political scientists alike. The criteria by which persons were selected for participation tell us much about the extent to which the dominant minority respected indigenous concerns; the powers exercised by those chosen tell us much about the extent of autonomy remaining in local hands.

Systems of imposed external rule can be placed along a continuum, whose poles frequently are deemed direct and indirect rule. Let me draw the contrast sharply, perhaps more starkly than the evidence below justifies, to point up the basic tendencies. Indigenous participants in systems of direct rule have no power or status without the overlord's backing. They exercise control delegated from the ruler, lacking legitimate foundations in their own right. They may have attributes useful to the dominant minority, such as willingness, efficiency, linguistic proficiency, and a seeming commitment to the objectives of the conqueror. But they cannot claim to represent popular wishes: they are imposed. Indigenous participants emerge in systems of indirect rule. They enjoy substantial power and status in their own right. Considered legitimate rulers within the particular society, their rallying to support of the dominant minority helps legitimate it. Adjuncts of this sort reduce the victor's need for coercion; popular acquiescence is achieved by the adherence of influential strata. The point is that external rulers had options available. They could tend more toward *selection* of *subalterns* in their own image, or more toward *recognition* of junior *partners* in the image of the administered society.

The direct-indirect rule antinomy leads to the second question, the responsibilities, resources, and relative autonomy of the subalterns/junior partners. In systems of direct rule, power is bequeathed; in systems of indirect rule, power is recognized. Let us assume that those without significant political and social resources of their own—the "outs"—rally more rapidly to support the dominant minority than do those whose resources are threatened. Gaining the opportunity for power through close association with the conqueror, the "outs" gain what earlier had been denied them. They may be content with the crumbs of control proffered them. Indigenous leaders accustomed to wide-ranging control may be induced to cooperate (and their subjects' fealty maintained) only if they retain considerable power. Other factors enter in, to be certain. The resources available for governing may be so scanty that indigenous administrators—presumptively cheaper than expatriates—must be employed. The dominant minority may lack the power to impose direct rule after conquest, but perforce must rely on the potentially fickle support of surrendered leaders. In zero-sum terms, the greater the control the dominant minority feels it can or must retain, the less the responsibilities, resources, and relative autonomy indigenous associates enjoy.

As one might expect, each setting for rebellion fell at a distinct place along this direct rule-indirect rule continuum. The clearest example of indirect rule came in relations between the Nizam of Hyderabad and the government of British India. British advisers were despatched to the princely state, but the reins of power on internal matters were firmly clutched by the Nizam and his entourage. Hyderabad did not enjoy total autonomy vis-a-vis Her Majesty's Government—but the state remained outside the sphere of direct imperial interest. Of more direct concern to our interest in rural rebellion was the relationship between *deshmukhs* and the court. The court did not interfere in the *deshmukhs*' extractions. This ultimately undercut the system as a whole, with the post-World War II violation of the subsistence ethic. The near-total exclusion of Hindus from the State's administration polarized the society along communal lines. Such lines were not sharply drawn in Imperial China. The Ch'ing dynasty used the examination system for recruitment, leaving district magistrates and their administrative superiors a degree of autonomy as long as rural tranquility remained undisturbed. Han, not Manchus, filled the great majority of government positions. Villagers had no say in who occupied the yamen, however. As we shall see below, the Manchu rulers divided rather than delegated duties. Distrusting local initiatives, they encouraged conformity and caution. Chinese did participate in the system up to the highest level, however, in sharp contrast indeed to Hyderabad and the two African colonies. The British and Belgian governments drew Africans of Kenya and the Congo only into lower administrative echelons. Such "chiefs" (as often created by colonial action as by popular recognition in acephalous societies) were restricted in their duties to village questions. For the Kikuyu and Pende, direct rule above the local level most accurately characterized their position. Indigenous rulers with large followings did not characterize these ethnic groups, making indirect rule an unlikely option.

It should be apparent that "appropriately qualified" individuals were judged by two conflicting sets of criteria, those of the alien administration, and those of the indigenous populace. Selection in accordance with the latter set followed local customs and practices. Qualifications rested on acceptability within indigenous values, as determined by the administered groups. Selection in accordance with the former set of qualifications obviously differed. "Traditional" or parochial legitimation was less important than identification with the administration's goals. Such persons could be tagged, unkindly but not necessarily inaccurately, as puppets. Their power and status derived from the colonial master; their local legitimacy was negligible.

"Appropriately qualified" varied as well with the bureaucratic requirements of positions to be filled. A village chief might have had little need for education; a potential high-level bureaucrat required extensive training. Greater duties demanded higher qualifications—an irrefutable logic that led to discriminatory consequences were recruitment circumscribed. Requisite skills could be set at levels so high indigenous personnel had no prayer of recruitment, an item that fanned discontent among the excluded. It should be no surprise that the examination system provided Chinese an opportunity to advance under the Ch'ing dynasty far higher than could Africans in the Belgian Congo, to whom entry to university, and hence recruitment to senior civil service echelons, was barred essentially until the death throes of colonialism. The openness of the four systems, and accordingly their contributions to legitimation, thus varied widely.

The dominant minority confronted an inescapable dilemma in controlling indigenous personnel, especially those chosen more on the indirect rule model. Were they incorporated fully into the administrative machinery, their local legitimacy might be forfeit; yet outside it, their compliance with government decisions could not be guaranteed. Control by command might be used at village levels, where the consequences of personnel change were less; spontaneous field control was close to impossible, save where (as in the mandarinate under the Ch'ing dynasty) the interests of the alien rulers and their local allies coincided in large measure. The usual strategem was direct field control, a mixture of blandishment with discipline, based on supervision by members of the dominant minority. Dilemmas remained, however, taxing the administrative ingenuity of those seeking to legitimate rule based on the premises of inequality and alien domination.

Ultimately, alien domination was sustained by what brought it into being: military force. Although this fact might have been veiled by indigenous collaborators or by minimization of local change, coercion remained the last refuge of the imperialist. The administration required troops on call, in accordance with the fourth maxim:

Be ready to employ coercion to support minority control when necessary, but do not use it indiscriminately lest an uncontrollable explosion result; remember the limited number of those in control.

The use of force by privileged minorities involved profound risks. Though power cows, and absolute power may cow absolutely, no minority government can in fact exercise total control. Force necessary to preserve domination under any circumstance might, in the cl sic riposte, destroy the society in order to save the principle. The privileged group could not staff repressive forces to meet all contingencies without co-opting some members of the majority — whose obedience under stress was open to question. Racial stratification marked the armed forces and police in the four societies. Officers were drawn from the dominant minority, rarely if ever from the dominated majority; the rank-and-file were drawn from low prestige groups in the populace, known for their political sluggishness and loyal to the incumbents, and often selected (in accord with divide and rule) from groups other than those they patrolled.

Imperial China and Hyderabad — and, to a lesser extent, the two African colonies — were plagued by military indiscipline. To reduce maintenance costs, the governments on occasion required troops to meet their own living expenses. The results rarely endeared soldiers to the rural populace. It was quicker and easy to requisition, without payment, than to provide for themselves. Corruption was endemic, most notably in the declining years of the Ch'ing dynasty. The combined result, as can readily be imagined, were parasitic, predatory military groups, perhaps more feared by the peasantry than the enemies against whom they were guarding.

Such military exactions could go too far, provoking widespread discontent. If exaction turned into action, problems multiplied. Ill-trained troops endangered the incumbents' position. Heavy-handed or inept repression further inflamed popular feeling. Doses of coercion (if necessary) should have been measured, neither inadequate nor overwhelming. Such advice can be easily given, followed with difficulty. The governments' use of violence against dissidents exacerbated relative deprivation, and sparked collective political violence. Attempted repression, in other words, helped convert dissidents into insurgents, an assertion evidence from the four rebellions (to be examined in Chapter 5) confirms.

What I have asserted thus far points to the incumbents' overall vulnerability. Widespread coercion was a last resort for the dominant minority. Yet it was a means that worked. The shortcomings of incumbent troops did not entail corresponding strength of insurgent troops. The Taiping, Mau Mau and Kwilu partisans were suppressed by government soldiers, drawn from rural milieus similar to those from which the rebels sprang. Many reasons accounted for the insurgents' defeat: quality of military leadership, training, and armaments; the deliberate demilitarization of indigenous society; the absence of outside aid for the rebels; ethnic isolation. But this is to leap ahead in our analysis. We must now examine, case by case, the ways in which the dominant minorities maintained and reinforced the control they had gained by the use of violence.

China: The Manchu Maintenance of Rural Control

From its earliest days, the Ch'ing dynasty followed the precepts of governance developed by preceding dynasties. No radical changes resulted from the imposition of Manchu domination. The rhythms of rural life continued in their time-honored forms; the yamen (office of the district magistrate) reminded villagers that the Son of Heaven needed revenue and dispensed justice; the imperial government courted the support of gentry and scholar-officials, seeking through their acquiescence to guide the rural populace. As a minority acutely aware of its small numbers and cultural debts to the Han, the Manchus justified their rule by reinforcing the tried and true, by reviving what had worked for previous dynasties.[7] The Ch'ing dynasty tried not to disturb the traditional agricultural patterns on which rural life depended, although in the late seventeenth and early eighteenth centuries it encouraged prosperity through new incentives. In general, the ruling house realized it lacked the ability to *transform* rural society—but it could try to *control* rural society by utilizing local mores and leaders. Co-optation thus was central to alien domination. Legitimation came through maintaining the rural status quo as far as possible.

It should not be assumed, however, that the government shared identical outlooks with their supporters. Among the issues which the Ch'ing dynasty faced in the nineteenth century, the following problems presented different aspects to rural dwellers, local gentry and scholar-officials, and the imperial court:

poor harvests, with human misery compounded by official mismanagement of public works, famine relief, and like;
"squeeze" imposed on villagers through unauthorized tax surcharges,

falsification of records to favor local influentials, and similar steps that facilitated concentration of land ownership;

intense competition for entry to bureaucratic employment, with the consequent disappointment of many qualified candidates;

an increasingly sclerosed imperial administration, rigid in its procedures and far more concerned with control than with efficiency;

seeming imperial inability (especially later in the dynasty's history) to curb local extortion, banditry, and other signs of dynastic decline;

rural protest, mounted against administrative inadequacy and encouraged by traditions of villagers' right to rebel against a group that had lost the "mandate of Heaven";

a sense, when the ethnic chips were down, that the Manchu interlopers should be replaced by authentic Han rulers; and

external pressures from Western powers for trade and territory, backed by greater military might than the dynasty had previously confronted.

Most of these danger signals, to be certain, were not exclusive to the Ch'ing. They marked periods of decline in most bureaucratic empires, in which the desire for central control extended beyond the governments' abilities. The wishes of the center became attenuated en route to the periphery. Local officials, despite their purported subservience, could turn their distance from the capital to personal and group advantage. A tug of war between center and periphery often resulted (as we shall see below in the case of Hyderabad) in imperial inability to curb excessive extractions and their concomitants, rural protests.

The dynasty believed the gentry and scholar-officials held the key to rural calm. Recognized as socially preeminent, the support of both groups could be obtained by careful co-optation. This had been the pattern of pre-Ch'ing rulers; it was to serve the Manchu overlords with a similar degree of efficiency. Rural calm was abetted by recognizing the substantial stake of gentry and literati in the overall order. Social deference based on the values of Imperial Confucianism meant—ideally—that harmony prevailed, with the maintenance of proper relationships (father to son; ruler to subject; husband to wife; et cetera) ensuring no part was out of joint.

What was fine in theory was considerably vitiated in reality. Few effective safeguards existed against exploitation of the weak. The elite (gentry and scholar officials in particular) could turn to advantage the power they enjoyed by Imperial recognition and the status they enjoyed by success in examinations or acquiring property. Traditional Confucian platitudes notwithstanding, the peasants bore the brunt of gentry and officials' exactions. The imperial court proclaimed its intention "to benefit the people"; its agents as often benefited themselves. As Hsiao notes in his critical study of late Ch'ing administrative practices and local responses, the interests of the dynasty were not synonymous with the interests of its admininistrative adjuncts:

> The central aim of the emperors was to maintain their regime for "ten thousand generations." In order, however, to make the conditions of the empire favorable to their continued rule, they sought to make their subjects, both gentry and commoners, generally contented with their lot or at least not seriously dissatisfied with it....Under ordinary circumstances, the gentry tended to use that doctrine of benevolent government based on paternalistic, authoritarian rule to serve their private interests in the name of "the people," without challenging the imperial authority....A subservient gentry lived symbiotically with a generally submissive rural population, and a measure of political stability prevailed in the empire.[8]

Recognizing the long-term dangers of elite disaffection, the Ch'ing dynasty could not impose overly strict sanctions, lest elite acquiescence be forfeit. Recognizing also the profound threat of popular revolt, the Ch'ing dynasty attempted to meet prevailing expectations of what the government could and should do. More was needed than reiteration of Confucian principles of harmony between ruler and subjects. As long as "ordinary circumstances" prevailed, what precise steps did the ruling house take? In what respects did it follow the maxims for imperial control?

Rather than keep the rural populace untutored, the dynasty sought to inculcate the virtues of conformity. Rural lectures (hsiang-yueh) were to be delivered, twice a month, to the elders, scholars and commoners of a neighborhood.[9] The people were exhorted to remain in the strait and narrow as defined by Imperial Confucianism. Take, as examples, the following precepts from the Sheng Yu (1670):

> Perform with sincerity filial and fraternal duties in order to give due importance to social relations;
> Instruct your sons and younger brothers in order to guard them from evildoing;
> Work diligently at your proper calling in order to give settlement to the aims of the people;
> Pay your taxes fully in order to dispense with official urging.[10]

Rural schools brought official beliefs to the general populace (although the harsh requirements for survival meant few children could afford the time for education). To avoid unsettling teachings, the government compiled, selected and distributed textbooks.[11] Older persons received official gifts—far more as a measure of social stabilization than as a type of pension or social security. The examination system, with its stress on Imperial Confucianism, provided another channel by which these beliefs could be inculcated.

The homilies of the *hsiang-yueh* lectures struck a discordant note for many villagers, however. Precepts collided with reality. Peasants had no need to be urged to work diligently; their survival depended on it. The taxes they handed over seemed more to maintain officials' luxury than to improve their own living condtions. Families pushed into penury may have had no choice other than "evil-doing." "Proper" social relations were undercut by corruption. In short, these efforts at rural instruction—at inculcating values justifying the stratification of power, status and wealth—ran counter to the concerns of rural dwellers under most circumstances. They were concerned with survival; all else was irrelevant. Official exhortation notwithstanding, "the bulk of the rural inhabitants paid little attention to anything beyond the immediate exigencies of their everyday living. They were neither positively loyal to the existing regime nor opposed to it. Generally resigned to fate and to the dispensation of Heaven and the deities, they toiled patiently, trying to make a living as best they could."[12] They wanted, in other words, to be left to their own pursuits.

The fabric of Chinese rural life, as already suggested, continued substantially unchanged under the Ch'ing dynasty. Calm required the collaboration, or at least the acquiescence, of local notables. This in turn necessitated the recognition—indeed, the encouragement—of values justifying the stratification of power, status and wealth. To attract and maintain gentry and literati support, the Manchu rulers exempted officials and titled scholars from labor levies[13]—thereby, of course, shifting the burden to others. The government winked at other abuses of privilege. Officials and gentry enjoyed an inside track in avoiding land taxes. Official land and tax registers were both inaccurate and liable to falsification; the social respect accorded members of the elite, and their close ties to local officials, enabled them to bend the system to serve themselves. Various exactions could be heaped on the populace, enriching the supposed servants of the people while further angering and impoverishing the majority. The dynasty (especially in the nineteenth century) could do little about these unauthorized but widespread instances of petty corruption. Omnipotent in theory, the Son of Heaven and his immediate subordinates seemed powerless to stop such exactions. "An officialdom which became increasingly inept and corrupt as time went on, a populace that remained generally helpless and indifferent, ready victims of official and gentry corruption, a vast countryside with very few facilities for communications and transportation—all these conditions posed problems that were practically impossi-

ble to solve....On the one hand, the imperial government seldom received
the full amounts of the taxes that were legally due; on the other hand, taxpayers in the villages often had to pay much more than was due . . ."[14] The
"satiation of the middle," the enrichment of those siphoning off funds between the court and the peasantry, could not always be borne with
equanimity. The people clearly would not remain politically untutored or
inactive when subjected to such injustices.

Natural disaster — flood, drought, pestilence — posed a further threat to
the regime's stability. Human suffering could be accentuated — and unrest
increased — by inadequate official preparation. The Ch'ing dynasty accordingly decreed the creation and replenishment of rural granaries; "past experience had shown that a grain reserve was one of the best ways of maintaining imperial peace in times of stress."[15] Ambition exceeded administrative capacity or commitment. Most granaries had fallen into
neglect by the middle of the nineteenth century. Supplies could not be
guaranteed; in times of real need, they were liable to inequitable distribution. Efforts to palliate the unfortunate stresses of natural disasters could
bolster support for the alien minority. The failure of such efforts, however,
undercut its legitimacy. The dynasty could be judged by its goal "to benefit
the people." To the extent that Confucian precepts of good government
conflicted with the actual conduct of Ch'ing officials and their gentry-
literati allies, calls for justified resistance found sympathetic hearers. The
right of rebellion, as we shall see in Chapter 7, provided an ideology for
collective political violence that had afflicted other dynasties prior to the
Manchu conquest.

Ch'ing achievement of the third maxim — provide channels through
which appropriately qualified indigenous persons could participate in governance — suffered from many of the shortcomings just described. Promise
often outstripped reality. Take, for example, the examination system.
It both legitimated the government, and provided fresh administrative
talent. It held out the hope for prosperity and status based on educational
attainment to all Chinese; the barriers of caste in India, or job assignment
by race in some parts of colonial Africa, had no parallel in Imperial China.
Hallowed by centuries of tradition, the examination system was revived by
Ch'ing rulers immediately after assuming control. This step gained, and
helped to maintain, the support of the officials. With the exception of the
first and closing years of the dynasty, no official was known to have harbored — or at least to have acted upon — treasonable designs against the
government.[16] The officials, overwhelmingly Han, had been tamed; their
participation and various imperial controls kept them docile.

The aspirants for office far outnumbered the officials, however. Disappointment was the lot of most degree recipients: there were not enough

positions to be filled. (It should be recalled that district magistrates administered a quarter-million people.) The pool of qualified individuals exceeded the need; those who remained outside provided fertile recruiting grounds for collective protest. The examinations themselves were not free from "fraud and deception."[17] Sale of degrees provided a ready source of government revenue, but further undercut the legitimacy of the system. Above all, examinations based on Confucian ethics were at best a slender protection against the attractive opportunities for corruption. Those allegedly qualified for office may not, in the popular eye, have merited such recognition.

The qualification for office that most concerned the ruling minority was loyalty. Ch'ing policies promoted what Hsiao saw as administrative sterility and conformity to avoid challenge. Administrative functions were divided rather than coordinated. The dynasty distrusted initiative from below. Its rulers were, in Hsiao's judgment, "consistently more interested in making officials obedient and subservient than in evolving an efficient administration"[18] — a statement, it should be added, that has been called increasingly into question. Literary skill, not bureaucratic competence, marked the successful products of the examination system; time-and self-serving characterized all too many Ch'ing officials. *Chin-shih* and *chu-jen* degree holders may have been "appropriately qualified" as far as the dynasty was concerned — and certainly were respected by the populace for their academic achievements — but they suffered from limits inherent in the way the dynasty encouraged training and let them exercise their responsibilities by the nineteenth century. The Confucian education degree holders received could not ensure their honesty in a corruption-prone setting, nor could it equip them to respond with speed and effectiveness to the unusual challenges of the British and of the Taiping rebels.

The various instruments of ideological conformity and acquiescence were supplemented by coercive control. The Ch'ing dynasty realized, however, that the empire could be won but could not be ruled by the men on horseback.[19] In fact, the inauguration of Manchu rule brought a period of peace after an enervating period of civil war.[20] The means described above were supplanted by force only when the government found itself in desperate straits. By far the most effective control sprang directly from the rural populace. Not surprisingly, a cardinal objective of the dominant minority was the eradication, at the village level, of "banditry" and other acts likely to weaken, or to demonstrate the weakness of, the imperial government. The *pao-chia* system thrust upon local inhabitants the detection and reporting of all acts that violated imperial law or disturbed local order.[21] All rural dwellers — including gentry and scholars — were incorporated; the head of each group of 10, 100, and 1,000 households (respectively *p'ai, chia,* and *pao*) was responsible for reporting transgressions to appropriate authorities. In times of relative prosperity and rural tranquility, the system deterred crime reasonably effectively. When conditions worsened, and unrest became common, "the *pao-chia* was no more able than any other instrument of imperial control to operate with its peacetime efficiency (or, more accurately, semi-efficiency)."[22]

A second means of coercion short of direct imperial action came through local defense units—*hsiang-yung* (rural braves) and *t'uan-lien* (regiment and drill corps.)[23] Some arose spontaneously from the need for protection against roving bandits; others resulted from imperial urging. The unsettled conditions that made the Taiping rebellion possible made the initiation of local defense units imperative. Where Imperial forces could not provide adequate protection, or where they threatened to be as disruptive as bandits, villagers often had to take matters into their own hands. As might be expected, however, the Ch'ing rulers had little stomach for such local initiatives, which countered the subordination and conformity they favored.

It is difficult accurately to estimate the size of the imperial armed forces on the eve of the Taiping rebellion. Payrolls were often padded, generals pocketing part of the funds intended to maintain the troops. In training and discipline, the armed forces were mediocre at best. Acutely aware that dynasties had been overturned by military leaders (the ouster of the Ming by Li Tzu-cheng serving as an obvious example), the Manchus took heed to keep the armed forces small and dispersed. Such a policy had the added benefits of holding down costs and reducing the negative impact on rural dwellers. When major challenges confronted the regime, however, its military response was likely to be belated, ineffective, or unnecessarily brutal. There should thus be little wonder that the Ch'ing dynasty kept a low profile militarily. Isolated from external enemies by sea, mountain, jungle, and desert until the Opium Wars interrupted their assumptions, the rulers of the Middle Kingdom believed they had more to fear from their own mutinous troops than from invasion.

Manchu emperors, in summary, assumed control over a society with a long, rich history of bureaucratic rule allied to local privilege. Drawing on institutions, groups and values that had served earlier houses well, the Ch'ing dynasty heeded the four maxims suggested in the preceding pages. The thorough integration of Chinese into the administrative structure, the neutralization of officials' threats to the regime's stability, and (above all) the continuity with earlier practices, meant the dominant minority avoided effective nationalist pressures for much of its history. Continuity and control over subordinates exacted certain costs, however. The dynasty profited far more from passive compliance than from active loyalty.

Reliance on the relatively privileged, though long the accustomed pattern, made possible an exacerbation of internal strains. Ch'ing rule was judged by rural dwellers not in terms of what went on in Peking, but what affected livelihood in their villages. The actions of the dominant minority's allies impacted directly on the peasantry and on the ambitious literati excluded from official circles. When officials and gentry abused their privileges, and the central government appeared unwilling or unable to stop rural exactions, discontent was bound to mount — and could couple hostility based on incipient nationalism with nascent class antagonisms.

The qualifying phrase, "under ordinary circumstances," appeared more than once in the paragraphs above. Manchu rule could smooth over normal domestic stresses. When these were intensified by growing corruption and further compounded by external pressures, traditional solutions no longer sufficed. The Ch'ing dynasty, to be certain, was far from unique in having its later years tested by increased domestic violence. It, like other dynasties, could not escape the cycle. Manchu emperors faced what their Han predecessors had confronted — and, on occasion, succumbed to. "Ordinary" circumstances meant the foreign roots of the Ch'ing had little political relevance. The discontinuity between the indigenous majority and the dominant alien minority never touched the usual life of villagers. With dynastic decline, however, the context changed; Manchu impositions, such as the wearing of the queue, aroused active resentment. The increasingly sclerosed nature of the dynasty after 1840 encouraged rural dwellers to repond to an appeal for radical change, in which nationalist sentiments played a part. It was thus accelerating ineptitude, not the simple fact of Manchu control, that focused popular resentment on the dynasty and its local allies.

Telengana: British "Paramountcy" in Theory, Muslim Dominance in Fact

The Hindu peasants of Telengana lived under a dual colonial regime. Closer to them was the government of the Nizam, a Muslim-dominated remnant of the former Mughal Empire. It existed in the shadow of the British Raj which asserted its superior position in a series of treaties and in evolving practice. The British government reserved the right to intervene in the domestic politics of Hyderabad. The Nizam lacked the full attributes of sovereignty — despite the 21-gun salute to which he was entitled and his high-sounding title of "His Exalted Highness." The arrangement was distinctive, a species of indirect rule quite distinct from the direct intervention of the British government in colonial Kenya, but equally distinct from the Manchu co-optation of indigenous allies.

Hyderabad survived the eighteenth century collapse of the Mughal Empire largely through the vigorous leadership of Chin Qilich Khan (also known by his Persian title, Asaf Jah). Given temporary charge of the Deccan plateau in 1713, and named its governor in 1724, he fended off both the British East India Company and the Maratha confederacy until his death in 1748. His successors reached accommodation with "the Company" in a series of treaties. The most important, signed in 1800, brought Hyderabad into a "subsidiary alliance," at a cost of providing 9,000 horse and 6,000 foot soldiers.[24] The Nizam agreed not to deal directly with foreign powers.

The state over which the Nizam presided bore little resemblance, through most of its history, to a modern, bureaucratized country. It was a ramshackle feudal structure, built upon Muslim military freebooters in search of rapid wealth. Afghans, Persians, Arabs, Turks, Mughals and others were attracted to the Deccan area by the lure of profit. Members of the dominant minority were, in the eyes of one observer, "for more than five centuries a military oligarchy superimposed on a client population of a different religious and ethnographical texture, which outnumbers them ten to one. They have never been absorbed and are separated from the Hindus today [1934] as rigidly as when they first conquered the South."[25]

That Hyderabad was not absorbed into British India resulted from British choice, not effective resistance from the Asaf Jahi dynasty. There was little need for incorporation, in fact, since the government of Hyderabad had to yield to the interpretations of Her Majesty's Government when differences arose. The sticky wickets, as might be expected, were the Nizam's profligacy and the internal administration of the state. The 1800 treaty placed no restrictions on the Nizam's internal authority, such authority being regarded as "unquestionable"[26] at that time. The 1853 treaty eroded this power, by sequestering revenues from the most prosperous part of the state (Berar) to meet debts resulting from improvident spending (including, one must add, maintenance of the military force stipulated in the 1800 treaty). In 1860, Lord Canning set forth two principles governing British relations with the princely states: first, their integrity should be preserved by perpetuating the rule of the princes; secondly, flagrant misgovernment must be prevented or arrested by the timely exercise of intervention by the Paramount Power.[27] By 1902, Lord Curzon intervened to make the Nizam limit his personal expenses and appoint a British finance minister. When the Nizam claimed in 1925 that he and his predecessors were "independent in the internal affairs of their State just as much as the British government in British India," he received an icy response. This letter merits quotation to illustrate the powers H.M.G. could choose to exert:

The Sovereignty of the British Crown is supreme in India, and therefore no Ruler of an Indian State can justifiably claim to negotiate with the British Government on an equal footing. Its supremacy is not based only upon treaties and engagements, but exists independently of them....The right of the British Government to intervene in the internal affairs of Indian States is another instance of the consequences necessarily involved in the supremacy of the British Crown. The British Government has no desire to exercise this right without grave reason. But the internal, no less than the external, security which the Ruling Princes enjoy is due ultimately to the protecting power of the British Government, and where Imperial interests are concerned, or the general welfare of the people of a State is seriously and grievously affected by the action of its Government, it is with the Paramount Power that the ultimate responsibility of taking remedial action, if necessary, must lie. The varying degrees of internal sovereignty which the Rulers enjoy are all subject to due exercise by the Paramount Power of this responsibility.[28]

These claims notwithstanding, the British government found few "grave" reasons for intervention in Hyderabad. In internal policy matters, the British left the court a fairly free hand, as long as the state did not go into debt. The Nizam was advised, not compelled. Although economic links with British India were fostered, political contacts were limited. Hyderabad, like many other princely states, remained relatively unstirred while Gandhi's *satyagraha* campaigns and the repercussions of the 1942 "Quit India" resolution washed over British India. The few British advisers attached to the Hyderabad government seemed to take no steps to forestall the explosion in rural Telengana.

The colonial oppression rural dwellers in Telengana experienced was not that of the distant British Raj, but that resulting from the economic position, religious exclusivity, and political dominance of the Muslim community, compounded by intensified exploitation by Hindu landlords. Lower Muslim orders were employed primarily in the army, police, lower civil service, and households of great nobles. Given the distinctly communal complexion of the Hyderabad administration, the Muslims of the state might have agreed, "L'état, c'est nous."

The origins and administration of the state made it nearly impossible to build a Hindu-Muslim community. As already suggested, the Nizam's government was weak and inept for much of the nineteenth century. Court and public expenses remained hopelessly entangled, and usually in deficit, until Salar Jung's reforms in the 1880's. Muslim adventurers (largely disbanded mercenaries) grabbed petty fieldoms, extracting relentlessly from the Hindu peasantry. Barriers between the two groups stayed in place. Most Hindus felt no attachment, psychological or social, to Muslim-dominated Hyderabad. Their affinities cut across state borders to their colinguists in the Madras Presidency, or the Central Provinces. Some Muslims experienced similar pulls, as in the Khalifat dispute or the stirrings of what became Pakistani nationalism. By the end of World War II, no overarching community of interests had been created — or perhaps could have been created — between minority and majority.

The economic position of the *deshmukhs* stemmed in large measure from the fiscal improvidence and lax administration of nineteenth-century Nizams. They presided over an inefficient feudal system, support being maintained by granting key retainers land and taxing rights. The central problem was keeping subordinates' support once a *jagir* grant had been made. In this system, a retainer of the Nizam received land revenues that otherwise would have gone directly to the government; he received as well the necessary powers to collect and appropriate these revenues, and to administer the area. In theory, such a grant was revocable; in practice, it became hereditary. Approximately one-third of Hyderabad fell under *jagir* tenure — and one may safely assume that the services rendered were minimal. Almost all the remaining lands[29] were government (*diwani*) lands, revenues from which could enter government coffers without intermediary. Mughal practice was to auction the rights to revenue collection, a process in which well-to-do Hindus could compete. A change in this practice had significant consequences for economic stratification. Pavier has described the process as follows:

> *Deshmukhs'* origin can be traced to the administrative reforms of Salar Jung I, prime minister of Hyderabad state in the 1860s and 1870s. The reforms abandoned the previous practice, of auctioning off the revenue-collection in the government-administered areas to farmers, in favour of direct revenue collection by the State. The 'revenue farmers' were given land in compensation. Most of them availed of the opportunity to seize as much of the best land as they could. They also received a pension. The *deshmukhs* were thus given a dominant position in the rural economy which they proceeded resolutely to strengthen during the succeeding decades.[30]

There should be no wonder that an informal alliance born of mutual dependence emerged between *deshmukhs* and the Nizam. Each sought to squeeze the peasantry as far as possible.

With these background facts in mind — the British Viceroy theoretically limiting the Nizam's power but actually leaving a free hand; the haphazard administration of Hyderabad for much of its history; the diverse origins and self-interest of Muslim *jagirdars*; the Muslim hammerlock on official positions; the unreponsiveness of *deshmukhs* to local concerns — we can now assess the principles suggested earlier in this chapter.

The first maxim for alien rulers suggested that the populace be kept politically untutored and socially divided, and that the direct impact of government on rural life be minimized. Whether by inadvertance or intent, the Nizam and his administration followed this prescription in most respects. The Hyderabad populace was fragmented by caste, language and community. The 1931 census counted 14,436,148 residents of Hyderabad, 7,554,598 of them living in the 10,064 villages and cities of the Telengana districts.[31] In the state as a whole, Hindus totalled 12,176,727 (84.4 percent), Muslims 1,534,366 (10.6 percent), with animists, Christians, Buddhists, Sikhs, and other sects accounting for the remainder.[32] Thirty-four major castes of Brahmanic Hindus were enumerated, plus two groups of AdiHindus (the "untouchables"; in effect the lowest rung of all, save for tribal peoples.)[33] Most crafts were dominated by single castes, as should be expected, given the occupational nature of most *jati*.

Taking formal education as the chief basis for political awareness, Telengana peasants were backward. Educational opportunities barely existed outside urban areas. One-third of all the state's teachers and professors lived in Hyderabad City, which, with 466,894 inhabitants, represented only 3.2 percent of the total population.[34] Access was limited and the period of schooling short. The 1931 census revealed 4,041 primary schools, with 242,422 pupils; 173 secondary schools, with 51,881 pupils; and eight colleges, with 818 students.[35] Literacy was infrequent — even rare for lower castes. For all Telengana districts including Hyderabad City, literacy among males over five years of age was 9.8 percent, among females 1.6 percent. Excluding the city, the respective overall percentage dropped to 3.6 percent.[36] English remained an exotic language in 1931, with scarcely one percent of males and 0.1 percent of females literate in it. Four major languages were spoken by 96 percent of the state's residents: Telugu by 6,972,354; Maratahi by 3,786,838; Kanarese by 1,620,094; Urdu by 1,507,272.[37]

Communal separation reflected the differing life styles of the two major communities. A mere 8.7 percent of the Hindus lived in towns, they being (in the prose of the census) "generally a stay-at-home population, the place of birth, caste and traditional occupation having a stronghold on them."[38] By contrast, the 1941 census showed that 64 percent of Muslims lived in Hyderabad City and district headquarters where government offices were situated.[39] Compared to Hindus, Muslims were far more likely to be landlords, government administrators, and policemen. The following table, prepared from data in the 1931 census, points these contrasts.

Major Occupation for Selected Groups (percentages)

Group	Lived on Income	Lived on Rent	Public Admin.	Police	Military	Professional	Cultivator	Field Labor	Other
Muslim	–	6	7.5	6.8	–	1.2	26.3	10.1	33.1
Brahman	3.7	–	–	–	–	4.9	13.8	–	47.1[3]
Kapu	–	6	–	–	–	–	40.2	24.3	28.4
Kshatriya	–	–	–	–	43.9	–	6.9	–	45.8
Madiga (Untouchable)	–	–	–	–	–	–	9.7	20.7	58.2[2]
								19.5	4.5
Telaga	0.1	2.3	–	–	–	–	69.2		
Ango-Indian Christian	–	–	11	20.7[1]	–	0.9	–	–	58.5
European	–	–	–	90.4	–	1.1	–	–	5.4

1. "Public Force". Source: 1931 census, pp. 182-5.
2. Includes 29.7 percent "menial service."
3. Includes 25.8 percent "priests."
Notes: figures total less than 100 due to omission of categories.

Sharp as these contrasts were, they seem not to have become politically salient between the world wars. The reasons lay in the political ignorance and fragmentation of rural dwellers, and in the government's limited impact on them. The peasants' chief desire, it seemed, was undisturbed survival. Even the confusion and depredations of the nineteenth century had not upset the agricultural rhythms and the fatalism of *karma* that marked villagers. The greater administrative efficiencies (or, perhaps more aptly, the lesser administrative inefficiencies) of the twentieth century kept tax burdens stable; surpluses rather than deficits were the rule. On the other hand, for reasons to be explored in the following chapter, landlord exactions increased as cash rents became more common, and communal passions soared as pressures for partition of British India were aroused. The direct impact of the Hyderabad government on villagers remained muted until the razakars attempted to reinforce Muslim supremacy in a sharply polarized context, and the *deshmukhs* tightened their grip on the rural economy.

Minority domination, the second maxim suggested, required values rationalizing the stratification of power, status and wealth. These long had characterized India. For the maintenance of political docility and nescience, *karma* and caste differentiations served admirably. *Karma* justified one's rank in life as unavoidable; conformity to group expectations marked the virtuous person. The social distinctions of caste abetted stratification. The system had enabled waves of invaders to penetrate India, establish control, and eventually be incorporated, without basic alteration to the structure. Ideologies of profound change seemed not to take root — although more detailed historical investigations may qualify this observation. Millenarian revolts were rare, having flared chiefly among cultural minorities who had lost their customary security, occupations or status, and who suffered unusual deprivation by comparison with their own past and with those around them.[40] *Karma* may have quelled incipient revolt by reminding persons their next incarnation could be even more unpleasant; taboos on some caste contacts impeded collective action among several groups.

Note should be taken, as well, of the denigration of political action implicit in Hindu values. The contrast with Imperial Confucianism is sharp. The most prestigious social ranks in China were held by scholar-officials, who turned their learning to worldy use. In India, prestige was monopolized by Brahmans, who (to carry out their priestly avocation) were supposed to turn their backs to politics. Preeminent groups in China were identified with government; preeminent groups in India were identified with religion. Renunciation of mundane desires, not involvement in political affairs, marked the acme of achievement. Not surprisingly, Gandhi, the greatest political revolutionary in Indian history, never held political office, and remained at a distance from the Congress party that so benefited from his ability to stir mass support.

Channels for indigenous political participation and legitimation formed the gist of the third maxim. From what has been stated thus far, it should be obvious that the overwhelming majority of Hindus in Hyderabad were excluded from a share in governing. The Nizam's government was composed of, by, and for Muslims. Few opportunities for the majority existed even at local levels. *Panchayats* (caste and village councils) were peripheral politically. Village headmen were drawn from, or were allied to, the leading landlords.[41]

The British appeared to give scant political attention to Hyderabad, an attitude generally applicable to large princely states. The Nizam was a member of the Chamber of Princes, formally inaugurated in February 1921. Its powers were limited to matters affecting all rather than individual states; annual meetings offered little chance for sustained action. The 1935 Government of India Act, examined in the following chapter, made provision for the voluntary accession of states to the Indian Union, but this opportunity remained a dead letter with the outbreak of World War II, and the further inflaming of communal passions.

Finally, the Hyderabad police and armed services bore the stamp of Muslim dominance. The state's military origins meant its leaders were well aware of the importance of military efficiency and loyalty. In 1931, 4,081 Hyderabadis served in the Indian Imperial army, 21,527 in the state army, and 16,774 in the police.[42] Like the other societies discussed in this book, the dominant minority staffed army and police ranks by drawing upon

loyal indigenes — in this case, members of the Kshatriya caste, the traditional mainstays of armies in India. However, since there were no
Kshatriyas in Hyderabad, most came from the Rajput states of the north.
The protective arm of the British included a garrison in Secunderabad, the
British-administered twin of Hyderabad City. A few years before the uprising, it appeared as though the Nizam's government had effectively chan-
nelled coercion in its support. On this count, as in the first two maxims,
the dominant minority had acted in accordance with its long-term interests.

To sum up the observations of this section, the Muslim government of
Hyderabad avoided incorporation into British India by entering a subordinate alliance. What attention the British provided was directed far more
to the Nizam's private purse than to landlord-tenant relations. Formidable
obstacles to collective action existed, notably as a result of caste, although
communalism provided a ready basis for identification. Rural Hyderabad
remained a political backwater through World War II, the Nizam's
government willing to leave substantially undisturbed the calm based on
political apathy and belief in *karma*. The many inequalities villagers suffered might have persisted several decades had the war and devolution of
political power not dramatically aroused rural awareness in Telengana, as a
result of even greater landlord extractions and pressures for communal
and class action.

Kenya: Race Against "Paramountcy"

Alien settlers in Kenya were racially demarcated far more clearly from
African society than were the Manchu rulers of the Ch'ing dynasty, or the
Muslim overlords of Hyderabad. Bearers of a civilization they regarded as
superior in every aspect, early British governors and white farmers (many
of them drawn from the highly stratified setting of South Africa) imposed
sharp changes upon social and economic relations. Pastoral and agrarian
societies were wrenched into a cash economy. The drift of peoples to new
areas for farming was interrupted by the white intrusion. "Colour bar"
slashed through Kenyan colonial society as a whole, establishing clear,
racially defined areas of formal settlement. In certain respects, accordingly, the imprint of minority rule stood out more sharply in Kenya than in
any other rebellion. An understanding of the means by which British control was imposed and maintained must necessarily precede analysis of the
"Mau Mau" uprising itself.

A fundamental contradiction stood at the heart of colonial policy in
Kenya. It was oriented, on the one hand, to the social uplift of Africans.

The official doctrine, that of paramountcy, was enunciated in 1923. According to this statement, developed in connection with a Royal Commission investigating the status of Asians, African interests were to be paramount whenever conflict occurred between the interests of the various races.[43] "Paramountcy" implied a notion of trusteeship, in which the colonizing power, as mentor or tutor, would bend its efforts toward African well-being and progress. Many consequences would flow from these: education for Africans, which might enhance their political awareness; public health measures, which resulted in a population growth of 1.5 percent;[44] instruments of local administration, through which Africans retained responsibility for village matters and pressed for greater responsibility. On the other hand, responsibility toward the majority conflicted in many respects with measures to enhance the position of the minority. Official encouragement for white settlement was pressed practically from the moment the British government asserted its formal power over the East Africa Protectorate, as Kenya was initially named. The Uganda railway, built at a cost of £5.5 m., traversed fertile areas seemingly devoid of settlement. A vigorous, learned administrator, Sir Charles Eliot, translated a general assumption vigorously into policy. In the words of one historian,

> It was merely assumed that immigrants would be required to exploit the existing resources of the Protectorate and to develop commerce and agriculture. Scarcely a thought was given to the possibilities of African peasant agriculture. Africans were held to be so primitive that it would be years, perhaps centuries, before they could grow cash crops and participate successfully in an exchange economy.[45]

Presumed lack of African capacity to carry out development led thereby to policies that transferred resources from African farmers to European farmers, while at the same time the colonial government pledged to uphold the "paramountcy" of the majority.

This contradiction, to be certain, emerges starkly with hindsight. Its existence, if recognized at the time, was dismissed as a price of progress. During the colonial period, African advancement was not seen as fettered by European rule and settler agriculture. The advances of the immigrant-dominated commercial agricultural sector, it was believed, would spill over into the "traditional" sector. This view, as we shall see shortly, paralleled the Belgian belief in the desirability of plantation agriculture in the Congo. There was no notion of a zero-sum game, in which the gains of the Europeans would be the loss of the Africans: both would share in the social, economic, and (more speculatively) political progress that was being made.

An important aspect of British colonial rule rested in unity of mind within the dominant minority. Rarely were the fundamental assumptions tested in open debate. There existed a "high degree of agreement over fundamentals," namely, "that the colonized peoples were not capable of governing themselves 'under the strenuous conditions of the modern world,' and that the relationship between the interests of colonized and colonizer was an essentially reciprocal and creative rather than an exploitative and contradictory one."[46] Far removed from the political concerns of his constituents, the average British MP took little interest in Empire affairs, save when significant upheavals occurred. The "Mau Mau" rebellion was such an upheaval—and its suppression the last major occasion on which the British government sought to interpose its military power in defense of an overseas minority of its citizens. Only in 1960, after the African uprising had been crushed at a cost (officially) of £55,585,424 and over 13,500 deaths,[47] did the colonial government recognize that Kenyan Africans were ready to govern themselves: capability, pressed through guerrilla warfare, would be recognized at the constitutional negotiations.

Two fundamentally opposed goals, resulting from the contradiction noted above, marked the colonial period. One, simply expressed, was that of building toward African self-government; the other, "White Man's Country," in which settlers would hold political supremacy. In fact, neither expression was correct. Although the colonial administration was influenced by the pressure of both, it was responsible to neither. Strong encouragement for Europeans' settlement did not entail willingness to devolve control upon them. As much as the white community may have desired self-government on its own terms, and as much as its desires may have been acted upon in Nairobi, no Rhodesian-style grant of power was made from London. Kenya remained a Colony and Protectorate, in the official language, not a Dominion; the major decisions were made in Great Britain, especially as telegraph and later aircraft permitted closer official oversight. However the doctrine of paramountcy may have been expressed, by contrast, the colonial government considered itself the valid interpreter. The trusteeship that was exercised was expressed in terms largely defined by professional administrators. Advance would depend on decisions made within the colonial framework. Those who brought pressure outside the system risked exclusion. Having decided against devolution of power to the minority, the administration would decide to whom power should be devolved among the majority. Sir Philip Mitchell expressed thus the official view of what educated Africans (as opposed to "ignorant tribesmen") should aim for:

> If these politically mature groups are willing to accept and to collaborate without reserve in the central policy of the Trustee, then they have a right to be associated closely—indeed, I would say to be entrusted—with the expecta-

tion of it and the work will benefit greatly by their participation. But if they, or any one of them, reject that policy, they are in effect taking a position in opposition to high policy and cannot expect to be accorded anything more than the representation reasonable for a minority.[48]

Seeking thus to call the shots on African political advancement, the British government sought means of adaptation that would be concurrently, cheap, acceptable, and in keeping with its conception of "good" government. For a variety of reasons, local government provided the chosen avenue. Kenya never witnessed the elaboration of a major system of "Native Authorities," perhaps best exemplified in northern Nigeria. The pattern was far more that of direct rather than indirect rule. However, through a series of ordinances, gradually expanded powers were given to formally recognized and constituted agencies. Local Native Councils were established in the 1920s, followed later by African District Councils. Both were regarded as appropriate forums for African apprenticeship. The emphasis lay on "development from below," in Hicks's phrase.[49] Centrally-exercised authority by Africans was distrusted — a distrust, to look ahead, shared by the Belgians in the Congo. The secretary of state for the Colonies expressed concern in a 1947 despatch on local government, about the danger of starting at the top:

> [the naming of Africans to Legislative Councils] carries with it one danger for the future, in that it may result in the creation of a class of professional African politicians absorbed in the activities of the centre and out of direct touch with the people themselves....Local government must at once provide the people with their political education and the channel for the expression of their opinions. An efficient and democratic system of local government is in fact essential to the healthy political development of the African Territories; it is the foundation on which their political progress must be built.[50]

Implicit in this statement was the belief, or at least the expectation, that colonial officers drawn from different cultures understood the concerns and aspirations of the populace — an assumption not always borne out by the facts.

The several roots of this local orientation merit brief discussion. Gradualism and pragmatic response to prevailing circumstances were dogmas in British colonial policy. Organic development of "new" institutions should proceed from "traditional" institutions; it was assumed that "efficient and democratic" (later rephrased as "efficient and representative") forms of governance could in fact be born from customary and consultative units. A sudden ripping of the "natives" from their cultural milieus and political traditions, official belief continued, would spell unrest. (Indeed, contrasts between "old" and "new" ways of life were widely believed, during the Mau Mau rebellion, to have resulted in psychological disorientation; a movement with profound political, social and economic roots could thus be dismissed as an unexpected mental aberration.)[51] Existing, respected indigenous leaders and institutions should be adapted to changing circumstance, never straying too far from either indigenous support or contemporary responsiveness. The hand of the colonial administration, if not necessarily invisible, should be veiled, operating to a substantial extent with and through local agents. Accordingly, in the words of one classic expression, "It is obviously desirable that Government should be called upon as rarely as possible to intervene between the chiefs and people . . . ."[52]

Three obvious problems existed within this general policy orientation. First and most obvious, issues of concern to the African populace exceeded the authority and expertise of local and district councils. The provincial or colony-wide levels gave access to far more influence. Not surprisingly, African leaders sought what the settlers had much earlier achieved, namely direct participation in the Legislative Council. Secondly, the conception of local government rested to a substantial degree on models drawn from the Indian princely states, such as Hyderabad, and from hierarchical societies in Africa (for example, Buganda or the Fulani emirates). The starting point for indirect rule was an identifiable group or individual, in which political authority had been vested. Societies more fragmented in composition—especially acephalous societies, such as the Kikuyu—could not be fitted easily into colonial schemes for local government. Finally, despite the paramountcy doctrine, British rule in Kenya witnessed a substantial transfer of resources from indigenous to immigrant sectors of the economy. Those who participated in the process, were they African or European, obviously could not claim to have acted, always and directly, on behalf of the majority interests. Each point merits further discussion.

Local Native Councils (LNCs) were instituted as a belated response to post-World War I stirrings of African political awareness. Apart from *barazas* (public meetings) or informal, appointed advisory councils, European administrators had no direct link to what may be loosely called African public opinion. To be certain, District Officers (DO's) were regularly exhorted to "go on tour," in the 1920s a physically taxing and time-demanding effort through most of Kenya. This contact was supplemented by contact with missionaries, with interpreters, and (given commitment and linguistic skill on the part of the DO) with individual Africans. DOs' duties brought them directly into the political and social arena, for they had to ensure that taxes were collected, that indigenous courts meted out appropriate judgments, that roads were constructed and maintained, et cetera. But in the early performance of these tasks, they lacked the support of a *shen-shih* group, its raison d'être that of linking village issues to the national administrative apparatus. Educated indigenous clerks were distrusted, their values and outlooks presumably being at variance with the views of "the people themselves." Thus imposing their rule on an unreceptive land, the British did not find (unlike the Manchus or the British as they dealt with Hyderabad) an indigenous group both experienced in administration the colonial government deemed appropriate and marked by popular support. And, as will be shown subsequently, the development of indigenous groups affiliated with the colonial administration resulted in fragmentation during the rebellion between "Loyalists" and Mau Mau partisans.

The shortcomings just noted should not be unduly magnified. For the undoubted majority of Africans until World War II, administration at the local level, though modestly adapted from indigenous roots, sufficed. Customary law, as increasingly codified, could be drawn upon in disputes. The hand of the colonial administration rested lightly on many parts of Kenya. The greatest exceptions came in Nairobi, and in the increasingly crowded Kikuyu reserves. Within Nairobi, "tribal" forms of government could not be readily carried over. The city housed groups with divergent interests: Europeans, usually associated with the administration; Asians, heavily engaged in commerce, transport, some professions, and clerical work; Africans, drawn by the opportunities for personal independence and cash employment without the constraints of rural life. Nairobi did not predate colonial rule. In fact, the city's location, in a lowlying papyrus swamp, resulted from happenstance, namely the erection in 1896 of a railroad supply depot and later installation of railway headquarters. Nairobi in its early days was an Asian town, whose African population grew slowly, reaching 12,088 in 1921.[53] Those who left the African reserves were largely Kikuyu, as might be expected: Nairobi stood close to the densely settled Kiambu district. The Local Native Councils of Kiambu had no power in the urban area, which was governed under its own statute. Nairobi represented thus an area in which Africans desirous of escaping the "idiocy of rural life" could congregate. It became the locus of Kenya African politics.[54] From it stemmed much of the later impetus for rebellion.

A mounting Kikuyu population clustered in the reserves. Their 1923 population was estimated at 447,000; in 1931, at 493,500; and in 1948, when the first full census of Africans was taken, at 733,924. (For sake of comparison, Kikuyu living outside the reserves were estimated in 1923 at 50,000, in 1931 at 110,000, and in 1948 enumerated at 292,417.)[55] Particularly densely inhabited pockets developed near Nairobi (Dagoretti) and in Nyeri (North Tetu). The growth of population brought increased land tensions, migration, feuds, and other symptoms of social malaise, as indicated in Chapter 2. Local Native Councils could do nothing to expand the total acreage available; their restricted ambit meant they were incapable of responding to the most salient issue confronting the Kikuyu.

The impotence of institutions for indigenous African administration contrasted sharply with the access Europeans enjoyed to the corridors of power. The most important instrument was the Legislative Council, originally an advisory group to the governor, subsequently broadened to include representatives of interest groups. Established in 1907, "Legco" rapidly became the avenue through which Lord Delamere, E.S. Grogan, Michael Blundell, and other minority spokesmen pressed their views. They used various platforms to argue in favor of restricting African participation to the innocuous setting of local government, leaving to better educated Europeans the real business of administration. Take, for example, this 1946 statement by the Electors' Union:

> The European community should urge that the African should be given a gradually increasing part in local Government and that Local Native Councils should be given gradually increasing responsibility in controlling their own Reserves. Until that period of training has been successfully passed, African representation on the higher bodies should be limited to a point sufficient to ensure that their needs are fully voiced and the selection of representatives should be by Government nomination....[representation in the Legislative Council and on municipal and township councils] to be subject to gradual expansion in accord with the development of the African sense of civic responsibility with full recognition of the fact that for very many years to come, the African community will be unfitted to exercise the privilege of election of its representatives and that the power of selection must, therefore, rest with the Government or the local authority concerned.[56]

When this statement was penned, the majority population of over four million was represented in Legco by a single African.

A second set of issues connected with local government arose from the social organization of the Kikuyu, described at length in Chapter 2. Early British administrators sought to work through chiefs and headmen — most likely, clan (*mbari*) leaders — giving them responsibilities that had no parallel in the pre-colonial system. "Their obligations to government were strictly limited," according to Sorrenson; "for some years their only important functions, apart from keeping the peace, were to recruit labour and raise some taxes. If they did this efficiently, government did not inquire too closely into how they operated."[57] In other words, the power lent by association with the British *raj* could be turned to personal or clan advantage. I do not wish to imply that the decentralized nature of Kikuyu society enabled those recognized by the colonial government to profit. Similar solidification of privilege occurred in almost every setting in which indirect rule was employed, be it in *deshmukh* extractions or in the "squeeze" Ch'ing district magistrates could extort. The differential in power, prestige, and (more problematic for Kenya) literacy gave any indigenous associates immense advantages.

Granted, then, that limited political stratification marked the Kikuyu prior to colonization, what were the consequences of domination by an alien minority? First, as already noted, the way was opened to the emergency of petty chieftains lording over the indigenous peasantry. Secondly, the range of responsibilities in the hands of the local associates expanded well beyond the traditional ambit of decision making. Prior to the imposition of colonial rule, each *riika* (age group) attempted to settle disputes through its *kiama* (council). The issues that increasingly concerned the colonial administration — for example, land terracing or cattle culling — could not readily be resolved through "traditional" instrumentalities. Despite the desire for a slow, paced evolution of local government, pressures mounted instead for far more profound change.

The chief reason for the evolution of local government was the direct result of the disjuncture between the slogan of paramount African interests and the reality of settler dominance. The primary concern of the British administration until the outbreak of the rebellion, it can be fairly opined, was support for European agriculture. The model chosen was one of settler farming, not plantation agriculture. The two are qualitatively different. Plantation agriculture is managerial, involving contracts for supervisors and their presumed return "home" when their stint is over. Settler farming is much more sweeping in its impact on indigenous society. Not only the manager but his whole family must be accommodated; they expect some reasonable facsimile of the cradle-to-grave services they would have enjoyed in their native land. The true settler transfers his allegiance to his new home. Cutting ties to his former metropole, the settler may be expected rabidly to demand the right to control his own affairs — political, social, and economic.

Settlers in Kenya needed cheap labor. The Electors' Union, in its 1946 statement, put the matter directly:

> It is necessary that there should be a large floating or semi-permanent population of Africans in the Highlands area, because there their services are required as agricultural labourers. This type of employment will be valuable outlet for the proportion of the 'landless' population.[58]

The ingenuous nature of the statement, failing to ascribe landlessness to settler agriculture, need not detain us. What was important was the explicit recognition that Africans had to be pushed away from their lands in order to drift to the European farms. The intensification of such pressures, the following chapter will indicate, markedly enhanced relative deprivation among the Kikuyu.

The pressure on the majority took many other forms. Denial to Africans of the right to grow coffee; manipulation of railroad charges to favor European rather than indigenous agriculture; hikes in the poll tax; protective tariffs borne largely by the majority; railroad expansion assisting the minority at heavy costs to the Africans; these and other strategies (carefully analysed by Brett)[59] removed resources from the majority, whose interests supposedly were paramount. The funds thus extracted from Africans subsidized settler agriculture. Africans were forced out of subsistence agriculture, or precluded from cash crop farming, in order that their labor be available. The choice was clear. "Independent peasant production and capitalistic settler production therefore existed as sharply antagonistic modes, and any effective development of one necessarily precluded an equivalent development of the other in the same social universe."[60] The colonial government believed the transfer of resources to the alien minority represented the soundest strategy for development. Thus, to the extent the British defended policies designed more to capitalize settler agriculture than to defend African paramountcy, a clear contradiction existed — clearer and sharper, perhaps, than the contradictions already noted in China and India.

To what extent, accordingly, did British administration in Kenya keep the populace politically untutored and socially divided?

Both were obviously among the implicit goals of the European settlers. Since their assumption that African political and social progress required prior European economic advance was shared with the administration, the minority populace presented a united front. The relatively unmobilized conditions of most African inhabitants prior to World War II helped. Only where the weight of alien settlement was particularly heavy, or social change accelerated, did significant political action result. In areas of light governmental or settler impact, awareness of the colonial situation and widespread development of feelings of relative deprivation were retarded. The system of Local Native Councils, added to the continued emphasis on working through chiefs and headmen, resulted in little direct challenge to the "traditional" means of problem solving in much of Kenya. In other and cruder terms, the ethnic foundations of village and rural administration remained substantially intact.

Yet it would be incorrect to underestimate the long-term effects of even a minimal colonial presence. Poll taxes were levied on all adult males. Growing consumer preference for imported goods — usually subject to heavy tariffs — encouraged African participation in the cash economy.

Schooling, though in essence confined to primary education and far from universal in acceptance, helped implant perspectives transcending the village setting. Official encouragement for Christianity abetted another avenue of change. Embroilment in both World Wars accelerated for many their awareness of national and international issues. Most important, the colonial presence in Kenya was *not* minimal for many of its inhabitants. The alienating effects of land transfer, of religious disputes, of taxation, and of denial of political access were profound. The concept of paramountcy could be periodically dusted off to underscore contrasts between the rhetorical commitment to African advance and the actual rate of change. Ultimately, the colonial administration was supposed to work itself out of its job. Tutelage was to be bounded in time—despite the obvious differences between Africans and Europeans regarding the speed of accomplishment. This qualitative difference distinguished British colonial administration from the "internal" colonialism of the Ch'ing and Muslim rulers. Up until 1960, however, the prospects for full independence seemed limited.

Highly restricted avenues existed for African political participation. As underscored previously, the colonial administration reserved to itself the nature and pace of recruitment. Preference was accorded those drawn from respected families who were ready to work within essentially local contexts. The acceptable avenue for Africans lay through village settings—while Europeans could enter the Legislative Council directly. Jomo Kenyatta, with a graduate degree from the University of London and a facility in English Governor Mitchell regarded as equal to his, was advised to start at the bottom as well. Analogous rebuffs to those divorced from the village setting contributed to African grievances.

It accordingly appears as though British colonial rule only partially satisfied the third maxim for minority control. Selection of allies for governance from the majority precluded a small but significant sector of Africans. The urbanized and the nationally-oriented literate had little incentive to play by the British-established rules and confine themselves to rural issues—issues that explicitly excluded challenges to alien domination and the settler presence.

On the other hand, the British did co-opt Africans into support of the colonial mission. Administration required willing local adjuncts. Circumstance and preference combined: certain chiefs and headmen emerged, joining continuity with the traditional system to compatibility with British objectives. The ambivalence inherent in their responsibilities left ample ground for personal initiative. They stood between groups with non-congruent interests, often resolving conflict to their own advantage. What we observed in Imperial China and Hyderabad seemed applicable to the

Kikuyu under British rule: local collaborators in alien domination could turn their new-found powers to practices not officially authorized by the regime, but unofficially tolerated as the price of cooperation. To a substantial extent, the chiefs recognized by the British stood outside traditional sanctions. Their field for action reflected, among various factors, the absence of detailed colonial knowledge of and interest in local matters, the preference to relegate such matters to indigenous decision-makers, and the small number of expatriate District Officers. (In the five years prior to the Emergency, only 17 to 19 DOs served in Central Province; in sharp contrast, 218 DOs served there in 1955.)[61] Those who profited from low-level posts bore the dual onus of supporting minority rule and of profiting from it. There should be little wonder, accordingly, that rebellion often lashed out at local agents of alien oppression; when open conflict erupted, self-serving collaborators were its first victims. The interests of Ch'ing officials, of *deshmukhs* and *jagirs*, and of Kikuyu chiefs, seemed to lie with the outsiders who made their opportunities available.

Coercion provided the British colonial administration its ultimate basis for control over the Kikuyu. It was not a simple maintenance of the disparities in armaments that had facilitated the British occupation, but a reasonably sophisticated mixture of steps that discouraged Africans in Kenya from rebelling. Indigenous societies were kept demilitarized as far as possible. Stiff regulations prevented Africans from acquiring modern firearms directly; Europeans, by contrast, had ready access to pistols and rifles. (Not unsurprisingly, theft from Europeans provided Mau Mau fighters a major source of weapons. By early 1953, some 52,000 firearms had been registered in Kenya, these being overwhelmingly in settler hands.)[62] Traditional patterns of military training, as in age-set initiations, were discouraged. The British established tribal police, although in numbers that made them less than useful in combatting widespread collective political violence. (At the start of 1952, only 98 African constables, plus European officers, served in Central Province, with a population over 730,000.)[63] Backup for the police came from the King's African Rifles (KAR), two battalions of which were stationed in Kenya in mid-1952;[64] ultimate support came from British troops, who were airlifted into the colony during the Emergency. The colonial administration and Ministry of War manipulated the composition of the military to maximize its effectiveness and loyalty. KAR battalions (to adumbrate what appears in Chapter 8) were practically devoid of Kikuyu. British administrators preferred to recruit the rank-and-file from "martial races," whose major advantage was unswerving loyalty, and to draw officers from British subjects. Thus, white officers presided over African troops, whose composition in no way accurately reflected the ethnic mosaic of Kenyan society, but whose ability to follow commands made them crucial props of British rule.[65] All in all, the colonial administration in Kenya seemed to use force sparingly, and thus to heed the relevant maxim, until Mau Mau burst upon the scene. What was official policy did not, however, free the Kikuyu from coercion. The exactions of settlers, as we shall see again in the following chapter, magnified the Kikuyu sense of relative deprivation after World War II. Pushed to defend themselves against increasing exactions, the Kikuyu were to turn to collective political violence.

The Belgian Congo: Service through Domination

The *leitmotiv* of Belgian rule was provided by Pierre Ryckmans: "Dominate in order to serve." Until its near-collapse in 1959-60, the colonial administration in the Belgian Congo exercised a control whose impact exceeded what Kenya as a whole (though not Kikuyuland in particular) experienced under British control. Transformation marked all parts of Congolese society which, the Belgians seem to have felt, could be moulded in accordance with their wishes. The service to be rendered justified domination.

Rural transformation and disappointed expectations made the 1964 Kwilu rebellion possible. Both had their roots in colonial policies. The Belgians did not content themselves by simply presiding over a static rural society, as had the Ch'ing and Asaf Jahi dynasties. The vision held in Brussels and Leopoldville stressed economic development with substantial European participation. Religious training and intensive Christian proselytizing would provide moral elevation. Careful attention would be given health, primary education, and social welfare. Since the benefits of Belgian policies might not be obvious to the untutored, compulsion could be employed in (for example) cotton cultivation; in this fashion, economic development and education would be advanced. Political participation by Africans, in the Belgian vision, lay appropriately in local communes. As had British administrators in Kenya, Belgian officials in the Congo neither encouraged nor expected indigenous persons to serve in central political institutions until a thorough apprenticeship had been completed at lower levels. In brief, then, Belgian colonial administration coupled intensive alteration in the countryside with significant obstacles to African political participation. Economic and political advance proceeded at different speeds, along separate tracks.

Young has published an excellent survey of the basic premises of Belgian colonial rule. The points that follow owe much to his analysis.[66] Decolonization would be gradual, and graduated. The process would remain under Belgian control. Political construction would take place from the ground up, with economic and social transformation preceding the installation of political institutions. The Belgians assumed that African societies were pliable, that they could be bent in accord with imperial designs, that direct administrative action would hasten accomplishment of this design. Change might not be modest, nor the administration hesitant in applying strong pressures. In the words of one Belgian pressure group, "the more backward the population, and the more radical the reforms which its accession to our civilization necessitates, the stronger, more general, and more constant our intervention in native life must be."[67] Aiding the achievement of this vision would be an African middle class, who would come to share certain bourgeois attitudes with Europeans as a prelude to sharing political rights. It was further assumed that Belgians would continue — even after decolonization — to play an important part; a Eurafrican partnership might be established, avoiding both the Scylla of settler self-rule and the Charybdis of Congolese autonomy. Finally, the Belgian royal family would continue to serve as an important link between metropolitan and African sectors.

This brief description shows many similarities between Belgian colonial policy, as applied in the Congo, and British colonial policy, as applied in Kenya. The guiding slogans of both stemmed from a *noblesse oblige* attitude that Europeans, even while compelling Africans, were aiding the latter. "Dominate in order to serve" and "paramountcy" translated into what the local administration wished to do. Settlers exercised substantial influence. The extension of infrastructure was intended largely to benefit European undertakings, from which benefits would spill over to Africans. African involvement in governance would have to proceed from the grassroots, in accordance with timetables devised by the administration. Locally-staffed but European-officered armed forces were available to suppress local revolts. African participation in the cash economy would be encouraged where possible, pressured where necessary. Although the metropolitan parliaments could exercise supervision, they in fact tended to leave colonial civil servants a free hand; legislative interest rarely was roused in the sleepy days of colonial rule between the world wars.

A few contrasts should also be noted. Belgian economic development in the Congo centered more on mining and plantations than on settler agriculture, despite the presence of many settlers in Kivu; the white farmers of the Highlands and the Rift Valley enjoyed the limelight in Kenya. Evangelization reached a far higher pitch, with Belgian encouragement, than evangelization in Kenya; mission stations (669 of them Roman Catholic)[68] dotted the rural areas of the Congo. Compulsion, especially in cotton cultivation, was pressed in the Congo both for longer periods and more intensely than forced labor in Kenya. Also differing in degree was the recognition of indigenous leaders. The Belgians seem to have given far less attention to "traditional" means of selection than did the British, the contrast stemming from the greater British use of indirect rule. Extensive social benefits for Congolese, notably those in industrial employment, contrasted with the far more laissez faire practices used for Kenyans. Although political associations in both colonies were tightly reined, Kenyans were subject to somewhat fewer restrictions. The most significant contrast, however, came in the density of rural administration. Not until the Emergency and the implementation of the Swynnerton Plan did the British colonial presence among the Kikuyu attain what the Congolese had long experienced. "What differentiated the Belgian system from others in Africa," Young comments, "was the extent of its occupation and organization of the countryside."[69] The domination that was to serve Africans started *en brousse*.

The initial implantation of Belgian rule, as is well known, came through the personal efforts of King Leopold I in the 1880s. His International Association of the Congo lobbied to have its claim to 1.3 million square miles recognized by European powers; they, in turn, claimed "the right to annex African territory for their own advantage as long as the nominal consent of a certain number of African chiefs had been obtained."[70] The 1885 Berlin Conference granted Leopold absolute powers to establish effective authority in the occupied areas of the Congo basin. The Belgian parliament initially stood aside, leaving any link between the new state and Belgium as "exclusively personal."[71] The horrendous exactions by which the Congo Free State financed its activities aroused international concern, leading in 1908 to Belgian annexation. A score of years of exploitation had left deep marks on Congolese society. Lemarchand offers the following judgment:

> In terms of its psychological impact, the Free State left a legacy of latent hostility on which subsequent generations of nationalist leaders could capitalize to gain popular support for their cause. On the other hand, the ruthlessness of the methods employed under the Leopoldian regime left a legacy of fear and hopelessness which, initially at least, discouraged the emergence of nationalist activities.[72]

The checkered legacy of the Free State affected Belgian administrators as well. Determined to avoid the excesses and exploitation that marked the period prior to 1908, they evolved sharply paternalistic policies. Physical compulsion, though still employed, was rationalized as benefiting Africans rather than as profiting Europeans. (It was questionable, of course, whether those compelled could discern any difference at all.) Economic and social uplift became the keystones of policy. In practice, however, this meant heavy reliance on European initiative. The alienation of plantation areas to Huileries du Congo Belge was one of many examples of Belgian preference for large-scale European enterprise rather than for African production. Such sharp intrusions into longstanding patterns of indigenous life — "the more radical the reforms which its accession to our civilization necessitates" — made clear the Belgian desire for transformation. Minority rule, to reiterate, was justified in colonial eyes by the changes it wrought.

These preliminary observations suggest that the Belgians gave scant heed to the maxims discussed in this chapter. Take, for example, the idea that the populace should be kept politically untutored and socially divided, with the direct impact of the government on rural life as minimal as possible. The Belgian imprint on rural patterns was sharp. The intrusion of missionaries, of agricultural specialists, of health officers giving compulsory examinations, could not be escaped. Each encouraged actions that conflicted with African practices in some degree — not necessarily with beneficial results. The intense impact contrasted sharply with the continuation, under Belgian rule, of political and social division. Political parties could not be formed until the death throes of colonial rule; Congolese, however, could create ethnic associations, and it was by and from these that political participation was largely shaped. All groups experienced the homogenizing effects of colonial rule, but these could not, and did not, suffice of themselves to create a "nation" within Congolese borders. "Nationalism" based on anti-colonialism, yes; "nationalism" reflecting a submergence of ethnic perceptions, no. Social divisions remained under Belgian rule; the late overlay of political institutions meant ethnicity served as the chief basis for collective action. It should be reiterated, however, that Kwilu represented an unusual case. The multi-ethnic area rallied behind the Parti Solidaire Africain (with the exception of the Bayezi), a factor significant in explaining the region's 1964 support for rebellion. The PSA will receive closer attention in Chapter 6.

Prior to World War II, Belgian rationalization of differences in power, status and wealth remained "more an implicit assumption than an explicit political theory...the social and political immaturity of Congolese populations was so self-evident to the colonizer that no elaboration was required."[73] The greater care with which colonialism had to be justified after 1945 led to conscious enunciation of paternalism. The Belgians enjoyed superior knowledge, the transfer of which to Congolese could be accomplished only over several generations. European investment had brought benefits; not unnaturally, Europeans should enjoy greater salaries. Administration required skills, at the higher levels, that only university graduates enjoyed; the fact no Congolese attended a university until 1952 was incidental. Belgian nationality, required for appointment as a full civil servant rather than an an auxiliary, was a further barrier to the indigenes. Underlying paternalism, as already suggested, were beliefs in the plasticity of African institutions, in the ability of the Belgians to preside over the decolonization process, and (above all) in the firm conviction that economic and social transformation should precede political change, itself to start at the village or commune level. These arguments failed to impress Congolese of all backgrounds. The long-term elevation that was supposed to come through mandatory cultivation made little sense to Africans, who resented the interference and (in many cases) reduction in living standards this imposed. The barriers to African land ownership, to higher education, to administrative employment much above the clerical level, and to political advance concerned the educated.

Some groups in Congolese society obviously gained from their association with the colonial masters. But how open were the channels by which appropriately qualified individuals from the subject populace could participate in governance? Barriers to Africans attending university and the citizenship requirement, as suggested in the previous paragraph, precluded them from reaching senior ranks in the civil service. Despite this barrier, administrative service provided an attractive career — even though until 1959 Congolese could serve only as "auxiliaries," not as full civil servants.[74] They formed the basis of the "administrative bourgeoisie" so important in the early years of Congolese independence. Those "traditional," or not-so-traditional indigenous leaders recognized by the Belgians enjoyed ample opportunity for personal advancement. Abuses similar to those noted in Kenya marked the Belgian Congo as well. In Lemarchand's judgment, "The chefs de secteurs, officially regarded as 'the custodians of custom,' exercised quasi-dictatorial powers in their *circonscriptions* in violation of all customary prescriptions."[75] Belgian rule further abetted and enriched a few Congolese who rose (despite Belgian, Greek, and Portuguese competition) through trade. Finally, Congolese priests (500 or so in 1959, with new ones being confirmed at 35-40 annually)[76] enjoyed high prestige. The channels for participation, in other words, reflected the structure of control imposed by the colonial power; it corresponded in few details with indigenous patterns. Those who were recruited were relegated to inferior positions; there was little higher education, and accordingly little opportunity to reach senior posts; no significant degree of indirect rule existed, although local leaders could profit disproportionately; only the church seemed to offer opportunities for advancement less tinged by overt discrimination. Perhaps not surprisingly, many ex-seminarians provided leadership in the anti-colonial movement in the Belgian Congo; they saw clearly the gap between Christian presumption and political inequality.

The Force Publique was pressed into action when local disturbances threatened the *pax Belgica*. The Force Publique developed a reputation for ruthlessness in suppression, the Pende casualties in the 1931 revolt being a good example. The rank-and-file were Congolese, often selected from what the British called "martial races": relatively unsophisticated but trained in instant obedience; untouched by political consciousness; willing to make a career in the armed forces. Officers were exclusively white, a fact that (in the intensely political atmosphere of the first week of independence) was to lead to mutiny and a substantial breakdown of the machinery of government. The depredations of the Force Publique were feared during the colonial era, as might be expected. Its composition and activities underscored the inherent gap between Belgian rulers and Congolese subjects.

Readers will doubtless have noted that Kwilu has rarely appeared thus far in this chapter. This reflects the essential similarity of Belgian rule throughout the Congo. To be certain, variations existed: in Katanga in particular, and to a lesser extent in Kivu, European communities harbored dreams of settler rule. The rapid growth in expatriates—6,971 in 1920, 27,791 in 1940, 34,789 in 1946, 98,804 in 1956, and 114,341 in 1959[77]—brought numerous instances of racial discrimination. Large-scale European settlement did not mark Kwilu, however. The region's preminence in palm collection gave it one of the highest African per capita incomes in the colony—meaning, to be certain, sharper responses to economic interruptions. No unusual differences separated educational or mission activity in Kwilu from other parts of the Belgian Congo. Overall, accordingly, the inhabitants of Kwilu were affected by the colonial administration's acts of commission and omission, chief among these being the near-total absence of indigenous participation above the village or commune level. The short duration of the national political apprenticeship had its impact only after formal independence had been granted.

I have already made note of the partially homogenizing effects of Belgian rule. Colonial administration simultaneously enhanced ethnic awareness, and encouraged broader nationalism. The Parti Solidaire Africain represented a geographic area demarcated by Belgians for adminstrative purposes. The PSA developed from a federation of ethnic groups; it stood among the most militant Congolese parties in seeking independence; in a complex political situation, it favored centralization over the loose federalism preferred by the dominant party of the region. Perhaps most important for our investigation, the PSA became the conduit, after independence, through which the impetus for rebellion spread.

Here may seem to lie a contrast between the two uprisings in tropical Africa. The British administration in Kenya sought to discourage political change by banning seemingly militant groups: the Kikuyu Central Association in 1940, the Kenya African Union in early 1953, after its constitutionalist leaders had been jailed. The Belgian administration in the Congo sought to forestall further administrative breakdown in 1959 by belatedly recognizing political movements and hastening the transfer of power. Those who turned to collective political violence in Kenya did so in large measure because the British turned a deaf ear to claims for land reform and independence. Those who turned to collective political violence in Kwilu did so in large measure because the African successors to the Belgians seemed determined to exclude members of a vigorous party from a major political role. The seeds of collective political violence were planted in Kwilu prior to 1960, but harvested after independence by those unable to fulfill the inflated claims of what the Belgian departure would bring.

This chapter started with the suggestion that minority domination evoked rebellion. The reality, of course, is far more complex. Were the suggestion literally true, the 1964 "second independence" uprising would not have occurred; collective political violence, rather than being confined to sections of the populace, would have been far greater in its extent. Is there a ready explanation?

One obvious response is that the four societies were both polarized and pluralistic. Ruler and ruled were pitted against each other as polarization — and accordingly the potential for revolution — increased. Fragmentation remained among the ruled, however. Pluralism among the majority made rebellion a more likely form of collective political violence than revolution. The pathways for collective action had not been fused; ethnicity constituted the chief building block. Only Hung Hsiu-ch'üan, evoking Han solidarity, new-cum-old religious messages, and appeals to previous rural uprisings, could mount a broad challenge. The extensive history of peasant rebellions in China provided a model for collective action, into which a variety of grievances could be poured. The rural dwellers of Telengana, Kikuyuland, and (more problematically) Kwilu lacked such a ready model, or at least one extending beyond a relatively limited group. Particularism inevitably became prominent.

A further obvious response comes from the different international contexts, to which we have, as yet, given scant attention. The maintenance of minority domination — as the Nizam found in 1947-8, and the Belgians found in 1959-60 — became next to impossible when internal pressures for change were dramatically accelerated by ideas flowing from external sources. Colonialism became increasingly difficult to justify. The retention of minority control after World War II received greater and greater international criticism. The wave of new states that crowded into the United Nations made clear their abhorrence for denials of majority political rights. In the African settings we are examining, paternalism in the Congo appeared increasingly anachronistic; paramountcy of African interests seemed belied by the power and privileges of European settlers.

Alien domination by itself thus does not, and cannot, explain when, why and how rebellion bursts forth. Control by a culturally distinct group may be a *precondition* of collective political violence; it is not the *only* precondition, however, nor is it necessarily a precipitant. We must continue to probe for other contributing factors. In particular, we should focus on the interaction between minority rule and individual sectors of society, and on the pressures from outside that bolstered political awareness. The propensity for involvement in collective political violence varied among groups. Explanation of such variations requires attention to three types of interaction: of alien domination with internal strains, such as the distribution of power, status and wealth; of coercion to maintain privileges of the minority in the face of growing popular resentment; and of ideas from outside the particular society with indigenous notions of inequity and change. Interactions of this sort precipitated relative deprivation and crystallized it into collective political violence.

PART II

THE POLITICIZATION

OF DISCONTENT

The four chapters that follow explore a single phenomenon: the politicization of discontent. Rebellion cannot break forth without a sense of grievance both motivating participants and directing their concern against a seemingly culpable government and its agents. Analysis of the causes of collective political violence requires attention to the sources of discontent, and to the ways in which it is projected against the incumbents.

I need not minimize the complexity of the task. The interested scholar must try to grasp concerns perhaps far removed from his own experience. He must comprehend what pushed seemingly docile rural dwellers onto the "dangerous path," as the Chinese would have said. He must become aware of economic, political and social milieus far removed from his own. Detachment may bring objectivity. But it can also encourage erroneous assumptions, unchecked by critiques from participants distant in time, space, or outlook. The outside analyst may project sets of inappropriate assumptions on peasant societies. For example, rural dwellers have often been reprimanded—implicitly and explicitly—for being "pre-political." Marx, Wolf, Hobsbawm, and many others have insisted that awareness of the peasants' plight and achievement of a more sympathetic economic and political order can come only from outside the "idiocy of rural life." Such an approach risks seriously underestimating the ability and willingness of peasants to fight for a fairer share. Although they may not aspire to the style of life outside observers themselves favor, and although they may take far more interest in village than in national matters, rural dwellers are neither "pre-political," nor unable to assert and defend their interests. True, persons with broader backgrounds may catalyze uprisings; nonetheless, the chief participants and ultimately the setters of objectives are peasants. They are "mindful" of their concerns as Scheiner reminds us.[1] We must not impose inappropriate expectations or outlooks, nor magnify rebellion beyond its inherent limits. The danger of assuming "pre-political" behavior is thus complemented by the danger of seeing rural uprisings as embryonic revolutions. Rebellions and revolutions have much in common. To assume the former leads readily to the latter smacks of romanticism, however. Those who glimpse a peasant *foco* as a nucleus for profound change are liable to be disappointed. Rural rebels have their own objectives, to which revolutionary goals can be attached only with difficulty. We must thus pick a careful path between dismissing peasants as "pre-political," on the one hand, and viewing them, on the other hand, as the torchbearers of a new economic, political and social order. We must, in short, examine the participants *in their own terms* — as far as the data and informed supposition will permit.

How did the participants in the four rebellions view their roles? This broad question lies behind Chapters 4 through 7. Those who rose in violent anger did so as a result of various types of provocation. One such provocation was a perception of "relative deprivation." Individuals felt they were being denied rights and opportunities to which they were entitled. As a sense of personal resentment, the political consequences of relative deprivation may be restricted. As a sense of group or collective resentment, however, its political consequences may be great. What makes relative deprivation or frustration politically relevant is the aggregation of concerns, and their attribution to the government. Perception, generalization, and projection of discontent constitute the necessary steps. The "mere existence of privation," in Trotsky's phrase, does not lead by itself to politicized discontent. Feelings can be diverted: blamed on individual's shortcomings; attributed to unquestionable fate; presented as the result of outside interference. Only if problems are perceived as shared, as potentially susceptible to solution through joint action, and as due to official action or inaction, may discontent be translated into collective political action. Its further translation into collective political violence reflects a situation of conflict in which the participants turn to coercion, not compromise. Avenues for peaceful change having been closed off, force provides the only way in which claimants can be heard, incumbents defended.

The pages that follow thus adopt a multicausal explanation for rebellion. Collective political violence on the scale manifested in the Taiping, Telengana, Mau Mau and Kwilu uprisings resulted from many factors working in combination. The usual checks on overt, widespread conflict between rulers and ruled proved insufficient. Rebellion resulted from the combined impact of widespread relative deprivation (Chapter 4), elite weakness and ineffectual use of violence (Chapter 5), indigenous leadership and organization (Chapter 6), and a structure of beliefs that justified mobilization (Chapter 7). All these elements had to be present to bring about collective political violence of such intensity and scope.

The chapters of this section are based on a roughly chronological approach. Schematically, discontent gave rise to a sense of relative deprivation among persons who increasingly viewed themselves as members of an aggrieved group needing redress. Since discontent was not evenly distributed through the particular societies, certain groups took the lead in pressing for change. Their quest for reform, even if directed along channels recognized by the government, brought repression rather than rectification. The incumbents' attacks exacerbated discontent. When these attacks were countered by violence from the aggrieved, the general level of conflict rose, making compromise even more difficult. The need for coordination, and the desire to spread the message of change, encouraged the formation of political movements — often clandestine, given their objectives. Leaders explained their actions and motivated their followers through ideology. These generalized beliefs defined the aggrieved community, identified the reasons for collective political violence, and suggested the type of society that should be created. All these steps are subsumed in the simple phrase, "politicization of discontent." The process was neither automatic nor direct. Comprehension of the process requires a careful melding of theory and data, so that we can group the perceptions and actions of the participants — examples of the collective political violence rural societies have experienced, and doubtless will continue to experience.

CHAPTER 4 /

The Sense of
Relative Deprivation

Rebellion develops from popular discontent—but not all discontent gives birth to rebellion. Collective political violence on a mass basis is a relatively uncommon phenomenon. This does not mean that discontent is rare, but that discontent of the magnitude and concentration requisite for widespread revolt develops only under unusual circumstances.

Thus far, we have examined two major foundations of discontent. One sprang from within the four societies we have been considering. Contrasts in power, status and wealth were pronounced in all four. Such contrasts could evoke collective action, activated on ethnic, religious, class, or political foundations, or on varying combinations of these. Alien domination constituted the second foundation. The actions of the imperial minority and their local collaborators opened gaps in the affected societies. Only a handful of indigenous persons shared in the power, status and wealth effectively monopolized by the various ruling groups. The connections between internal strains and external domination brought into being a complex variety of discontents, from which collective action sprang.

The purpose in this chapter and the three following is to take the potential rebels a further step along the road to insurgency: the step of focusing resentments, felt both individually and collectively, on the government. Such projection may not seem difficult. Inequalities were manifest, inequities pronounced. But three preliminary cautions are in order. First, perceived *inequalities* need not give rise to perceived *inequities*. No direct translation of the former into the latter exists. Secondly, perceived inequities need not give rise to collective action. They may be shrugged off, attributed to causes beyond human control, or perceived as problems insoluble by common action. Thirdly, even were collective action to result, it might be directed against targets other than the political incumbents. Those who should bear the brunt of rural resentment may have been so far removed from the immediate world of those affected as to escape blame, or at least direct attack.

126

Speaking in general terms about collective political violence, the politicization of discontent, so obvious in retrospect, and no doubt clear in the minds of some participants, proceeds along an uneven, obstacle-strewn course. The causes of many frustrations cannot readily be attributed to political incumbents. Indigenous belief systems may attribute present misfortune to individuals' past indiscretions, seeming to foreclose the chance for immediate rectification. Existing models for collective action may be riven with internal contradictions, with the result that coordination among the aggrieved remains partial. Conscious steps by the governing minority to divide and rule compound the problems of would-be protesters. A general sense of rural impotence vis-a-vis existing inequities—at least under "normal" conditions—promotes general apathy.

One certainly can argue that collective political violence becomes inevitable under certain conditions, using the metaphor of spontaneous combustion. This comparison between chemical/physical processes and political/social processes does injustice to the complexity and distinctiveness of societal change, I believe. Spontaneous combustion smoulders, then blazes forth under known, measurable, and replicable conditions of volatility, volume, and ventilation (if the natural scientists will permit this alliterative explanation). A mechanical application of physical laws to social contexts would mean that a sufficient quantity of grievances, in the absence of opportunities for alleviation, automatically results in collective political violence—the political equivalent of fire. If grievances were more precisely quantifiable, and data more readily available, computer-assisted studies might relegate analyses such as this to a museum of historic relics. Difficulties in measuring perceptions of grievances, levels of leadership, and other personal and cultural variables, confront all scholars, however. The "flash point" for rebellion varies in ways that make precise prediction next to impossible. One can speak of tendencies or probabilities only. Collective political violence is not *inevitable*, though it becomes more or less likely under circumstances that can be compared.

Since rebellion constitutes a political act—that is to say, an attempt to change government personnel and/or policies through coordinated challenge to the incumbents' legitimacy and control of the means of coercion—the interested political scientist must devote prime attention to the politicization of discontent. This in turn requires concentration not only on the nature and scope of discontent itself, but also on the ways in which this discontent is focused on political institutions. Discontent, we shall see in the four rebellions, was never equal in its impact, nor unitary in its politicization.

The Uneven Nature of Rural Discontent

In retrospect, three major sources abetted the politicization of discontent, but did so in uneven ways. The first major source was socioeconomic, and focused on land issues. Access to land, and protection of a right to livelihood, obviously affected many rural dwellers. With restriction on either, the means by which problems were resolved came under increasing strain. Alienation of land, restrictions on tenants' protections, and similar reductions of the margin of safety played key roles in the politicization of discontent. Population pressures, marked and sudden increases in tax burdens, and extensive commercialization of agriculture to the detriment of subsistence farming appeared in the four rebellions as chief social and economic factors.

A second major basis for discontent was the use of force to buttress the transfer of resources from indigenous to exogenous persons or groups. Imperial conquest, punitive raids, suppression of local demonstrations, and enforcement of unequal economic, political and social relationships bore witness to the fact alien domination was imposed by arms, not welcomed with open arms. The use of force, in the view of those suppressed, both necessitated and justified counterforce. As will be presented later, rebellion in the four societies owed much to intensified violence by the incumbents. As in the economic issues just noted, discontent stemming from coercion varied regionally: force was neither employed nor countered evenly.

Further contributing to the uneven nature of rural discontent was the development of benefits, as well as drawbacks, for inhabitants. Dominant aliens, yes, used force to redistribute local resources. But what the ruling group had in its power to take away, it also had in its power to restore or award. The penetration of commercial agriculture into rural areas created many seeming losers, but likewise benefited others. The promise of resources and opportunities provided the third ground for discontent. As de Tocqueville and many others have noted, the nearer one approaches a goal, the more vehemently any remaining obstacles are resented; relaxation of oppression heightens discontent; "the most perilous moment for a bad government is one when it seeks to mend its ways."[1] Aspiration for what can be provided—in addition to concern over what has been taken away—fueled collective discontent.

Not only did sources vary; the interpretation followed different paths, only some of which led toward rebellion. Individuals and groups vary in their perceptions of discontent, and accordingly differ in their potential for collective action. Inequities are not experienced uniformly. Pronounced contrasts stem from age, sex, intelligence, personality structure, education, and all the other ways in which humans differ. Statistical techniques provide an understanding of the "normal" conditions. Aggregate measures — Gini inequality indices, Lorenz distribution curves, GNP per capita, demographic statistics — can suggest grounds for discontent,[2] but cannot fully predict the likelihood of collective political violence. Perhaps statistics are not always needed. When a dominant minority monopolizes governmental positions, or substantial numbers of indigenous inhabitants are thrust into unbreakable indebtedness, latent discontent is widespread and could be catalyzed into collective action. But a brief caution is in order. We are concerned with *perceptions* of *inequity* that — likely, but not necessarily — exist under *conditions* of *inequality*. Perceptions vary for individuals, over time, in accordance with many factors. The extent to which inequality is perceived as inequity by a given person at a given time cannot be determined through aggregate measures.

To my knowledge, no trained social psychologists assessed rural discontent in the four regions immediately *prior to* rebellion, although some economic and political information exists. Evidence is thus either ex post facto (memoirs penned by participants, justifying their involvement and actions, and presuming their concerns mirrored those of their supporters), or inferential (academic analyses also prepared after the fact, reconstructing the manners in which indigenous participants perceived the situation.) The results are often impressive, as in the work of Weiss and of Fox and her colleagues in Kwilu blending on-the-spot observation with disciplinary insights.[3] But there is no final word, only approximations of the ways in which tensions were transformed into collective political violence.

How, then, do discontented rural dwellers turn into active rebels?

A general lesson seems to be that the act of rebellion represents a culmination of several prior steps. Collective political violence was — and remains — unusual. It requires, as Smelser aptly suggested,[4] a "value-added" approach, in which combinations of factors, not any single Cause with a capital C, necessarily precede widespread group action. Accordingly, the scholar's task becomes that of presenting the interaction among variables, in order to illustrate their relative significance. Three major explanations for rural discontent have been sketched — socioeconomic transformation worsening the perceived lot of many; officially sanctioned coercion; and frustration stemming from promised but insufficient reform. It remains to suggest which may best account for the discontent that (once politicized) took shape as collective political violence.

At first blush, it appears that transformation of rural economic relationships most readily produces discontent, touching as it did the heart of basic concerns about survival. One of the largest international surveys ever carried out underscored the importance of economic issues. Hadley Cantril and his associates carried out several thousand interviews in twelve countries, finding that the "vast majority" of human concerns revolved around well-being.[5] Family, health, values and character were important—but far less so than individuals' economic circumstances.[6] Extrapolating from Cantril's findings, one can suggest that political movements promising to rectify widespread economic grievances, or to advance widespread economic aspirations, will find fertile soil—more fertile, it would seem, than those espousing narrowly political goals.

The Cantril data also suggested links between phases of development and patterns of human concerns. Higher levels of economic and educational development went hand-in-hand with greater individual confidence in bringing pressure on the government. Acquiescence to circumstances marked the initial phase. Since India serves as the chief example, Cantril's conclusions merit brief quotation. In his view, the people of India

> were still unaware of their problems; who were too depressed to have many
> ambitions for themselves; who were unaware, too, of the possibilities of ac-
> tion at the national level to improve their welfare; whose passivity derives in
> large part from an ancient and widespread fatalism which still makes it possi-
> ble for millions upon millions of Indians to accept their lot.[7]

What the survey suggested for India as a whole should not be indiscriminately applied to Telengana in particular. Its inhabitants—like the participants in the other rebellions with which we are concerned—seemed to have reached at least the second or third phase of Cantril's model (respectively, awakening to potentialities for change, and awareness of means to realize goals.) They appear to have experienced discontent more markedly than others. Though perhaps unaware of the "possibilities of action at the national level," they were willing to act at village levels. Local problems broke through the integument of apathy and fatalism Cantril suggested.

The evidence from Telengana should caution us against overly-quick application of national norms to local circumstances. Aggregate data are useful in underscoring the central importance of economic concerns, particularly where substantial portions of the populace survive on narrow margins. Concerns over livelihood lend themselves readily to politicization. Discontent—in the form of unrealized aspirations, or of actualized frustrations—is not evenly distributed by region or economic circumstance. Nor, one can add, is such discontent uniformly made politically relevant. The uneven *nature* of discontent thus accounts for some, but not all, of the uneven *politicization* of discontent.

The Uneven Nature of Politicization

Few discontents are narrowly political — but most are politicizable.[8] Further, it stands to reason that particularly salient concerns (such as personal economic status) can be translated into collective action more rapidly than less salient concerns.

Mass support for rebellion requires the belief that a wide variety of grievances can be resolved through collective political violence. Would-be rebel leaders must harness to their cause as wide and intensely -felt a spectrum of concerns as possible, and project them on political targets. These discontents may reflect conditions beyond the incumbents' control. Such is immaterial. Given marked disparities in power, status and wealth, it takes little imagination to attribute an extraordinary range of nefarious actions to the dominant minority. The translation of such discontents with the incumbents into coordinated steps against them involves politicization, as true in the events examined in this book as in other forms of collective action. Politicization is the means by which rebellion becomes possible.

Discontents arising from the direct impingement of government actions on individuals' lives lend themselves most readily to politicization, and thence to collective political violence. The imposition of new taxes, for example, has classically served as a cause of revolt.[9] Tenancy arrangements extorting additional obligations have likewise given birth to collective political violence. Desperation in the face of imminent loss of reciprocal bonds between landlords and tenants lends urgency to group action. As Scott has noted, "the vast majority of peasant risings with which I am familiar are without doubt largely *defensive* efforts to protect sources of subsistence that are threatened or to restore them once they have been lost....peasant rebellions are typically desperate efforts to maintain subsistence arrangements that are under assault."[10] Punitive raids, ill-disciplined police or troops, or unexpectedly heavy use of force against actions rural dwellers considered legitimate, are other frequent grounds for collective political violence. Coercion receives fuller attention in the following chapter; at this point, it is appropriate to note for the record the interaction between government-condoned violence and popular resistance to undesired impositions.

The evidence to be presented below does not prove that the ability to engage in collective political violence had to be imported, as it were, by persons from outside the particular social contexts. Violence was an indigenous response to situations widely perceived as intolerable, even if fanned and focused by those with broader awareness. To a substantial extent, the organization of collective political violence followed existing bases of social interaction—hence the ethnic or ascriptive bases to which attention has already been drawn. Expansion beyond this basis, however, posed a crucial issue to leaders. The uneven nature of discontent—exacerbated as it often was by particularism—put a premium on politicization. Presenting the acute grievances of some as the generalized grievances of all taxed the ingenuity of major rebels. As we shall see in this and the other chapters of Part II, Hung Hsiu-ch'üan expanded the scope of the Taiping rebellion further than that of the three other uprisings—in large part due to the longstanding Chinese tradition of peasant violence against an overbearing dynasty. The heritage of rural resistance was more restricted, and the power of the incumbents greater, in Telengana, Kenya, and Kwilu. In none of them, however, did a handful of leaders *invent* collective political violence as a means of grappling with the intractable issues. They followed the turn to popular resistance as much as they initiated it. It may have seemed the only appropriate option under the prevailing conditions.

Relative deprivation forms the organizing concept of this chapter. Thanks largely to the work of Ted Robert Gurr, relative deprivation has been elaborated into a complex network of hypotheses and corollaries. Central to Gurr's conceptualization are the frustration and anger stemming from perceived gaps between an individual's aspirations and his accomplishments. Most people can, and do, live with disjunctures between reach and grasp; rare are those whose every desire is satisfied. At some point, however, the distance between value expectations and value capabilities (to use Gurr's terms) results in deep discontent. The intensity of such feelings, and the extent to which profound discontent is widespread, help determine the intensity of relative deprivation; several steps later, collective political violence (in the form of turmoil, conspiracy, or internal war) may eventuate. Frustration makes individuals disaffected; it does not make them effective rebels, however. Discontent need not lead to collective action; collective action need not take the form of collective political violence; the scope and magnitude of collective political violence may be highly restricted. Gurr's theory—seventy-two hypotheses, fourteen corollaries[11]—provides a suggestive, valuable framework within which to pursue comparative analysis.

Whence stems relative deprivation? For "traditional" societies, what Gurr deems "decremental deprivation" appears to be the dominant pattern.[12] This pattern presupposes a relatively stable set of value expectations and a declining set of value capabilities. As a belief individuals can alter their environment for the better takes root, a different form of relative deprivation develops. Aspirations soar, while capabilities remain essentially constant; individuals expect more, though resources may be scant. "Incremental deprivation" (often called the "revolution of rising expectations") becomes common. Finally, aspirations may rise while capabilities simultaneously decline. This phenomenon, akin to Davies' J-curve model,[13] seems particularly well suited to explain rebellion on the scale we are discussing. For significant numbers of inhabitants, the gap between expectations and capabilities suddenly widened. A shared sense that something was grievously wrong, that those grasping political power were culpable, and that no means other than insurrection might offer rectification resulted in violence. Such beliefs lay behind the four rebellions in this book.

Gurr devotes few pages in *Why Men Rebel* to direct discussion of the politicization of discontent. His two hypotheses place much of the onus on the incumbents. The effectiveness and scope of past government actions in alleviating relative deprivation have a moderate effect on the intensity and scope of justifications for political violence, Gurr asserts, both of which also vary moderately with "proportional difference in allocation of regime resources to the alleviation of the relative deprivation of different groups."[14] In other words, governments that have been historically sensitive to group needs, and that continue to respond to such concerns, confront far less likelihood of politicized discontent. But Gurr's model is far richer than these sentences might suggest. Many factors account for the intensity and scope of relative deprivation, which in turn determine the potential for collective violence; the potential for collective political violence rests on the intensity and scope of utilitarian and normative justifications for political violence, taking account of the government's legitimacy and effectiveness in alleviating relative deprivation; the magnitude of political violence reflects the balance between the incumbents and the insurgents, in terms of both their institutional support and their coercive control.

To give adequate attention to all Gurr's hypotheses and corollaries for four complex rebellions would stretch this book well beyond the usual bounds of readability. I have accordingly drawn from, rather than adopted, Gurr's full panoply of explanatory variables. The key concepts remain: the intensity and scope of relative deprivation (the focus of this chapter); governmental response to perceptions of relative deprivation and claims for political advance (Chapter 5); mobilization for collective action, through the encouragement of group awareness (Chapter 6); justifications for violence (Chapter 7); the balance of support and control enjoyed by the challengers and the incumbents (Chapter 8).

The main purpose of this chapter is to illustrate what hindsight spotlights as a dramatic, sudden increase in the scope and intensity of relative deprivation. The decades prior to the outbreak of rebellion had witnessed a gradual intensification of discontent. For the most part, the affected rural dwellers seemed to bear their misfortune passively. Cowed by their relative political impotence, tied to the land by chains of indebtedness and absence of other opportunities, the rustic majority suffered in the silent ways that for centuries have seemed to characterize peasants. Most minimized the value expectations-value capabilities gap by keeping their expectations low. As did the Indian illiterates surveyed by Cantril, to whom reference was made earlier, they met adversity with passivity, social and political inferiority by minimizing contacts with their superiors. One cannot fault this strategy under most circumstances. The horizons rural dwellers shared were in most cases shaped by kinship and village. Unusual circumstances forced change, however. The gap between expectation and accomplishment suddenly widened. External events—in particular the social dislocations of war or dramatic expansion of a cash economy responsive to international trends—intruded on village society. The times were out of joint, the formulas of accommodation ill-tuned to the unexpectedly severe pressures rural inhabitants experienced. As long as a zero-sum game set of rules seemed to apply—the gains of the minority could come only from the slender resources members of the majority possessed—any increase in the power, status, or wealth of the dominant few provided grounds for further alienation. What Gurr calls limited or nonexpandable value opportunities seem especially prone to encourage a turn toward collective political violence,[15] an observation that appeared to be true in the four rebellions.

Four specific questions will be addressed in this chapter.

First, how did individuals perceive their own positions in society? What gaps between their expectations and capabilities existed? Were there marked widenings of these gaps within a relatively brief period? In short, what was the intensity and scope of discontent?

Second, how salient were the gaps individuals perceived? Might the discontents have been tolerated by personal adjustment, or did they threaten to push individuals into undesirable actions such as emigration, banditry, or further indebtedness? Given the centrality of economic issues (as demonstrated by Cantril's data), did concern stem more from short-term and potentially self-correcting economic and livelihood problems (such as drought leading to crop failure), or more from long-term problems (such as increased rents or accelerating land alienation) attributable to human agents?

Third, what was the flexibility of what Gurr calls "value stocks" within the society? Were new opportunities for individual and group mobility opening up, or did a converse restriction take place? What was the track record, as it were, of dominant groups in resolving previous issues?

Finally, what collective avenues existed to express discontent? To what extent could grievances experienced by individuals be brought together, and be perceived as affecting an entire group rather than a handful of scattered persons? How significant, in terms of the political system as a whole, was the group through which collective grievances were initially expressed? Did their demands for rectification strike a sympathetic chord among others?

To these key issues we now turn.

Taiping: Hakka Perceptions of Threats to Livelihood

What grew into the Taiping rebellion started with humble people in circumstances not that far out of the ordinary, but liable to sudden worsening. Founded in a part of China relatively isolated from the remainder of the country, yet peculiarly susceptible to external pressures, the Society of God-Worshippers gave little initial evidence of differing markedly from many secret societies or religious sects. The seeming proliferation of such groups hinted at the widespread economic, political and social disorder that characterized South China. Unrest was in the wind in China as a whole, but the wind blew more freely in Kwangtung and Kwangsi. Local factors compounded national trends. One must accordingly examine both the peculiar circumstances of South China and the general conditions in the country as a whole to explain the rise and wide spread of the "Great Kingdom of Heavenly Peace."

Careful research by generations of scholars has brought to light a great deal of information about the roots of the Taiping movement. The rebellion has fascinated scores of historians who—perhaps needless to say—have viewed it through different interpretive lenses. In broad terms, recent Chinese scholarship has divided along People's Republic/Taiwan lines.[16] The scattered nature of sources has complicated research. Despite the court-mandated destruction of Taiping documents, some material survived—but by no means all the scholar might desire. Assiduous combing of local gazeteers has furnished information, though not definite answers. The result is a variety of data and related profusion of approaches, rather than a complete picture. For example, few details (as contrasted with sweeping assertions) are readily available on the social composition of the Taipings. That there was widespread landlessness in South China cannot be doubted; however, we cannot at this point be as precise about rural indebtedness and tenancy on the eve of the Taiping rebellion as we can be about the Telengana and Mau Mau rebellions. Thus, the material presented in the following paragraphs lacks the empirical details of later parts of this chapter.

Preceding pages identified several sources of discontent in China of the 1840s: dynastic decline, the unsettling effects of the Opium Wars, the drain of silver, corruption, military indiscipline, population growth intensifying the pressure on relatively static agricultural lands.[17] To these were added factors peculiar to South China, especially land conflicts expressed in ethnic terms. The exacerbation of relative deprivation and the need for self-defense owed a great deal to economic differences, reinforced by Hakka group awareness and by a general militarization of rural society.

Conflict has always existed between landlords and tenants in some form. Economic circumstances provided the basis for many peasant revolts in Imperial China. A wise government could reduce the negative consequences of economic polarization. As was suggested in Chapters 2 and 3, various safety valves existed. The rich did not always remain wealthy; the poor could hope their sons, suitably educated, could join the ranks of imperial officials, since access to office meant opportunity to acquire land. Admittedly, myth and reality coincided for few. Inescapable indebtedness and insufficient capital with which to finance education or acquisition of land consigned most to economic and political subordination. Apathy and disengagement provided the obvious alternative to revolt or unfulfilled expectation. The exceptions justified hope for those who did not resign themselves to their condition; banditry provided an escape for others; only a few risked death by taking up arms against the Son of Heaven. Whatever the case, it was difficult to create coherent, continuing peasant unity. The peasantry in itself was not for itself. Though rural uprisings had often punctuated Chinese history, and illustrated a sense of economic awareness transcending local issues, such revolts usually stopped with local land redistribution, leaving the structure of Confucian values and bureaucratic institutions relatively intact. More sweeping changes seemed to require broader objectives, and a stronger sense of collective identity. These characterized the Taiping movement from an early point, although the distant court seems to have taken little notice. Differences between landlords and tenants became affected by ethnic solidarity, religious fervor, a growing sense of nationalism, and a concern for economic change more sweeping than dividing landlords' properties. In short, cultural, religious, economic, and political bases reinforced each other in the politicization of discontent.

Factors peculiar to the Hakka made them apt candidates to experience relative deprivation on a collective basis. As latecomers to South China, they had to squeeze their settlements between existing communities, cultivating hillsides others had previously spurned. Group unity was underscored in several ways: by dialect, by endogamous marriage, by the absence of foot-binding, by values of thrift and hard work, and by a cer-

tain rustic bumptiousness often expressed as a "reputation for conten-
tiousness."[18] Masters in their own homes, they were not always masters of
the lands they tilled. As has been noted previously, land tended to remain
under Punti ("native") control. The energetic, expansive Hakka found
their opportunities limited by the Punti. Each group felt a sense of
superiority vis-a-vis the other; each group willingly protected its rights and
interests. This "basic conflict between the Punti and Hakka villages"[19]
resulted in intense disputes, especially as population growth made the lack
of land all the more obvious.

There is little evidence to suggest the "guest families," the meaning of
the term Hakka in Chinese, were markedly worse off in objective terms
than their Punti neighbors. Hard work compensated for inferior soil. But
"objective" and psychological reality did not coincide. The Hakka felt
liable to eviction. They were attacked on occasion. Their sense of industry,
and their strong family and village loyalties, meant a threat to some could
rapidly be translated into an attack on all. Its effectiveness in protecting
Hakka interests explains why the Society of God-Worshippers enjoyed support from many classes, including "such normally disparate types as
landlords, scholars, schoolteachers, militarists, and humble charcoal
makers...."[20] Jen attributes their affiliation to "personal sympathy with the
religious and nationalist goals of the new movement."[21] Although I am
hesitant to question the conclusions of the Taipings' most thorough
chronicler, I believe defense of the Hakka provides a simpler, more accurate explanation of the society's initial growth. Success in defending the
"guest families" from administrative and Punti pressures abetted the early
development of the Taiping rebellion.

Unexpected disasters befell Kwangtung and Kwangsi in ways that indirectly intensified the Hakka-Punti conflict, as previously noted. British
military pressure played a great part. The Opium War displaced hundreds
of boatmen; the drain of silver and the consequent increase in rents forced
thousands into tenancy or banditry. Widespread local militarization marked South China, since imperial troops could no longer provide effective
protection.[22] (As previously noted, an 1849 memorial to the emperor
reported seven-tenths of Kwangsi had been overrun by bandits.)[23] The efficacy with which members of the Society of God-Worshippers defended
their interests enhanced the organization's support. Pestilence, drought
and famine in 1848-50[24] compounded the miseries already brought by
human actions. Disorder was widespread in South China; the Hakka enjoyed a cultural foundation and a proven organization for collective action
to combat widespread anarchy. The rapid worsening of conditions during
the 1840s encouraged the Taiping rebellion.

The evidence suggests the villagers of South China could not readily accommodate themselves to these worsened situations by the usual means. Migration (even if psychologically desirable) ran up against the ineluctable fact that little land was available. Economic squeeze had been intensified by official ineptitude as well as by the ripple effects of opium imports. The spread of banditry provoked a general climate of uncertainty and fear. Some took the "dangerous path" because they had little choice; others banded together for protection. Provincial governors were reluctant to take action; the court wanted reports of calm, not indications of unrest. There was little indication the difficulties would soon disappear. Many problems were systemic and unavoidable, such as Punti control of land; others, such as administrative weakness, did not admit of easy, local solution. That the government was failing to protect the rural populace was clear. The cause of concern was obvious: it was the bureaucracy, staffed by co-opted scholars, and their gentry colleagues. Relative deprivation could accordingly be focused on a political and economic target.

In Gurr's terms, little flexibility of value stocks existed. What the Hakka had eked out, the Punti or officials might seize. It was the old story of some profiting at the expense of others. Of course, this did not preclude new approaches to the problem — and, as we shall see in following chapters, the Taiping movement was marked by several adaptations of new and traditional beliefs. The military organization of the Society of God-Worshippers staved off loss; it was after 1851 to bring gains for many. But its origins were essentially defensive.

Kwangtung and Kwangsi in the 1840s were thus provinces in which many inhabitants were forced to ensure their own protection. The need for local defense confirmed impressions of the government's weakness and incompetence. Only mutual efforts could forestall further decline in individual and group value capabilities. Those who had something to lose, as well as those who had something potentially to gain, rallied behind the Society of God-Worshippers. By the end of the decade, it had become the most powerful organization in its restricted areas of operation. Defending against bandits, Punti landlords or agents of the administration provided experience of value later when Taiping fighters streamed into the Yangtse valley. The structure created by Hung Hsiu-ch'üan and Feng Yün-shan, combined with Hakka solidarity and a growing sense of grievance against the Manchus and their associates, eased the collective expression of relative deprivation. Multiple bases existed, and reinforced one another. Hung did not create *de novo* a new, elaborate institution; he built upon and extended indigenous foundations. Individual discontent quickly took organizational form in the troubled conditions of South China.

Unfortunately, I cannot provide specific data on who joined the Society. Although the names of a few adherents are known — especially those who brought entire clans or bandit groups into it—almost all followers are now lost to historical record. What is missing for individuals cannot readily be found for the aggregate either. We shall shortly examine statistics from Hyderabad that indicate the extent and geographical concentration of rural indebtedness. No comparable information exists for South China a century earlier, although Rawski has made useful suggestions.[25] Nineteenth century rural society in Kwangtung and Kwangsi has yet to be fully dissected by anthropologists, economists, sociologists, historians, and political scientists interested in how the Hakka related to their fellow Chinese. Educated inference must suffice; what is known clearly supports the contention that the two provinces suffered not only from conditions of overall dynastic decline, but also from conditions of local tensions. The Taiping rebellion was conceived in a setting in which relative deprivation, weak provincial and national governments, an existing medium for collective action, a visionary leader, and a set of beliefs that encouraged more effective defense came together. It started as a local response to local issues, but quickly mushroomed into a far broader movement for change at the national level. The intense relative deprivation of one area provided the basis through which other aggrieved areas might seek rectification. The significance of the Taiping rebellion for the entire nation seemed far and above the significance of the Telengana rebellion, though it too was seen by some as a springboard for changing the national government.

Telengana: The Intensification of Rural Indebtedness

For Telengana rural dwellers, the fifteen years between the Depression and the end of World War II marked a time of markedly worsening conditions. The peasants were whipsawed. Economic impoverishment marked the Depression era. The prices earned for cash crops plummeted, forcing cultivators into debt, and pushing many over the line into tenancy. World War II brought a sudden, sharp rise in crop prices, but little improvement in the lot of most peasants. The money-lenders and *deshmukhs* could capitalize far more readily on the upswing. The value of fertile land, particularly irrigated land, rose sharply, but rarely did ordinary cultivators profit. Instead, the *bhagela* found themselves liable to increased pressures and landlord expectations.

These economic shifts took place in an increasingly tense communal and political atmosphere. Congress and the Moslem League squared off to settle the future of the subcontinent. Echoes of their disputes reverberated throughout Hyderabad, despite the Nizam's desires to keep his populace politically deaf and dumb. As home rule came into view, the issue of who would rule at home aroused passions that in some areas exceeded the most pessimistic forecasts. It was a time, in short, of political ferment more intense than India as a whole had previously experienced.

To document the basis of relative deprivation in Telengana, I shall give close attention to the economic and political conditions characterizing the decade and a half prior to the rebellion's eruption. Two careful government surveys—a 1937-8 analysis of tenancy and indebtedness, and the 1941 census—provide clues to the downward spiral of rural conditions. Both reveal, through their statistical tables, an accelerating squeeze on cultivators and tenants, accompanied by intensifying communalism. These studies provide a richness of detail lacking at this point for Kwangtung and Kwangsi in the 1840s. Of course perceptive observers at the time did not require massive surveys to realize rural malaise existed in Telengana. Harbingers of unrest concerned the Nizam and his advisers. A series of laws enacted between 1935 and 1938 sought to arrest increasing tenancy; a new legislature was promised, in which Hindus would share responsibilities. With hindsight, one can judge the reforms to have been too late, too timid, and too poorly administered to have had any positive effect. Promised reform may have been worse than none at all—a message de Tocqueville had given a century earlier. Political protest and communal hostilities in Hyderabad were stimulated, not stilled, by the enactments of the mid- to late 1930s. The changes seemed cosmetic, maintaining the Nizam as unchallengeable ruler, and leaving undisturbed the rural hegemony of *deshmukhs*.

What precipitated collective political violence in Telengana was a dual collision, on the one hand between Hindus and Muslims, on the other hand between rural tenants-cultivators and landlords. The privileged—the Muslims and the landlords—increasingly used force to maintain their position against the rising claims of tenants. The attempt to keep the unequal division of rural assets collided with the increased desire of villagers to regain the autonomy that had ebbed away from them. This *prise de conscience* owed much to the incumbents' use of coercion and to political organizing, to which we shall turn in Chapters 5 and 6. The proponents of change in Telengana found a receptive audience, however, because of the earlier concatenation of economic immiserization with communal and class awareness.

The 1937-8 rural survey depicted a seemingly unbreakable cycle of impoverishment and indebtedness. Although more than half the cultivators and tenants in the sample were debt-free, the remainder carried an average indebtedness of Rs. 390 per family, the burden averaging six times the assessed value of the land. As one writer said, "In Hyderabad, the moneylender's credit supports the farmers as the rope supports the hanged."[26] The annual rate of interest, theoretically limited to 12 percent by legislation, averaged 17¼ percent in Telengana—and the true rate may have been "at least double" that figure.[27] Credit, to be certain, forms an essential part of farmers' lives anywhere. In rural Hyderabad, however, indebtedness was fraying the social fabric. The *sahukar* (moneylender) had played a role in traditional village India; but it was a subordinate role, he being more a servant than a master of the village. Prior to the British conquest and the widespread introduction of cash crops, land was not a commercial asset, meaning the *sahukar* had little reason to expropriate when his clients fell into arrears. Rates of interest varied with economic circumstance; agreements were usually oral rather than written; the relatively homogeneous composition of the village, and perhaps the power of the *panchayat*, meant social pressures on borrower and lender alike to respect mutual needs. All changed. British rule helped release the *sahukar* from *panchayat* control.

Contracts, even if "cooked," were to be honored. Cash crops and population growth meant land acquired value.[28] The Depression pushed cultivators further into the moneylenders' clutches. From 1928 to 1934, overall prices for commodities fell by half, while the cost of production went down only 15 to 20 percent.[29] Cultivators coped by growing more, but the gap was unavoidable. The survey showed nearly one-tenth of the total cultivated lands passed into moneylenders' ownership between 1920 and 1935. While the overall population of Hyderabad rose 14.7 percent between the 1931 and 1941 censuses, the number of agricultural laborers rose 29 percent, receivers of rent 33 percent, and moneylenders 114 percent.[30] In the 312 villages of the survey, *sahukars* numbered 5,274, cultivators 55,027.

Recognizing the magnitude and accelerating nature of the problem, and recognizing further the changing overall political context as exemplified by the 1935 Government of India Act, the Hyderabad government promulgated several laws. The 1935 Records of Rights Act (implemented, it should be added, with tortoise-like speed) sought to ensure accurate village land registers. The *minimum* amount that could be registered in the name of a single *pattadar* (cultivator) would be eight acres dry land, or one acre irrigated land; Qureshi estimated that one-seventh to one-third the holdings in Telengana fell below these government-set minima.[31] The 1936 Land Alienation Act sought to prevent transfer of property from poor to well-off. A cultivator whose lands carried an annual assessment of less than Rs. 500 per year—defined for purposes of the act as a member of a protected class—could alienate land permanently *only* to another member of the protected class and *only* if he kept in his own name land valued at least Rs. 50. A 1936 agreement—not, it should be noted, a legislative enactment—banned unpaid compulsory service (*vetti*) extracted from *bhagela*. The 1938 Money Lenders Act put ceilings of 9 percent interest on secured and 12 percent on unsecured loans, and prohibited compound interest. The 1938 Debt Conciliation Act established boards whose good offices between borrowers and lenders would slow the descent into tenancy.

Each of these laws showed serious deficiencies. The Records of Rights Act invited abuse. The *patwaris'* (village clerks') records could be doctored, the landlords being the usual gainers. *Patwaris* came into office by inheritance, and readily accommodated themselves to the more powerful *deshmukhs*. When registration came to Telengana in 1947, the would-be reform touched off a scramble by the landlords to grab a few bits more. Evictions mounted, because of another reform that would have granted security of tenure to tenants cultivating the same plot for six or more years. The Land Alienation and Money Lenders Acts, and the restrictions on *vetti*, were universally flouted. The various conciliation boards, by 1947, had "not touched even the fringe of the problem, and considering the present speed of their work, they are not likely to reduce the present burden of debt to any considerable degree, in any reasonable amount of time."[32]

Prosperity resulting from World War II further accelerated the concentration of land. Major commodities more than doubled in cost between 1939 and 1944, making it more profitable for landlords to mandate cultivation of cash crops, rather than allow tenants to concentrate on subsistence agriculture. For example, rice rose from 103 to 223; wheat, from 101 to 272; jawar, from 108 to 234.[33] Serious shortages developed. Food was drained from Hyderabad as a result of the war. Each month, British and Indian defense needs absorbed 5,000 cows, bullocks, and buffalos, 16,666 sheep, 16,666 goats, and 66,850 chickens.[34] Higher prices did not halt land alienation. Fertile plots became all the more valuable, encouraging *sahukars* to dispossess indebted small landowners as rapidly as possible. The irrigated lands of Telengana were prime targets.

The provisions sent to British India should remind us of the subordinate economic position of Hyderabad as a whole. What had been essentially a rural subsistence economy at the start of the twentieth century had become significantly commercialized by 1946. Castor seeds and grain flowed from the princely state into markets outside it. The political position of Hyderabad—an illusion of full autonomy, given the powers the British government held in reserve—was paralleled by the state's economic position. Not an island unto itself, Hyderabad was progressively being enmeshed in the Indian economy as a whole.

Much of the land turned to commercial purposes was withdrawn from food production, although castor seeds could be cultivated in arid, low-fertility soils. The varying returns from cash crops (witness the roller coaster prices cited in the preceding paragraph) provided little surety to farmers. Higher receipts were mixed blessings at best. Many farmers, perhaps most, preferred certain subsistence to uncertain commercialization. But pressure from *deshmukhs* encouraged the spread of cash cropping. Tenants' contracts became more rigid, more detailed, more onerous, and less responsive to indigenous needs. As we shall see in the following section, the Kikuyu tenants of European-owned farms in Kenya suffered from similar conditions during and after World War II. Profits from commercial agriculture rested ultimately on cheap labor. The need to ensure a docile, inexpensive agricultural proletariat motivated major landowners in both Telengana and the Kenya highlands. The bonds of reciprocity that had marked landlord-tenant relations and the subsistence ethic were eroded. In its place, the government of Hyderabad had to devise legal strictures to mitigate the negative consequences of commercialization. The need for a formal code thus emphasized the increasingly polarized conditions of rural Telengana. That peasants had to be protected from landlords illustrates a setting in which relative deprivation spread quickly and widely. The real question was whether bills enacted in Hyderabad City could curb the practices of *deshmukhs* who, in reality ruled as village kings.

According to 1946 legislation, all tenants who had been cultivating the same lands for six years or more would not be liable to eviction, if they had paid their rents punctually and had not injured the land. The bill also provided a minimum lease period of ten years, a provision that could profoundly have transformed the insecurity of *bhagelas*. (The 1929-30 rural survey showed that about three-quarters of all tenancies in Warangal, heart of Telengana, were tenancies at will, which could be abrogated at any time by the landlord.)[35] To combat this abridgement of their powers, Hindu *deshmukhs* carried out large-scale evictions in 1946 and 1947, to prevent their tenants from claiming the rights proffered by the act. Once again, reform backfired; the sense of relative deprivation increased and landlord-tenant relations worsened. (Parenthetically, one might ask why this legislation was passed. Impetus came mainly from a reform-minded prime minister, Sir Mirza Ismail, who resigned in mid-May 1947. For information on his views, see footnote 14 in the following chapter.)

Could sufficient reforms have been effected to avoid militant confrontation? The cards seemed stacked against peaceful change. The *deshmukhs* and the state government made gestures toward reform, then failed in implementation. Their alliance of convenience precluded any fundamental approach to the problems of rural indebtedness and land alienation. These could not be resolved without basic changes in the entire system. In Pavier's judgment,

> Such explicitness would have entailed an attack on the landowners and moneylenders who were, after all, the social basis of the State. Therefore, the efforts to reform agriculture were essentially efforts to 'reform' landlords and moneylenders. It should have been clear to the State that while the land-owners and moneylenders could dominate the countryside by exacting 'feudal' dues and exorbitant rates of interest, such supportive efforts were as effective as whistling up the wind.[36]

The Nizam, himself an eccentric ruler, presented an insurmountable political obstacle. He had, in the contemporary expression, a good thing going.[37] Unwilling rapidly to divest himself of power, and unable to call into being a non-landowning Hindu-Muslim group with whom to share control similar to the communal coalition that governed the Punjab until 1947, he clung to the hope of making Hyderabad an independent state. Given the flux of the times, such a hope was anachronistic. To understand the bases of the Nizam's hopes, we should return at this point to the 1930s, and trace the political and constitutional changes mooted at that time.

As pressures for *swaraj* — self-government — mounted on the subcontinent, the British government tried to puzzle through the necessary steps for peaceful change. The princely states posed vexing problems. The overwhelming majority of the 560 + were trivial principalities: the smallest 300 totalled just over 6,000 square miles and one million inhabitants. The large states, by contrast, represented potential obstacles on the road to independence. Constitutionally speaking, they were not part of British India; their participation could be encouraged, not coerced, though the Paramountcy concept severely limited their autonomy. The extraordinarily complex Government of India Act (1935) attempted to effect the peaceful integration of the states. According to its provisions, a new federal Indian union would be formed by voluntary accession. States' rulers could, prior to joining the proposed federation, circumscribe central jurisdiction over their states; internal matters would remain under their control; one-third of the lower house and two-fifths of the upper house would be nominated by the rulers, the remainder chosen directly by "separate electorates." Congress objected strongly to permitting the princes to take such a major part in the proposed new political order. When World War II started, the inconclusive, sporadic negotiations between the British government and the various states were suspended.

The provision for "separate electorates" recognized the communal fragmentation and minority fears that marked India. But the provision may have exacerbated both. The establishment of communal safeguards whetted the appetite for more. Guarantees in the 1935 act for the representation of Muslims, Sikhs, Indian Christians, Anglo-Indians and scheduled castes in some respects intensified rather than calmed communal tensions. The effect of reform (as in the Hyderabad land legislation) was further tension — an ominous development for Hyderabad, with its autocratic Muslim administration. As identification based on religion increased, polarization marked the state.

The 1941 census report furnishes abundant evidence of the communal sensitivities being fanned. The commissioner noted that upheavals in British India

> had some repercussions in Hyderabad. Communal and party dissensions and feelings of bitterness were traceable to political causes. The political consciousness of even the Depressed Classes was quickened to a surprising degree by the events occurring elsewhere in India. When a community or party felt aggrieved that its share of rights and privileges were either withheld or denied, it manifested its displeasure in an unconstitutional manner and open clashes occurred.[38]

Since essentially Hindu political movements had been banned in 1938, the resort to demonstrations should not have been surprising. A few steps were taken, such as the banning of songs likely to incite class or communal hatred, or the rewriting of history texts to expunge communal references.[39] They could not stem the rising tide. "Vehement Hindi propaganda" during the census period helped account for an increase of 111.5 percent in declared speakers of that tongue.[40] Urdu — spoken by 10.4 percent of the Hyderabad population in almost every census since 1891 — suddenly rose to 13.4 percent; the total number of Urdu speakers jumped 45.1 percent, from 1,507,272 to 2,187,005.[41] Admittedly, part of the increase resulted from the spread of education (there were 408,462 pupils in Hyderabad schools in 1941, compared with 291,930 in 1913),[42] since Urdu served as the compulsory language of instruction in all primary and elementary schools.[43] "Propaganda," in other words, did not come from one side only.

From separate electorates, it was a short step to total separation. Communal pressures, in the context of declining British ability to control the situation, forced the separation of Pakistan from India when independence was granted in 1947. The major impetus for partition came from the Moslem League. Led by the barrister Mohammed Ali Jinnah, the League expressed, and perhaps magnified, Muslim fears of being swallowed in a Hindu-dominated *swaraj*. Communal balloting seemed an inadequate safeguard, particularly given the territorial concentration (as in East Bengal and the northwestern provinces) of Muslim majorities. The key step came in 1940. The League, in convoluted language whose political import was clear, announced it would reject all British plans for constitutional change unless "geographically contiguous units are demarcated into regions which should be so constituted with such territorial adjustments as may be necessary that the areas in which the Moslems are numerically in the majority, as in the northwestern and eastern zones of India, should be grouped to constitute 'independent states' in which the constituent units shall be autonomous and sovereign." The communal cat was out of the bag; the Muslims had given notice they considered survival impossible in an undivided India.

Pressures of World War II profoundly affected British ability and determination to maintain the Indian empire. All efforts had to be directed to prosecuting the war against the Japanese, who seemed ready to sweep to the gates of Calcutta. In March 1942, Sir Stafford Cripps sought wartime support from Indian political parties and communities, in return for a pledge of dominion status — independence — after the war. The offer was sweetened by assurance that the Indians, not the British, would frame the new constitution via a constituent assembly. The issue of the Princely states once again bedeviled negotiations, while communal pressures could not be forestalled. Congress rejected the British proposal, since states' rulers were to nominate representatives; the Moslem League likewise turned down the offer, since the possibility of partition seemed foreclosed. In August 1942, Congress adopted the "Quit India" resolution, as a result of which the party was banned. Political ferment could not be stilled by emergency restrictions, however. The defeat of the Axis by no means restored the status quo ante bellum. The authority of the British *raj* evaporated. Escalating communal hostility, riots in Calcutta, mutiny in the Indian Navy, and other instances of violence showed the situation rapidly deteriorating. Under such pressures, the British government decided to "divide and quit" in Moon's phrase.[44] The man who did not become the king's first minister in order to preside over the liquidation of the empire had been replaced at 10 Downing Street; the Labour government was more sympathetic to colonial advancement. The decision was made: independence would be granted, partition implemented. What would happen in the large states remained unclear.

What were the effects of these constitutional and communal wranglings on the illiterate villagers of Hyderabad? No pollsters took opinion surveys in Telengana as the war ended and moves toward self-government accelerated. Evidence of rural awareness comes largely from partial sources — biased as well as incomplete. Hence, the assertions that follow cannot be proven; they are surmises based on available evidence.

First, the approach of *swaraj* quickened the political pulse throughout the region. For the Muslim minority, it seemed imperative to reinforce their control of the state—cutting counter to the tentative steps taken in the legislature to share power between the communities. A consequence was the violence unleashed by razakars pledged to retain the Nizam's rule, as will be examined in the following chapter. For the Hindu majority, the long slumber seemed to be ending. The Andhra Mahasabha, and later Congress and the Communist party of India (CPI) enlisted followers. The Telugu foundation of the Andhra Mahasabha and its 1944 efforts to improve the lot of the rural poor (to be discussed in Chapter 6) bore the greatest fruit after World War II ended.

Secondly, as suggested previously, implementation of various tenancy laws exacerbated tensions. Landlords sought to evade the new provisions, tenants sought to have them enforced. The economic inequalities the *bhagelas* had suffered in silence were now descried and decried as inequities. Tenants, encouraged by the Andhra Mahasabha and (less directly) by Gandhi's appeals to depressed groups, showed evidence of militance. The task was not easy. Centuries of subordination and *karma* had engrained a deep sense of resignation. In the ferment of the times, however, and with landlords obviously bent on entrenching their control, the once-passive had to become active.

Thirdly and most speculatively, the general climate of reworking the political and social framework encouraged villagers to believe they might recover their prized but much-reduced autonomy. The extractions of *deshmukhs* and *sahukars* would disappear; the taxes remitted to the Nizam and his government would instead remain in local hands; the prized old order would be restored. The people of Telengana seem not to have desired the world turned upside down, only the world turned back to what they believed they once enjoyed. They were, at heart, far more rebellious than revolutionary. The roiled conditions of postwar India helped push them into acton. Like their Kikuyu fellows, the rural dwellers of Telengana wanted land under their own control.

In summary, it appears that almost all sectors of Telengana rural society experienced growing relative deprivation by the end of World War II. Widespread eviction of tenants to circumvent protective legislation affected the indigent. The ethic of mutual obligations that had bound *deshmukhs* and *bhagelas* had substantially collapsed, as shown by the heavy extractions of *vetti* labor. Small landowners were caught in credit squeezes. Since landlords often doubled as money lenders, the threat of expropriation, of descent into tenancy, hung over the heads of middle and poor peasants. Even relatively well-off peasants found themselves in a squeeze as title registration drew near, for the village officials entrusted with registration belonged to the most privileged group.

Perceptions of relative deprivation were heightened by the unsettling conditions of war and partition. Growing commercialization of agriculture ate away at the fabric of rural society. "Value stocks" were neither flexible nor increasing. Few options existed for Telengana villagers. What the *bhagelas* and tenants surrendered, the *deshmukhs* gained. Local government offered no recourse, given the hereditary power of *deshmukhs* and *patwaris*. For the residents of Telengana, decremental deprivation focused on land provided the basis of rural discontent — as had been the case a century earlier in southern China, and was the case simultaneously in Kikuyuland.

Mau Mau: Alienation of Land and Alienation of Support

The title assumed by Mau Mau fighters — the Land and Freedom Army — indicated the chief goals of the rebellion, and the major causes of relative deprivation. Alienation of land to Europeans had hemmed the Kikuyu into increasingly crowded reserves; settler pressure had sufficed to deny meaningful political progress and recogniton of majority rights. Freedom in choicés of land, and liberty in the selection of the government, were the twin planks of African spokesmen. What was desired was a reversal of the presumptions inherent in "White Man's Country": that Kenya would be run by and for European benefit; that paramountcy would remain a slogan devoid of political content.

Rural discontent in Kenya varied markedly among provinces. Central Province, as documented in earlier pages, felt the brunt of the settler and administrative impact. Relative deprivation reached far higher levels there than in areas where the British encouraged indigenous agriculture. As crowding intensified in the reserves, and as the settlers placed more onerous requirements on the "squatters," the sense of relative deprivation grew apace. Official attempts to improve African agricultural productivity collided with practices the Kikuyu considered socially and economically more appropriate. The scope and intensity of relative deprivation thus mounted sharply in Central Province after World War II. The politicization of discontent was characterized by significant regional contrasts as well. The Kikuyu area had long been marked by political action. This heritage of grievance profoundly and directly influenced the course of events. Kikuyu had been sensitized, as it were, to the political significance of land. Not only was land central to their sense of social identity, through the *mbari* system; it was also the basic issue with which they approached, and reproached, the colonial government. The resentment popularly felt was thus made more prominent by collective protests orchestrated by Kikuyu leaders, based on a long-standing tradition of concern. No other part of Kenya matched this combination of intensifying discontent with a heritage of political protest.

The years immediately after World War II witnessed an accelerating divergence of views between British and Kenyan leaders. They differed fundamentally on the extent and consequences of deprivation. Even more basically, they remained at loggerheads regarding the means of solution. During the period reviewed in this chapter, British administrators entertained few, if any, notions of a rapid achievement of majority rule. They believed strongly in the trusteeship they were exercising over the African populace. Economic transformation should precede political advance—a notion identical, it should be noted, with the Belgian vision of "dominate in order to serve." Although the colonial administration harbored no illusions about the settler community being granted autonomy, officials in Nairobi seemed far more concerned in their actions with the relatively small (though growing) European community than with the majority Africans. Indigenous spokesmen stood for majority rights. Their supporters demanded land—satisfaction of which required basic political alterations. Until and unless the British government was willing to replace what Africans perceived as settler domination with equal access to land, no ready solution could be found. It was in the widening gap between indigenous discontents, as these were increasingly politicized, and seeming colonial intransigence, as this was manifested in pressure on Kikuyu cultivators, that the Mau Mau rebellion took shape.

The French refer on occasion to a *dialogue des sourds*—a conversation between deaf people. Postwar Kenya fitted this descriptive phrase. African aspirations and British projections sprang from different assumptions, and pointed in different directions. To harmonize these views peacefully became impossible; by 1952 Kikuyu and British alike had turned to force, each in the hope of imposing or insuring their particular solution. In the absence thus of a "meaningful" dialogue, and in the presence of mounting pressures for change, the groups were bent on collision. Indeed, the contrasting views of each on land and on appropriate steps for majority political advance indicate how readily existing discontent could be translated into political action.

The British recognized the obvious, that the introduction of settler agriculture had affected the Kikuyu. The British denied, however, that significant lands had been "stolen" from them. The typical rebuttal included the following points:

in terms of land alienation, it was not the Kikuyu but the Masai who were the major losers; far more European agriculture was based in the Rift Valley or the Laikipia plateau than in Kikuyuland;

Kikuyu land claims had been thoroughly investigated in the early 1930s by the Kenya Land Commission, chaired by Sir Morris Carter; the resultant additions to the reserves were, in the official perspective, more than adequate to compensate for any eviction of Kikuyu;

traditional Kikuyu practices did not recognize land title as known in "civilized" countries,[45] thus making it appropriate to make settlements on group rather than individual bases, even though such steps opened the opportunity for abuse by British-installed chiefs insulated from the traditional checks and balances;[46]

restrictions on Kikuyu cultivation of cash crops, notably coffee, were justified since inept native agricultural practices might spread disease to European farms;

the "problem" of overpopulation in the reserves was in fact a consequence of wasteful agricultural practices that, if rectified, could adequately feed all resident Kikuyu;

forest reserves, compulsory terracing, cattle culling, and similar steps against soil erosion were necessary antidotes to these wasteful practices;

economic progress for the entire colony was best assured by settler cultivation of major export crops rather than by indigenous cultivation (although increasing official encouragement was given Luo planting of coffee and cotton);

efficient European agriculture required a stable, settled group of rural laborers whose prime attention would be devoted to owners' lands.

This combination of points, it can readily be seen, represented a point of view essentially unchanged from that of Sir Charles Eliot in 1903, with the exception of administrative intervention in indigenous agricultural practices. The presumed greater efficiency of settlers remained the backbone of official policy. Indigenous export-oriented agriculture—the mainstay of Uganda, for example—would supplement rather than supplant European agriculture. The European impact, marked in the early years of British rule, had become profound by its fiftieth year. Long-established policies thus stayed in force, and were in fact reinforced in the face of growing popular resentment.,

Although colonial administrators realized the emotional significance of Kikuyu land claims, they underestimated its political significance. It was an issue *par excellence* for politicization. British officials failed to foresee the profound discontent that obligatory communal labor would create in the reserves, and that new contracts for "squatters" would create in the White Highlands. To the Kikuyu who felt the brunt of both changes, the consequence was further alienation: the force and pressure employed, described in the following chapter, compounded the already noticeable sense of relative deprivation. The gap between official land policy and indigenous concerns should become even more obvious by looking at the latter.

Major Kikuyu points relative to land can be summarized as follows:

European penetration of the Highlands came in the wake of a series of natural disasters that had temporarily reduced the population but by no means extinguished *mbari* rights;

mbari lands were the focus of Kikuyu social structure, meaning that restrictions on customary practices undercut the cohesion of the entire ethnic group;[47]

land title in fact existed and was widely recognized in Kikuyu society, even if not necessarily embodied in the written form of which Europeans were enamoured;

despite the Carter Commission and similar bodies, the history of European settlement in Kenya was one of steady erosion of African areas, meaning the administration failed in its mandate to protect paramount indigenous interests;

it was not African agriculture but European agriculture that was wasteful, given the relatively small portion of settler land actually under cultivation, especially before the World War II boom;

African cash cropping had proven efficient and responsible, as in

Tanganyika and Uganda, thus showing European claims to be little more than a strategem to monopolize the market and justify subsidies;

creation of forest reserves had removed a safety valve for population growth and had directly jeopardized many Kikuyu.

These points were not new in 1952, when the Emergency was proclaimed. Just as British policy remained consistent in its support of settler agriculture, Kikuyu discontent remained consistent in its stress on land rectification. The desire of settlers for abundant, cheap lands and abundant, cheap, pliable labor ran headlong into the desire of the Kikuyu to maintain their way of life, free from the coercion and disruption inherent in European farming. Indigenous complaints about land alienation were viewed by the British as an unavoidable cost of change. They saw resistance to improved agricultural techniques as unfortunate manifestations of popular backwardness, accentuated by "agitation." Perhaps because the claims seem historically to have varied little, the colonial administration may have misread the widespread, intense feeling of relative deprivation that underlay them, and to have underestimated the substantial intensification of rural discontent that emerged after World War II.

It is appropriate at this point briefly to depict Kikuyu concerns in historical terms. The settler and administrative impact intensified over time. Initial accommodation in the 1890s was followed by gradual incorporation of ridges under the British Crown. Kenyatta suggests an early feeling of amity between the races: "When the Europeans first came into Kikuyuland the Kikuyu looked upon them as wanderers . . .who had deserted from their homes and were lonely and in need of friends . . . . . As such the Europeans were allowed to pitch their tents and to have a temporary right of occupation on the land . . . . "[48] The decentralized nature of Kikuyu society meant coordinated resistance was not mounted against the British. Rather, the colonial presence gradually enveloped the Kikuyu, enclosing them in an increasingly rigid framework from which relief was impossible. Not having been conquered, the Kikuyu were nonetheless subordinated. As Rosberg and Nottingham aver, "the tribe as a whole avoided the overall, crushing disaster inflicted in other parts of Africa on people who either were smaller in number or whose social and political organization permitted substantial tribal mobilization against the intruder . . . . there was no symbolic movement of surrender to the new authority."[49] That Europeans denied *mbari* land rights, or interpreted temporary usage of land as permanent alienation, came as a rude, bitter, and continuously irritating surprise. Chief Koinange in 1950 expressed this concern poignantly:

> When someone steals your ox, it is killed and roasted and eaten. One can forget. When someone steals your land, especially if nearby, one can never forget. It is always there, its trees which were dear friends, its little streams. It is a bitter presence.[50]

Instead of overtly resisting the waxing settler presence, the Kikuyu turned literally for decades to relatively modest, moderate channels of constitutional protest regarding what they perceived as denial of land rights. Rather than remain sullenly resigned to a *fait accompli*, Kikuyu leaders pursued almost any possible source of rectification. Protest was political instead of military or millenarian, and developed in Kiambu district, to the west and north of Nairobi prior to World War I.[51] Spokesmen such as Chief Koinange complained to the administration of the debilitating effects of white settlement.[52] The Young Kikuyu Association and the Kikuyu Central Association, founded respectively in 1921 and 1924, referred to the "stolen lands," return of which was essential.[53] Support for these groups, it should be pointed out, was not confined to those directly deprived of land (about 4 percent of the Kikuyu population), but spread to districts relatively untouched by the European presence.[54] The 1928 Hilton Young Commission received KCA representatives in Kenya. Even more important for subsequent politics, Jomo Kenyatta (together with P.G. Mockerie) traveled to London in 1929, in order directly to present Kikuyu land concerns to the Parliamentary Committee on Closer Union in East Africa. He met with Sir Morris Carter in London, after unsuccessful attempts to obtain a hearing at the Colonial Office on land claims.[55] While in Kenya, the Carter Commission received more than 300 petitions regarding *mbari* land. The resentment the Kikuyu felt thus was translated into petitions for rectification. The "bitter presence" of lands removed became the central theme by which relative deprivation was politicized.

The intensity and scope of relative deprivation owed much to geographic propinquity. The extensive agriculture of European areas contrasted markedly with intensive cultivation of the reserves. The overwhelming majority of the Highlands remained unfarmed prior to World War II. Between 1920 and 1938, rarely was more than one-ninth of the more than five million acres alienated to settlers actually tilled.[56] Why, many Kikuyu asked, should Europeans squander such lavish resources while the indigenous people went hungry?

The intensity and scope of relative deprivation owed even more to labor policies. Settler preference was clear: Africans would become economically active under European auspices, as resident workers rather than as relatively self-sufficient squatters. As Furedi has aptly emphasized, oscillations occurred in the relative strength of squatters and settlers.[57] In the first twenty years of the century, European agriculture was negligible, due in part to low factor input (limited capital and labor); African squatters emerged as independent producers in their own right. The collapse of the world market in the 1930s weakened the settlers' position, and correspondingly strengthened the indigenous tenants' position. By contrast, during the 1920s and even more markedly during World War II, rapidly expanding exports encouraged European farmers to restrict laborers. The amount of time Africans were required to spend tilling settlers' crops increased; the amount of stock Africans were allowed to keep decreased. Both exacerbated the discontent Kikuyu felt. No surprise, then, that political activities accelerated in the 1920s and after 1945. A direct correlation existed between pressure on the squatters and Kikuyu political militancy.

To substantiate this assertion, let us look more closely at the consequences of World War II for the Kikuyu agricultural populace. The economic situation of the squatters took a sudden nosedive after 1945. The war had brought settlers unparalleled prosperity. The unsettled conditions and the high demand for agricultural workers had given the Kikuyu a degree of bargaining power that Europeans found (with apologies for the pun) unsettling. White farmers pressed, through the District Councils they controlled, for implementation of the Resident Labourers Ordinance. The basic intention of the ordinance was the transformation of squatters into resident laborers, a process that entailed stripping away much of the security Africans had managed to acquire. (For example, the Nakuru District council limited each resident laborer to 15 sheep and two acres for cultivation, plus an additional acre per wife for polygamous workers.)[58]

The government's impact on squatters was unmistakable. Registration was undertaken under the Resident Labourers Ordinance, with 42,183 Africans enumerated in 1945.[59] Police were used to clear European farms of unregistered laborers and of those who refused to sign the new, far more restrictive contracts. The Kenya colonial administration showed its continuing commitment to settler agriculture by working with the British government on schemes for veterans' settlement. With official blessing, white ex-soldiers arrived, gained special loans, and often comported themselves in ways that made clear their unstinting support for European supremacy. They fled from Socialist Britain to find an archaic way of life based foursquare on racism. Such persons carried with them, in the words of the man responsible for their settlement, "an almost fascist concept of organization and massed emotion," being both "racialist and strongly reactionary" in their views.[60] Some 8,000 new settlers arrived after 1945.[61]

Yet another avenue of impact on rural areas came through increased administrative commitment to agricultural improvement. Sir Philip Mitchell, who came briefly to our attention in the previous chapter with his urging Jomo Kenyatta to serve his political apprenticeship in the impotent Local Native Council, displayed an unshakable concern for reform in traditional farming practices.[62] His strongly paternalistic outlook accorded well with the authoritarian, hierarchical, guardian-like outlook of British field officers (District Officers and other members of the provincial administration responsible for all facets of a particular territory, not for technical services alone). Berman has convincingly captured the ethos of such men. "They understood administration as ameliorative and protective: it corrected the disruption and exploitation introduced by uncontrolled changes and the intrusion of individual selfishness."[63] The real business of government, one might say, was that of protecting the African majority against the excesses and distractions of politics and individualism, and of preserving African welfare through the strength and benevolence of the provincial administration. As we shall see in the following two chapters, the field officers viewed African political associations (in Berman's words) as "unnecessary, premature, even unnatural phenomena."[64]

Grievances other than land characterized colonial Kenya. Relative deprivation marked the cities as well as the villages. The end of World War II ushered in a period of intensely disappointed expectations for the growing African communities of the major towns. The colonial administration wished, at almost any cost, to avoid a floating urban population. Labour Control Officers tried to slow the influx to Nairobi and Mombasa. It was, for example, illegal for an African to remain in Nairobi more than 36 hours without employment, or to remain outside after a 10 p.m. curfew.[65] Housing remained abominable—yet city life appeared to offer an opportunity no village could match, let alone a precarious contract with an alien settler. Evidence of racial discrimination struck urban Africans as acutely as those living near the White Highlands or Rift Valley. Segregation marked almost all public institutions. Unequal pay remained the rule, a lowest grade clerk with white skin receiving up to £420 per annum, with black skin up to £54 per annum.[66] Labor unrest increased, similar to rural militancy and responsive to the same types of European pressures.

The frustrations and disappointments experienced by the economically depressed Africans were paralleled by the frustrations and disappointments felt by the more mobile Africans. Denied the opportunity for substantial political advance and faced with an administration seemingly bent on prohibiting any indigenous organization with a mild whiff of militancy about it, Africans willing to work within the "rules of the game " found the British seemingly unwilling to abide by these. Kenya seemed to stand apart from other dependencies. India received independence, the transfer of power having been greatly accelerated by World War II and internal pressures for change. The continuing close connections between Kenya and the Indian subcontinent spread news of change quickly. Alterations in British-ruled West Africa also came to the attention of those attuned to broader streams of political development. Kwame Nkrumah—organizing secretary at the 1945 Manchester Pan-African conference attended by Jomo Kenyatta—became identified with a direct demand for "Self-Government NOW." If Nkrumah's Gold Coast could be promised independence based on majority rule, why should Kenya lag so far behind? The small settler minority, seemingly able to twist the government in Nairobi to its own ends, stood intransigently in the path of African rights. As will be presented more fully in Chapter 6, impediments to indigenous organizations pressed African political, social and economic concerns increasingly into clandestine channels, in which ethnicity provided a chief basis for common action.

Demobilized African veterans—later to provide Mau Mau with military leadership—felt an acute gap between their expectations and their achievements. Having fought, in the words of Karigo Muchai, "for our country and for democracy," and having been told "that when the war was over we would be rewarded for sacrifices we were making," they found instead little opportunity for their talents, and scant recognition of their contributions. "The army talk was false propaganda . . . . "[67] The "40 generation" (*Anake wa 40*) was to come to the fore. Armed with guerrilla skills, desirous of recognition and advancement, veterans brought added strength to African protest. Their aspirations, skills and impatience with unresponsive means of constitutional petitions were to inject an important element in what became the Mau Mau rebellion.

The discontent just recounted by no means touched all parts of Kenyan African society. The blows dealt to squatters by the Resident Labourers Ordinance, to urban workers by wage stagnation in the face of their growing demands, to educated Africans by the continued denial of political rights, and to inhabitants of the Kikuyu reserves by government insistence on obligatory agricultural improvements, aggrieved substantial portions of the Kenya populace. Many groups were far less affected, however. Pastoral groups remained largely apart from the issues of urban wages and reserved agricultural land. Access to education remained highly uneven; in general, overt hostility to colonialism seemed directly to reflect the extent of schooling. Ethnic groups in Western Kenya prospered—for, unlike the Kikuyu, the colonial administration permitted them to grow coffee. To be certain, inflation eventually touched all; the veterans were particularly concentrated among the Kamba, giving the government some cause for concern; workers came to Nairobi and Mombasa from many parts of Kenya. Yet the pronounced exacerbation of relative deprivation occurred in parts of the colony most closely linked to the settler agricultural economy and to the urban commercial and industrial economy, in areas with relatively higher opportunities for African education, and in areas where individual discontents could be coordinated and reinforced through existing avenues for collective action. These characteristics fitted the Kikuyu regions most aptly.

I do not wish to convey the impression that the grievances felt by the Kikuyu led, simply and directly, to collective political violence. Once again, deprivation was a *relative* phenomenon. Perceptions of what was wrong were shaped in several ways: by actions of the colonial administration, directly through pressures on affected groups, inadvertently through turning a deaf ear to requests for reform that might have accommodated discontent; by actions of African groups, willing to utilize indigenous grievances as levers for change; by an ideology of ethnic unity and militant struggle. Each of these interconnected factors will be treated in separate chapters below. It remains, however to probe the widening chasm of distrust that marked the Kenyan political scene. The *dialogue des sourds* on land issues were paralleled by seemingly irreconcilable views over the appropriate nature and speed of political change.

Among the settlers, the chief political desire can best be described as maintaining their British connection while reinforcing local control over the Africans. Some, it is true, hankered for a Rhodesian- or South African-style solution, in which His Majesty's Government would transfer full control over domestic affairs to resident whites. The small size of the European community (despite postwar additions) rendered such hopes impracticable. By strengthening a continuing, Ulster-type relationship with the Crown, however, many settlers felt their privileged status could be protected, despite their lack of numbers. The European community accordingly used every occasion to proclaim their loyalty to imperial objectives, and to stress, for all it was worth, the ties of culture and kinship that bound them to Great Britain. With respect to the majority population, the minority was clear: Africans would remain in subordinate roles. The settlers wanted tight control over the "large floating or semipermanent population of Africans in the Highlands area, because their services are required as agricultural labourers."[68] Local government would be encouraged in the reserves in indigenous hands—the long term desire being "a system of government free from the direct influence and intervention of the Colonial Office over African problems."[69]

The official position remained that of trusteeship and paramountcy. Great Britain was obliged as trustee to safeguard the interests of the majority; conflicts between races supposedly would be settled in the Africans' favor. Responsible self-government remained the long-range goal. Such lay in the distant future, however; an actual transfer of power in Kenya seems not to have been seriously considered by British officials until the mid-1950s, when the costs of suppressing Mau Mau raised doubts about the wisdom of propping up the minority community in the face of widespread majority resentment. Until that fundamental reassessment came, the independence granted India in 1947, or promised the Gold Coast in 1949, seemed highly unlikely for Kenya. One piece of evidence comes in the post-World War II European settlement schemes. Those brought to the colony were granted 44-year leases—a commitment, in their eyes, to the maintenance of the status quo during their lifetimes.

Yet it would be unfair to regard the 1945-55 period as one of political stagnation. It was in fact a time of basic questioning in the British Empire as a whole, and of important administrative adjustments in Kenya itself. Reforms were made. For the increasingly politicized Kikuyu populace, however, the reforms fell into the classic too little-too late syndrome, enhancing rather than abating the sense of relative deprivation. The increased economic extractions seemed far to outweigh the political adjustments made on behalf of the Africans.

A guiding British principle remained that of gradual change from the base up. Through expanding skills gained through local administration, Africans would gain the experience necessary for broader responsibilities. In the previous chapter, I mentioned certain problems with this "development from below" approach, perhaps the most important of these being the fact key political issues remained outside local control. An apprenticeship in trivia stretching potentially over a few score years had little attraction for aspirant African politicians—nor could it necessarily reduce the popular discontent fed from several sources.

A second guiding principle, this particularly associated with Governor Mitchell, was that of economic advance preceding political advance. The African populace would better their economic status through agriculture. Mitchell's concern for increased productivity led him directly to encourage extensive administrative intervention in Kikuyu farming practices. The reserves' inhabitants came to feel the direct impact of the colonial government as never before. As we shall see in the following chapter, official enthusiasm for agricultural betterment translated into growing pressure, into a use of force that accelerated the politicization of discontent. The delays in constitutional change seemingly countenanced by this gradualist approach exacerbated the sense of relative deprivation.

Also espoused by Governor Mitchell was the concept of multiracialism. Kenya's future would best be assured, he held, by explicit recognition of partnership among the major communities. "High policy" made greater African involvement in the central government appropriate, even while training through the Local District Councils was in process. The first African to serve in Legco was named in 1944; by 1948, the number of African representatives had increased to four. European representatives gained quasi-ministerial responsibilities, supervising government departments. The reform pleased few of the politically articulate, however. Europeans resented efforts to treat all races impartially;[70] Africans resented their minute representation in Legco and the continued restriction of the franchise. Multiracialism, like economic change in the reserves and stress on local government, seemed far removed from any serious implementation of self-government based on paramount African interests.

It should be clear from this review that relative deprivation was fed by many sources in postwar Kenya. New grievances were added, old grievances intensified. Africans living in the Highlands and Rift Valley were assailed by greater demands on their time and labor, by evictions, and generally by a declining economic situation. Those living in the reserves were confronted by the unprecedented administrative measures in agricultural change, and by the exacerbated crowding. The Kikuyu experienced decremental deprivation sharply. They believed their security and standards of living were being reduced. The political steps encouraged by Mitchell fed the growing sense of indigenous discontent, especially among educated and urbanized Africans. Modest reforms made the remaining obstacles all the more salient. Kenya after 1945 increasingly seemed to fit the "white man's country" slogan. The gap between value expectations and value achievements thus widened for many Africans, and certainly for most Kikuyu, especially after World War II. They enjoyed few avenues for effective relief. "Value stocks" were both inflexible and fixed. With their livelihood and culture seemingly threatened, the Kikuyu were susceptible to appeals for change achieved by violence in the default of other means. Ethnic awareness provided a basis for collective action. As violence was mounted against them, so they in turn prepared to respond in kind. Their response was in many respects an act of desperation. Just as desire for what should have been achieved by independence was to affect villagers of Kwilu, a longing for restoration of what had been seized by aliens marked villagers of Kenya's Central Province.

Kwilu: Aspiration Denied

When relative deprivation was politicized in rural Kwilu, it spread with incredible rapidity, and aroused equally great expectations. Belgian policies had created a pressure cooker atmosphere that exploded (once certain restraints were removed) to an extent that dizzied the colonial administration, and may well have surprised indigenous Congolese leaders. Events in the Congo seemed to confirm what de Tocqueville had written over a century earlier:

> For it is not always when things are going from bad to worse that revolutions break out. On the contrary, it oftener happens that when a people which has put up with an oppressive rule over a long period without protest suddenly finds the government relaxing its pressure, it takes up arms against it....Patiently endured so long as it seemed beyond redress, a grievance comes to appear intolerable once the possibility of removing it crosses men's minds.[71]

The "rural radicalism" that blossomed in Kwilu betokened a sudden widening between aspirations and achievements. Value expectations skyrocketed with the approach of independence; value capabilities plummeted with post-independence disruption of the area's economic and political fabric. Perhaps nowhere else in Africa did rural dwellers feel they had so much to gain from self-government; in few areas indeed were their inflated expectations so quickly punctured.

Let us turn first to the sources of rising expectations. A chief source lay in hasty decolonization, in the extraordinary contrast between the suffocating presence of the Belgian administration one day, and its seeming evaporation the next. The crucial time in the lower Congo (Leopoldville Province) was January 1959, when three days of violence in the capital "came as a virtual death knell for the system."[72] Not since the 1931 Pende uprising and the 1944 Luluabourg mutiny had Belgian rule been so forcefully challenged.

Leopoldville, located in the heart of Bakongo country, mushroomed after World War II, its population more than trebling from 96,116 in 1945 to 290,377 in 1955.[73] A decade of prosperity turned in 1955 to stagnation. Mounting economic troubles of the Belgian Congo as a whole resulted in increased unemployment: between 1955 and 1958, the percentage of unemployed African males rose from 4.41 to 18.94.[74] The Bakongo, with 60 percent of the total population, dominated the urban scene[75] —yet Lingala served as the official indigenous language, illustrating the degree of ethnic mixing. As might be expected, the non-Bakongo immigrant population was relatively young, predominantly male, and economically ambitious. Such a setting was conducive to economic, political and social rivalry being expressed in racial terms (Africans versus Europeans) or in ethnic terms (Bakongo versus other Congolese groups, such as the Bangala or Baluba).

The first major indigenous political movement in Leopoldville — or, indeed, in the Belgian Congo as a whole — was ABAKO (originally the Association for the Promotion of the Kongo Language, later the Association des Bakongo). Founded in 1950 as a cultural association among the elite, its initial aims were modest: "It seems timely to those of us who constitute the nucleus of the Congolese elite, to take care to improve our mother tongues."[76] These objectives, we shall see in Chapter 6, were remarkably close to those of initial movements among the Kikuyu and in Telengana. ABAKO fostered solidarity among the Bakongo. It became the first major indigenous political group to demand total and immediate independence;[77] it parlayed 46 percent of the vote in the 1957 Leopoldville municipal elections into 133 of the 170 seats.[78] Perhaps most disturbing to the colonial administration, it sought to redraw frontiers on ethnic lines. Such an action could have balkanized the Belgian Congo, and profoundly altered the tribal complexion of Angola and French-ruled Moyen Congo.

The infamous riots broke out on the evening of January 4, 1959, after Belgian refusal to let ABAKO hold a public meeting. The myth — "Il n'y a pas de problèmes au Congo" — was irretrievably shattered. Participants lashed out at symbols of their subjugation (social centers, Catholic missions, Portuguese-owned shops); the turmoil was suppressed at an official, and doubtless understated, cost of 49 lives.[79] The explosion, in other words, was unexpected, powerful, and politically diffuse; it vented sharp African frustrations with the colonial situation, but had no readily visible leadership or political goals; it made abundantly obvious the need to speed the pace of self-government; it testified to the depth of relative deprivation, at least in some parts of the Congolese population.

The Belgian reaction to the riots seemed unwittingly designed to foster further politicization of discontent. First, a hasty change was made in a long-planned reform: on January 13, 1959, King Baudouin announced Belgium's intention "to lead the Congolese peoples, without fatal hesitations but also without ill-considered haste, to independence in prosperity and peace."[80] Political violence, even of the anomic type manifested in the riots, seemed to have worked. Pressure from the majority appeared to make the colonial edifice crumble. Further pressure became all the easier. Secondly, the administration tried to restore urban calm by expelling agitators. In the process, they lost the countryside. The region between Leopoldville and the chief port of Matadi slipped inexorably away from Belgian control. Africans cut themselves off from the Belgians and their collaborators.[81] The promise of hasty, belated reform in the face of indigenous unrest made de Tocqueville's suggestion valid.

Decolonization, the Belgians had assumed, would be gradual, based on amity between the withdrawing imperial power and indigenous leaders. The militancy of Congolese political parties in demanding total and immediate independence gave the Belgians pause to consider; the mutiny of the Force Publique (to be discussed in Chapter 5) gave the Belgians reason to flee. The top layers of the public service were quickly depopulated. Merlier notes that, of 8,200 high-ranking expatriate civil servants at independence, only 1,600 remained two months later.[82] Congolese who moved upward did so with explosive speed, perhaps well beyond their greatest expectations. Inauguration of provincial assemblies and the National Assembly gave indigenous politicians ample opportunity for status, power and wealth. Employment in the public sector swelled, the government resorting to heavy deficits and consequent inflation (almost 95 percent in the first twenty four months of independence).[83] An estimated 150,000 Congolese benefited materially from decolonization.[84]

The rise of the few indirectly profited some, since social norms in the Congo stressed sharing with kinsmen, but directly cost the many. Promises made in the heady preindependence days, when politicians competed for support by advancing ever more extravagant claims, remained unsatisfied. The growing contrast between the sudden affluence of the political "class" and the continued impoverishment of most Congolese could not be masked. In these conditions, the sense of relative deprivation was bound to grow. What had been great prior to independence increased in several ways.

Congolese cities became a locus for sharp discontent. Prior to independence, the Belgian government had maintained relatively tight controls over urban settlement. The phenomenon of the urban squatter, fickle in his politics, uncertain in his employment, was something the colonial administration wished to avoid. Self-government brought the abandonment of influx controls; within a year, the population of Leopoldville leaped from 378,158 to 733,170.[85] Over half the men were unemployed.[86] The quality of urban public services declined, the consequence of both the spiraling populace and the resignation or flight of most expatriate officials. Salaries for municipal employees fell in arrears. Policemen eked out their existence by extortion and petty corruption. The limited largesse spread by the profiting few could not mask the fact of urban misery.

The rural situation was but slightly better, even though subsistence agriculture gave most inhabitants a margin of protection. Public services declined sharply: dispensaries ran out of medicine, schools were overcrowded and short of supplies, bribery became widespread. What had happened to the golden promises of independence? Commentators on Congolese politics agree that a wide social division opened after independence. An indigenous ruling group succeeded an alien ruling group; neither seemed to take direct interest in popular wishes; personal enrichment appeared to motivate the new elite. The temporary unity of protest faded away. Common opposition to the Belgian administration had linked Congolese of all backgrounds; different fortunes once self-government was achieved affected all. Independence permitted some to rise rapidly, but required most to swallow the aspirations they had been encouraged to express.

As sketched thus far, the situation might appear to have resulted in a classic polarization between haves and have-nots. A few caveats must be entered. First, the cleavage was partially diminished by redistribution through the extended family system. Those temporarily out in the cold might hope for a turn of fortunes, through which they might enjoy an opportunity to gorge at the public trough. Hope for turnover in the elite mitigated the severity of conflict; hope for benefits in the rural areas undercut local expressions of grievance.

Secondly, the vertical fragmentation of class—the political/administrative bourgeoisie versus the urban and rural proletariat—was in fact counteracted by the horizontal fragmentation of ethnicity. The impending division of the spoils, once the Belgians conceded independence, accentuated perceptions based on tribal factors. Ethnicity, not income, became the primary basis for political identification. At least some part of the blame must be ascribed to Belgian policies. Indigenous organization of political movements was precluded until the terminal phase of colonialism. Those parties that emerged in the heady atmosphere of 1959-60 frequently sprang from ethnic roots. The intense electoral competition of that period not only gave birth to ever-more extravagant claims; it also witnessed increased awareness of ascriptive givens. A clear split between ruler and ruled thus ran up against an ethnic basis for collective action.

The extent of polarization was affected, thirdly, by the extent of politicization and the post-independence level of public services. It has occasionally been presumed that the Congo in late 1960 dived straight into anarchy. Such was not true. Some areas were sharply affected by declining government efficiency; others were not. Some sections had been strongly mobilized against the Belgians; others were but lightly touched. The sharpest combination of politicization and diminished services came in the western Congo, including Kwilu. Popular defiance and deliberate inculcation of noncooperation (as in, for example, not paying taxes) complicated government tasks. The "super-enthusiasm" of rural dwellers was fanned rather than quieted.[87] If local political leaders were excluded from the governing coalition, as was to characterize some parts of Kwilu, polarization could be marked; if local political leaders were incorporated, and if a satisfactory level of expected services remained, discontent might not reach a critical level. As will be shown below, the Mulele branch of the PSA (Parti Solidaire Africain) found itself in opposition—and hence out in the political cold from late 1960. The ruling elite appeared bent on excluding representatives of one of the most politicized districts of the entire Congo. When added to ethnic solidarity, party mobilization, and the ideological appeal to which subsequent chapters turn, relative deprivation in Kwilu became sharply politicized.

It should be recognized, fourthly, that polarization takes time to develop. In the Congo after independence, inflated expectations were not immediately punctured. Hope remained: urban migrants, that they would find profitable employment; rural dwellers, that onerous requirements would be removed. All politicians know that "Prosperity is just around the corner" can, for a while, allay popular disgruntlement—though at the cost of an eventual credibility gap. Multiple disasters are required, Chapter 1 noted, before millenial beliefs become widely credible. The repeated shocks of military and police raids, especially common in Kwilu because of its opposition to the government in Leopoldville, contributed to polarization; these raids only became marked late in 1963.

Taking the Congo as a whole, discontent was thus unevenly distributed, politicization subject to major local variations. For Kwilu, the proximity of Leopoldville encouraged political activity; the radicalism of the rural populace gave special strength to party claims. The district was in many respects unusual. The enthusiastic reception accorded PSA demands—indeed, the intensification of these demands as a result of pressures from below—indicated the widespread desire in Kwilu for change. The intensity of relative deprivation was reflected in the rapidity of politicization. But what was common in Kwilu was not necessarily as intense elsewhere in the Congo; polarization within a segment can readily coexist with overall pluralism, as we saw earlier for China, India and Kenya.

The immediate euphoria of independence over, Congolese politicians learned that discontent could be more readily aroused than allayed. The contagion of success—or, expressed in different terms, the bandwagon phenomenon—crowned efforts at rural politicization. Prior to independence, ABAKO and the PSA had in effect supplanted the Belgian government in local matters. The apparent ease with which the Belgians were pushed into retreat gave African participants an unduly elevated sense of what politically could be accomplished. They sought first the political kingdom, assuming all else would be added later. But the disappearance of the colonial administration removed the prime political target. That the expected blessings did not soon materialize could not be ascribed — immediately, directly or totally — to the new Congolese elite. Its members, after all, were linked to sectors of the indigenous populace. Ambivalent feelings existed, those who succeeded the Belgians being simultaneously castigated for their indifference to the people, admired for attaining positions of power, status and wealth. The focusing of discontent became more complex as the political target itself became more diffuse. The marked political and cultural distinction between Congolese and Belgians was thus succeeded by a far more complex set of gradations. The increasingly ethnic character of competition diffused rather than concentrated discontent. Once the racially defined masters had effectively disappeared, other forms of identification and conflict became paramount. Pluralism far more than polarization marked the Congo as a whole after independence. Rural discontent found expression in antagonism based far more on "tribal" than on class perceptions. The implications for collective political violence on a widespread basis should be clear.

Another effect of high aspirations should be noted. Gurr has suggested, I believe correctly, that decremental and progressive patterns of relative deprivation increase the potential for collective political violence more than aspirational patterns.[88] The Taiping, Telengana and Mau Mau rebellions appear in retrospect to have borne the clear stamp of decremental deprivation. Direct threats to the well-being of agricultural peoples marked all three. Landless laborers were pushed by exigency and incumbent violence into collective political violence. In Kwilu, given the prominence of the *coupeurs de fruit*, the attachment to land that characterized the other uprisings did not appear. The "second independence" rebellion was directed against politicians, not landlords. Unfulfilled aspirations, more than fulfilled fears, lay behind rural unrest in the Congo as a whole; Kwilu was an area in which a progressive pattern of relative deprivation (a combination of rising value expectations with declining value capabilities) became prominent. Alexis de Tocqueville had expressed an applicable truth.

In concluding this chapter, I must again refer to a seemingly unavoidable problem. Because collective political violence occurs, it is tempting to lay much of the onus at the door of relative deprivation. The careful scholar — and certainly the inventive one — has little difficulty in eliciting evidence of discontent that (appropriately politicized) figured in subsequent events. *Post hoc* reasoning is so, so tempting! Ideally, generalizations about relative deprivation within a particular system should incorporate evidence from all its sectors. The focus of this chapter on areas characterized by rebellion may be misplaced; it might have been better to attempt a study that directly contrasted the Kikuyu with other groups in Kenya, or the low-caste Telaga laborers of Telengana with other depressed castes in India, rather than to compare, across cultures and historical periods, societies in which collective political violence burst forth. So be it. I believe reasonable academic grounds exist for confining detailed investigation to those social groups distinguished by involvement in rebellion. It is the translation of relative deprivation into collective political violence, not the mere existence of relative deprivation itself, that concerns us in this book. The proof of the pudding....

Yet a basic question remains unanswered: does relative deprivation theory provide the most suitable means to explain the collective phenomena examined in *Anatomy of Rebellion*? One of the most perceptive analysts of collective political violence has developed a different line of reasoning. In Scott's view, peasant rebellions erupt as a result of violation of the "subsistence ethic," mention of which was made in Chapter 1. Scott offers his "moral economy" theory as a more satisfactory explanation than relative deprivation for uprisings similar to the four described in this book. To quote him directly,

> The critical shortcoming of this explanation [that "men in these circumstances are angered by the loss of what they once had or thought they would have"] and of the frustration theory in general, however, is that by beginning with some crude "want-get" ratio they fail utterly to do justice to the moral indignation and righteous anger that characterize most peasant explosions. This failure is inherent in interpretations that begin either with individual or with objective welfare comparisons, because they ignore the social context of the peasant's actions—his expectations about his rights in society.[89]

In Scott's view, once rural leaders refuse "to recognize the peasantry's basic social rights as its obligation, the elite thereby forfeits any rights it had to production and will, in effect, have dissolved the normative basis for continued deference. Defiance is now normatively justified."[90] This argument—provocative and important—seems nonetheless to have a significant gap. It appears as though once rural presumptions have been denied, collective political violence is not only morally appropriate, but may in fact be highly likely, unless government coercion has recently and effectively quelled resistance. The leap in Scott's theory from peasant expectations to peasant actions occurs abruptly—more rapidly than the instances studied in this book would suggest is in fact justified.

I concur with Scott that mechanistic treatment of relative deprivation demonstrates marked weaknesses. Particularly given the absence of compelling documentation regarding perceptions, the expectations-achievement gap can only be inferred. The same argument, however, can be applied to assertions about a "moral economy." Violation of the subsistence ethic, it would appear, can be deduced from the fact of rebellion. Thus, relative deprivation and the subsistence ethic suffer from a similar post hoc weakness. Both are vitiated, further, by their combination of presumed comprehensiveness with seeming monocausality.

Gurr and Scott, to be certain, are sophisticated social scientists, aware of the limits to which their arguments can be pressed, and chary of reductionist approaches to complex social phenomena. In their alternative approaches, however, they give limited attention to factors that appear key, based on the cases in this book. Gurr, for example, devotes far less concern to the politicization of discontent than seems appropriate. Scott does not sufficiently recognize the angering effects of government repressive actions. Although he points out that "the peasant is more often a helpless victim of violence than its initiator,"[91] and further indicates the snowballing effect of initial success when the regime is challenged,[92] Scott underestimates the galvanizing effect of coercion. When representatives of the government or the dominant group attack those demanding justice, discontent rapidly becomes politicized. Should coercion be indiscriminant or collective in its impact, violence from above may well be countered by violence from below.

To some extent, those active in rebellion had already shown evidence of action. The Kikuyu had long been at the forefront of Kenya Africans seeking redress from British policies; the Pende had proven themselves sensitive to economic changes and protested decline by revolt. Such experience with, and hence memory of, collective action probably facilitated later politicization of discontent. Yet the other cases suggest that prior involvement in violence is neither a necessary nor a sufficient condition. Cultural pride of Telugu speakers, and the industrious clannishness of the Hakka, provided cultural identity; they connected indirectly at best with willingness to take up arms. Kannarese-and Marathi-speakers in Hyderabad suffered from land crowding; the Punti of south China were marked by economic stratification as were the Hakka. What this suggests is a "value-added" approach similar to that used by Smelser.[93] A conducive structure for collective action represents only one of the many steps that lie between relative deprivation and collective political violence.

The unevenness of both discontent and its politicization put a premium in all four societies—and, by extension, in any society in which collective political violence might be undertaken—on establishing or extending a basis for collective action. Were a foundation already in existence, politicization could seem easier, if the foundation could be expanded so as to incorporate significant sectors of the population. Ethnically heterogeneous societies pose special problems. Ethnicity provides a readily politicized avenue by which aspirant leaders can marshall support, or by which rural dwellers can identify themselves with particular leaders, policies, or concerns. The avenue may be narrow, however. It must be widened in some fashion, as by emphasis on a widespread grievance, organization, or propagation of a set of beliefs encouraging extensive participation.

The evidence presented thus far suggests the importance of economic deprivation as a primary basis of discontent. Those faced with clear and present dangers to their means of livelihood seem (with the usual caveat, other things being equal) more disposed to turn to collective political violence. Feelings of economic insecurity can be readily politicized. They seem far more translatable into action among rural people than do feelings of political subordination. Individuals can survive without civil liberties; they cannot survive without food, shelter, and perhaps a modicum of economic security. Recognition of this fact need not lead to a crass economic determinism, nor to mechanistic application of relative deprivation theory or the idea of "moral economy." Rural dwellers may prefer political disengagement to involvement—but when the chips are down, they may throw themselves into actions designed to gain (or, better perhaps, to regain) the necessary basis for security.

Safety and survival are concerns common to all humans. When actions of a government threaten both, response must be expected. In all four rebellions, the politicization of discontent was bolstered by incumbents' actions. The coercion intended to quell dissidence had a contrary effect of enhancing discontent. Our survey of the politicization of discontent must accordingly move on to the use of force. Ineptly used by those in control, violence begets counterviolence; protesters turn into rebels. The politicization of discontent, it seems, is enhanced by inept repression, more than some leading scholars of collective political violence have asserted.

CHAPTER 5 /

Incumbent Response and
the Actualization of Violence

Governmental Protection and Coercion in Rural Areas

Despite the conditions sketched in the preceding chapters, violence was not inevitable. Spontaneous combustion is a law of the natural sciences, not a proven regularity of the social sciences. Yet conflict becomes more likely—and certainly was provoked in the rebellions under review—by inept repression. Collective political violence gained significant impetus from official acts, or from provocations by armed groups linked to the politically dominant.

Stated in such bare terms, the major hypothesis of this chapter calls out for clarification, specific application, and (above all) for justification. I have no doubt it will be questioned by those who view violence as inherent or inescapable in settings as divided as those described in this book. Those at the bottom rarely accept the inequalities or inequities of minority control. To the extent that property is theft, echoing Proudhon, resentment is built into the system. Resentment need not lead to collective action, however. As has been noted frequently, discontents may be sublimated, be redirected toward the bread, circuses and cults the dominant either tolerate or encourage, or (most simply) be dismissed as matters individuals could not effectively challenge. The central point, it seems to me, involves collective violence *legitimately* and *appropriately* directed against the political incumbents who had sought to reinforce their control by violent means.

My argument, in brief, is that coercion to maintain the status quo increased both the scope and magnitude of discontent; attempted suppression turned protest towards rebellion; the indigenous inhabitants considered their own use of violence fully appropriate, as a response to what had been inflicted on them. The level of hostility escalated as both parties felt justified. Acts of protest (quite likely peaceful) by members of the subordinate group provoked repression by the incumbents, thereby inciting a violent response from the aggrieved, leading in turn to further and wider attacks by the dominant, bringing about widespread mobilization by

169

what had become now "rebels." The rebuff to petition—"illegitimate" coercion unleashed by the dominant group—necessitated a militant reply, a "legitimate" collective violence directed against the status quo. The successive steps may have been linked, but were not automatic; the step-by-step progression toward internal war could have been slowed, or perhaps reversed, at many points along the way.

Several questions require close attention.

First, why did the incumbents turn to repression rather than reform or redirection? Was there careful consideration of the costs and consequences of coercion rather than concession? If not, why? What information did the government have in hand regarding the objectives, composition and support of the protesters? To what extent did officials perceive the political consequences of indigenous protest?

Secondly, what were the popular perceptions of the violence used increasingly by both parties? How did each justify its actions? Did collective political violence arise naturally, as it were, from existing foundations for collective action, or was an essentially new, more militant basis created? Did support for either side result more from fear (individuals concerned about potential loss from failing to acquiesce in the wishes of the more powerful), or more from hope (individuals desirous of gaining new opportunities in the increasingly polarized situation)?

Thirdly, what consequences flowed directly from the escalation of conflict? Under what conditions did violence more effectively unite the aggrieved, and under what conditions did it splinter their cohesion? At what point did the costs of coercion become too onerous for either party to bear? What alternative strategies to achieve desired ends were then employed?

Violence was but one of many possible strategies the politically powerful might have employed. Faced with protest, they could have reacted in several ways. Particular demands could have been: 1) accepted and fully acted upon; 2) taken note of, with varying degrees of implementation; 3) ignored, if not necessarily forgotten; 4) rejected, without prejudice to those raising the demands; or 5) vigorously combatted, with sanctions taken against the claimants. The action most significant for rebellion, I suggest, was the last. Rejection coupled with retribution introduced—or more likely exacerbated—direct conflict between the incumbents and the protestors.

Accepting this for the nonce as a working hypothesis, it remains necessary to suggest why violence was the response chosen by those atop the political hierarchy. Two tentative suggestions come to mind, familiarity and fear.

Repression may have been the strategy best known to the governments. Historically, their control had been undergirded by coercion. Conquest had achieved Muslim superiority in Hyderabad, Manchu rule in China, and European colonialism in tropical Africa. Earlier revolts in all had been militarily quelled, and, perhaps more important, had been quelled largely by indigenous troops under alien command. The mailed fist ultimately appeared through the velvet glove. The incumbents' seeming belief in the efficacy of a "whiff of grape" did not die easily, reinforced as it was by success in combating previous uprisings.

This willingness to use the tried and familiar was reinforced by fear of the consequences of "caving in" to indigenous pressures. The dominant minority recognized their numerical disadvantages. The strategies for control were far from fool-proof. Acceding to demands—especially conceding under duress—might abet discontent. Acceptance of a claim could be interpreted as a sign of official weakness, or as implicit recognition of the legitimacy of the demand. Either interpretation led to the slippery slope: a misstep would worsen the situation. Thus, coercion was not only familiar; its antithesis, concession, risked escalating rather than reducing demands. The use of force admittedly entailed risks of its own, but these appeared less dangerous under the prevailing circumstances—at least as interpreted by the incumbents.

The slippery slope perception owed much to the distribution of resources. The dominant minority, I have suggested, monopolized power, status and wealth, sharing these only with trusted subalterns. Any significantly wider distribution would have cut into what the few possessed. The minority would have had to surrender what the majority would receive—the classic zero-sum game. As suggested in previous chapters, the potential for discontent was writ large in this situation. Faced with growing popular discontent (manifested in the politicization of discontent), and finding the old nostrums of co-optation and diversionary beliefs less effective, the government played the one trump still in its hand. Repression ultimately sustained the control of the privileged. Unwillingness significantly to share what they had seized—at least under the conditions and timetable suggested by the protestors—helped push the incumbents toward repression.

One should not assume that government troops alone stirred the tensions that bubbled forth into rebellion, however. Members of the dominant minority protected their privileges not only through the central military and police; they also buttressed their power by local means. In South China, *t'uan-lien* irregulars enabled Punti landlords to squeeze Hakka peasants; in Telengana, *goondas* and razakars buttressed the power of the *deshmukhs*; in Kenya, European farmers coerced Africans with little fear of punishment; in the Congo, party officials helped maintain their control by employing faithful, armed retainers. To a great extent indeed the acts and depredations of such groups touched off the collective responses with which this chapter is concerned. To the affected rural dweller it made little difference whether official or unofficial toughs in the landlords' employ were used. The effects were the same.

The manner in which protest came to official attention merits brief note. In all four rebellions, central government concern was belated and partial. Confronted by issues of greater salience when initial information about discontent filtered upwards, administrators paid little heed (so it would seem) to the rumblings of discontent. Their actions were often taken hastily, on the basis of incomplete and potentially misleading information. Relying on familiar policies, and fearful of the consequences of inaction or concession, they dispatched force to meet challenge. The consequence — possibly unanticipated — was escalation of a dispute into a disturbance. The politicization of discontent took a further step with the government's violent response, insufficient to erase the threat, sufficient to intensify conflict.

The clarity that hindsight permits suggests the incumbents misinterpreted available information about the protestors. Their errors grew as much from incorrect perception as from incomplete information. Let me illustrate briefly with examples. Hung Hsiu-ch'üan and the Society of God-Worshippers were perceived, or at least portrayed, as typical "bandits," or as a run-of-the-mill religious sect. The appeals of the Taiping ideology in the distressed conditions of South China were not readily grasped in the Peking court. Telugu-speaking villagers in Hyderabad suffered landlord exploitation. The court had no way of telling this exploitation was perceived more acutely in Telengana than elsewhere, a consequence of the landlords' power relative to the Nizam's ability to curb excesses. In Kenya, British administrators appeared to suffer from a dual perceptual screen in dealing with incidents in the Highlands and reserves. They initially dismissed rural violence as insignificant, apolitical, or the price of progress; then (as "Mau Mau" increasingly was brought to public attention) ascribed such violence to the evil hand of Jomo Kenyatta, manipulating gullible followers. The role of settlers or administrative officers in promoting discontent tended to be minimized. The government of the Congo, finally, seems to have been totally oblivious to the plans of Pierre Mulele until he disappeared into the Kwilu forests with groups of followers. Absorbed in the lucrative game of using power, Congolese leaders underestimated popular antipathy toward themselves, grievances that could neither be resolved nor placated by repression.

Just as the protestors believed their grievances to be legitimate, so too they considered the incumbents' rejection and attempted suppression as illegitimate. Coercion could not and did not satisfy indigenous objections.

Nor (using hindsight once again) was it sufficiently harsh to extirpate protest — although a relatively strong response (as in Kenya after proclamation of the state of emergency) might bring a temporary lull. The sword was two-edged. Violence exacerbated protest, turning it into counterviolence. The protesters could draw upon existing foundations for collective action, refining them where appropriate into more efficient means for combat. Ineffectual use of coercion by the incumbents thus helped precipitate collective political violence.

I may, in using the adjective ineffectual, seem to commit the error of Monday morning quarterbacking. The point is not that collective political violence became inevitable, only that it became probable. Government actions drove many of the wavering into active opposition. There seemed to be little reason to support the incumbents, whose ham-handed actions benefited only the few and who enjoyed little popular legitimacy. Any evidence of success by the protestors naturally broadened their support, and further increased the likelihood of collective political violence. Once the lion's tail had been tweaked without harm, others were emboldened to do so. The vaunted, or at least presumed, repressive power of the incumbents was tried and found wanting. Acts of violence could spread along the lines of communication already defined for collective action. A bandwagon effect thus occurred, enabling the protestors to apply pressure against the hesitant. Within individual villages, the initiative passed to the (by now) rebels. Government supporters or members of the privileged minority had to retreat for personal safety, their violent riposte to indigenous claims having further inflamed popular feelings. Successful resistance to the incumbents' acts of violence boosted the dissidents' support; success bred success.

This last observation leaves unanswered the question of when the costs of rebellion might outweigh the gains presumably derived. In all four uprisings, the insurgents "failed": they were defeated militarily. The dominant minority may have won the war but lost the peace, however. Policies of repression had to be coupled (at least in Telengana and Kenya) with significant reform. The pacification thereby achieved was to embody many of the protestors' original demands as these related to land and to political change. Where suppression was not accompanied by some rectification (as seemingly in China and in the Congo), the potential for further violence remained. Festering grievances continued to highlight the inadequacies of the existing system.

Before we turn to the initiation of combat in the four rebellions, a final set of cautions is in order. These concern the fuzzy distinctions between "personal" and "political" acts of violence, as these are carried out by individuals.

This book centers on collective political violence, that is to say, on organized force openly directed against the central government or its representatives to help accomplish objectives affecting a significant part of the society. Such acts of collective political violence are thus intended for general benefit. They are distinct — at least in theory — from individual acts of violence, motivated largely by personal gain or vengeance. What is clear theoretically is often muddled in fact. Collective political violence is constituted to a great extent by individual acts against political targets, and to some extent by "ordinary" violence (if "ordinary" is the correct adjective). To illustrate the analytical problem, consider the murder of a government-appointed chief or landlord known for his corruption. Does his death signal the presence of "political" violence? Yes, one might respond, were his execution both intended and perceived as a warning to other corrupt officials unless they changed their ways. No, one might respond, were the killing an act of direct personal vengeance by a person who had suffered. The outside scholar faces obvious difficulties in ascertaining the "real" motives for the murder — let alone in determining how the act is interpreted, popularly and officially. Perceptions can only be inferred from actions.

The climate of social unrest that precedes and accompanies widespread violence — "political" or not — illustrates a weakening of both social norms and government effectiveness in detecting and punishing criminals. (To be certain, the government may not be particularly active in searching for supposed lawbreakers whose exploits make them popular heroes — a not uncommon precursor of weakened political legitimacy.) The setting thus is one in which essentially individual acts might be garbed in the raiment of "political" acts. Motives may be impugned that, quite simply, did not apply. Too much can be read into acts of violence that sprang naturally, as it were, from an environment in which usual constraints were inoperative. For example, the Corfield report on the origins and growth of Mau Mau claims as "political" many incidents whose roots were far more personal and mundane. Settling of personal scores may be paraded as evidence of political fervor when vengeance provides a simpler explanation.

A quite separate problem arises, however, from incumbents' dismissing violence as totally non-political. The characterization of the Society of God-Worshippers as ordinary bandits accorded far more with the formulas of imperial administration than with the facts of the situation. It was, and is, easy to see banditry stemming from personal vendettas or desires, harder to detect the seeds of rebellion. As explained in Chapter 1, banditry may be endemic in areas at the periphery of effective government administration. Such regions obviously attract would-be guerrillas, seeking secure bases for their operations. A connection nonetheless exists—for those opposing government authority.

What I am suggesting is that a government may systematically, if unintentionally, distort its understanding by overlooking the generalizable goals of resisters. Seen as reprobate thieves by the incumbents, the opponents may in fact have goals that go far beyond the personal. Attempts to treat them as criminals whose acts lack popular support not only will have little effect; they may enhance the resisters' popularity, as has already been suggested. Should the efforts at repression be countered successfully, the resisters may change thereby into insurgents, enjoying an even higher degree of popular support.

To be certain, a government can go to the opposite extreme, treating discrete acts of vengeance or theft as rebellions in the bud. What may be non-political in origin and intent can be misinterpreted: personal violence is not identical with collective political violence. A government able to make the admittedly complex, judgmental differentiations may successfully withstand challenges to its authority. Effective protection remains the *sine qua non*. If a government cannot defend its subjects—a facet we shall see shortly in all four rebellions—it itself becomes a target.

We thus arrive at a paradox. The spread of collective political violence reflects insufficient protection as well as overabundant coercion. Inability to maintain order in rural areas—particularly under conditions of economic, political and social stress—encourages persons to shift their support away from the incumbents; would-be reestablishment of order—particularly when accompanied by belated and extensive coercion—hastens this transfer of allegiance.

To summarize, acts of coercion mounted by the dominant minority bolstered the cause of the protestors more than they reinforced the power of the few—at least in the short run. In the long run, however, the greater resources of those on the top came into play. The initial shock of confrontation, and the anger intensified by the "illegitimate" violence of the incumbents, passed. Fear of loss or injury succeeded the burst of rage. The force and blandishments the incumbents could mount countered the potential rewards and risks the insurgents could offer. Individuals were forced to choose sides as open conflict came to the fore. The opponents had to contest (in the by-now hackneyed phrase) for the "hearts and minds" of people, as well as for their strong right arms. The politicization of discontent advanced.

Taiping: Imperial Ineptitude and Power Deflation

Weaknesses of the imperial government encouraged the growth of the Society of God-Worshippers. The Ch'ing dynasty lacked effective means by which to administer many parts of the empire, especially the strife-torn provinces of Kwangtung and Kwangsi in the 1840s. The Opium War and increased banditry suggested the dynasty's military strength was insufficient both to repel foreign invasion and to maintain domestic tranquillity. Hung Hsiu-ch'üan could offer security the provincial government could not.

In many respects, the decline of Manchu military efficiency came as a surprising development.[1] Banner troops had regularly demonstrated their strength and esprit through the end of the eighteenth century. Some decline might have been expected, as the dynastic cycle rolled on; on the other hand, the Ch'ing dynasty was less than 200 years old at the time of British pressure, a relatively early time for imperial senescence. Speculating on the causes of inadequacy, I feel four factors provide partial explanations. The court, first, was understandably far more concerned about military pressures around the capital than similar pressures 1400 miles south of Peking. Kwangtung and Kwangsi were separated, physically and to some extent psychologically, from the North China plain with which the rulers were both more familiar and more concerned. Problems of communication contributed. Despite special courier service, information to the court and directives from it consumed at least a month. Secondly, members of the government underestimated the tenacity with which the British would attempt to "open up" China, or the strength with which the "long noses" (as some Chinese deemed Europeans) could pursue their objectives. What westerners might do was still relatively unknown, for their prior impact (as the Portuguese at Macao) had been limited and local. No Chinese thought Europeans would try to conquer China without changing their ways. Proclivities of the court constituted a third factor. The Taokuang Emperor (ruled 1821 to 1850) appears to historians as a weak, ineffectual ruler, far more concerned with calm on the surface than with long-term conditions for peaceful development. Subordinates reinforced his outlook. Governors ignored or covered up events belying the emperor's image of peace and prosperity.[2] Without imperial encouragement, cautious bureaucrats were unlikely to report, or to counteract vigorously, acts of local unrest. Ignorance and inaction constituted the wisest policy. Finally, the court may have perceived its own armed forces as a clearer threat to its power than scattered rebels. Military commanders were selected for loyalty more than prowess; an undermanned, decentralized army was a lesser danger than threat of invasion or peasant unrest. The Opium War clearly disproved this assumption, but by this time the rot had penetrated deeply into the imperial forces.

The conditions that thus attended the initiation of the Taiping rebellion differed from what we shall observe later in this chapter. The uprisings in Telengana, Kikuyuland, and Kwilu reflected a rapid, unexpected increase in government coercion in rural areas. In those areas, attempts to reinforce central control sparked local discontent; the power of the dominant minority was demonstrated all the more clearly. Not so in South China. The decade of the 1840s witnessed a marked decline in Ch'ing power. What Talcott Parsons has aptly deemed "power deflation"[3] came to characterize rural Kwangtung and Kwangsi. The government no longer met its paramount obligation, that of protecting the populace. Administrative weakness, and deliberate encouragement, allowed local gentry to seize local power for their own ends. It would be an exaggeration—but not a great exaggeration—to speak of a Hobbesian state of nature at that time and period. Many of the usual restraints evaporated. Landlords could extract more, hiring local "bare sticks" to help in rent collection. Bandits operated over wider and wider areas, as previously pointed out. The subsistence ethic was violated in many villages. The tacit acceptance that buttressed the dynasty's authority wavered—or, perhaps more accurately, the village- and family- centered concerns of many were affected by events that influenced their perception of the political system as a whole. Force became increasingly utilized, its effectiveness being reduced in the process. The legitimacy of the entire system of government could be—and was—questioned.

It may seem paradoxical to see the seeds of decline in an imperial reform. An attempt to extirpate opium addiction, in the judgment of a distinguished scholar, shifted the balance of power in Kwangtung and Kwangsi decisively from the local administration to the gentry.[4] Military assistance seemed necessary to achieve the designed reform. In 1839, the imperial commissioner sanctioned local milita, levied and controlled by landlords. The gentry-led militia perpetuated themselves, and reinforced the power of the already privileged. Class antagonism reinforced already embittered Hakka-Punti relations. The disasters noted in the preceding chapter encouraged further disorder, leading in 1850 and 1851 to the creation of local militia. In Wakeman's words,

Once formed, the *t'uan-lien* were used by the Punti (original settlers) landlords against their Hakka (guest families) tenants, who began to join an obscure sect called the Society of God Worshippers. The society of the province quickly polarized: Punti landlord militia against Hakka tenants' "God Worshippers." And so the communal brethren of obscure iconoclasts became the militant brotherhood of the *T'ai-p'ing t'ien-kuo*.[5]

Few echoes of these disturbances reached Peking, at least in their early days. Competition took place in a setting officially marked by calm. Reports sent the court commented on peace and prosperity—a far cry from the unruly reality. Cheng Tsu-ch'en, the governor of Kwangsi, contributed by inaction. "Perhaps equally devoted to Buddhism and to the solaces of an impotent old age, Cheng would have nothing to do with violence and forbade local officials to kill bandits or to disturb his spirit with reports of local disorders. It was this aspect of his provincial administration that made possible the unimpeded initial expansion of the Society of God Worshippers...."[6] By implication, firmer administrative resolve might have crushed the Taiping rebellion in its South China nursery. The inattention that permitted the banditry and landlord excesses to flourish encouraged other means of self-protection—including a group willing to contest the hold of the central government and its Confucian ethic.

Thus, a seemingly conscious renunciation of coercion by the Ch'ing dynasty abetted the Taipings. It did so in two ways. First, the government lost some of its mantle of legitimacy. Unable to protect all its subjects, it could not claim full support. Secondly, the Society of God-Worshippers could inherit what the provincial administration had forfeited, and what the Punti gentry had tried to seize. The society could become, in effect, an alternative government. Elite ineptitude vis-a-vis British and bandit pressure became obvious to many. Dissidents could easily resuscitate the belief the dynasty was rapidly approaching its predestined end. They could turn against Punti gentry the resentments that had festered for centuries, and had been exacerbated by events of the 1840s.

Apparent renunciation of coercion by the government led to little, if any, reform, however. Perhaps the bandits and religious heretics would leave of their own accord, Governor Cheng seems to have believed. His sources of information—biased by the fact he wished optimistic reports—played down the importance of Hung and his followers. The Society of God-Worshippers was viewed in the same light as "ordinary" bandits or sectarians; the unusual features of the society's organization and beliefs, to which we shall turn in the following chapters, were either unknown to the provincial administration, or uncommunicated by it to Peking. It was one of a not inconsiderable number of heretical sects spawned by the disordered times.

The local administration had lost almost all initiative by 1850. The gentry-led *t'uan-lien* brought little credit to the Ch'ing dynasty and its officials. The government had condoned, indeed encouraged, the landlords' use of militia—similar in many respects to the razakars we shall encounter shortly in Hyderabad. An ill-disciplined military force betokened a weak administration. Reliance on forces outside the control of the provincial government did it no good. Initiative passed to the gentry, whose self-serving militia units helped push militant religious enthusiasts into active rebels.

Governmental inadequacies were thrown into high relief by the preparedness and esprit of the Society of God-Worshippers. In terms of military material, the two sides differed slightly. Neither imperial nor rebel troops had access to heavy equipment or precision rifles. Hand weapons predominated—knives, swords, spears, and the like, fabricated by local blacksmiths.[7] As we will later see, the incumbents in the Telengana, Mau Mau and Kwilu rebellions started with significant advantages in equipment over the insurgents; in the Taiping rebellion, resources were far more even. Further, Hung Hsiu-ch'üan had instilled a discipline and fervor that gave the insurgents a real advantage in manpower. Despite their smaller numbers, the Taipings fought with greater enthusiasm. One measure comes in their successful escapes from five encirclements in 1851-2. They fought for goals transcendent as well as material; their opponents lacked such motivation. Imperial soldiers ranked near the bottom of the Chinese social hierarchy, with good reason. Members of the military were often forcibly conscripted, or pushed into service by personal disaster. Their training was far from extensive, their willingness to risk their lives for corrupt officers questionable. Faced with a determined, coordinated opponent, imperial troops wilted under the impact. Indeed, as chronicled in Chapter 8, it took many defeats before the court overrode its usual caution and authorized the recruitment of special troops to counter the "long hairs."

The mountain forests of the Kwangtung-Kwangsi hinterland concealed initial organization and training. Feng Yün-shan located an encampment at the foot of "Mount Thistle"—in reality, eighteen close peaks of "considerable" height, linked to the world outside by two primitive mountain roads.[8] This geographically marginal area, inhabited by aboriginal Yao as well as by Hakka unable to find salubrious land, lay beyond the reach of effective government action. There the Society of God-Worshippers established its base in 1848-9, moved in mid-1850 to the village of Chin-t'ien. Religious, military and political solidarity could be reinforced in the remote setting. The Taiping base area conformed to most characteristics suggested in Chapter 1. The rebels-in-training grew in numbers as groups (including some bandit gangs) offered their support.

Several factors indicative of the government's weakness thus can be discerned. The willful inattention of the provincial administration and its reluctance effectively to counter either landlord exactions or insurgent manifestations, versus the increasing size and effectiveness of the Taiping nucleus; imperial troops' limited equipment and their even more limited knowledge of local terrain, versus the rebels' stockpiling of weapons and their careful choice of encampment; the low morale and limited training of gentry-led *t'uan-lien* and imperial troops, versus the religious enthusiasm, careful discipline, and cohesiveness of society members: all these enter the picture. Added to the intense local discontent, the shortcomings of the Kwangtung-Kwangsi administration facilitated the rise of dissident groups. Dynastic weakness thus contrasted sharply with the growing militance of the Society of God-Worshippers.

Our story would be incomplete at this stage, however, were we not to turn our attention northwards. The really marked expansion of the Taiping rebellion came in Hunan and Kiangsi provinces. The move of Hung and his followers into the Yangtse valley brought them into contact with readily mobilized groups anxious for betterment. Landlessness and unemployment were rife. For example, a shift in export trade in the 1840s had thrown an estimated 100,000 porters out of work at the Mei-ling pass between Canton and central China.[9] Unemployed boatmen and coolies, and tenants enmeshed in crushing debt, seem to have flocked to the Taiping banner. There had been 20,000 combatants and a total army of 40,000 in late 1851; by early 1853, the total had swelled to 500,000.[10] Hung and his converts brought a message of promise to the destitute, challenging imperial weakness with a militant organization and elaborate set of beliefs. We shall turn to these in later chapters.

Finally, we should note that many concurrent irritants plagued the imperial court. Hung was but one of several rebel leaders active in the late 1840s-early 1850s. Although the Taiping rebellion dwarfed others, it reflected conditions that pushed other groups, such as the Niens or the Moslems, into action. Life was being drained out of the Ch'ing dynasty by numerous local effusions. Individual hemorrhages might be stanched—but at some point the Manchu superstructure would give way. Previous dynasties had collapsed under the dual pressure of internal rebellion and external invasion. Protection of the center was essential. Well aware of history, the government in Peking risked few of its resources on what appeared a far-from-unusual uprising well removed from the imperial court. Not until the Taiping rebels had crossed into the densely settled Yangtse valley did the administration seriously ponder its next steps.

Weaness and inefficiency had taken their toll of the former Manchu efficiency, so that obscure squabbles over land, flavored with ethnic particularism and religious fervor, could mushroom into a national challenge. Local issues turned into widespread rebellion in the conditions of imperial ineptitude. The Tao-kuang emperor, who died as Hung was proclaiming the "Heavenly Kingdom," exemplified an attitude in which reform and repression was equally insufficient. A seeming lack of will paralyzed the court. In such a setting, well-organized groups could turn their own coercive strengths and political appeals against the incumbents.

Telengana: Village Initiation and Landlord Response

In simplest terms, the Telengana rebellion resulted from the interaction of increasingly militant groups with an India-wide atmosphere of communal violence and Communist encouragement of redistribution in the villages of Nalgonda and Warangal districts. The revolt itself arose from conditions peculiar to the princely state—but open conflict might not have occurred without the general inflaming of political and communal awareness that characterized the entire subcontinent. Hindu peasants, the first major group involved in violence, responded just after World War II to the prior extractions landlords had made. Their spontaneous seizure of *deshmukh* and *jagir* land brought immediate relief to the landless, and led to the "village soviets" the CPI was later to trumpet. Relatively little violence occurred in these land occupations. The second group was composed of militant Muslims, anxious to preserve the political dominance they had possessed for centuries. Their efforts at self-preservation, and the later Hindu counterattack, was to cost tens of thousands of lives. The upwellings of both groups reflected the overall escalation of communal consciousness and group violence that preceded—and bloodied—the grant of independence to India and Pakistan. The general climate, in other words, was one in which open conflict became the most prominent form of problem resolution.

By the eve of independence, 14 August, 1947, most of the usual constraints on the use of violence had been severely weakened. Communal tensions created an atmosphere of profound distrust. Indigenous army and police units, their impartiality tested by religious and language appeals, found it almost impossible, in several parts of the subcontinent, to stop waves of killing. British troops, soon to be withdrawn anyhow, were kept on the sidelines. The confusion inherent in dividing politically integrated units, such as Bengal or the Punjab, increased the levels of uncertainty and hostility. Government authority evaporated in some areas despite Gandhi's incessant appeals for calm. Few bases existed on which Hindus and Muslims could mutually resolve problems.

As the Telengana peasants became increasingly active, so too did their landlords. In some areas, thanks to the *goondas* they employed, the *jagirs* and *deshmukhs* preserved their economic dominance by force. In other areas, the tenants were able to squeeze out the detested, well-off landlords. Success in acts of violence encouraged further recourse to it.

It should be noted that the "struggle" — if this is the correct word — began in a very low key. Dating the start of the rebellion from the killing of Doddi Komarayya, 4 July, 1946, only ten insurgents had been killed by the end of the year.[11] This suggests the government of Hyderabad was unwilling and/or unable to mount a speedy campaign against the rebels, whose armaments were little more than sharpened sticks, muzzle loaders and slingshots, or that it did not regard the scattered local actions as politically significant. What seems to have happened, in a nutshell, was the rapid erosion of the power the privileged had enjoyed. Landlords no longer could command the respect from which they had earlier profited; their seeming abrogation of the subsistence ethic through eviction of tenants, insistence on *vetti* labor, and food requisitions could no longer be borne. Small-scale dramas were enacted in villages. Rapacious landlords were deprived of their power, forced to pay "protection money" when they visited their estates,[12] or hauled before "people's courts" to retract their actions. (The lack of a Hindu precedent for these "courts" suggests the degree of Communist influence.) Many *deshmukhs* temporarily withdrew from the scene. Others, as suggested above, turned to hired local toughs for support. Needless to say, *goondas'* actions further polarized landlord-tenant relations, and continued the escalation of local violence. On an essentially village-by-village basis, the underprivileged of Telengana started to take power and land in their own hands.

What started on an ad hoc basis gradually expanded: local success encouraged other villagers temporarily to put aside their caution. The targets were clear. Large landlords bore the brunt of accumulated resentment, intensified by the growing indebtedness and landlessness documented in previous chapters. All rural strata could unite in opposition to wealthy *deshmukhs* such as the Janareddy family, which owned 160,000 acres. The division of *deshmukhs'* lands and cancellations of debts followed the classic pattern of peasant revolts. The subsistence ethic had been violated; little outside encouragement was necessary to initiate small-scale village change. The violence landlords had employed in squeezing their tenants, and had continued through their hired toughs, was visited upon them. Communalism as such played little part. The targets were marked by riches, not religion. Matters of local import — above all the sense injustice had been wrought — accounted for the manifestations against the *deshmukhs*.

The acts of the razakars proved important nonetheless in the actualization of violence in Hyderabad State as a whole. These Muslim "volunteers"—many of them urban or refugees from India after partition—tried to perpetuate minority dominance by unbridled coercion. They were concerned with the state as a whole, not individual villages. The government of Hyderabad appeared unwilling to put a halt to their actions, despite strong urgings from British and Indian officials. The razakars' ranks swelled after the November 1947 standstill agreement, which maintained the status quo pending detailed discussions between the Hyderabad and Indian governments.[13] One may infer that the Nizam, increasingly uneasy with the reforms suggested by Sir Mirza Ismail and others, faced the escalation of violence with equanimity.[14] The doors of the state were opened to refugees. As Muslims streamed into Hyderabad, victims of communal tensions elsewhere in India, force seemed increasingly necessary to preserve the minority's privileges. Hyderabad City was Muslim-dominated; the Nizam and his courtiers, remaining in the urban area, may have had little accurate information about rural Hindu wishes. Pressure from India for the accession of Hyderabad continued unabated. The imbroglio in Kashmir encouraged the belief in Hyderabad that no Indian military action against the state would be possible, thereby permitting Hyderabad to maintain a tenuous autonomy. Nonetheless, the Nizam agreed to increase his army, attempted to purchase arms from Czechoslovakia, and countenanced an incredible growth in the razakars. V. P. Menon, chief Indian negotiator for the state's accession, estimated 200,000 of them were engaged in violent acts by August, 1948.[15]

The third major element in the Telengana rebellion was the Communist party of India (CPI), members of which had taken an increasingly important part in cultural-cum-political organizations such as the Andhra Mahasabha. It would be incorrect to ascribe the initiation of the uprising solely to Communist influence. Encouragement and advice provided after peasants had started to take matters into their own hands do not, in my view, "prove" that CPI agitation "caused" the rebellion. As has been mentioned previously, the Party adopted a Mao-come-lately perspective on the uprising. The Communists hesitated; cadre involvement assisted what was already in being. Not until December 1947 did the party officially begin to show interest; it then started directly to assume a role in what already had been accomplished in scores of villages. The following quotation from a leading party organizer illustrates what I have been asserting:

> But *in spite of our hesitation*, the Telengana people's discontent and upsurge was [sic] so deep and great, that *by their spontaneous activity*, of course guided by our party, with all its limitations, they put an end to *vetti* (forced labour), illegal exactions, and compulsory grain levies and started to reoccupy the lands seized earlier by the landlords and deshmukhs . . . .[16]

It is important to note that the rebellion in Hyderabad did not spill beyond Telugu-speaking areas. Kannarese-and Marathi-speaking inhabitants of the state, though also susceptible to relative deprivation and razakar violence, remained apart in the 1947-9 period from collective political violence. Why? I have no evidence that razakar actions were more severe in Telengana than in other parts of the state. The reasons seem to be economic and political. Rural indebtedness and landlessness were more sharply defined in Telengana than elsewhere in Hyderabad. Economic inequities weighed heavily on villagers, notably in Warangal district. These inequities took political form through the organizations described in the following chapter. Telugu awareness had been aroused and extended; cultural pride led to political militancy, more markedly in Telengana than in other parts of the state. Communists were to abet this transformation, especially when they pressed after February 1948 to expand the uprising. The bourgeois nationalist government of Jawaharlal Nehru became the target, the Nizam and *deshmukhs* local examples of what eventually should be swept away. Before moving to the larger scene, however, a secure local foundation had to be created. The "left" policy adopted by the CPI seems romantically to have envisaged Telengana as India's Yenan. The violence with which peasants had attacked landlords and countered razakar raids would be turned toward the government in Delhi. More of this story anon.

The Communists were thus preparing for a struggle against India; the razakars were entrenching Muslim privilege and preparing as well to fend off Indian pressures. What was perceived as an informal entente emerged between the two during 1948.[17] Despite the active involvement of Communists in the Telengana rebellion, the government of Hyderabad lifted its ban on the party in mid-1948. (The ban originally had been imposed in 1943.) By this time, the CPI had adopted its militant ideology, in which the inhabitants of Telengana were presumed to play a major part. Local pressures against landlords, encouraged by Telugu-speaking communists (some from neighboring Madras) but firmly rooted in indigenous conditions; militant Muslim pressure on the Nizam to remain separate from India; razakar acts of violence against Hindus; verbal CPI commitment to an intensified, broadened armed struggle; Indian military intervention designed to subdue the perceived threat to stability; Hindu communal violence against Muslims following the "police action": these were successive steps in the rise and fall of collective political violence. The Telengana rebellion intensified and took on communal coloration as a consequence of razakar actions designed to retain minority political control. The roots of the uprising, however, lay more in economic inequities and in a sense of Telugu solidarity. These require exploration in organizational terms as well as in terms of coercion.

Mau Mau: Nationalist Agitation or Incumbent Provocation?

The chief contemporaneous explanation of the Mau Mau rebellion — the official version, as it were — ascribed the outbreak of violence to manipulative Africans. According to this view, incidents of cattle maiming, harassment, and assassination were provoked by ambitious indigenous leaders. They exploited grievances, blowing them far out of proportion. The colonial administration bore little blame, according to this perspective. Though its members had failed to heed warnings of unrest, they had acted honorably albeit naively. Government officials had erred by being insufficiently firm in their response to provocations. Such was the authorized explanation in October 1952, when the state of emergency was declared, and remained the usual interpretation for years thereafter, particularly in circles favorable to pre-1960 British policy in Kenya. One of its bluntest spokesmen was F.D. Corfield, whose officially sanctioned report expressed both a clear view of Mau Mau ("... there was, in my opinion, no justification for *Mau Mau*, which was wholly evil in its conceptions")[18] and an equally clear explanation of its cause ("It was the deliberate exploitation of the western ideals of freedom by the more extreme African nationalists which placed the Government on the horns of that dilemma; and it was the inability of that Government, faced as it was with these outside influences, to resolve this dilemma, which was a decisive factor in the spread and near victory of *Mau Mau*.")[19]

Standing in sharp contrast to this view are interpretations that depict Mau Mau as a last-ditch indigenous response to pressures from above. Perhaps the bluntest statement of this genre — that the turn to violence stemmed primarily from actions of the colonial government — comes from Berman. In his judgment, declaration of the emergency represented "a preemptive attack carried out by the incumbent political authorities against a significant segment of the African political leadership of Kenya and its supporters."[20] The colonial administration, in other words, was the aggressor.

The differences between these views are more than semantic. They reflect fundamental contrasts in the approach to collective political violence. To Corfield and others sharing his views, violence carried out by Africans impeded the implementation of trusteeship; to Berman and others sharing his perspective, African violence alone pressured the colonial government into accelerating its languorous schedule for achieving majority rule. The dispute thus turns on the efficacy and appropriateness of violence under the prevailing conditions. Was the Kenya administration in fact capable of moving speedily toward rectifying land, labor and political grievances without the unambiguous evidence of indigenous discontent the rebellion offered? More broadly, was violence legitimate or illegitimate under the prevailing circumstances?

Speaking abstractly, it would seem the majority and minority alike had reason to employ coercion. Many Africans believed existing opportunities for reform and change could not accommodate what they desired; many Europeans believed that opening of settler agricultural land to Africans and significant steps toward majority rule totally jeopardized the rights due them as purveyors of Western standards and as mainstays of the Kenyan economy. It was the interaction between positions seen as irreconcilable that turned the Central Province of Kenya into a battleground in the early 1950s. Once again, the poor struck in the name of justice, the privileged in the name of order.

In this section, I shall consider incidents of violence leading up to the declaration of the state of emergency first from the perspective of the affected Africans (most of them Kikuyu), then from the perspective of the involved Europeans. This evidence should help clarify whether the violence of Mau Mau reflected more a manipulated, unjustified response to assorted grievances or a spontaneous, justified riposte to unbearable violence mounted by those in control.

In the view of many Africans, declaration of the state of emergency was neither the first nor the last step taken by the colonial administration and its settler allies to repress Kikuyu discontent. It capped a series of restrictions placed on African political claims; it justified a series of further coercive steps. Freed of many checks on its actions, the Kenya government could pursue its policies of suppression and pacification, to which Chapter 8 gives attention. Our concern here is with the period from roughly mid-1944 to October 1952. During this time, the administration and the Kikuyu edged toward overt conflict. British-condoned steps necessitated collective political violence, it seemed to many in the majority.

Rural dwellers, and particularly the squatters, felt the pressure of the immigrant community most acutely in the postwar period. Their sense of security declined; their presumed rights were denied by the settlers. What motivated the abridgement of the squatters' position can be simply explained. World War II had made settler agriculture profitable. Despite the extensive transfer of resources from indigenous sectors of the economy, European farms prior to 1939 never fully satisfied the enthusiastic claims made for them. Population statistics make the point starkly. The Depression had interrupted the growth of the settler community: the 1,183 active European farmers in 1920 had risen to only 1,890 by 1938.[21] At least three-quarters of Kenya's exports prior to the War came from African sources.[22] The proportions changed dramatically with the stimulus of fighting, and with postwar encouragement for colonial production of foodstuffs. It was to the obvious benefit of settlers to reduce competition from Africans, turning their labor from competitive to subordinate cultivation; squatters would become resident laborers, the landless a floating agricultural proletariat.

Labor had been at a premium during the War. For example, the colonial administration (with strong settler urging) introduced obligatory labor for essential agricultural production in March 1942. The 1937 Resident Labourers Ordinance was not enforced, lest African discontent be fanned at a time of labor shortage.[23] But the unusual conditions of 1940-5 did not last. By the end of the War, European farmers, through the district councils they controlled and through other pressure on the administration, introduced new restrictions on the large African population of the "reserved" areas. Transformation of the squatters into a rural proletariat, into wage workers temporarily residing on lands alienated to Europeans, collided with the relative autonomy Africans had enjoyed. Having gained relatively during the Depression, when many settlers had turned to "Kaffir farming" (in which Africans sharecropped on European farms—an arrangement generally profitable to them) and having consolidated these gains during World War II, the squatters had no desire for further restriction. The implementation in 1944 of a Nakuru District Council order, mentioned in the preceding chapter, foreshadowed what was to come. Africans were to be "put in their place," the paramountcy principle being construed as the implantation of wage labor.

The Resident Labourers Ordinance mandated the registration of all Africans living on European farms. There were, in 1945, some 42,183 squatter workers—plus more than 200,000 dependents.[24] Each family, of course, maintained its own domestic animals and cultivated areas for subsistence purposes. By various sorts of squeeze—restrictions on livestock; greater obligatory cultivation—settlers could enhance their position. The effects were dramatic:

> The Kikuyu squatter, who hitherto provided a labour rent of 90 days per year, having five to six acres of land with 25-30 sheep and goats, was in 1946 forced to work from 240 to 270 days, while reduced to having one and a half acres of land and limited to owning five sheep. The monthly wage of eight to

nine shillings (while at work for the settler) was not raised so that the drop in real income of squatters was anywhere from 30 to 40 per cent.[25]

In such a situation, African unrest and defensive measures emerged naturally. "Outside agitators" did not have to remind Kikuyu squatters of the threat they faced. A return to the reserves held little hope of improvement, for landlessness was shooting up under the impetus of population growth. D.H. Rawcliffe (to whom belongs the distinction of having his detailed book banned in Kenya) estimated that, by 1953, fully half the African populace of Kiambu was without land.[26] As European farmers stepped up their pressures, including eviction, the squatters responded defensively. Furedi, the most thorough student of the social dynamics of Mau Mau, offers the following judgment:

> ...mass oathing campaigns...pledged the Kikuyu squatters to solidarity against the European and to fight for the return of lost land....This use of oathing was necessitated by the need of the squatters to protect themselves from the gradual erosion of their status as tenants. This need for an active movement of defence led to the crystallization of an organization — which was to be known as the Mau Mau.[27]

Contributing to this defensive orientation was the "Olenguruone affair," to which Rosberg and Nottingham have given close attention.[28] In brief summary, squatters under the Resident Labourers Ordinance were settled in a block of 34,700 acres (54 square miles) acquired from the Masai. The area, given a special legal classification as a "Native Settlement Area," was seen by Kikuyu as recompense for land previously seized by Europeans, and by administrative officials as a controlled area in which improved agricultural techniques could be introduced. These conflicting views made Olenguruone an area of direct confrontation. Its transfer in 1947 to Rift Valley jurisdiction made clear that Europeans were to inherit the land. Unity among the subject populace was essential were Kikuyu to resist growing pressure from settlers and the administration. The oath provided "an instrument to ensure mass obedience in a situation of open defiance to constituted authority."[29] The Kikuyu were forcibly evicted in early 1950 after a remarkably strong, prolonged African rejection of administrative rules. Although compelled eventually to bow to *force majeure*, the evictees had proven the efficacy of oathing. Olenguguone became "a national symbol of sacrifice and martyrdom," whose participants typified "unity and defiance of Government on the part of men, women, and children, all of whom had been oathed and had stood firm."[30]

Administrative pressure intensified in the reserves through campaigns for agricultural improvement. Faced with a burgeoning population and eroding soils, the Kenya government embarked on intensive programs of terracing. Sir Philip Mitchell stood strongly behind what appeared to him to be sensible conservation measures — and was firmly convinced of the correctness of his judgment. His marked paternalism toward Africans ("people who have never been able to look ahead...simple, ignorant, witch-, and magic-ridden people at the mercy of many enemies....")[31] fitted closely with the racialist views of most administrators and settlers. The majority peoples of Kenya, whose interests were paramount, might have to be forced to be free. Pressure in the name of indigenous interests was no error. District officers were thus given marching orders: halt the continuing slide in living standards in the African reserves by encouraging, and if necessary by conscripting, communal labor. Cattle culling, terracing, crop rotation and similar imposed alterations of indigenous practices swelled the chorus of African discontent. That resentment was felt and some resistance organized against these steps should not come as a surpirse. Why, many Kikuyu may have reasoned, should we be cooped up in grossly inadequate areas when abundant untilled land still exists in the Highlands and the Rift Valley? Obligatory communal labor in the reserves, and eviction from Olenguruone and European farms made Kikuyu feel besieged. Defense against such pressures required unity — and each incident of standing firm encouraged further acts of resistance, while simultaneously pressing the colonial government toward sterner measures.

Concerned by evidence of "lawlessness," manifested in mass rallies against terracing and the equivalent of rural sit-down strikes, Kenyan administrators sought an answer. As might be expected, many leaned to a simplistic explanation. Some guileful, malevolent intelligence must be guiding and coordinating the various manifestations. The Africans, Europeans believed, could not spontaneously organize boycotts; a covert organization had evoked the collective rejection. This outlook led directly to the proscription of the "Mau Mau Association" in August 1950.[32] That European presumptions strayed far from reality should be apparent at this point. It was in large measure the intensification of the European impact that brought defensive oathing.

In simplest terms, the ban on the "Mau Mau Association" was intended by the colonial government to halt the increasingly prevalent, increasingly militant oathing ceremonies. The official mind-set believed that a central hand or organization guided the upsurge of Kikuyu solidarity, as previously noted. British officials appeared reluctant to accept the idea that unrest could arise without agitation; they assuredly did not agree in a "spontaneous generation of protest" theory. Thus, the Nyeri District Commissioner, a month prior to the proscription, wrote to Nairobi about a "theory" that persons "centrally trained and directed" aimed eventually to disrupt the government's activities and authority, The DC was forced to admit, however, that this belief may have stemmed more from speculation than reality: "The evidence in support of the theory is at present meagre," he wrote, "although there is considerable belief, both on the part of officers and chiefs, that such an organization does exist."[33] European settlers fully subscribed to this belief. Was it in fact accurate?

The historian of the rebellion must pick his way through a welter of contending interpretations, as noted at the start of this section. The official version, most fully expressed in the noted—one might better say infamous—Corfield Report, stressed conspiracy. Otherwise peaceful Kikuyu were gulled into violence by master manipulators, especially by Jomo Kenyatta. Believing Kenyatta to be the brains behind oathing, and further believing that what had been evoked by him could be halted by him, British officials put strong pressure on Kenyatta unambiguously to denounce Mau Mau. What might best be described as a cat and mouse game ensued, colonial administrators demanding a strong public statement, Kenyatta recognizing the popular sentiment that lay behind the oathing ceremonies and thus expressing his thoughts in masterfully ambiguous terms.[34]

Why did the British ascribe so much power to Kenyatta? The answer lies partly in personality, partly in his role in the KCA. An almost pathological distrust of Kenyatta had surrounded him after his return to Kenya in 1946. He had, in the settlers' and administrators' eyes, done almost all the wrong things: visited Moscow; kept a white mistress during part of his fifteen years in Great Britain; refused to serve a political apprenticeship in the Local District Council; thrown himself enthusiastically into collecting funds for a teachers' training college that Europeans considered a front for self-enrichment; drank too much. Kenyatta epitomized the "detribalized native" the British detested, even feared. Able to use the white man's tricks against him, Kenyatta could not be cowed by the means of control Europeans in Kenya customarily employed; supposedly able to manipulate African desires, Kenyatta enjoyed a basis of support no other Kikuyu could claim. He built for himself, in Murray-Brown's words, "an unofficial status as an alternative source of tribal authority to the government."[35] To the Kikuyu masses, the accomplishments of Kenyatta proved that a local boy could "make it" despite British opposition. He threw himself energetically into political organizing; he stressed Kikuyu pride, accomplishments and unity after his triumphant return in September 1946. His political sensitivities honed by years abroad, Kenyatta stepped into a situation not of his own making—but engaged in actions that made him the clearly recognized spokesman for Kikuyu interests. He might be pressured into public comments on Mau Mau, but he was not ready totally to disown what may increasingly have appeared to be the only way the intransigent administration might have been moved. Kenyatta enjoyed the undisputed mantle of being the major Kikuyu spokesman for political advance. His early role in the Kikuyu Central Association and his testimony in England for land claims could be matched by none. Given thus his hold on crowds, his 20 + years pressing for African rights, and his tinges of radicalism, Kenyatta understandably became the focus of settler and administrative distaste and of Kikuyu aspirations. In thus concentrating on an individual, however, the British seriously underestimated the deeply rooted character of African resentments Kenyatta and others voiced. They did not fully recognize the effects of squatter evictions and compulsory agricultural improvements. In the honored parable, they looked for the mote in the other's eye.

Yet an element of political opportunism did exist. Appearances by Kenyatta influenced Kikuyu conduct vis-a-vis administrative efforts. Smouldering resentment, fanned by evictions and agricultural compulsion, was on occasion intensified by Kenyatta and other prominent spokesmen. But their actions were markedly different from the promptings of "rural radicalism" in the Belgian Congo. This had been the product of a suddenly lightened colonial weight; Kikuyu grievances, by contrast, had been the product of an increased colonial presence. Desperation rather than hope motivated popular demonstrations in Kenya. Instances in which the British were forced to suspend their efforts naturally strengthened Kikuyu resolve to resist. Successful resistance — even if (as at Olenguruone) the colonial administration emerged the Pyrrhic victor — was capitalized upon by indigenous leaders.

Force was not absent from the majority. The Intensification of oathing, to which we shall return in Chapter 7, involved the use of violence against the recalcitrant. Ostracism or even assassination increasingly befell those who refused to swear the oath after mid-1952. As the confrontation with the British sharpened, still stronger elements were incorporated into oathing. The relatively spontaneous pledge of group solidarity resulting from European pressure was supplanted by a relatively planned expansion of Kikuyu unity resulting from Kikuyu militants. Such adaptation of a defensive oath to offensive possibilities marked an important stage in the Mau Mau rebellion. Force used by the minority would be countered by force mounted by the majority. Active resistance against the enemy, and sanctions against those who dealt with him, increasingly characterized Kikuyu society. The declaration of the state of emergency in October 1952 came at a time when the great majority of the ethnic group had by oathing expressed support for ethnic solidarity; subsequent British steps were to help transform this sense into a popular revolt with widespread backing.

The departure of Sir Philip Mitchell in mid-1952 serves as a convenient divide. European settlers and administrators in Central Province believed the situation to be getting out of hand. What Corfield called the "rising tide of subversion"[36] aptly characterizes their views. Nothing more concerned the Europeans, I believe, than fear of losing control. The few, scattered, white farmers could not hope to withstand a major outbreak of rural violence. Colonial officers accepted the need for African advancement, but wished it to be both peaceful and in accord with a timetable negotiated with leaders the British considered valid. They dismissed "urban riffraff" and "semi-literate malcontents," to use two common epithets, as self-seekers unrepresentative of popular wishes. Jomo Kenyatta and fellow officers of KAU (Kenya African Union) appeared untrustworthy, since they would not denounce Mau Mau in terms the British considered sufficiently strong. Nothing, in short, seemed to slow the breakdown of "law and order." And, most disturbing to the colonial government, violence was clearly on the upswing. Drastic action appeared necessary.

European members of the Legislative Council forced the colonial administration publicly to admit that unusual circumstances prevailed. On 10 July, 1952, Michael Blundell moved an amendment urging the government to take steps against the "increasing disregard of law and order."[37] The Member for Law and Order (an official) observed that all crimes should not be ascribed to Mau Mau (to which Blundell acidly wrote later, "It seemed to me that our country was going up in flames and the head of the fire brigade refused to acknowledge even the smoke"),[38] an observation restive Europeans could not accept. Viewing the agitation as a dispute over whether Africans or European settlers should eventually govern Kenya, the European Elected Members Organization met twice with the acting governor in August, urging a statement that African nationalism on the lines of West Africa — in other words, majority rule and independence — was not Her Majesty's Government's policy, and that any statements suggesting such would be considered seditious.[39] The interim appointee, Henry Potter, had little desire to accept what the European legislators urged; this would have contravened official policy. Potter also showed little enthusiasm for invoking the Emergency Powers Ordinance, as urged by Blundell and his associates, to permit arrest and imprisonment without trial. Meanwhile, the pace of oathing increased.

It should not be assumed that the colonial administration did nothing in the face of the perceived challenge. The steps taken, however, exacerbated Kikuyu discontent more than subdued it. Additional police were posted to affected areas; curfews and collective fines were imposed.[40] These tried weapons were not true; they had little effect on a populace, up to ninety percent of whom had taken the oath of unity. The colonial administration had refused reform at earlier times, largely as a result of settler pressure. Now the settlers pushed strongly for action against the "subversion" of

Kikuyu beliefs. In the new governor, Sir Evelyn Baring, they found a man willing to listen, energetic in his touring, and trusted by the Colonial Office to make difficult decisions.

An important precipitant of Baring's decision to proclaim the Emergency was the assassination of Waruhiu, one of three senior Kikuyu chiefs and an outspoken assailant of Mau Mau. His car was ambushed 7 October 1952, barely a week after the new governor had been sworn in. In the words of a top-secret telegram to the Colonial Office:

> It is now abundantly clear that we are facing a planned revolutionary movement. If the movement cannot be stopped, there will be an administrative breakdown, followed by bloodshed amounting to civil war....We are faced with a formidable organization of violence and if we wait the trouble will become much worse and probably lead to the loss of so many lives that in the future bitter memories of bloodshed will bedevil all race relations.[41]

Strike, in short, while the gun was still smoking.

The themes of the British decision are shown clearly in this message. More than simple agrarian unrest existed; sweeping political change was being sought by an organized, active "revolutionary movement." Compromise presumably would be impossible, concessions might not diminish the appetite for change. The British intended to retain administrative control, "breakdown" being the prelude to major domestic violence. The insurgents seemed to be effectively organized. Delayed British response would further strengthen their hands. A preemptive move, as had been urged upon the governor, seemed in order, Inaction in the past had resulted in an explosive situation; strong action immediately was necessary.

Baring's proclamation, approved in advance by the Colonial Office, took effect 20 October 1952. Of the government responses to the four rebellions, this was the most clear-cut and soon the most sophisticated. The initial *modus operandi* proceeded from the themes just identified. Since the movement was presumably organized, arrest of its leaders would throw it into quick confusion. The detention of 183 African leaders (overwhelmingly Kikuyu) appeared to be the quickest, simplest means of decapitating revolutionary tendencies. Major military action would be avoided, although the First Battalion of the Lancashire Fusiliers arrived at 6 a.m. the day the Emergency was proclaimed, followed a day later by the 4th and 6th King's African Rifles. Dramatic expansion of the Kenya Police and Police Reserve started. But the initial military moves were primarily intended to protect government supporters among the Kikuyu from retribution.

The sudden arrest of African political figures caught most by surprise. Bildad Kaggia, one of the most prominent militants, asserted he "never" believed the government would declare the Emergency.[42] At one fell swoop, most public figures of Kenyan African nationalism disappeared from the scene. This might have ended strong pressures for change, were it not for the simple facts that the grievances were too strong, the movement of Kikuyu unity sufficiently advanced, and the commitment to struggle so great on the part of some, that the die had been cast. Unrest in some fashion would continue, irrespective of British action against the purported leaders. The fact is that "Operation Jock Scott," as the round-up was dubbed, removed many constitutionalist Kikuyu leaders and left untouched many far more extreme in their views—including some who had already commenced guerrilla exercises in the forests. Violence became more diffuse, and in some respects more intense.

In the short run, the colonial administration came close to breaking down in the Central Province. Its intelligence services seemed woefully ill-informed. Even when the depth of Kikuyu resentment had been communicated, it was dismissed as the inevitable consequence of agrarian reform (the dominant administrative view under Sir Philip Mitchell), or as the carefully orchestrated result of subversion (the dominant settler view, shared to an increasing extent within the colonial government). Repression appeared to be the correct response, yet the local forces of law and order could not possibly have handled such an assignment. Scant political base existed among the Kikuyu supporting the colonial presence; African opinion, I have suggested, strongly favored Mau Mau goals of land and freedom. It soon became obvious that rebellion could not be terminated by coercion alone. For as Rosberg and Nottingham have written, "The declaration of the emergency did not head off an incipient mass revolution, but rather precipitated further mobilization for small-scale, violent resistance in the rural areas, along with increased violence in Nairobi."[43] Administrative action thus initially encouraged what it was supposed to prevent. The Mau Mau rebellion ultimately owed more to governmental steps than to the agitation of Jomo Kenyatta.

Kwilu: Military Indiscipline and Public Discontent

Rebellion in Kwilu reflected, in good measure, a response to incumbent violence that provoked widespread resentment. An ill-trained national army served the Congolese government poorly. Post-independence anarchy resulted from the collapse of the Force Publique; the spread of the "second independence" uprisings reflected the contagious spread of defiance. The inadequate discipline of the armed forces was manifested in mutiny, extortion and unnecessary brutality; their military shortcomings (a tendency to flee rather than fight) led to the hiring of mercenaries. In short, inept official coercion both helped foment collective political violence and scarcely defended the central government.

To trace adequately the role of military repression, we should give attention to the Force Publique, the colonial precursor of the Armée Nationale Congolaise (ANC). The Force Publique was a Belgian creation, intended for domestic operations. Though militarily unsophisticated in comparison with European armies, it enjoyed more than enough firepower to suppress internal disturbances in the Congo without reinforcement from Belgium. The rank and file came overwhelmingly from relatively disadvantaged or marginal Congolese groups who found the Force Publique an opportunity for employment and prestige more rewarding than other possible pursuits. The Force Publique acquired an unsavory reputation, due in part to the recruitment of convicts and apparent official willingness to condone heavy-handed repression. The bloody termination of the 1931 Pende revolt stands as mute evidence of the tactics pursued.

The racial stratification that marked the preindependence Congo clearly applied to the Force Publique. Whites controlled and composed the officer corps. The highest rank to which Africans could aspire was that of sergeant-major. The Belgians, similar to other governing alien minorities, believed their rule best protected by compliant troops schooled in instant obedience, and by culturally homogeneous commissioned officers sharing in full the assumptions and views of the dominant group. Even for the Belgian Congo, schemes for preparing indigenous officers were noteworthy by their languorous pace. As Young notes, "At the end of 1958, when the Working Group was completing work on a plan which foresaw Congo independence in perhaps five years, a scheme was announced with great fanfare which would have produced fourteen second lieutenants after 10 years."[44] The essential conservatism of the military establishment became obvious. Rapid Congolese advance in political circles contrasted sharply with continued Congolese subordination in the armed forces. It was this disjuncture that sparked the mutiny of 5 July, 1960 — perhaps the crucial date in the Congo's tortured post-independence period. The precipitating incident was General Emile Janssens' proclamation to restive troops, "Before Independence = After Independence."[45] Again to quote Young, "The first mutiny in modern times of an army against its entire officer corps began."[46] Attempts to calm the troops by dismissal of Janssens and promotion by a rank failed; the central government decided to dismiss all Belgians, reengaging a few as advisers rather than commanders. Shorn thus of military protection, the skittish Belgian community started to flee, their haste increased by incidents of pillage, assault and murder. The copper-rich province of Katanga seceded, with obvious Belgian encouragement.[47] Thus, national unity was compromised, the national army profoundly shaken. A return to the former status quo was manifestly impossible.

The political status of the military changed dramatically. Formerly on the sidelines, a feared prop of alien rule, the Force Publique moved front and center into a prominent, and eventually a dominant, role in Congolese politics. The secession of Katanga was followed by the split between the Leopoldville and Stanleyville governments (more fully discussed in the following chapter) and the proclamation of an "independent" South Kasai. The Congolese armed forces were thus divided into four antagonistic sectors, echoes of which reverberated long after the Kolwezi incident of May 1978. The ANC became in reality a series of private armies.[48] Squabblings among politicians opened the opportunity for ambitious military leaders to superimpose themselves on the government. On 14 September, 1960, Colonel Joseph Mobutu announced the army had "neutralized" both President Kasavubu and Prime Minister Lumumba; university students in the "Collège des Commissaires Généraux" would run the country.[49] Although a compromise prime minister was named in July 1961, when Parliament met in enforced isolation on the Louvanium University campus, the political muscle of Mobutu had been flexed. No civilian government could hope long to survive without due regard to the needs and demands of its armed supporters.

The impact of the military was not confined to the political summit. The weakening of discipline afflicted Congolese of all walks of life. Soldiers and police gained license for popular extortion. One might see in this a continuation of the pre-independence pattern. During colonial days, the Force Publique had served as "hated and despicable tools of the white conqueror."[50] This negative image was reinforced by military self-serving. Bullying and badgering provoked popular resentment. The seeming inability of civilian leaders to curb such excesses added to the growing belief politicians cared for none save themselves and their immediate retainers.

As might be expected, military exactions tended to be levied more heavily in regions without strong representatives in the central government. Kwilu suffered from such liabilities. PSA leaders Antoine Gizenga and Pierre Mulele threw in their lot with the breakaway Stanleyville government, as will be shown more fully in the following chapter. Gizenga was imprisoned in December 1962, while Mulele travelled to China to acquire expertise in guerrilla warfare. (Ironically, Mulele was one of a handful of educated Congolese who had served in the Force Publique—and, irony of ironies, served in the same unit as the man who countenanced his later execution, Mobutu.) As the opposition of the Mbunda and Pende (respectively the ethnic groups of Mulele and Gizenga) to the Leopoldville administration remained unrelenting, repression increased. "The central government not only offered no counterbalance to the abusive authority of the bureaucracy and to the caprices of the forces of law and order," Verhaegen writes, "but to the contrary pursued its own policy of repression against the Pende and Mbunda political leaders."[51] Chiefs of villages suspected of sympathy for Mulele were bound and dragged behind trucks; soldiers requisitioned girls. Such crude tactics were far more successful in politicizing discontent than in quelling dissidence. As had the Punti *t'uanlien* and the razakars of Hyderabad, the Congolese army incited popular antipathy without extirpating resistance.

Not all the blame for military indiscipline and depredations should be placed on the shoulders of the Armée Nationale Congolaise, as the Force Publique had been rebaptized at independence. The *sauve qui peut* atmosphere, coupled with declining administrative efficiency, pulled the attention of political leaders away from the armed forces. In view of Mobutu's intervention of September 1960, this assertion may seem surprising. The immense problems of reuniting the sundered sections of the former Force Publique, of incorporating new officers, and of making appropriate international arrangements, seemed outside the interest of most politicians; they appeared content to let Mobutu "get on with it."[52] Soldiers and police climbed abroad the gravy train, their salaries respectively being increased to 347 and 240 percent of their preindependence rates of pay.[53] Perhaps political leaders felt that such hefty increases would curb soldiers' appetite for power; perhaps the raises reflected the bargaining position the forces of coercion had attained. Whatever the cause, the burgeoning costs of the military weighed heavily on the Congo's rickety finances. However, a salary promised is not necessarily a salary delivered. Pay arrears contributed to the police mutiny in Leopoldville 3 May, 1963, suppressed only with the intervention of the gendarmerie and the dismissal of many members of the police force. Taking a leaf from the colonial administration's handbook, the provincial government repatriated several to Kwilu — where a few months later some joined the Mulelist *maquis*. Aware both of the use of arms and of the central administration's fragile underpinnings, some of these discharged constables played roles analogous to those of veterans of the King's African Rifles in the Mau Mau rebellion, or of Malagasy veterans in the 1947 Madagascar insurrection.[54]

The people of Kwilu had little defense against the various military or police pressures on them. As had many other Congolese parties, the PSA had organized a militia, but this served party officials primarily as a ceremonial bodyguard and in crowd control. This *milice* was by no stretch of the imagination a crack guerrilla unit, nor a well-armed military formation that could provide widespread protection. The organization of a *maquis* ready and able to confront regular ANC troops represented a major departure from the practices of Congolese politicians, who had generally been willing to work within the system—and to reap from it significant financial rewards. In theory at least, the Mulelist *maquis* also constituted a departure from an ethnically homogeneous group raised for defense purposes. Not a *levée en masse* nor a reincarnation of an age set, the guerrilla army of Mulele was to be marked by political awareness. The ideological departure represented by such adaptation of Maoist beliefs to African realities will be explored in Chapter 7.

To what extent did the mounting indiscipline of the ANC contribute to the politicization of discontent in Kwilu? This broad question can be answered only by seeing military violence as both cause and consequence of politicization. Illegal levies and raids could only diminish the already low regard with which the armed forces were viewed. Independence alone could not convert the former Force Publique into a national army, disciplined in its conduct, broadly representative of the populace, and restrained in its use of coercion. Internal checks were lacking. Little constrained individual soldiers from taking the law into their own hands and, in so doing, further reducing the legitimacy of the central administration. The acts of indiscipline were far from random, however. The well known antipathy of parts of Kwilu to the Adoula government meant military infractions there were unlikely to be detected or corrected. With the decision 3 September, 1963 to organize military expeditions into "troubled regions" of Kwilu Province, any remaining restraints disappeared. Against some of the most politicized and discontent people of the Congo, repression became the chosen instrument. Policymakers in Leopoldville found the easiest solution to dissidence in intensified coercion. Thus the cycle of discontent-challenge-riposte-repression-internal war began in rural Kwilu.

The violence of the ANC thus must be placed in its political context. Coercion was particularly resented because discontent and popular awareness were already high. Military steps further confirmed, in effect, what the rural inhabitants of Kwilu already realized: legal opposition brought little benefit; government coercion would have to be countered by popular mobilization. The prior existence of the Parti Solidaire Africain, and the various ideological precepts of Pierre Mulele, further abetted the politicization of discontent and its transformation into collective political violence. Discussion of both are reserved for later chapters.

What we have examined in this chapter has been more the initiation of collective political violence than its maintenance in time and its extension in scope. Insufficient government protection, I suggested, abetted the rise of self-defense groups. The Society of God-Worshippers and Mau Mau oathing efforts arose under circumstances adverse to significant parts of the populace. Retention of land and rights made both essentially defensive in their origins. We still need to explain how and why expansion occurred. What turned defense on behalf of a few into offense on behalf of the many? In what manner did protection of the aggrieved turn into attack on the incumbents?

Part of the answer lies, of course, in the obvious, direct role of the incumbents in acts against the rural majority. Administrative complicity in razakar raids, or inaction in the face of widespread corruption and extortion, made clear the lack of enthusiasm of those in control for what villagers considered just. The zero-sum game seemed to operate in favor of the already powerful and privileged. The politicization of discontent reflected the fact government officials were involved in suppression. What they did, in terms of extraction, and what they did not do, in terms of protection, could readily be interpreted in political terms.

But another part of the answer lies in the deliberate acts of the protestors. They turned into rebels through their willingness to challenge official coercion in its own coin. They sought to portray the attacks on some as threats to many. They suggested that infringements on rights would increase; they noted that the incumbents' rhetoric of concern for the majority scarcely matched their actions. Most important, the protestors argued the necessity for collective counterviolence. No satisfactory alternative existed to taking on the central government. They turned to rebellion with the decision to fight and, if necessary, carry the struggle beyond the circle of those immediately affected.

Effective challenge to the incumbents required expanding the awareness, numbers and unity of those aggrieved. Individuals might react on their own, betokening the disgruntlement of others, yet prove unable to bring significant change. United with many, however, they might successfully translate discontent into action. Politicization and organization proceeded hand-in-hand. The following chapter examines the third facet in the politicization of discontent, namely the creation and expansion of organizations directly antagonistic to the government. It was in and through such groups that collective political violence effectively countered the violence visited on many citizens by official policy and ineptness.

CHAPTER 6 /

Leaders, Organizations, and the Coordination of Dissent

The Personal Bases of Political Institutions

In the words of Montesquieu, "Dans la naissance des sociétés ce sont les chefs des républiques qui font l'institution; et c'est ensuite l'institution qui forme les chefs des républiques"[1] This famous aphorism — loosely translated, "It is men who first make institutions, thereafter institutions form men" — aptly suggests the dual concerns of this chapter. Rebellions of the scale described in this book required leadership and organization. They were not leaderless "mobs," spontaneously called into being by the prevailing circumstances. Nor, on the other hand, were they tightly coordinated, planned manifestations bearing the impress of a single mind. Individuals — a Hung Hsiu-Ch'üan or Pierre Mulele — might crystallize discontent and organize a framework for collective political violence. They could not, and did not, control all aspects of the resulting actions. Only with existing bases of resentment, directed, coordinated and perhaps magnified in the process, were the concerns of individuals translated into group action. Collective political violence thus developed from the interaction of existing elements (such as relative deprivation), crystallizing events (such as government actions perceived as illegitimate and the rise of leaders), and ongoing organization (such as the entities to which we shall turn in this chapter).

Traditions of resistance to government, in some form, characterize all societies. Such ideas coexist with the traditions of acquiescence or resignation we have already noted. The format may vary, the sustaining beliefs differ. They can be drawn upon at times of social distress to justify change and collective political violence. The rebellions with which we are concerned were typical, in this regard: all partook of "traditional" elements of protest. The Taiping rebellion, for all its seeming Christian trappings, seeming nationalist elements, and awareness of class distinctions, retained Confucian overtones; the Maoist ideologies attached to the Telengana and Kwilu rebellions remained esoteric grafts onto hearty indigenous stocks of resistance to economic exploitation; the oathing that attracted so much notoriety to Mau Mau represented an adaptation of practices "typically Kikuyu"[2] to especially oppressive circumstances. To these we shall turn in Chapter 7.

The contributions of specific persons must be assessed against this backdrop of continuity coupled with change. They were revivers, in some measure. Equally important, however, they were innovators. The individuals to whom we shall turn in the following pages sought to embody social discontent in ongoing organizations. These entities, in turn, were intended to attract adherents from different backgrounds. Ascription no longer accounted for persons' involvement in and of itself. The evidence seems clear. The Society of God-Worshippers broadened from its Hakka base; although language and communal issues restricted support for the Telengana rebellion, most castes and rural strata in the affected districts gave support, and the CPI sought an even greater widening; the expansion from the Kikuyu Central Association to the Kenya African Union indicated political concerns for the colony as a whole; the multi-ethnic character of the PSA and Mulele's use of class categories represented significant innovations. Organizations of this sort might initially take shape in secretive conditions, among members of a restricted group. Their potential support was far wider, however, thanks to organizational adaptations.

A further area of innovation came in adaptations of militant resistance. Collective political violence could be initiated and sustained in "traditional" ways. Yet important changes came here as well. As we shall see shortly, some of those who rose to prominence contributed special military skills. Their training, whether in conventional or unconventional warfare, gave them a sense of what force might obtain, and how coercion might be organized. Such skills may have been rare in the particular societies and hence all the more effective (since unexpected) when turned against the incumbents. In this regard, the prominence of veterans should be noted: especially in the two African rebellions with which we are concerned, former military or police personnel filled crucial positions as conflict itself took armed forms.

A third area for adaptation of existing patterns, and inclusion of new concepts, came in ideological justification. Folk wisdom, as already suggested, cherished examples of resistance, as well as homilies of acquiescence. When incumbents overstepped the bounds of appropriate conduct, resentment and response would be just. The grounds for popular resistance gained new twists from leaders. They provided an additional layer, in a sense, of ideological explanation. By criticizing the old order, depicting the new order to be created, asserting its legitimacy, and establishing bonds of common identification transcending narrower forms of community, they contributed yet another basis on which discontent could be politicized.

These varied combinations of "old" and "new" reflected the political circumstances prevailing in these societies. Severe restraints existed on indigenous economic and political advance. The dominant minority feared, or at least distrusted, any group claiming to represent majority interests. Central to the old order was concentration of decision-making in the hands of the privileged few and their chosen allies. Those at the top reserved the right — perhaps I should say *asserted* the right — to decide by whom the subject populace might be represented. The cultural superiority presumed and cultivated by the dominant few made them loathe to make significant alterations in patterns of stratification. The strategies of retaining power reviewed in Chapter 3 left little place for open expression of majority concerns, insofar as these challenged the prevailing assumptions. Rhetoric of responsibility, good government, or trusteeship notwithstanding, the reality was one of restricted opportunities for indigenous persons. Concerned lest their control be weakened or modified, the ruling group accordingly placed many legal, psychological, organizational and other obstacles in the path of would-be indigenous organizers.

One consequence was clandestine efforts, often clad in cultural rather than political garb. Shadowy areas of political endeavor came into being. Many guises or concealments existed. Rural dwellers confronted outsiders with distrust and icy response. Active planners of revolt tested the waters cautiously, rarely disclosing their possible resort to resistance though parading their concerns for majority interests. As might be expected, the greater the degree of secrecy required, the more restricted the circle of activists remained. Such necessary caution had the natural effect of confining direct participation to those presumed trustworthy by background, and made available by propinquity. Those linked by communal identification often met both criteria. Accordingly, the degree of ethnic homogeneity in early stages of rebellion in multi-ethnic societies should come as no surprise. Organization may most readily grow from roots already sunk in the indigeneous setting, for these roots provide a necessary degree of concealment, sympathy, and ease of mobilization.

Recognizing the dangers inherent in indigenous organizations, the ruling groups encouraged divisions and diversions. We have already noted them. Among the strategies discussed in Chapter 3 was co-optation of significant or influential social sectors. The objective was to build a cadre of indigenous supporters, diminishing thereby the chance of revolt. Expressed in simplest terms, the risks and benefits potentially derived from rebellion differed within the subject population because of this policy. Those with stakes in the existing order remained lukewarm to change threatening their privilege—an observation buttressed by historical evidence as well as intuitive obviousness. In all four societies, as we shall see in Chapter 8, many of those who sat on the fence, and most of those who rallied to the incumbents' position, shared bonds of sympathy with the dominant group. Those whose bread was buttered through association with the ruling class remained loathe to jeopardize such benefits—particularly if they were singled out as targets for rebels' vengeance, yet enjoyed protection from the incumbents. The conflict between "government" and "rebels" thus became internecine. Civil war was the result, the level of hostility reflecting splits within the local society as well as confrontation of the rulers and the ruled. Avoiding such divisions within local society, we shall see in the following chapter, became a leading objective of ideology.

A continuing issue in the study of collective political violence is participation. What groups might most likely throw themselves wholeheartedly into conflict? Possible candidates include the most deprived, the most disappointed, the most hopeful, and the most militant. Let us look briefly at each, reserving for later pages more detailed information on the social composition of rebel movements.

A " . . . you have nothing to lose but your chains" approach tends to equate maximal participation in collective political violence with minimal share in the status quo. Were this the case, we should find the most active supporters of rebellion coming from backgrounds of humble origins and limited achievements. The "wretched of the earth" would furnish the shock troops; social and political reordering should come by and through them. By contrast, the relative deprivation approach suggests that individuals and groups who experience the greatest gaps between expectations and achievements would be disproportionately involved. Those at the bottom of the social hierarchy may have adjusted their hopes downward; a long heritage of subordination can, after all, be translated into minimal expectations for betterment. No such stricture applies to the upwardly mobile: their desires may rise far more rapidly than their attainments, making them feel relative deprivation most acutely. The most hopeful may thus have nothing to lose, but a great deal potentially to gain. "Intellectuals" fall into this category. I put the term in quotation marks to stress its relative nature. The severe restrictions on education in the societies under review meant that literacy, especially in the language of the ruler, gave individuals special status, this translatable on occasion into aspirations outstripping achievements, and into awareness of the chinks in the incumbents' armor. This combination of aspiration with disappointment would prove explosive. One might finally expect the greatest involvement in collective political violence to be manifested by the most militant. Persons skilled in the use of arms, such as demobilized soldiers or police, might combine such talents with a flair for organization. Those who had collided with the government—bandits or other outlaws; former official employees dismissed for various causes; perhaps scions of families whose heads had been killed resisting the politically powerful—might provide impetus. Their grievances would seem likely to lead directly to encouragement of revolt.

Distinctions among these four categories are obviously not hard and fast, however. They represent types of backgrounds, not necessarily coherent strata in themselves. Information about the social origins of participants suggests the ways in which discontent is experienced and politicized. The combinations among these four groups (the most deprived, the most disappointed, the most hopeful, and the most militant) help account for the varying paths collective political violence took.

A further complex question is that of leadership. Not only must we try to uncover the characteristics of rebels, but we must also seek the reasons for differentiation between the leaders and the led. It may be that answers can be found along the lines just suggested: the crucial initiative for collective political violence perhaps comes from those most deprived, those most cognizant of presumed deprivation and potential gain, or those most militarily-inclined. Special attention must be given here to the "intellectuals." To the extent one accepts Marx's view (as applied by numerous epigones) that the rural multitudes constitute a class in themselves rather than for themselves, assistance from outside their milieu is necessary. Those with special skills and awareness might awaken the "rustics" from their "torpor" and at the same time channel the energy of the rural aggrieved into broader movements for change. Such would-be transformation of endemic discontent into focused revolution has become a contemporary shibboleth. Since Mao Tse-tung's assertions regarding the revolutionary potential of Hunan peasants, his imitators have become legion. An upsurge of the rural masses, along lines drawn by the politically more conscious, provides the chief twentieth century recipe for profound change in developing countries. The evidence of this chapter, as extended in the following and the concluding chapter, should more fully sensitize us to the revolutionary implications of rural rebellions. The transformation of these into rural revolutions comes rarely. Those who lead, irrespective of their backgrounds, face major obstacles indeed.

Of the biographies of political leaders, there seems to be no end. Be they hagiographic, debunking, or "objective," such works provide useful information and should form the basis for a flourishing industry of comparative study. What common factors, if any, mark those who rise to the top of the political heap? More narrowly, what characteristics seem to distinguish leaders of rebellions from their fellows? The answer ultimately may smack of circularity: their obvious hallmark is the desire to lead.[3] Some revolutionary figures have been examined under neo-Freudian microscopes: for example, Gandhi and Luther by Erik Erikson; Lenin, Trotsky and Gandhi by E. Victor Wolfenstein.[4] Study of presidential character earned James Barber[5] appropriate recognition. Concern about socioeconomic background provided writers of Marxist bent a basis for comparative study of political leadership. Concern for "political culture" has given a link between individual qualities of leaders and national or cultural parameters for leadership.[6] It is from approaches of this last sort, I believe, that the most useful information about rebels can be sought. Leadership in collective political violence rests to a very great degree on unique factors inherent in each setting.

Context is the key word in assessing individuals' contributions to collective political violence. Cross-cultural commonalities may exist in such broad phenomena as relative deprivation. Its politicization, however, varies along lines unique to the particular society. The reason is simple. If each culture has, in some fashion, an indigenous tradition of political resistance, persons who best tap it likely come from within that tradition. Although they will doubtless try to extend and modify this tradition, they and their followers are constrained by it. The interaction between leader and led occurs in a specific setting. The context helps define the ways in which collective political violence is expressed. The manner in which discontent thus becomes politicized and translated organizationally into attacks on the incumbents reflects particular as well as universal characteristics. Recognition of the peculiar factors must be with us as we probe more deeply into the structures of the four rebellions and, by extension, of other instances of collective political violence.

Taiping: The God Worshippers and Other Organizational Types

The popular appeal and military success of the Taiping rebels owed much to their organization. Buoyed by religious fervor, bound into a tightly-knit group, members of the Society of God-Worshippers confronted the Ch'ing dynasty with a challenge qualitatively different, and quantitatively greater, than any other internal challenge it faced. The origins of the society were humble and obscure, as we have seen in earlier pages. The message it brought, and the goals it sought, enabled the society to spread well beyond its local, Hakka roots. Under the leadershp of Hung

Hsiu-ch'üan and Feng Yün-shan, a foundation was created open to others, universalistic in its appeals.

Hung Hsiu-ch'üan came from a significant sector of Chinese rural society, the scholars *manqués*. Esteemed for their learning—for only those versed in the classics would dare sit for examinations—such persons counted among the most respected members of village society. Local administration rested in large measure on the willing assistance of such persons. Sharing the Confucian norms, if not necessarily the formal degrees, of those in the administrative hierarchy, they helped ensure rural calm. Yet, as was noted in Chapter 2, inherent strains existed. The aspirant mandarin, disappointed in his hopes for office, might turn against the system. Such was the case with Hung.

Hung enjoyed the advantage of bringing a message melding "old" and "new" elements. His visits to Canton brought him into contact with Christians who, as we shall see in the following chapter, furnished several new ideological themes. In other settings, or at earlier times, the Christian alternative would not have been available. Hung's message thus differed in significant respects from the millenarian Buddhist or Taoist beliefs, and from the redistributive ideals of some secret societies, that provided the customary alternatives to Confucian norms. The Society of God-Worshippers brought disrupted areas of Kwangtung and Kwangsi a militancy and sense of organization from which many of the aggrieved profited. Let us, accordingly, turn first to the types of organization through which collective action has been fostered in rural China, then look specifically at the adaptations made by Hung Hsiu-ch'üan.

Three traditional formats for collective action existed in Imperial China: clans, secret societies, and religious sects. The latter two shared several characteristics. Clans were based on descent, secret societies and religious sects on initiation. None was *ipso facto* ethnically exclusive, although intermarriage preserved the essentially Hakka character of many clans. None was confined to a single class, although the socially and economically disadvantaged derived the greatest advantages from secret societies, given their many connections with banditry. None preached a clear political message, although many sects (most notably those drawn from the White Lotus groups of North China) called for expulsion of the Ch'ing dynasty and restoration of the Ming dynasty. All linked a sense of rough equality among members to a marked distinction between leaders and followers; yet all held out the promise of rewards for the faithful.

Kinship-based clans (*tsu*) introduced to a village "a principle of cohesion which would not otherwise have been present."[7] In South China particularly, rural and clan leaders were virtually identical. Landowners, in other words, were able to direct the *tsu* for their own ends: "The gentry supplied the active, and the commoners the passive, components of the kinship group."[8] Ritual land gave many clans their financial foundation and (in Hsiao's words) "it was ritual land also that rendered gentry domination a natural and perhaps inevitable consequence."[9] The economic and political interests of clan members were thus not congruent; the ascriptive basis of the *tsu* gave many gentry a means of expanding their own power. Clans did not protect the interests of all their members; the already well-to-do were more equal than others. In many respects, *tsu* were responsible for local violence, notably where powerful lineages competed for resources.

Secret societies provided a second organizational format open to villagers. Despite their historical significance, secret societies remain relatively unexplored by scholars.[10] It is as though a continued veil of concealment separates observers from participants. A simple explanation exists: in South China in particular, secret societies merged imperceptibly into bandit gangs. The various Triad brotherhoods attracted a wide variety of participants—small merchants, yamen workers, gangsters, pirates, and smugglers.[11] Many secret societies practiced banditry and extortion. In times of dynastic ineffectiveness, however, they might protect the common people. To quote a late nineteenth century memorial from Kwangtung:

> *Hui-fei* [society bandits] have been most rampant in Szechwan, Hunan, Kweichow, Kwangsi, and Kwangtung. At first they were lawless, wandering people who burned incense and organized societies. When their organizations have waxed strong and their members become numerous, they rely on their strength to tyrannize their neighborhoods and victimize the good people. The humble people, being helpless, may join their societies for self-protection.[12]

Despite the official bias of the statement, its import is clear. Secret societies offered a modicum of safety for their members, an alternative to the standard Confucian order, and opportunities for "the persecuted and . . . those who had no voice or power in the existing political and social structure . . . . The societies were secret orders of all those who had no other way to defend themselves against the pressures of the state and the privileged social leaders."[13]

In important respects, secret societies esteemed as virtues what Confucian values derided. Popular religion rather than orthodoxy; social banditry; opposition to the "five relationships" of social conduct: these characterized secret societies.[14] They drew support largely from poor peasants, urban and rural *déclassés*, and the "pre-proletariat"[15]—the same groups that furnished the bulk of recruits to the Society of God-Worshippers as it expanded from its Hakka nucleus. Such similarity in followers' social origins, and the influence of secret societies on Hung's beliefs and practices, should not be interpreted as making the Society of God-Worshippers "just another" secret society.[16] Millenarian elements gave it many of the trappings of a heretical sect, the third major genus of rural collective action.

Sects enabled rural dwellers to unite their efforts in search of an alternative to an unpleasant present. There were many ways in which secret societies and heretical sects overlapped; differences between them in many respects reflected contrasts between North and South China.[17] In the former, rebels against the prevailing order could tap into a rich vein of heterodox beliefs. Millenarian ideals, transmitted through chains of teachers and disciples, could prod believers into rebellion. As Naquin has aptly demonstrated for the 1813 Eight Trigrams uprising, local events (drought, flood, appearance of a comet) were proclaimed as heralding the collapse of the old order. Only members of the sect might benefit from protection and safety amidst the chaos.[18] In some respects, peasants experienced rebellion in religious terms, finding through it a reknitting of the raveled family structure.[19] Others found nourishment. Many peasants flocked to the Eight Trigrams for food.[20] Sects differed in kind from bandit gangs or many secret societies, in which promises of benefits or violence were rendered immediately, not deferred until the new age was ushered in,[21] food being the exception.

The conditions that encouraged heretical sects thus fostered rebellious groups of many sorts, including bandit gangs, secret societies, and entities as skeptical of the Confucian order as the Society of God-Worshippers. Social disruption intensified relative deprivation, and manifested the weaknesses of the *ancien régime*. The search for substitutes, as it were, led to forms of social organization other than Confucian paternalism. Groups adapted to the changed exigencies provided an alternative to the existing pattern of gentry domination. The transformation of the small, seemingly innocuous Society of God-Worshippers into the *T'ai-p'ing t'ien-kuo* — the Heavenly Kingdom of Eternal Peace and Prosperity, claiming the right to rule all China — provides a case in point of organizational adaptation.

The society was born of religious enthusiasm, itself in some measure the product of personal frustration. A few months after Hung's fourth failure in the provincial level examinations, he and his cousin Li Ching-fang baptized themselves. Feeling what Jen calls "an exhilarating sense of release from his former anguish and of dedication to a great new task,"[22] Hung started to impart his message to others. His dedication led him to occasional excesses, for he dared to profane the Confucian foundations of village life. By smashing the tablet of Confucius in the village school, Hung brought himself into direct conflict with local leaders and, not incidentally, was fired from his teaching position. In the spring of 1844, the iconoclastic Hung and his cousin Feng Yün-shan trekked for two months from their Kwangtung home into southeastern Kwangsi. Seven months' work among fellow Hakka brought more than 100 converts. Hung then returned home; perhaps sobered by his earlier experiences, he resumed teaching, and poured his energies more into writing than into preaching. The reports of his apocalyptic visions we shall examine in Chapter 7 were penned at this time. Meanwhile, the movement expanded under Feng's impetus. The fivescore adherents had grown to more than 3,000 by mid-1847.[23] Hakka families started to gather at the foot of "Mount Thistle," their interests aroused by reports of Hung's visions. Feng took the initiative to organize the new converts into the Society of God-Worshippers, with Hung the supreme earthly leader.

As a religious brotherhood, the society stressed the fraternity of all true believers. Members pledged to worship God, since they "would not have calamities and sufferings, and those who refused to worship Him would be hurt by snakes and tigers."[24] They would regard Hung as the "true lord" and the elder brother. A semimonastic order prevailed. Adherents turned over all their money and valuables to the society's treasury, which then provided for their needs. Men and women were segregated.[25] Baptism, confession, and common worship united members. They differentiated themselves from the populace and, not incidentally, manifested a political message by refusing to plait their hair into the Manchu-ordained queue.[26] Long, unkempt hair was as much a political symbol in imperial China in the 1850s as in the industrialized West just over a century later.

As a militant and increasingly military organization, the society drew from the rules traditionally ascribed to the Duke of Chou, brother of the founder of the Chou dynasty (ca. 1122 to 418 B.C.). These regulations set forth, in elaborate detail, the hierarchical organization of the armed forces and the appropriate flags and insignia.[27] The basic unit was the squad, composed of twenty privates, five corporals, and a sergeant. (The western terms are here used for convenience.) Members were enjoined to be on good behavior during the march and in camp.[28] Ill-treatment by soldiers long had marred Chinese history; Hung promised a change. Increasingly virulent anti-Manchu messages were used to stir popular support. But the organization was never forgotten at this stage for the ideology; both were closely linked. Those who joined the society entered a comprehensive framework—Michael goes so far as to call it "totalitarian" in character.[29]

The widespread militarization of South China, to which we gave attention in the preceding chapter, put a premium on effective coordination. It is not to be wondered that, in their limited immediate surroundings, the followers of Hung Hsiu-chüan steadily increased in number. Defense against Punti-led militia was not the same as a forthright attack on the Ch'ing dynasty and its Confucian values, however. The transformation of the Society of God-Worshippers into the *T'ai-p'ing t'ien-kuo* permitted the transition from religious and communal protest to nationalist rebellion. From January 1851 on, Hung and his followers were in full, open opposition to the Ch'ing dynasty.

The Taiping rebels were far from unique in their willingness to use arms against the inept government. Dynastic decline by the mid-nineteenth century evoked many uprisings beyond that of Hung Hsiu-ch'üan. As the power of the administration waned, bandits, malcontents, dispossessed peasants, and disgruntled literati found scope for their discontent. The Taiping were not unique, merely unusual. The disrupted circumstances of South China facilitated the transformation of their religious sect into a rebellious nucleus. The organic development of the Society of God-Worshippers into the "Heavenly Kingdom" occurred naturally and directly, given the prevailing conditions and unorthodox beliefs of the leaders. Although various Christian concepts to which we turn in the following chapter contributed, institutional transformation came about internally. Those who built the Society presided over its reincarnation and expansion as the Taiping movement. In contrast to the Telengana rebellion, outside influences and organizational adaptations were limited, despite the overtly Christian elements.

Special about the Taiping rebels were their cohesion, fervor, and increasingly elaborate ideological justification. They seem, in retrospect, to have brought to their crusade a vision and organizational framework other rebellious groups could not match. Ideology plus organization provided the basis for the Taipings' widespread challenge to the Manchu rulers. The regulations elaborated by Hung and his immediate associates became meaningful, within the setting of transcendent beliefs, these having been emphasized by the overall conditions of social distress. Discontent was readily politicized as the Taiping rebels proclaimed their intention to unseat the dynasty and their gentry minions. Religion, far from being the supposed opiate of the masses, provided the basis for sweeping challenge to the political status quo.

Telengana: Communal and Class Bases for Conflict

Partisan politics entered Telengana from two sources. From Hyderabad City came the Majlis Ittehad-ul-Muslimin, the "Council of the Union of Muslims." With impetus from British India came the Andhra Conference, the Communist party, and Congress, to take the most important groups.

In their early days, these groups catered to the limited Hyderabad intelligentsia. Little incentive existed, under the benevolent despotism of the Nizam, for encouraging political awareness in rural areas; the government permitted seemingly innocuous cultural organizations, not explicitly political organizations. Although the prohibition on politics was not as marked as in Imperial China, the fact remained that resentment initially followed cultural lines.

Growing polarization between Hindus and Muslims took its toll on all associations in Hyderabad. Communal passions—some seeping into the state from British India, others inherent in the minority nature of the government—inflamed the political scene, especially after 1936. One witnessed, in effect, a competitive mobilization that spread to rural areas. Muslims flocked to the Ittchad; Hindus increasingly identified their interests with explicitly Hindu groups including the Arya Samaj ("Aryan League"). Communalism impeded the formation of political alliances cutting across religious lines. Once a group was perceived as disproportionately enrolling or catering to the interests of a single community, any pretense at bridging the religious gap collapsed. And, one must add, the Nizam's government was quick to pin the label of communal on groups that threatened its interests.

It is too simple to depict Hyderabad politics as revolving around the Hindu-Muslim dichotomy, however. Other political and economic issues gave rise to party activity. Major parties, including Congress and the CPI, eschewed communalism. Though the distribution of population imparted a Hindu tone to both, they stood nonetheless for a secular India.[30] It is erroneous as well to presuppose total agreement within the major communities. Differences of opinion marked both as witnessed by the millions of Muslims who willingly remained in India following partition. To most villagers, the religious make-up of the governing elite had little effect, an observation true for the subcontinent as a whole, not merely Hyderabad. Villagers' horizons and expectations were determined far more by the landlords' economic demands than by their religious affiliations. The landlords of Telengana were largely Hindu, *deshmukh* families who had accommodated themselves to the Nizam's rule with mutually advantageous results. Conflict in the countryside thus tended to be intracommunal: a matter of Hindus separated by caste and class differences. As long as "politics" remained confined to a restricted, urban minority, communalism per se did not touch the rural Hindu majority. The early 1948 actions of the razakars considerably intensified communal passions that had been relatively insignificant. Even the overlay of communalism in rural areas could not mask the intra-Hindu, land reform-oriented emphases of the Telengana rebellion.

Communal and class conflicts became inescapable and intertwined, I believe, because of the court's reluctance to update its major presuppositions and the *deshmukhs'* insistence on extracting as much as possible. Elite intransigence has contributed to many revolutions and, it follows naturally, to many rebellions. The major task of this section is to examine political shortcomings in Hyderabad that exacerbated existing discontents. The absence of means for reform in the long run undercut the ruling house and the well-off landlords associated with it.

The Nizam and his courtiers had little taste for competitive party politics. The reason was simple. One man, one vote elections would have spelled the end of the Asaf Jahi dynasty's unquestioned control. Official policy was accordingly one of avoiding concessions that implied acceptance of majority rule. Popular sovereignty, a constitutional monarchy, responsible government: all were resisted by the court in ways that abetted the politicization of discontent springing from economic and social factors. The court stood firm against political reform in the 1930s and 1940s, when other parts of India were changing with dramatic speed.

Congress, aided by the widely-reported and widely-supported actions of M.K. Gandhi, built a popular political foundation through British India by the early 1930s. Through nonviolent noncooperation and *satyagraha* campaigns, Congress made clear its desire for Indian self-government, *swaraj* replacing the British *raj*. The mass efforts seemed to have had little direct echo in Hyderabad. Not attempting to organize in the state until 1938, Congress leaders at the time concentrated on areas under direct Imperial rule. Hyderabad and other princely states were exempted from the partial implementation of the 1935 Government of India Act. As noted in Chapter 4, provisions for the accession of the princely states had not been implemented when World War II abruptly halted constitutional negotiation. The provinces of British India, however, took a fundamental political step with the installation of elected assemblies and cabinets. (Congress controlled seven provinces, the Moslem League two; coalition governments took office in the remaining two provinces.) Dominion status—independence—represented the logical next step. The principles of popular sovereignty and responsible government had been established in British India by 1937. These concepts applied quite differently in Hyderabad. Under pressure from several sources, including British advisers, the Nizam established a constitutional reform committee in September 1937. Its report, submitted eleven months later, included the following restatement of the Nizam's power:

The head of the State represents the people directly in his own person, and his connection with them, therefore, is more natural and abiding than that of any passing elected representatives. He is both the supreme head of the

State and the embodiment of his "people's sovereignty." Hence, it is that, in such a polity, the head of State not merely retains the power to confirm or veto any piece of legislation, but enjoys a special prerogative to make and un-make his executive or change the machinery of Government through which he meets the growing needs of his people. Such a Sovereign forms the basis on which our constitution rests, and has to be preserved.[31]

Such a blunt statement issued while the Hyderabad State Congress was pressing for official recognition gave little hope to those defining "people's sovereignty" in democratic terms. It meant that the political concerns of the majority had to be veiled, or presented in terms the governing minority would not reject out of hand, were organizations to get off the ground.

The Telugu-speaking Hindu intelligentsia (drawn from Madras as well as the princely state) took the first steps toward expressing majority concerns. Political desires could not be openly expressed in Hyderabad. It was through the medium of culture that the first steps were taken, with the cue coming from British India. In 1921, the Andhra Jana Sangham was formed, followed three years later by the Andhra Kendra Jana Sangham. Their official aims included establishing libraries and reading rooms, according respect to scholars, spreading knowledge through booklets and speeches, and propagating Telugu.[32] These efforts were broadened in 1930 by the establishment of the Andhra Conference, an annual session officially for cultural discussions, unofficially for expression of Hindu political concerns as in, for example, the 1937 request to the Nizam's government to devise means to lighten agricultural taxation.[33] None of these groups seemed prepared, prior to World War II, to devote time, energy, and funds to organizing rural protest. They spoke, in the muted tones intellectuals sometimes use, of cultural uplift, not of the very real problems of coordinating and politicizing popular discontent. These tasks were later assumed by individuals linked to the Communist party.

Let us look first at the Hyderabad State Congress, the largely Brahmin local offshoot of India's major nationalist party. Established by a provisional committee in July 1938 — the month before the constitutional reform committee denigrated the importance of "passing elected representatives" — the State Congress sought the seemingly impossible. It called for a noncommunal evolution toward a constitutional monarchy and electoral democracy. In the words of its statement of purpose, the State Congress favored

the attainment by the people of Responsible Government under the aegis of H.E.H. the Nizam and the Asaf Jahi dynasty. This object is to be achieved by all peaceful and legitimate means and by promoting national unity, fostering public spirit and developing and organizing the intellectual, moral, economic and industrial resources of the country.[34]

The Nizam and his advisers rejected these objectives, or at least the leadership of those who proposed them. Two days before the organizing conference was to be held, the Hyderabad State Congress was declared illegal. "The movement, ostensibly political, is in fact a cloak for subversive, communal activities," the banning notice read.[35] Leaders of the movement responded with the weapon that seemed so effective in British India, a *satyagraha* campaign. A two-month campaign in Hyderabad, in which nearly 400 were imprisoned, was called off by Gandhi himself.[36] A purportedly noncommunal expression in fact became virulently communal, with the Arya Samaj ("Aryan League") and the Hindu Mahasabha conducting simultaneous *satyagraha* campaigns. Congress's claim to represent the entire population, not only the Hindus, had been impugned. Gandhi preferred to suspend activities if the Hyderabad State Congress could not enjoy support from all sectors—a close to impossible goal, given the increasingly militant desire of Muslims to maintain untrammelled control. In the words of a Muslim newspaper, "Our aim regarding the political goal of Hyderabad is to maintain permanently the Islamic State of Hyderabad as it *is*... the Hindus of the State shall have to place perfect trust on the Musalmans and banish the idea of their being in a majority."[37] Not until July 1946 was the ban on the Hyderabad State Congress lifted. By this time, the rural dwellers of Telengana had already launched their rebellion. Congress thus could take little direct credit for the awakening of political awareness among Telugu speakers.

The shallow roots Congress was able to sink resulted from internal inattention and external suppression. By concentrating its organizational efforts on British India, Congress paid scant heed to the princely states. Even where such efforts were made, the various rulers could obstruct Congress workers. After August 1942, Congress had to confront British power as well. Its leaders spent most of World War II in prison following the "Quit India" resolution and the party's immediate proscription. Other groups seized the opportunity to entrench their own positions. The Communist party of India, which had already achieved a significant local foundation in Hyderabad and adjacent parts of Madras, was among the beneficiaries.

Communist activities in Hyderabad must be viewed from both regional and national perspectives. As we shall see more fully in the following chapter, the CPI became closely identified with the "Andhra movement," the attempt of Telugu speakers to achieve a linguistically homogeneous state. Cultural associations like the Andhra Conference furnished CPI members a logical basis from which to pursue their political goals. The spontaneous actions in rural areas provided another ground. Telengana villagers had, by late 1946, already taken important steps toward economic redistribution that gave an opening Communists were soon to recognize — although, as we shall shortly see, chief impetus came more from the landed than the landless.

The rural foundations of Communism in Telengana and other Telugu-speaking areas contrasted sharply with its urban bases elsewhere in India. The CPI had gained its main footholds in cities and working class centers, natural enough given its concern for the proletariat. Throughout the 1920s and 1930s, the party remained small, its membership reflecting its origins from "a number of nebulous groups of romantic Indian ex-patriates — students, intellectuals, and political exiles and emigres — who tried to build a Communist movement in India from abroad."[28] From 1935 on, the CPI cooperated with Congress in an anti-imperialist united front. Its junior partnership gave the CPI little scope for independent action — until the proscription of Congress in 1942.[39] The two parties had already devised separate approaches to communal awareness. As we shall see in the following chapter, the CPI increasingly encouraged self-determination on linguistic lines, a policy reflecting the roots it had sunk in various Telugu-speaking areas, as well as its assessment of the demand for a separate "Pakistan."

It was through the younger, rural-oriented members of the Andhra Conference that Indian Communists cemented their links with Telengana villagers. The abortive efforts of the Hyderabad State Congress led directly, I believe, to pressure for change from below — with the growing encouragement (surprising as it may seem) of middle landlords.

Disgruntled by the Nizam's continued rejection of petitions couched in the genteel language of well-educated Hindus, several groups favored direct action based on mass support. Peasant involvement — as Gandhi was bringing to Congress in British India — would strengthen the hand of those wishing major reform. The most important persons in reorienting political protest in Telengana were not peasants but well-off Reddis with higher education who started their efforts in the late 1920s. A dozen sons of rich and middle Telengana peasants who attended Osmania University[40] walked 110 miles through rural Hyderabad, to spread word of the 1928 Andhra Mahasabha meeting. Ravi Narayan Reddy took a leading role — as he did in the 1938 *satyagraha*, when 125 Telugus continued their non-violent resistance despite Gandhi's prohibition.[41] Their efforts were not appreciated. Congress distrusted the militancy some deemed necessary. The constitutionalist-direct action split that marked the Mau Mau uprising affected the Telengana rebellion as well. The "left" in the Andhra Mahasabha favored organizing the rural majority, the "right" preferred petition from the educated minority; the "left" pressed for economic change, the "right" called for political advance. The two schools of thought parted in 1944, with a split in the Andhra Mahasabha. Those closer to the CPI demanded the abolition of *vetti* labor and of rack-rents, confirmation of title deeds, abolition of *jagirdar* grants, drastic reductions in taxes and rents, and compulsory survey settlements.[42] Economic improvement based in the villages, versus constitutional change based in the city: this encapsulated the contrasting objectives. Given the economic and social conditions Telugu-speaking peasants experienced, the relevance of the Communists' goals should be abundantly clear.

Once again, however, I must add a word of caution. The paragraph above might be construed as meaning awareness was imported to the villagers. The usual school of thought suggests effective action on behalf of the peasants comes only with outside assistance. I agree that the rebellion was prolonged, and its class character emphasized, by CPI assistance. As Elliott wrote about Communist cadres entering Hyderabad from adjacent Telugu-speaking areas of Madras, "This leadership was crucial to the transformation of the initial peasant uprising into an organized rebellion against the Nizam and the entire feudal system."[43] These were contributory, not initiatory, however. Outside assistance came thus in *organization* and (to a lesser extent) in *ideology*; the village contribution came in *objectives*, *support*, and *initiation*. There was ample indigenous awareness of exploitation. What had to be added were means of effectively expressing this awareness, given the Hyderabad government's apparent deafness to calls for change. The ideology to which we turn in the following chapter combined objects of widespread peasant concern with appeals to cultural unity, class solidarity, and opposition to the *deshmukhs*. Internal and external elements were united in the popular beliefs of the Telengana rebellion.

Seizure of *deshmukhs'* lands in the post-World War II ferment marked the initiation of the rebellion. Partisan politics without popular elections could not bring any real change in the conditions confronting peasants. The methods Congress espoused appeared irrelevant in Telengana. Militancy among the Hindu rural majority crept in on little cat feet. What villagers discovered and Communists proclaimed opened the door to change.

Finally, we should give attention in this section to the actions of the Muslim minority. The growth of razakar activity represented a growing concern among the Nizam's entourage, and even more among middle class Muslims of Hyderabad City, about the basis of their power. Their actions, as suggested in the preceding chapter, added to the overall climate of violence.

Muslim organization started with the Majlis Ittehad-ul-Muslimin. Created in 1927, the Ittehad espoused cultural and religious objectives (such as overcoming sectarian differences) as had the parallel Andhra group. Political aims soon came to predominate. The Ittehad was converted into a proselytizing entity: conversion of Untouchables and other Hindus would help create a Muslim majority in Hyderabad.[44] The waxing strength of Congress in British India, and its threat to the status quo in the state, obviously concerned Ittehad leaders. In December 1940, for example, the Ittehad resolved to "resort to every such step as will make the existence of the State Congress and its formation abortive."[45] Ittehad militancy and threats of direct action pushed the Nizam into conceding communally defined electorates; it temporarily blocked acceptance of the standstill agreement in 1947 (Chapter 5, footnote 14). Obviously, the greater the emphasis the Ittehad laid on its Islamic roots, the less useful it became for building unity among all Hyderabadis.[46] Growing division among the communities resulted, the *mulkis*[47] losing their significance as a bridging group.

The razakars sprang from the belief that, if nothing else worked, force might preserve Muslim dominance. Organized by Kasim Razvi, third president of the Ittehad, the razakars marched onto the political scene after India and Pakistan had gained independence. Many of its members were Muslim refugees from India, victims of communal strife anxious for their own pounds of flesh. During the travails of partition, the Hyderabad government encouraged resettlement within its borders, with more than 200,000 Muslims arriving.[48] As might be expected given the unsettled conditions, the number of razakars grew rapidly. Border incidents increased, to the obvious disquiet of the Indian government. Equally disturbing were assertions attributed to Kasim Razvi: "The day is not far off when the waves of the Bay of Bengal will be washing the feet of our Sovereign"; the 45 million Muslims of India will be "fifth columnists" in any showdown between Hyderabad and India.[49] Razakars took an oath to "fight to the last to maintain the supremacy of the Muslim power in the Deccan."[50] The reported presence of 200,000 razakars and 42,000 troops in the Hyderabad forces indicated the willingness of the Nizam's government to defend itself.[51] Communal antagonism thus grew apace; the class antagonism evident in Telengana interacted with the efforts of Muslim extremists to preserve their dominance.

There is thus an intriguing parallelism in the evolution of Hyderabad politics. Cultural, linguistic and religious ties furnished the initial basis for organizing. The Andhra Conference and the Ittehad catered to groups defined on ascriptive lines. Congress reflected the constitutional orientation of its constituents, but received short shrift from the Nizam's government. The militancy of villagers, egged on by Communist organizers and further encouraged by the razakars' violence, illustrated the weakening of any "political" approaches. Efforts at reform were blocked by major landlords. Confrontation replaced accommodation, adaptation and apathy as the usual approaches to politics. Discontent became focused along communal and class lines. The conditions were ripe for ideologies of violent struggle, as well as for organizations directed toward collective political violence. As in Kenya, it seemed as though no avenue for peaceful change remained.

Mau Mau: Constraints on African Political Expression

The British long have prided themselves on the rights enjoyed by His Majesty's subjects. Embodied in longstanding practice, in legal codes, and in a general attitude of political tolerance, political freedoms extended to those under the Crown. Such was the practice for British subjects; but such was mostly the theory for British "protected persons." In the colonial realm, the exercise of rights taken for granted in the U.K. was restricted. Those living in a protectorate such as Kenya remained liable to significant abridgements of political freedoms.

Kenya obviously posed a complex problem for British administrators. The paramountcy principle—the concept that the interests of Africans should prevail over those of other races—contrasted markedly with the manner in which many early administrators reinforced settler privileges. Some, indeed, had encouraged the belief that the minority community could achieve substantial powers of self-government. The year the Devonshire Commission enunciated paramountcy, Southern Rhodesia gained internal autonomy; there, a relatively small settler group exercised full control over the African majority without interference from London. As long as Kenya was regarded as "white man's country," the British government would be subject to pressure for transferring powers from the local administration to the settlers.[52] Dominion status remained the Europeans' goal. Political control would gravitate into their hands; they felt themselves best qualified to judge Africans' needs, and felt that the economy depended on their contributions. As was suggested in Chapter 3, many British administrators shared this belief in the advisability of devolving internal control to settlers. A substantial group in Nairobi and in London thus favored a Rhodesian-style solution as the basis for responsible self-government.

Countering this set of preferences were the concepts of trusteeship and paramountcy, expressed in the Devonshire report. In its words, "in the administration of Kenya His Majesty's Government regard themselves as exercising a trust on behalf of the African population, and they are unable to delegate or share this trust, the object of which may be defined as the protection and advancement of the native races."[53] Such a principle seemed to preclude transfer of control to any group other than the majority. The task of the British administration would be preparation for self-government in African hands. Though responsibility might rest *pro tem* with officers of the Colonial Service, the long-term goal meant, in effect, their working themselves out of jobs. A classic image, most clearly enunciated by Margery Perham, was that of scaffolding: erected by His Majesty's Government, it would be dismantled once local, majority-based institutions had proven their capabilities.[54] Which concept was the more important: political advance by the settlers, or political advance by the Africans?

The contrast between promise and reality, between the long-term evolution toward African self-government and the short-term denial of (for example) the franchise or the right to organize political parties became increasingly obvious to the majority in Kenya. The extension of education played a part, as did the example of movement toward self-government in other parts of the colonial empire. The proclamation of 1923—"the interests of the African natives must be paramount"—was stressed by African spokesmen far more than its immediate qualifier, "His Majesty's Government cannot but regard the grant of responsible self-government as out of the question within any period of time which need now to be taken into consideration."[55] The conflict between minority and majority was sidestepped by simply proclaiming the Africans incapable of governing until they had served a prolonged tutelage.

Constrained space precludes recounting how these conflicting perspectives were shaped and brought into practice. What requires attention at this point are the implications for African political organizations in Kenya. The conditions under which these could operate, and the areas of concern the administration permitted them, have direct implications for our central concern. Collective political violence in Kenya was in large measure the product of denied opportunities and blatant exploitation. The sense of inequity aroused by colonial rule found an outlet in rebellious groups when possible channels for peaceful settlement were choked off.

Combining administrative responsibility for trusteeship with the paramountcy of African interests and with encouragement of settler agriculture required squaring the political circle. The result was a series of compromises, untenable in the long run, among these conflicting tendencies. The usual pragmatic solution involved distinguishing between separate and hardly equal areas of political initiative each major race might exercise. Europeans enjoyed access from an early period to the powers exercised from Nairobi. The key institutions were the Legislative Council and Executive Council (Legco and Exco). Both grew from advisory bodies of officials and nominated persons serving the governor, into elected groups enjoying legislative rights or supervising government departments.[56] The first elections for Legco were held in January 1920; elected Europeans assumed ministerial responsibilities shortly after World War II. These official opportunities were buttressed by informal ties between administrators and settlers that resulted from race, language, culture, belief in the inherent superiority of European civilization, and acceptance of a long-term responsibility for the minority community. Such links, official and attitudinal, meant an apparent unity of view when it came to African political rights. Though some might be granted in due time, the "strenuous conditions of the modern world," in the words of the League of Nations Covenant, made the early achievement of African rule unlikely. What the majority thus perceived as a monolithic European bloc stood willing to counter any significant moves toward majority responsibilities.

The sphere of responsibility commonly assigned to Africans was local government. The 1947 proclamation, quoted in Chapter 3, emphasized apprenticeship in village and district councils. The settler community concurred in this stress, to the extent its members countenanced any African exercise of political rights. Local Native Councils were to provide basic training in governmental skills, presumably on a nonpartisan basis. Growing expertise would, in time, permit the exercise of wider responsibilities. Such development from below could coexist, albeit uneasily, with the superstructure of Legco and Exco. Accordingly, as long as Africans were willing to accept starting with basics—with sanitation measures in local markets or with grazing ordinances—the British government, and some parts of the settler community, would acquiesce. Once Africans pressed for rights akin to those Europeans exercised, informally as well as formally, the hackles of the settlers rose, and bureaucratic caution came to the fore. The line was drawn in the 1940s, and well into the 1950s, against indigenous movements seeking majority rule in any pattern other than that prescribed by HMG. The combination of postwar African militancy with more pronounced settler rigidity and with greater administrative involvement reawakened and expanded political awareness. The lines for confrontation were drawn.

The earliest major stirrings of African political awareness owed much to World War I and the steps taken by the European community immediately thereafter. Settlers wrested an increasing degree of control from the colonial administration, in the process showing little affection for those sent by London. (One spokesman more noted for his acid tongue than his sense of political moderation welcomed the new governor in 1919 with a frontal asssault on the minions of the Colonial Office: "We hold that the Secretariat has no function in governing this country...men of little more brain than the creatures that crawl about at the bottom of the sea...The time has come for them to go.")[57] The East African Protectorate became the Crown Colony of Kenya in mid-1920. European veterans were offered land for settlement gratis. Africans were required to obtain and carry a registration certificate (*kipande*), intended to reinforce administrative control over them. Court cases brought home to the majority the tenuous nature of the rights they enjoyed under the 1915 Crown Lands Ordinance, which formally vested title in the Crown; meanwhile, property directly controlled by settlers increased. To the official African death toll in the war of nearly 24,000 was added 100,000 deaths in Kikuyuland alone in a postwar influenza epidemic.[58] A proposed cut in African wages in mid-1921 added the seemingly final straw to the accumulation of grievances. The discontent among the majority populace, and most noticeable among the Kikuyu, began both to take organizational form and to attract administrative pressure. The Kikuyu elite and some European supporters—more specifically, some influential African headmen and chiefs from southern and central Kiambu, many of them Christians, and a few missionaries led by Arthur Barlow—moved to protest. Their catalogue of grievances covered a wide area, ranging from increases in taxes to the proposed cut in wages, from the limited opportunities for education to the alienation of land and imposition of the *kipande*. That these concerns were voiced by the Kikuyu elite with a modicum of European encouragement should be noted. Moderate reform through existing channels, rather than continued exacerbation of indigenous grievances, might have resulted. However, the support of many influentials was forfeited when a young, relatively well-travelled Kikuyu named Harry Thuku sent telegrams in the other notables.[59] The elite was thus outflanked; the younger and more militant seized the initiative. The colonial administration in turn became increasingly concerned about the slide toward open, popularly-based protest. The arrest of Thuku in March 1922, an attempted general strike in Nairobi, and police firing on a group estimated at six to seven thousand Africans resulting (officially) in twenty-one deaths, marked the confrontation. Although the East African Association quickly declined, the events of 1921-2 "lingered long in the general political consciousness, and the African version of what happened became part of the political education of new generations."[60]

To see parallels between Kenya after World War I and Kenya after World War II is easy—perhaps deceptively easy. Settler desire to exercise great control remained, with the selection of a European elected member to the Executive Council akin to the 1920 opening of the Legislative Council. Land settlement schemes were proposed for European veterans; Africans who fought in World War II felt excluded from any recognition. The *kipande* grievance lingered, with Europeans angrily rebuffing any attempt to provide identity cards for all races in 1947.[61] Educational opportunities for the majority remained minimal. Above all, the weight of the alien presence mounted, as noted earlier, relative to pressures on squatters and agricultural improvements in the reserves. The handful of African representatives in Legco could show little evidence of their pleas for reform falling on receptive ears. More militant approaches to concerns held by many Africans became increasingly attractive as legislation seemed insufficient. The early 1920s had witnessed a split over tactics between the Kikuyu influentials grouped in the Kikuyu Association, and the more urbanized, "detribalized" Africans grouped in the East African Association. The late 1940s witnessed an analogous divergence in tactics—though certainly not in goals—between the Kenya African Union (KAU) and the more radically inclined veterans and trade unionists sheltered under its umbrella.

These similarities should not conceal important differences between the two post war settings. The entire context of imperial rule had changed from 1918 to 1945. For example, India after World War I had barely embarked on the modest Morley-Minto reforms, while Congress had only started to find mass expression through Gandhi. India after World War II was in the throes of partition and a transfer of power far more rapid than expected. Anti-colonial uprisings in the Dutch East Indies and French Indochina indicated the weakening of European political control; the Chinese revolution suggested the potential militancy of peasants. The actions of the United States and the Soviet Union, amplified through the United Nations with its growing membership, further ripped the fabric of imperial control. The Cold War introduced a clear bipolarity into international relations absent from earlier decades. The British colonial empire expanded after World War I; it started dramatically to shrink after World War II. From many sides, accordingly, the seeming cavalier disregard for indigenous rights that characterized the 1920s came under increasing question in the 1940s and 1950s. Imperialism had to be justified, meaning that rights of labor and political organizing and more conscious steps toward indigenous development entered the colonial context. In Kenya itself, this entailed stress on rural economic improvement—Sir Philip Mitchell's schemes for land reclamation in the reserves—and a conscious approach toward multiracialism.

In preceding chapters, I attempted to clarify the grounds of discontent on which Mau Mau was to thrive. It remains more specifically to indicate the backgrounds of the uprising's leaders and the organizational forms they sought to use.

Mau Mau was, from its inception, a series of Kikuyu parallel protests against the British presence emanating from the squatters, the landless of the reserves, the urban lumpenproletariat, and the "40 generation" of young men. It would be fairer to say that leaders were developed as a result of mass actions, rather than mass actions developed as a result of leaders, in the preparation for collective action, the high regard felt for Kenyatta notwithstanding. Given the profound sense of Kikuyu discontent, few could have halted its propagation. Early actions in the Emergency, notably the enforced return of squatters to the reserves, accentuated discontent.

Noting that discontent arose from multiple sources does not mean an absence of leadership, however. The transformation of the potential for collective action into collective political violence required individuals willing and able to take a crucial step, to use guerrilla-style confrontation. Such persons rose to the top through British action. Because those oriented toward constitutionalist steps had been incarcerated at the start of the Emergency, leadership gravitated to younger, more impetuous, more militant persons. On their shoulders, not on those of Jomo Kenyatta, rested leadership in the armed phase of Mau Mau. They responded to, and in turn encouraged, the rural radicalism that had erupted among the squatters, and the urban radicalism that the underemployed of Nairobi manifested. The most discontented, in other words, furnished the impetus, the most militant the direct leadership.

The armed phase, however, occurred after other avenues of change had been explored and found wanting. Reforms of the nature Africans increasingly wished could not be encompassed within the values and timetable held by the colonial administration and the European settlers. Demands Europeans regarded as nonnegotiable were viewed by indigenous Kenyans as basic rights. No wonder, then, that Kikuyu concerns remained relatively unchanged during the colonial period. What Thuku telegraphed to London in 1922 remained on the agenda for action thirty years later—while Thuku, in turn, had based his telegram on items that had weighed increasingly on Africans since the Europeans' advent.

The Kikuyu were not the most economically aggrieved of indigenous Kenyans; they were, however, the most discontent. Their adaptability to changed circumstances, their thirst for education, and their quest for upward mobility accentuated what geographic proximity had initiated. Rather than cling tenaciously to pre-colonial ways of life, Kikuyu wanted to enjoy and incorporate aspects of the modern age. The barriers to achieving these confronted all members of the ethnic group, irrespective of their backgrounds. Some may have gained from association with the colonial power; all were aware of restrictions. The differences we shall consider shortly regarding tactics should not be allowed to overshadow the unanimity with which Kikuyu agreed that "stolen lands" should be returned and that constraints on their economic and political initiative should be lifted.

To the broad unity of goals, we should add acceptance of Jomo Kenyatta as the leading Kikuyu spokesman. I have already sketched some of the grounds for his popularity. Prolonged absence may have helped his political status: he avoided intra-Kikuyu feuds of the 1930s and early 1940s, returning unsullied as well as respected. His decades of association with indigenous protest, his ability to help bring a halt to several administrative schemes for compulsory agricultural improvement, his spellbinding oratory, and his educational and literary achievements, gave him a unique aura. Kenyatta came to mean many things to many people. His name could be — and indeed was — invoked in support of many goals. The question remains, to be certain, regarding his direct contribution in the drift toward militancy. Was Kenyatta more the active encourager, the passive observer, or the skeptical opponent? Was the man recognized as the leader of the Kikuyu in fact the leader of the Mau Mau rebellion? I believe no, his tactical preference being more for negotiation than for armed confrontation. His skills, after all, could be better employed in fostering public protest and in negotiating with the English whose language and ways he understood than in leading a guerrilla struggle he knew might be suicidal.

It was over questions of tactics that the Kikuyu divided, not over questions of goals or Kenyatta's preminence. After World War II, as after World War I, many members of the elite — and especially those from the more cosmopolitan Kiambu district — sought reform; their step-by-step strategy appeared to the more impatient, the younger, and often the less educated, to be doomed to failure. If the existing channels had proven impotent in the past, little hope existed for them to become powerful in the future. Yes, Great Britain could be urged to make good her promises to translate the paramountcy principle into meaningful steps toward land reform and majority rule; however, history offered little reason for optimism. The more militant preferred to lunge for the entire loaf, rather than nibble at the crumbs the British might let drop. The actions of the colonial administration described in the preceding chapter gave greater credence to those who favored force: reasoned approaches such as constitutional moderates favored seemed unreasonable to those petitioned for change.

Scholars seem generally agreed that Kenyatta was aware of the drift toward confrontation. He could do little to slow it, let alone reverse the current already flowing. There were, after all, many roads to political advance; negotiation often came only after both parties had paraded their strengths. Kenyatta, far more than other Kenyans, was aware of Nkrumah's "positive action" campaign in the Gold Coast, the principles of Congress expressed in the "Quit India" resolution, or even the actions of the Sinn Fein. He may well have suspected that moderation would not triumph over a group that gripped power as tenaciously as the European settlers of Kenya, supported in most respects by the colonial administration. The endemic discontent of the Kikuyu, made more manifest by political organizations, provided a godsend to moderates and militants alike: the moderates could claim they represented the better alternative, the militants could claim popular wishes supported their claims. Even a response as determined as that brought by the state of emergency temporarily advanced the Kikuyu sense of grievance. The politicization of discontent made tactical questions paramount. How could the numbers and concerns of the African majority be turned most effectively against the European minority?

To shed light on this question, let us examine the means whereby the seemingly voiceless sought to proclaim their political objectives. Achieving Kikuyu and Kenyan African unity became the desideratum, the spread of oathing the major means. As had workers' groups in the Industrial Revolution,[62] African groups translated the potential of numbers into the strength of numbers by pledges of unity.

Three sources of oaths must be noted: the defensive oath employed by squatters in the Highlands, the leadership oath spread among the Kikuyu elite at Kiambu, and the oaths of the urban militants.

Among the squatters, solidarity was needed in the face of administrative and settler pressure. The European objective, as noted previously, was the transformation of squatters into resident agricultural laborers. The squeeze on their livelihood was marked. Africans had numbers, Europeans had power; only by mobilizing the majority into an unshakeable alliance might the balance be righted. Strikes were difficult, migration affected by the shortage of land in the reserves and settler solidarity. Oathing was accordingly defensive in origin, "necessitated by the need of the squatters to protect themselves from the gradual erosion of their status as tenants."[63] The Olenguruone expellees utilized oathing for analogous reasons.

A second source of oathing was the Kikuyu elite itself, as grouped within the Kikuyu Central Association (KCA). KCA had been formed in 1924. It linked, according to Rosberg and Nottingham, "the elements within the tribe that psychologically did not fully accept European dominance . . .[and] from the beginning the KCA represented...a solid nucleus of the tribe in their rejection of the racial and authoritarian scaffolding erected over them."[64] The group was banned in 1940 on grounds it was plotting insurrection. KCA leaders spent World War II interned in the arid, isolated outpost of Kapenguria (in 1953, the celebrated locale of the trial of Jomo Kenyatta and five others). After their release, all former KCA branch officers and committeemen took an oath of solidarity. This "loyalty" oath, according to one specialist, was limited in extent to "reliable, experienced, generally older men, not for the young militants among the ex-World War II servicemen . . .".[65] Its moderation may be compared with the pledge of loyalty made to the British Crown by members of Local Native Councils in the 1920s, that inspiring in turn oathing within the KCA itself.[66] Selective oathing in the Kikuyu Central Association in fact entailed a gradualist rather than a radical approach. Rosberg and Nottingham suggest the ceremony was intended "slowly to persuade the elite to join the nationalist movement through taking an oath."[67]

The mass oathing of the squatters lay behind the 1950 proscription of the "Mau Mau Association"; the mass oathing of persons in the reserves lay behind the 1952 declaration of the state of emergency. The latter extension reflected the injection of a new ginger group in Kenyan politics. It was urban militants who encouraged the significant extension of solidarity through oathing. Working in and through KAU (the Kenya African Union), World War II veterans and labor leaders such as Bildad Kaggia and Fred Kubai pressed for confrontation rather than moderation. They took over the important Nairobi branch of KAU. Friction grew between KAU leaders and its Nairobi offshoot, since the former (in Kaggia's words) "continued to oppose most of our plans because they regarded us as extremists."[68] Extension of oathing, including use of coercion, came from the militants. Again in Kaggia's words,

> We decided that the movement could not succeed unless it was a mass organization. We ordered the oath to be administered to as many people as possible. All means were to be used to get people to come over: persuasion, bribes, and even force, where necessary.[69]

Political advance would have to be accelerated. Pressure from the KAU radicals put the organization on record, in its 1951 conference, as favoring independence in three years—the first direct espousal by Africans of such a rapid timetable. The lines of confrontation were hardening.

At first blush, the mobilization for collective action achieved by Mau Mau leaders is impressive. By mid-1952, a vast majority of the Kikuyu had taken the initial oath. This outpouring of support must be viewed against the background of the ineffectiveness of, and the profound Kikuyu alienation from, existing institutions. Local District Councils provided little if any scope for reform. Political parties had little reason for existence: trade unions were confined in essence to Nairobi and were proscribed from political activities.[70] What may be seen as an organizational vacuum existed. Relative deprivation was high, the sense of grievance marked, potentially countervailing institutions ineffectual. Taking an oath seemed to present few risks to initiates. The act of initial commitment was relatively simple, from mid-1950 to the proclamation of the Emergency, the scope of obligations seemingly minimal and unclear. Acquiescence shading into passive support was thus achieved in the face of a government concerned with many matters other than rural Kikuyu discontent.

The scope of support according Mau Mau, I have already noted, stopped well short of a majority of rural Kenyans. I would ascribe this to the endemic conflict within KAU between the moderate wing of Kenyatta and the militant wing of Kaggia, Kubai, and (more speculatively) Kimathi. The division was epitomized in the 1951 KAU elections. To avoid "tribalism," Kenyatta warned, officers chosen must represent Kenya's ethnic and regional diversity—in other words, avoiding charges of narrow tribalism by recognizing that all tribes had a stake in political progress. The Nairobi branch of KAU, dominated by Kaggia and his allies, walked out, believing (correctly) that this *dictat* was as motivated by Kenyatta's fear of urban Kikuyu radicalism as by his desire for pan-tribal unity. Kaggia et al. desired intensity of commitment and militancy, even at the cost of leaving non-Kikuyu in the lurch; Kenyatta et al. wanted the veneer of interethnic collaboration, even at the risk of alienating the *aile marchante*. Confrontation triumphed; according to Rosberg and Nottingham, "the radical militants succeeded in ousting the constitutional nationalists and gaining virtual control of the national executive committee."[71] The conference called for independence in three years (a pan-African recognition, perhaps, of Kwame Nkrumah's electoral victory in 1951 with the simple slogan, "Self-Government NOW"). Paced, gradual political progress—even had the British been willing at that stage to negotiate it—had few defenders within KAU. Murray-Brown described the situation thus:

> The atmosphere grew heavy with fear, suspicion and hatred. Despite Kenyatta's attempt to make KAU inter-tribal, the Kikuyu were cutting themselves off from the rest of the Africans in Kenya, and the moderates among them were isolated.[72]

There certainly were efforts to spread militancy beyond the Kikuyu. Paul Ngei (a Wakamba) and Achieng Oneko (a Luo) served on the KAU executive committee. But several factors militated against the transference of grievances. Among the agricultural groups of Kenya, the Kikuyu had felt most strongly the consequences of European settlement. The turbulent setting of Nairobi communicated concern and discontent, but essentially to the Kikuyu. Terracing and destocking campaigns were felt most heavily by the Kikuyu, as were the tightened restrictions on agricultural labor. Those useful harbingers of political awareness, education and participation in the cash economy, had already differentiated the Kikuyu from other groups. Local political institutions appear to have absorbed energies among the Kamba, for example, but not among the Kikuyu. Summing up these observations, one may conclude that the Kikuyu constituted the "leading edge" of Kenyan African politics, whose solidarity and commitment to change could be depicted as tribal chauvinism. The greater militancy became, the more clearly the Kikuyu nature of KAU emerged. No organization could mask this basic fact.

Finally, we should note that, even among the Kikuyu, the tactics the militants favored appealed disproportionately to some groups. Young males have traditionally provided cannon fodder; the Mau Mau rebellion was no exception. Uprisings motivated by land grievances have traditionally drawn most supporters from the poor and landless; again, the Mau Mau rebellion seems no exception. The geographic origins and ties of leaders affect the composition of followers; once again, the Mau Mau rebellion accorded with what one might expect.

Old men — over 40 — were rare among the forest fighters of the Aberdares and Mount Kenya. This arose naturally from the context of Kikuyu society. The *batuni* (platoon) oath, to which we give attention in the following chapter, was administered to males aged sixteen to thirty. Karari Njama indicated the great majority of the fighters were twenty-five to thirty.[73] Women rarely were recruited as combatants, filling instead roles as nurses, cooks, and companions for the leaders; and in any case Mau Mau women were substantially outnumbered by men.[74] As the young dominated the partisans, correspondingly the old controlled the Kikuyu Home Guard. The cleavage suggests, though does not prove, a recurrence of a customary handing-over of control from one Kikuyu generation to another. The *itwika* ceremonies had traditionally marked the accession of a new group to power, but colonial policy had driven the practice underground. Mau Mau hymns extolled the responsibility of the "young men to rise up in arms," while the elders should "shut up."[75] It may be, accordingly, that the Mau Mau rebellion drew part of its justification from longstanding tribal rhythms that should be honored, despite the colonial presence.[76] Evidence once again, it would seem, of the mixed "traditional"-"modern" nature of the Mau Mau rebellion.

I cannot — regretfully — furnish precise information on the economic circumstances of Mau Mau fighters. Furedi has documented the important leadership role of traders, artisans and farm teachers in the white highlands.[77] The bulk of those oathed, however, came from the squatter population, whose parlous state we have already considered. It stands to reason that the rootless had the most to gain, the least to lose. The rebellion appears not to have developed a clear ideology of class struggle; the Kikuyu as a whole experienced a sense of deprivation relative to the Europeans, yet were divided along economic and regional lines. The overwhelming significance of land in Mau Mau claims, and the undoubted

prevalence of landlessness in the reserves, seem to give credence to suggestions that those with property threw in their lot with the British, those
without property struggled for change. The composition of the Kikuyu
Home Guard, examined in Chapter 8, provides some basis for this claim.

Were landlessness the sole basis for recruitment of fighters, one might
have expected Kiambu district to have furnished a substantial share. It did
not. Mau Mau partisans were drawn disproportionately from the northern-
most Kikuyu area, Nyeri district. This reflected, it seems clear, the
geographic origins of the major forest leaders, Dedan Kimathi and Stanley
Mathenge. Their militancy was most readily accepted by those sharing
loyalties sustained by location. To some extent, differential access to
education affected recruitment into Mau Mau. Kiambu district had long
enjoyed a lion's share of schools, part of whose curriculum included British
Empire history—which, in turn, was studded with examples of suppressed
indigenous dissidence. Such information may have influenced the
educated.[78] Illiterates who joined Mau Mau might glory in their resuscita-
tion of the warrior tradition; literates who shied away from militancy
might congratulate themselves on their prudence. The rank-and-file guerrillas enjoyed little book learning—further reason for their seeming exclusion from the rewards the colonial administration sprinkled among the
Kikuyu. The educated enjoyed greater access to official positions—further
reason for their willingness to remain on the fence while others retreated to
the forests. Despite the ideology of ethnic unity, the fact remained that
Mau Mau activists constituted a fraction, and a small one at that, of the
entire Kikuyu populace. Though all felt discontent, only a few entered the
forests to engage in guerrilla struggle. It was a difference observable far
more clearly in Kenya than in Kwilu, where the indiscriminate repression
of Congolese soldiers afflicted all.

Kwilu: The Rewards of Opposition

Pierre Mulele served his political apprenticeship within a legal movement. The Parti Solidaire Africain (PSA) controlled Kwilu when independence came 30 June 1960; its leaders became ministers in the central
government. PSA officials filled, among other positions, deputy prime
minister, minister of education, and president of Leopoldville Province
when independence was granted. These testify to the support the party
mobilized in Kwilu. Given the influence the PSA could wield, its involvement in rebellion may thus seem paradoxical. Rebellion was to come in
part because the high aspirations of independence could not be sustained,
the composition of the government changed, and the party split. One section
of the PSA passed into opposition, thence into collective political violence.

The rewards Congolese leaders dealt out remained confined to a privileged few; aspirations denied proved potent basis for politicization.

The organizational opportunities afforded the PSA contrasted markedly with the clandestine conditions under which the preceding rebellions were initially organized. The early followers of the Society of God-Worshippers met in secret, their political aims subsumed within religious messages; the activities of various Andhra groups remained screened behind cultural objectives; the Kikuyu Central Association was forced underground by proscription, while KAU enjoyed only a restricted field of initiative. A group seeking major change but required to work in a covert manner confronts many obstacles. A premium on secrecy, perhaps a sacrifice of widespread proselytization in order to create a secure, dedicated nucleus: such are clear impediments to organizing a large-scale popular foundation.

Admittedly, the extent of secrecy necessary depends on the surveillance the incumbents choose to mount, or are able to mount. Dynastic inefficiency and distance gave Hung Hsiu-ch'üan reasonable initial latitude; the Nizam's government paid little heed to Telengana villagers in the turbulent days of 1946-7; in the late 1940s, officials in Nairobi appear to have considered reports of Kikuyu unrest exaggerated. The extent of necessary secrecy varies as well with the manner in which change would affect the particular group. An oppressed group whose members enjoy scant opportunity for reward or advancement obviously provides a far more secure basis for clandestine activity than a subordinated group with some opportunities for mobility based on service to the dominant group.

In Kwilu, the move into secrecy came after the rural areas had been openly politicized. I shall concentrate in this chapter on the period of public electoral competition. This period—from February 1959 through early 1962—marked the rise of the PSA in rural Kwilu, its leaders' brief incorporation into government positions, a rupture in the central administration leading to the exclusion of PSA leaders Pierre Mulele and Antoine Gizenga from major posts, and the fragmentation of the PSA into two hostile wings. The support the Gizenga-Mulele wing of the PSA had mobilized was later converted into backing for collective political violence. The major struggle thus came *after* the political foundations for collective action had been laid. Success born of striving for votes differed in kind from success born (as in the Taiping or Telengana rebellions) of violently displacing village leaders.

As was true for many Congolese political parties, the PSA initially took shape in Leopoldville among upwardly mobile immigrant groups. The political ferment of the city, manifested in the 1959 riots, had clear and direct impact. Non-Bakongo groups took up the call for rapid political advance. Kwango and Kwilu district citizens residing in Leopoldville founded the Parti Solidaire Africain February 1, 1959, its objectives being "Emancipation of the African people in all domains [and] accession of the people to independence (by defined steps)."[79] Worthy of note is the reference to African people: the party sought a role wider than district, province, or perhaps even the Congo itself. Also meriting note was the party's intention "to combat any obstacle to political parties' extending themselves into rural areas . . . ."[80] Concern for popular mobilization thus emerged early in the party's history.

From May 1959 on, the PSA rooted itself in the Kwilu district of Leopoldville Province and, to a lesser extent, in the Kwango district. A powerful conjunction of elite and mass aspirations took place. Both hungered for changes of the sort immediate independence offered. Evidence of the strong local desire for rapid alteration came in the sale of PSA membership cards: funds flowed into the party treasury more rapidly than cards could be printed and distributed. Payment of the subscription fee, many seem to have assumed, was equivalent to payment of taxes. Local enthusiasm, aptly characterized by Weiss as "rural radicalism,"[81] was fueled by inflated promises. The masses wanted independence to bring economic advancement; the party was ready to promise better conditions for all. A PSA electoral poster of early 1960 sketched a rosy picture of what independence would bring:

VOTE PSA

A PSA Government

Promises You Immediately

1. Total reduction of unemployment and work for all.
2. Multiplication of schools especially in rural areas. Free primary and secondary education.
3. Increased salaries for all.
4. Improved housing in rural areas.
5. Free medical care for all non-salaried people.[82]

A massive social promotion and implied economic redistribution were to result from political advance. Benefits would be fully shared by the rural majority.

With elections for the Provincial Assembly and the National Assembly over, however, the locus of political activity returned to the cities. *Politi-*

que de coulisse replaced mass politicization. The thoroughly aroused rural populace was to leave to its elected representatives the task of making these inflated promises good.

The PSA formed a key bloc in the coalition Prime Minister Lumumba assembled just prior to independence. PSA President Gizenga became deputy prime minister, PSA Vice-President Mulele minister of National Education and Fine Arts, and PSA directeur-adjoint of the Political Bureau Joachim Masen minister of Labor — all these, though the PSA controlled only 13 of the 137 National Assembly seats. At the provincial level, the PSA obtained 35 of the 90 Provincial Assembly seats (perhaps surprisingly, two more than ABAKO). Cleophas Kamitatu (head of the PSA in Leopoldville Province) became president, with Norbert Leta, Celestin Kalunga and Sebastien Balongi receiving important portfolios.[83]

Operating at national and provincial levels took its toll on the party. The heterogeneity of the PSA made it a ready target for fission. Contrasts in orientation — the national view in Leopoldville versus the provincial view in Kikwit — in personality, in ideology, and in ethnicity opened up.[84] First to open was the contrast based on the geographical locus of the particular decision-maker. Concern for local autonomy was at the heart of political feelings among citizens of Kwilu. As Weiss has written, "For them, political action at first meant primarily emerging from the dark rural hinterland: they wanted to have a sense of involvement in their and their country's future. The frustration of not having been able to do this before engendered the virtual explosion of energy with which they established the PSA organization in the Kwilu district, but it also meant that they resented taking orders from Leopoldville or any implication that they were less sophisticated."[85] This rural-urban split, as it were, was reinforced by personality and *amour propre*. Tensions grew between Kamitatu on the one hand and Gizenga and Mulele on the other. These rivalries were in turn linked to the split between the Lumumbists and the supporters of the central government. The latter two, having been closely associated with Lumumba, took prominent positions in the rival government established at Stanleyville.[86] When efforts were made to conciliate the rival factions, Gizenga and Mulele initially acquiesced, then changed their minds. Gizenga returned to Lumumbist capital Stanleyville in August 1961, and was arrested in January 1962; Mulele in the same period went to Egypt as ambassador of the Stanleyville government and remained outside the Congo until mid-1963, at which point he returned home to prepare the rebellion — the training he had by then received in China to be pressed into service. Kamitatu by contrast threw in his lot with the new national government of Cyrille Adoula. Kamitatu became minister of the Interior in July 1962, minister of Economic Coordination and Plan in April 1963. His *modus operandi* changed as well. By 1962, he had shed his populist trappings; he became, in Young's judgment, "radically different"[87] from the local, agitational role he had filled prior to independence. Gizenga and Mulele, by contrast, clung to their Lumumbist beliefs. Finally, ethnic factors obtruded as well. The Kamitatu wing of the PSA received Mbala support; the Gizenga-Mulele wing received Pende and Mbunda support. The tribe of the leader, in other words, helped determine those who became affiliated. Such was not a matter of choice by those at the top of the party. Formally, they stood strongly against such manifestations of ascription. Their backing, however, depended on delivering goods and services to those of like background. As Weiss notes, "the modern elite leaders in the PSA were being viewed — or perhaps had been viewed all along — as delegates of ethnic interests within the party rather than as 'guides' who would be followed unquestionably." Once the ethnic character of the two wings had been established, recreation of party unity became next to impossible, given the number of divisive issues.[88]

Independence won, the division of the spoils started to differentiate those who profited from those who paid. After 30 June 1960, Congolese parties suffered from progressive inanition. It was no longer useful for party leaders to stir popular passions; those in control favored a calming of the tensions and expectations they had encouraged a few months earlier. The PSA was one of the few that still favored rural change, and thus fell increasingly into disrepute with the Leopoldville government. Military intervention, the installation of the short-lived Collège des Commissaires, and the attempt by followers of Lumumba to establish a separate government in Stanleyville, brought the Gizengist wing of the PSA into disrepute. The armed forces closed the Kikwit office of the Party in November 1960; it was not to reopen for more than two years.[89] One might have assumed that politicization in Kwilu had proven evanescent, flaring up in the pre-independence inflation of participation, collapsing after mid-1960 in the post-independence deflation of expectations. Such an impression mistook surface calm among the rural populace for acceptance, or at least acquiescence. Although the formal trunk of the PSA organization may have gone by the boards, its rural roots were still deeply embedded. In some respects, the PSA had been strengthened as a basis for collective action. Party identification and ethnic identification had in essence fused by this point. Thus, even though public activities by the Gizengist wing of the PSA may have ceased, the network of connections remained. Collective action in the interests of the Party/ethic group could still be roused. Rural radicalism was not dead, but temporarily dormant.

Rural radicalism had a spokesman in Mulele, who (after the dismissal of Lumumba) remained apart from the central government of the Congo, and thus could direct his critical barbs against those who profited from independence. At this point, it is appropriate to pause and furnish relevant biographical details. Mulele was among the handful of educated Congolese with military experience. Born 25 July 1929, in the Idiofa area, he graduated from the Ecole Moyenne in Leverville, having earlier quit the Jesuit seminary at Kinzambi also attended by Gizenga and Kamitatu.[90] Mulele's exposure to the Force Publique came after he left school, as part of the compulsory service he had to provide the government. He moved to Leopoldville, becoming in 1956 vice-president of his alumni association. Politically most important in 1959 were his visit to Guinea (at the time, the most radical state in tropical Africa) and his election as assistant general secretary of the PSA. His selection for Lumumba's cabinet followed his election to the National Assembly in May 1960.[91] The success that marked his career made Mulele a hero to many persons in rural Kwilu, particularly fellow Mbunda.

What turned Mulele from a cabinet minister pursuing a peaceful, profitable parliamentary calling, into an advocate of collective political violence based on village dwellers? His decision apparently was made the same year as Lumumba's execution. By September 1961, when he and other Congolese leaders then living in exile compared notes on what they should do, he already had decided to travel to China. The launching of the Kwilu rebellion was thus not a spontaneous eruption; it stemmed from the conjuncture between a willing leader and a ready set of followers. Mulele had come to believe that only force could displace the government fattening on the fruits of independence. I cannot offer a simple explanation of his decision. One possible cause may have been his exposure in Cairo to the echoes of the Algerian revolution. What Fanon was writing about the role of peasants Mulele wished to put into practice. His more radical bent — a consequence perhaps of his links to the mobilized populace of Kwilu — estranged him from the government in Leopoldville. He could not (having thrown in his lot with the Stanleyville government) penetrate the inner circle of decision-makers, or persuade them to adopt redistributionist policies of the type he favored. Knowing thus the unsatisfied fervor of probably most Congolese, at least in Kwilu, and aware as well of the limited support the central government enjoyed, Mulele became an aspirant revolutionary who directed a regional and ethnic rebellion. His aims were abetted by the decline of party strength.

Political organizations in the Congo had turned almost full circle between early 1959 and late 1963. The Belgians had regarded parties as harmful to their colonial interests; only ethnically defined associations had been permitted until little more than a year before independence. The sudden lifting of restraints brought a florescence of political parties, most of them ephemeral and but a step removed from the ethnic associations whence many had sprung. Parties served the Congolese elite and mass well in accelerating the handover of power. When independence had been granted, however, the tactical need for mobilization disappeared. Calming rather than arousing political passions became the order of the day. In the view of most African leaders, parties seemed unduly to stir rural concerns. Popular pressure on the government seemed, to those in Leopoldville, an unwelcome distraction from the tasks of governance. Political movements that remained outside the official fold, such as the Gizenga-Mulele wing of the PSA, became liable to hostility from the center. Pressures mounted on opposition movements, some of which chose to take the "dangerous path" of rebellion. The consequent stress on conspiracy meant planning was confined to the most trusted—who, in turn, usually shared common cultural origins. The PSA split took on ethnic overtones; the Mulelist rebellion confirmed these. Even the espousal of the ideology of class conflict could not mask the increasingly ascriptive basis on which discontent was politicized. The organization had to be adapted to the tribal realities of collective action.

A common problem confronted the organizations surveyed in this chapter. In their early stages, none was avowedly violent, let alone revolutionary. Each had to remain nonpolitical, given the hostility of the dominant groups. Circumstances changed, however, and the disaffected were pushed toward militant involvement to which they were imperfectly attuned. The Society of God-Worshippers started with a message of personal salvation; in the unsettled conditions following the Opium War, it turned toward group protection. The Andhra Conference united intellectuals concerned with their cultural heritage more than their political status; the Kikuyu Central Association fostered ethnic interests. Only the Parti Solidaire Africaine operated *ab initio* as an open political movement built on a federation of ethnic associations. A great deal of organizational adaptation was accordingly necessary, were any to become the nucleus of radical change brought by violent means.

A shift in character—from religious or social to militantly political; from open encouragement of cultural pride to covert preparation for revolt—in effect required wholly new bases. All moved, in the incumbents' view, from groups on the edge of legality to organizations clearly treasonous. They became illegal associations, built on bases possibly inappropriate to collective political violence. Difficulties arose in converting from cultural to political foundations. Fraternities founded on affinities, Wakeman reminds us, may be inept in political matters—notably in the inhospitable settings we have been considering.[92] There were, admittedly, some compensating features. Cultural affinity eased initial expansion.

Bases for collective action already existed. Common experiences and the sharing of certain outlooks abetted communications among leaders, and between leaders and followers. Secrecy might be maintained more readily. On the other hand, seeming communal exclusiveness put an upper limit on expansion. Unless a basis other than ethnic affinity were found, unity within the group led to isolation from other groups. The need remained (as was noted in Chapter 2) for a broader basis and appeal—hence for organizational transformation.

Such transformation was eased by incumbent violence. The obvious challenges to safety and livelihood made some form of response necessary. Groups in being might be turned more readily toward defense than new groups created. Even further steps were necessary to move from defense toward offense. Taking up the sword to pursue government troops and to attempt to unseat those in power required levels of commitment far beyond those required for protection. New ideas, additional militancy, had to develop. The proclamation of the *T'ai-p'ing t'ien-kuo*, for example, was more than cosmetic. It symbolized willingness to go beyond defense to direct attack on the source of the problem: in short, on the government itself.

Many adaptations proved necessary—showing, if further comment were required, the complexity of politicizing discontent. First, bases of recruitment were changed, from cultural and ascriptive to political, economic, and presumably universalistic. Secondly, the *modus operandi* was revised. Defense against governmental pressures and landlord extractions became offense against both. Thirdly, those involved had to submit to quasi-military discipline. Plotting required secrecy; attack required order. Unless the incumbents were themselves weak and disorganized—as were Ch'ing troops sent against the Taiping in its early years—the would-be insurgents might be crushed. Rebels lacking martial skills, equipment, and basic discipline could not survive long against determined defenders. There was little sense in issuing a clarion call for resistance if most were too cowed to obey, or too divided to act together effectively.

The open, wholesale recruitment of followers characteristic of "political" organizations does not always fit conspiratorial groups. Yes, rebels require a milieu of support; survival is difficult against a determined opponent in a lukewarm environment. But the insurgents may require, even more, a means of effective coordination in moving from defense to offense. Leaders must be able to impose sanctions when necessary against recalcitrant fighters. The enthusiasm of believing that injustices might be reversed required buttressing. As examples of sanctions, I would cite the *batuni* oath of Mau Mau fighters ("If ever I am called to accompany a raid or bring in the head of an enemy, I shall obey and never give lame excuses")[93] or the regulations of the Taiping army ("When the trumpet sounds, let everyone immediately hasten to the royal premises, there to hear orders to slaughter the devils; let none shirk his duty by hiding or fleeing").[94]

Preparations for insurrection can never be totally concealed. Would-be rebels must bank on a certain amount of official laxity, inattention, or misinterpretation. An inefficient government may in fact be a precondition for early insurgent successes.[95] Especially as D-Day draws nigh, the circle of those requiring information grows. Leaks of plans are likely without steps to preserve secrecy, such as restricting knowledge to a minimum number of persons known for their close-lipped natures. Once again, a relatively open, popularly based organization seems maladapted to these exiegencies.

Given these considerations, it should not be surprising that there often existed, in effect, concentric organizations. Conspiracy was confined. An inner circle of plotters took cover within a more open organization. Kenya gives the clearest example among our four rebellions of seeming success — albeit briefly. British administrators appeared so convinced of Kenyatta's leadership and direct encouragement of Mau Mau by KAU officials that they rounded up the constitutionalists who had appeared in public and left an open field for the aggressive militants. The adaptations in Taiping thought and organization effected by Feng Yün-shan and Yang Hsiu-ch'ing (whom we shall glimpse more fully in the following chapter), and the use Pierre Mulele made of PSA support to incite *maquis* action, offer further evidence. Circles within circles represent a more common means of organizational transformation in rebellion than the deliberate creation of a totally new organization. Montesquieu notwithstanding, institutions can be *re*made by individuals with results potentially as striking as those derived from institutions created *de novo*. Organizational adaptation was thus an imperative, in order to turn existing bases of collective action to rebellion.

One major element remains in the politicization of discontent. Ideology eases institutional transformation. Systems of belief help justify turns to violence. Organizations direct discontent into political objects; ideologies justify rebellious acts. Both must be coupled. Just as no rebellion can be said to be fully spontaneous — for it requires an organizational nucleus around which to crystallize — so too no rebellion can be said to be devoid of justification in its protagonists' eyes. The real issue remains the effectiveness with which ideology and organization alike turn discontent into challenge to the status quo. Having now surveyed the organizational factors, we must turn to the ideological.

CHAPTER 7 /

Ideology and the Justification and Direction of Rebellion

Four Functions of Ideology

> The mere existence of privations is not enough to cause an insurrection: if it were, the masses would be always in revolt. It is necessary that the bankruptcy of the social regime, being conclusively revealed, should make these privations intolerable, and that new conditions and new ideas should open the prospect of a revolutionary way out.[1]

In these justly-noted and often-quoted words, Leon Trotsky emphasized the central role of systems of belief in collective political violence. Rebellion springs from many sources, not the least of which are ideas. As a guide to action, as motivating force, ideology lies at the heart of popular uprisings.

But Trotsky may have overstated his case in emphasizing *new* ideas. The annals of rebellion, and of revolution as well, make frequent reference to old ideas, to deep-rooted conceptions of the appropriate limits to government involvement in rural life. Collective political violence rests in large measure on traditions handed down over generations, constituting the "folk" wisdom of particular societies. Heritages of rebellion have helped evoke widespread responses against government actions.

In this chapter, I intend to show ways in which "ideology" has been employed as justification, guideline, and aggregating principle for rebellion. Rural uprisings of the scale we have been examining did not spring solely from popular discontent, government repression, and institutions adapted to violent means. The four insurrections required awareness and commitment made possible by widespread popular beliefs. I call these beliefs ideology, recognizing that the term covers widely divergent items--popular slogans, arcane and elaborate belief systems, an intermediate range of formulations.

The beliefs manifested in the four uprisings differed markedly in terms of expression and background. All existed in popular form, as a series of simplistic ideas about the desired political format. Beyond these local formulations existed the outlines of national policies. The Taiping and Kwilu rebel leaders in particular enunciated complex and seemingly comprehensive systems of ideas, even if translation into precise consequences for the participants fell far short of what was claimed. It is difficult precisely to indicate the extent to which ideology accounted for the relative successes and failures of the particular uprisings. In each, however, collective action rested on a foundation of beliefs that, in Trotsky's words, illuminated the "bankruptcy" of the existing system, made privations "intolerable," and opened the prospects for change.

Two sources of justification for collective political violence exist, in terms of origins. Each society has a particular heritage of beliefs and conditions that may foster rebellion; relatedly, each society is open (though in varying degrees!) to the implantation of different beliefs and models. In other words, both indigenous and exogenous systems of ideas can be drawn upon to justify popular resistance to government actions. A fascinating point about the uprisings delineated in this book is the coexistence in each of parallel belief systems or ideologies for collective political violence. The "traditional" logic of mass protest existed side-by-side, as it were, with a set of more "modern" ideas identified with certain leaders, drawn to a substantial extent from outside the particular society. There thus existed dual bases for collective action: on the one hand, "folk" conceptions of revolt; on the other hand, "elite" conceptions of revolution. Their uneasy juxtaposition helped bring about large-scale rebellion.

Most scholars assume that political consciousness can be brought to rural dwellers only from outside. The "idiocy of rural life," in Marx's trenchant phrase, means external assistance is required. Peasants cannot act for themselves, in their class interests. This theme, sounded in *The Eighteenth Brumaire* (quoted above in Chapter 2) and accepted by later scholars, sees rural uprisings as consigned to futility. Villagers presumably lack sufficient political awareness or organization to press for more than minor revisions in the existing system. Such a view must be questioned. The beliefs of rural dwellers may be more radical than the views of leaders. Rustics can envisage a good society, quite unlike that in which they are embedded; this vision can motivate collective action benefiting them both individually and conjointly. There exist, in short, rural models of political change that, in large-scale rebellions, interact with the more elaborately formulated models of change held by the leaders.

Ideology, be it "folk" or "elite," serves four functions in rebellion:

1. as a critique of the existing social, economic and political order;
2. as a vision of an alternative order, seen by rural dwellers and their leaders as more legitimate;

3. as a means of asserting collective identity and interests, on the basis of which collective action can be undertaken; and

4. as a guide to how the existing order can be ousted in favor of the alternative order.

Each of these ideas mertis more extensive discussion.

Rebellion is a major act of collective discontent. As such, it necessarily involves identifying the shortcomings of the status quo. The first function of an ideology, in the sense used here, is thus that of criticism. The shortcomings of the *ancien régime* must be highlighted, pinpointed, ascribed to human acts. A set of beliefs that considers misfortune the result of divine malevolence irremediable by human action gives little reason for resistance unless, to be certain, life in the hereafter or in the next incarnation seems preferable to current miseries. If Fate is seen as the cause, then Fate alone can bring change. It should not be assumed, however, that rebellion cannot occur given such a belief — far from it! Millenarian revolts, in which the miraculous plays a key role, have been among the most sweeping events in rural settings. Such uprisings, as delineated by Cohn, draw their energy from movements picturing salvation as collective, terrestrial, imminent, total and miraculous.[2] The millenium would be ushered in for the faithful by divine acts. This did not preclude widespread violence by and for the convinced. Revolutionary millenarians proclaimed boundless aims and premises. They developed large followings only under unusual circumstances, however. According to Cohn, such individuals flourish only in situations marked by recurrent disasters, social disorganization, and emotional need for unquestionable authority.[3] These characteristics can aptly be applied to the uprisings under review; they arose in settings, as suggested in Chapters 1 and 4, in which sudden, sharp declines in living standards had occurred.

The shortcomings of the status quo are contrasted with the promises of the alternative. Ideologies of rebellion serve secondly as visions of a different social, economic and political order. Some conception of a different set of social arrangements — or perhaps various conceptions — precedes major acts of collective political violence. The imperfect nature of the present is thrown into sharper relief by the vision of the other, be it set in a bygone golden age, or promised as the result of future transformations. One should not necessarily expect a single vision of what change might hold, however. The combination in our four instances of "folk" and "elite" beliefs meant a variety of justifications for collective political violence existed. The ideologies referred both to past and to future — either presumably better than the current situation.

Ideology serves thirdly as a means of community building. The group to carry out collective political violence not only must be brought into existence; its members must also be motivated to risk life and property in the quest for the desired order. Ideology becomes thus a means of identification. Those participating should come to share both awareness of goals and a sense of the importance of cooperation. To be certain, long before violence erupts, latent bases for group solidarity may exist. In the "folk" ideology, these may be furnished by language, tribe, race, or some other ascriptive characteristic. In the "elite" ideology, by contrast, the foundations for collective action may be based on economic status or other achieved characteristic. Most likely, as the four rebellions illustrate, elements of both will be combined. The new community will be rooted in the old. Solidarity in the pursuit of common goals remains the central objective.

The new order must be established from the ruins of the old. The final function of ideology is an instrumental one, to justify collective action, including violence. The targets and pathways of change are indicated. The shortcomings of the *ancien régime* become grounds for specific alterations—"Destroy the Ch'ing, restore the Ming," in a rallying cry used by many secret societies allied to the Taiping. Here again, contrasts might be expected between the means of change upheld by leaders—focused, for example, on the seizure of power centrally—and the objectives sought by rank-and-file participants—motivated, for example, by the need to gain sufficient land for family subsistence.

The four points raised extend the functions of ideology listed by other scholars. Gurr, for example, relates the effectiveness of ideology—"symbolic appeals"—in promoting collective political violence to the extent to which these appeals 1) offer plausible explanations of the sources of relative deprivation, 2) identify political targets for violence, and 3) provide symbols of group identification.[4] Although he is aware of the importance of alternative futures, Gurr does not, I believe, give them sufficient attention. The importance of establishing a community for collective action receives little attention from Hagopian; his desiderata for ideology include 1) critique of the old regime, 2) affirmation that a better society is both desirable and possible, and 3) strategic guidance on the means to carry out sweeping change.[5]

To what extent did the rebellions described in this book follow the prescriptions for rural revolution written by Mao Tse-tung and Frantz Fanon? Both intellectuals in their societies, they recognized and sought to capture the explosive energy of peasants for national restructuring. Violence—coordinated, disciplined, and directed—was required for revolutionary purification. Peasants with urbanized leaders provided, in their view, the crucial foundation for change. Neither believed revolutionary alterations could result from the peasants, for the peasants, or by the peasants alone; alliances were necessary.

Mao and Fanon enjoyed the undoubted advantage of describing success. The Chinese revolution attracted international attention. In a seemingly brief period, the world's most populous nation threw aside traditions dating back millennia and bourgeois institutions installed for decades. The rapid advance of Mao's peasant armies surprised the world; the myth of guerrilla invincibility received a tremendous boost. The glory of the Chinese revolution was also the vindication of Mao Tse-tung. As military leader, spokesman, and dominant figure, he embodied and proclaimed the changes China experienced.

Fanon, though not a leader in the field of combat, emerged as the most articulate spokesman for the Algerian revolution. The bitter struggle against the French found no writer as passionate. He brought vividly to the world the traumas of rural change, in which the violence inherent in the colonial situation evoked a corresponding indigenous violence. Few other writers have matched the scorn he heaped on the national bourgeoisie who acceded to power when colonial territories gained independence.

Mao and Fanon mixed fact with theory, guerrilla practice with broader speculation. Their evocation of the revolutionary potential of peasants may be construed as a "myth,"[6] other factors proving more important in the eruption of violence.[7] The qualifications scholars have suggested are important in illustrating the peculiar as well as the universal factors in Mao's and Fanon's works. For the would-be guerrilla practitioner, however, the broad lessons rather than the specific details or caveats constitute the heart of the matter. Pierre Mulele did not require detailed information about the impact of Japanese armies in North China as part of the background to the Chinese revolution: he wanted basic principles and precepts with which he could instruct his *maquisards*. More useful thus for Mulele — and, by extension, for others desirous of a guerrilla career — were simplified maxims from Mao than analyses from scholars' pens.

In the final analysis, however, the sources of ideological beliefs may have been less important than their consequences. Each set of imported ideas was filtered through indigenous perceptual screens. What Mulele had to preach, for example, supplemented rather than supplanted existing, indigenous justifications for rebellion. I do not believe that the introduction of revolutionary ideas by themselves touched off resistance. They added to the politicization of discontent already in process; they fired the enthusiasm of some; they furnished an aura of international comparability. They did not and cannot, in and of themselves, provoke collective political violence. Ideology added a further element to perceptions of relative deprivation, to resentment about regime retribution, to would-be organization of aggrieved persons. These elements in combination permitted the politicization of discontent to take the form of collective political violence. Ideology helped justify or legitimate efforts by the wretched of the earth to better their condition, in ways mixing indigenous and exogenous patterns. Systems of belief helped strengthen organizations designed to rebuff attacks by the imcumbents and reduce the discontent that had afflicted many.

Taiping: How Christian? How Confucian?

The beliefs of Taiping leaders have been scrutinized from almost every conceivable vantage point. Despite court-mandated destruction of rebel documents, enough survived to give scholars and latter-day ideologues the basis for thousands of pages of analysis and dispute. Was Hung Hsiu-ch'üan a direct precursor of peasant revolution? Was he instead an early Westernizer, trying to bring (through Christianity) a new foundation for government practices? Or did he rather delve into the Chinese past, taking from it beliefs and themes that justified what was basically a larger-than-normal rural revolt? Did he stress nationalism decades before the Ch'ing dynasty collapsed?

The answers to these questions carry more than academic interest. Certain beliefs of the Taiping differentiated them from most earlier Chinese rebels; the prominent place of religious practices gave Hung Hsiu-ch'üan's followers a distinct, collective identity. Of the four uprisings surveyed in this book, the Taiping rebellion probably drew most heavily on ideology in the politicization of discontent. According to the most thorough scholar, "There is not the slightest doubt that the religious element in the Taiping ideology was the fundamental unifying force of the Taiping movement . . . . Religion gave the Taipings a crusader's zest, and politics gave them a practical direction."[8]

By closer examination of ideology, we may better determine how the uprising mingled elements of rebellion and revolution. Some scholars deem the *T'ai-p'ing t'ien-kuo* a "failed revolution,"[9] a "revolutionary movement"[10] or, at a minimum, "basically different from former dynastic upheavals."[11] Judgments of this sort rest to a substantial extent on the practices and goals of Hung's followers. The ideology of the Taiping insurrection mixed "new" and "old" elements. It justified the organizational steps briefly noted in the preceding chapter; it directed discontent against political targets; it held out transcendent goals that mingled economic, religious, nationalistic and political elements. All these points have been made in general terms earlier in this book. The occasion is now appropriate to dissect Taiping ideology, enabling us to compare its basic presumptions with other justifications for collective political violence.

The following aspects merit attention: the sources of Taiping beliefs, Chinese and non-Chinese; the contributions of individuals, notably Hung Hsiu-ch'üan, Yang Hsiu-ch'ing, and Hung Jen-kan; the changes in emphasis over time, as the movement as a whole rose, peaked and declined; and the relationship between ideology and Taiping practices, particularly in military organization, land distribution, and civil administration. On any one of these subjects, an entire volume could be written. What appears below is but a sampling from diverse, fascinating sources, for exhaustive treatment would extend this book beyond the bounds of normal readability, and could only repeat what more thoroughly versed scholars have already published.

Change of ruling house figured in Chinese thought millenia before Taiping leaders announced their intention to unseat the Manchus. Dynasties waxed and waned in accordance with an ancient pattern. A ruler who failed to protect his subjects' welfare abridged one of the chief Confucian relationships. The Mandate of Heaven would be forfeit. Social disturbances and natural disasters heralded the end of a ruling house. Those who succeeded in rising to the top themselves gained the Mandate; those who failed were stigmatized and usually liable to that peculiarly Chinese form of execution, death by slicing.

By establishing the *T'ai-p'ing t'ien-kuo* in January 1851, Hung Hsiu-ch'üan acted in accord with this traditional pattern. Although he did not proclaim himself emperor — "Heavenly King" (T'ien Wang) sufficed as a title — he conformed to the steps previous pretenders had taken. The phrases used to inaugurate the new dynasty enjoyed ample precedent. Monarchy remained, a change from one dynasty to another justified by the incumbents' shortcomings. Hereditary titles provided continuity with prior practice.

In their system of military ranks, Taiping leaders turned to the venerable *Chou-li*. Giving thereby the "aura of classical sanction to their organizational measures,"[12] they conformed once again to precedent. Taiping leaders, as we saw above (Chapter 6, footnote 26), drew on longstanding themes of ethnic pride. They followed the practice of several secret societies in espousing the overthrow of the Ch'ing. They promised subsistence to followers. Social stratification crept into the Taiping movement. Elaborate regulations prescribed the color, decor and size of officials' gowns, sedan chairs, carriages and flags. Even the examination system, that longstanding means of recruitment, was revived by Hung and his associates. Many of the concepts used, in short, had been handed down for generations. Old wine had merely been transferred to new bottles. Continuity with the past placed the Taiping uprising in a genus familiar to millions of peasants.

A great deal of new wine went into new bottles, however. Non-Chinese sources, especially Christianity, provided Taiping ideologues an unusual opportunity. They could (even while using titles sanctioned by time) introduce new ideals and objectives. Classical sources and analogues to what Hung Hsiu-ch'üan preached no doubt bolstered their acceptance. The Taiping leaders went even further. They introduced some elements entirely new to Imperial China, at least in the intensity associated with the Taipings. Jesuits at Macao, for example, preached Christian messages to a few; Hung Hsiu-ch'üan wanted to spread his good words to admonish millions. Hung claimed a divine foundation. God's wife had given birth to Jesus Christ, then to Hung. What Hung commanded as "Heavenly King" thus enjoyed God's sanction. Though Chinese emperors were traditionally accorded the title "Son of Heaven," they neither claimed divine descent, nor accorded their pronouncements the status of holy writ. Visions of Heaven and Hell loomed large in Taiping thought. Only those who accepted the word would be saved from eternal torture. To be certain, millenarian Buddhism incorporated the idea of salvation for the elect, as the Eight Trigrams uprising exemplified. The Taipings took this belief a step further. Death was not an occasion for mourning[13]—a sharp reversal of Confucian custom. Further, the message of the Heavenly Kingdom applied to all potential adherents irrespective of race, age, or sex.

Women apparently enjoyed opportunities in the Taiping movement they were otherwise denied. They served in military regiments organized separately from the men's. Foot-binding and prostitution were formally abolished. Women gained equal rights in inheriting land. Since the Taipings regarded adultery as the most serious offense, the sexes were segregated. This enforced separation was never fully implemented and was in fact abandoned in 1855, as we shall see shortly. Nonetheless, the legal status of females received a great boost from the Taiping movement; of our four uprisings, the Taiping gave by far the greater opportunities to women.

The iconoclasm of Hung—recall his smashing of a memorial tablet to Confucius a year after his fourth failure in the examinations—was carried over into the movement as a whole. Earlier rebellions in China had been mounted with imported religious beliefs; however, those who propagated non-Confucian ideas were, according to Muramatsu, "always dependent on court or government patronage and thus were usually ready to make an ideological compromise with established authority."[14] Taiping leaders were the exception. They were totally unwilling for several years to reach accommodation. One of the most striking discontinuities between Taiping beliefs and previous Chinese practices thus came in the attitude toward the classics. Confucian texts were explicitly proscribed;[15] participants were to turn their attention to the Bible. Once again, exigency later necessitated the abandonment of the anti-Confucius emphasis; as we shall see in the following chapter, nothing aroused greater gentry opposition than the Taipings' impious attitude toward the revered source of the traditional social order. In attacking Confucius, Hung Hsiu-ch'üan assailed the formal basis of Ch'ing society.

A less spectacular example of Taiping assault on the old order came in the calendar initiated in early 1852. Old practices and superstitions were swept aside "with the simple explanation that every day was a good and lucky day for the believer in God."[16] As did the revolutionaries of the First Republic in France, Taiping leaders sought a new beginning in basic respects. Even so, this act had ancient roots: every new Chinese dynasty established its own calendar.

Hung Hsiu-ch'üan and his immediate group joined their religious enthusiasm to political and military objectives. The message of the Heavenly King required the removal of the Manchu "devils," which in turn necessitated armed mobilization. The new Jerusalem the Taipings sought lay in China. Their ideology was not one of resignation to fate, nor of trusting to divine intervention. The Taipings organized against the Ch'ing dynasty and its gentry supporters. Ideology played a crucial practical role. In trying to overthrow those who had lost the Mandate, the rebels united the traditional goal with unorthodox justifications.

In shaping Taiping religious beliefs, Hung Hsiu-ch'üan played the leading role. He claimed to have received messages directly from God, and convinced others of the reality of his visions. The most dramatic message came in 1837, when Hung was twenty-five and had just suffered his third examination failure. Hauled before God (who wore a high-brimmed hat, a black dragon robe, and golden whiskers that ringed his face and covered his stomach), Hung was commanded to drive out the "square-headed, red-eyed demon."[17] Christ entered with a host of angels; God proclaimed that the "ultimate guilt for inciting the demons" lay on Confucius, "whose books of teachings are very much in error."[18] Hung, armed with a golden seal and sword, battled his way down through the thirty-three levels of heaven, gaining from God the title of T'ien Wang (Heavenly King). Proclaiming "I am sent by Heaven as the true ordained son of Heaven to exterminate the depraved and preserve the upright,"[19] Hung did not decide to undertake this onerous responsibility until six years later, when he glanced through a brief Christian tract, "Good Words to Admonish the Age" and was reminded of his vision. Hung communicated his enthusiasm to his cousin Hung Jen-kan and friend Feng Yün-shan. From these apocalyptic visions, the religious message of the Society of God-Worshippers began.

The concept of charisma may be overworked, but its appropriateness to Hung Hsiu-ch'üan and his early followers seems obvious. His supposed direct contact with the Heavenly Father bestowed a unique gift of grace on Hung. He was endowed with a special aura. Individuals could identify themselves and their aspirations with Hung. Putting their trust in a man of such extraordinary and unusual powers, members of the Society of God-Worshippers could cope more adequately with the frustrations that were their lot. The widespread discontent and militarized conflict of Kwangtung and Kwangsi encouraged thousands to harken to Hung's message. The unsettled conditions of south China in the 1840s, when the customary bases of authority were proving inadequate, clearly facilitated the rise of Hung as a charismatic figure.

To endure, charisma must be "routinized."[20] Two figures, Feng Yün-shan and Yang Hsiu-ch'ing, carried out this important task, Feng took the main responsibility for creating the Society of God-Worshippers; Yang transformed the *T'ai-p'ing t'ien-kuo* into an efficient, ordered military enterprise, though his quest for preeminence cost the movement greatly. The founding of the Society of God-Worshippers came through Feng's initiative, for Hung was (in 1845-6) occupied with teaching and writing. To attract more than 3,000 members Feng stressed the miraculous: "Always at the center of his teaching had been the story of Hung's ascension into heaven to receive a divine mandate."[21] Feng chose the Mount Thistle site where religious messages and group discipline were carefully instilled. Fervor was thus complemented by community, enthusiasm channeled into coordinated action. Feng started the adaptation of tradition that marked Taiping military steps. He drew on old sources for his ideological and organizational innovation. Each army (theoretically 13,155 members) followed patterns adopted from the *Chou-li* (Chapter 6, footnote 27). Officers had their own flags whose size, color and inscription proclaimed their rank. Army commanders trained and administered their troops; strategic command was invested in inspectors. As a result, Taiping armies manifested considerably greater coordination than had earlier rebel units.

The steps taken by Yang were both ideological and organizational. By late 1851, he had wheedled and pushed his way into dominance. As "Tung Wang" (East King), Yang served as chief of staff, determining what the Heavenly King should formally proclaim. Through him came a definite sharpening of the anti-Manchu tone of Taiping pronouncements. Religion and virulent racism fused in the following proclamation issued by Yang:

Awake! Awake! Those who follow Heaven shall be preserved; those who rebel against Heaven shall perish. Now, the Manchu demon, Hsien-feng [the Emperor], being in origin a barbarian, is the mortal enemy of us Chinese; moreover, he has induced mankind to asume demon shape, to worship evil spirits, to disobey the true spirit and to greatly rebel against the Great God; Heaven cannot tolerate him and therefore he must be destroyed.[22]

The rhetoric escalated: Manchus were depicted as foxes, monkeys, dogs, or swine. Those who took up arms against the "barbarians" from beyond the Great Wall were following Heaven and would be richly rewarded; "those who disobey Heaven shall be publicly executed."[23] Those "who in the past mistakenly served in the demon's camp and aided the demons in rebelling against Heaven" — in other words, imperial bureaucrats and their gentry associates — had to join the T'ien Wang's ranks lest they "become ugly and evil ghosts eternally consigned to the eighteenth layer of hell, to suffer unending and ceaseless torments."[24]

A third person who influenced Taiping ideology was Hung Jen-kan, cousin of Hung Hsiu-ch'üan and one of the movement's earliest advocates. (He and Feng were the first two converts made by Hung.) Unlike most Taiping leaders, Hung Jen-kan was at ease in the company of Westerners. He served in Hong Kong, for example, as a staff member of the London Missionary Society; his studies incorporated natural sciences, economics, military science, and public administration.[25] Hung Jen-kan also avoided becoming enmeshed in the fratricidal struggles that afflicted Taiping leaders in 1856, since he remained outside rebel-held territory from 1849 to 1859. Hung Hsiu-ch'üan quickly heaped his returned cousin with duties — Generalissimo of the army, leader of all ministers, chief examiner of government examinations, minister of the board of appointments minister of foreign affairs, and holder of a mandate that "everybody in the Kingdom must be under his control."[26] Such trust was well-placed. Hung Jen-kan proposed a series of reforms[27] that, if implemented, would have constituted a great leap forward nearly a century before Mao Tse-tung popularized the term. Take, for example, Hung Jen-kan's prescription for avoiding clique intrigues:

> If clique intrigues are uncovered and brought out into the open without the possibility of suppressing them, then the court will be undermined and the consequences will be disastrous. However, at a time when the country is militarily strong and wealthy, when public morals and customs are pure and correct, when there are steamships and trains which can start at one place in the morning and arrive at another in the evening, and when there are newspapers to publicize treacherous plots, all treachery and intrigue will find it difficult to escape the light of the sun.[28]

He wished to introduce "secondarily precious" objects such as clocks, thermometers, telescopes, and "revolving guns," with only the "most precious" Trinity of Heavenly Father, Christ and the Holy Spirit coming before.[29] Establishment of post offices, public suggestion boxes and newspapers; promulgation of law and education for all; contact with countries advanced in technical skills: all figured in Hung Jen-kan's prescriptions. He lauded the "Flowery Flag Country" — the United States — as the "most righteous and wealthy country of all," and cited with approval if not accuracy the election of officials.[30] No less than 28 specific proposals were made to establish "rule by law." His wide-ranging list included the need for railways, highways, banking, mining, postal services, and hospitals; other proposals included bans on infanticide, slavery, wine, opium, tobacco, temples and monasteries, and dramatic performances.

Proposals as sweeping as these surpasssed the capacity of Hung's government. Problems in implementation bring us to our final two concerns about Taiping ideology, namely shifts in emphasis as time passed, and the extent to which announced goals were in fact implemented.

Ideological change reflected, and was in turn reflected in, the different conditions the Taipings encountered. Its initial character as a tightly knit brotherhood of believers was supplanted by an explicit, coordinated system of military and civilian organization. The charisma of Hung Hsiu-ch'üan, and the message of his encounter with God, shared the ideological billing with protonationalist pride. As a would-be replacement to the Manchus, the Taipings drew on themes of racial purity, the notion that Han alone should rule other Chinese. After a period of internecine strife, there occurred a brief, aborted phase of explicit modernization, followed in turn by the progressive loss of group cohesion. Each phase is worthy of brief consideration, in showing the complex relationships between beliefs and practices.

All contemporary observers and latter-day scholars agree on the religious fervor and initial military effectiveness manifested in the Society of God-Worshippers. The gospel according to Hung fell on ready ears. Its millenarian elements offered respite from the multiple disasters that had assaulted citizens of Kwangtung and Kwangsi. A great deal of time was devoted to religious ceremonies. The sense of group identification was sharpened by defense needs, and further strengthened by success. The military organization described above proved effective against most Green Standard and banner troops sent against the Taipings. Although Hung's armies eventually had to bypass several heavily fortified cities, they clearly enjoyed the upper hand south of the Yangtse.

Success in battle bred further success in support. The expansion in Taiping numbers offers ample confirmation: literally millions joined Hung's armies. As would be expected, the mobile (especially the poor) most readily attached themselves to the Taiping forces. The anti-Confucian tone of Hung's pronouncements, and the increasing stridency with which the Manchu rulers and their allies were denounced, meant many officials and gentry fled as the Taipings approached. What they abandoned could be collected and redistributed. So long as Hung remained on the move, the multitudes could be fed and integrated into the structures developed by Feng Yün-shan and Yang Hsiu-ch'ing. Taiping ideology and organization were better suited to expansion than to consolidation. Lacking an effective basis for local administration (a point to which we shall return in the following chapter), the Taipings unwittingly fell into a trap of their own making. Interruption of the armies' momentum meant inadequacies were brutally exposed.

Success in numbers came at a cost as well. The intense spirit of God-Worshippers huddled together at the foot of Mount Thistle could not be maintained. Organizational coordination supplanted spiritual enthusiasm with the expansion in size and the move into the Yangtse valley. Establishment of the Heavenly Capital at Nanking—chosen in part since it had served as capital for the Ming dynasty—turned energies and tension inwards. With its military expansion halted, the Taiping movement turned back on itself. What might have been a period of consolidation, of establishing a base area from which to launch a decisive assault, became instead a period of decay. The efforts of Hung Jen-kan could not stem the rot. Though he tried valiantly to rekindle religious fervor, and to join this to a new emphasis on updating technology and institutions, he failed. His suggestions remained untranslated into policy. Hung Hsiu-ch'üan's beliefs and charisma had been organizationally captured by Feng; military action against the alien dynasty had been organizationally expressed by Feng and Yang. It was the fate of Hung Jen-kan that his beliefs, born of extended contact with Protestant missionaries, were shuffled aside. Ideology devoid of action, of expression in organizational terms, had little effect on the decaying movement.

In terms thus of phases, we may see Taiping ideology linked to organization as follows. The first phase was intensely personal: Hung's communicating his miraculous vision to a few close friends, and risking social ostracism as a result of his anti-Confucian zealotry. The second phase witnessed Feng's creation of the Society of God-Worshippers, especially attractive to Hakka under landlord pressure. The third phase started with the January 1851 creation of the *T'ai-p'ing t'ien-kuo*; traditional beliefs in removing a dynasty whose mandate had expired, and in placing Han once again on the throne, were joined to a carefully elaborated military basis. This period of rapid expansion through the Yangtse valley was followed by a fourth phase of ideological stagnation and organizational decline, briefly interrupted by Hung Jen-kan's attempts at revivification. The creative burst, as it were, came in the early years of Taiping history. From roughly 1848 to 1855, the movement blossomed, beliefs and coordination advancing apace. Thereafter, mired in a confined setting, the Taipings declined as a real alternative to the government in Peking. Their ideology no longer vital, their organization in shambles, they seemed in later years scarcely to differ from those they sought to replace. Taiping promises and Taiping practices were increasingly out of joint as time passed, as we shall see in the following chapter.

Taiping ideology served to question the existing order, to present an alternative order, to assert collective identity, and to indicate how the *ancien régime* might be ousted.

Two major shortcomings of the Ch'ing dynasty recurred in Taiping statements: its alien nature and the exploitation it permitted. Both themes were linked to a sense of moral rectitude; neither was original. Rebel beliefs had long included ethnocentric characteristics.[31] Presentation of the Manchus in bestial terms had ample precedent; the idea Chinese alone should rule over their kinsmen had become a fixed value in appeals for dynastic change well before 1850.[32] As examples of Taiping opposition to economic exploitation and unsettled conditions Hung Hsiu-ch'üan's odes furnish apt examples:

> The fourth kind of wrong is robbery and thievery;
> Injustice and inhumanity are not proper.
> Those who form gangs and are disorderly, Heaven will not protect;
> When iniquities are excessive, calamity will surely follow.[33]

> In the present day so many brave men
> Have wounded themselves with the opium gun.
> With regard to the love of wine, this is also a wrong.
> Successful families ought to warn themselves against the
>   family-destroying juice.[34]

> When the prince is correct, the people comply with his commands.
> When the prince is incorrect, his relatives will rebel against him.
> When the prince is correct, the whole empire will trust him.
> When the prince is incorrect, calamities because of his vices multiply;
> When the prince is correct, blessings because of his goodness are enjoyed.
> When the nobles are incorrect, they will at length be overthrown by
>   others;
> When the rich are incorrect, their riches will eventually be annexed
>   by others . . . .[35]

The fault lay in the system expounded by Confucius—despite the clear Confucian overtones of what I have just quoted. In the words of Hung's vision:

> The Heavenly Elder Brother, Christ, also accused Confucius, saying, 'You created books of this kind to teach the people, so that even my own blood brother [Hung Hsiu-chüan], in reading your works, was harmed by them.' All of the angels also proclaimed his guilt.[36]

As Yang Hsiu-ch'ing's influence grew, so did the vitriol of statements regarding the Manchus. Further quotation is not needed.

Of greater importance is the vision of an alternative order. Once again, we encounter a longstanding theme, egalitarianism. One scholar has called slogans for equal division of lands "shrewdly conceived propaganda efforts to rouse the peasantry and secure their loyalty and support."[37] If this is so, the noted "Land System of the Heavenly Dynasty"[38] falls in the tradition. It was never put into practice, but remained, in Jen's words, "a utopian scheme embodying significant departures from Chinese tradition...illuminating in a singular way the basic social and economic ideals of the revolutionaries."[39] The document called for equal lands for all adults, irrespective of sex. Abundant harvests would be moved to areas of shortage; those in famine areas might themselves be moved. All persons would share God's blessings blissfully: "There being fields, let all cultivate them; there being food, let all eat; there being clothes, let all be dressed; there being money, let all use it, so that nowhere does inequality exist, and no man is not well fed and clothed."[40] Persons would be grouped into armies of 13,156 families—a clear parallel to the highly successful military organization—with rewards for the virtuous.

In the ideal order, subjects should obey their sovereign and worship Heaven. They should not question their lot, as the following ode makes clear:

> Let each be content with his vocation,
> Be he scholar, farmer, artisan, or merchant.
> Let him constantly read the heavenly book.
> The heavenly doctrine is bright and clear;
> If thus they obey the several commands,
> Complying with Heaven they will become illustrious.
> All you common people,
> Be not disobedient, be not forgetful.
> If you dare offend against Heaven,
> You will be considered transgressors,
> You and your children will be killed,
> Your family broken and the people destroyed.
> But if you are honest and good,
> Your filial piety and loyalty will render you fragrant.[41]

The Confucian presuppositions of these lines are obvious,

In what manner could the existing dynasty be ousted? The terms were simple: obey the injunctions of the leaders. The Taiping military organization, to which we have already given attention, proved superior to most official armies until 1854 or so. Follow commands constituted, in effect, the basic instruction. This was linked, however, to belief (once again longstanding in Chinese history) in the mandate passing. Hung Hsiu-ch'üan's ode of mod-1850 serves as an apt example:

> In recent times the murky atmosphere has greatly changed;
> We know that Heaven means to take heroic leadership.
> The Sacred Land has been betrayed; it will not easily fall again;
> God should be worshipped, and he shall be worshipped...
> From times of old deeds have been done by men;
> The black mists are dispersed in the face of the sun.[42]

In other words, don't wait for God to overthrow the infidels; move ahead under Taiping leadership.

Finally, collective identity came through the *T'ai-p'ing t'ien-kuo*, building from the earlier basis of the Society of God-Worshippers. The concept of unity derived from several sources, including the personal attraction of Hung's beliefs, Hakka identity, military efficacy, distaste for the declining Ch'ing dynasty, and (especially in the first two phases) a deep sense of religious fervor. Complemented by a comprehensive organizational framework, the Taiping ideology thus provided a vigorous challenge to the Confucian framework of the Ch'ing dynasty. Continuity between Taiping beliefs and earlier rebel ideologies enabled Hung and his followers to tap a current of resentment that had previously overflowed into collective political action; innovation in Taiping beliefs enabled Hung and his followers to present a message that was new as well. The combination was a powerful one, as we shall see in comparing it to systems to belief in the other rebellions.

Telengana: Maoist Maladaptation?

From February 1948 to 1951, the Communist party of India took the strongest public stand in favor of agrarian struggle. It threw its weight behind the Telengana rebels, hailing their struggle as a model other rural groups should emulate. It is tempting to view the unrest in Nalgonda and Warangal districts as "organized along standard Communist guerrilla lines with wholesale land redistribution and parallel village government"[43] — these, indeed, are the words of Selig Harrison, one of the more sensitive analysts of the social context of Indian communism. To assume these features came into existence only after the Communist party took the plunge into insurrectional politics, or to overlook other sources of peasant unrest, results in distorted understanding of the functions and sources of the Telengana ideology, however.

What I shall suggest in this section is that participants sought material objectives, notably land and debt reduction; that a strong sense of linguistic pride preceded the effort at rural organizing based on class and party ideology; and that language, caste and economic grievances provided foundations on which political awareness and action developed. All these suggest a point generally borne out by the available evidence. Justifications for rebellion existed on more than one level. What appeared in *People's War* or *People's Age* (the chief CPI weekly publication) should not be construed, in other words, as the sole ideological foundation for collective political violence. Many sources bolstered the villagers' belief they could reach their goals only through violent means.

Aside from caste and village ties, the strongest ties among Telengana Hindus came through language. Propagation of Telugu, indeed a revivification of the culture as a whole, lay behind the formation of the Andhra Kendra Jana Sangham. Given the resolutely Urdu nature of the Hyderabad administration (incidentally, the only princely state in India not to use the majority tongue of its inhabitants as the official language),[44] language and politics were intertwined. A resolution from the 1935 Andhra conference urging the Nizam to consider the appointment of more Telugu speakers stepped dangerously close to the line that (in the Nizam's view) separated sedition from permitted expression. Any discussion of linguistic affinity led logically to the possibility of redrawing political frontiers to accommodate homogeneous communities—and this was the objective of the "Andhra movement." Building upon and thereby strengthening the bonds of language, the "Andhra movement" took early steps toward criticizing the existing political order and delineating the basis on which a different order might be established. But, since literacy was limited, leadership in the "Andhra movement" reflected education—which, in turn, betokened relative prosperity.

The political problems in creating Andhra prior to the 1948 police action need little discussion: they would have required the dissection of India's most populous princely state, Hyderabad, and British India's most complex province, Madras. But it was an appeal with which to assail Muslim and British overlords alike. It could ignite popular enthusiasm in a way the more distant vision of a unified India might not. The many daily reminders of the division of Telugu speakers gave a basis in fact to the theories of divide and rule. The poverty of the Telengana region contrasted with the relative affluence of the Nizam and Hyderabad City; the absence of colinguists in the state administration further reminded Telugu speakers of their inferior status. Pointing thus to seeming discrimination, proponents of Andhra could attract support. In the words of "Vishala Andhra," published in 1946 by one of the chief exponents of the rebellion, "The British keep up the Nizam, and his satellites in spite of this backward state of agriculture, only to keep our people divided and to suppress our common freedom movement."[45]

One must place the "Andhra movement" in the broader context of Indian nationalism. On the one hand, emphasis on language and culture risked undercutting the unity needed to oppose British imperialism. On the other hand, emphasis on language and culture (while recognizing an obvious fact) intensified the freedom struggle by attaching it to an obvious social base. During the 1940s, Congress and the Communist party of India tended to split along these tactical lines. Congress, as befitted the oldest, largest, and most widely supported indigenous political movement, claimed all Indians could achieve political advance through it. The party was to mirror the aspirations of the entire subject populace. To oppose Congress would be akin to heresy: anything else would necessarily be narrower and schismatic. Its leaders were genuinely committed to a noncommunal approach. They had little patience with those who catered to exclusive audiences, accusing them of retarding the advance toward independence, and often underestimating their popular support. The Communist party, by contrast, expediently favored a federative type of nationalism, in which the aspirations of many groups would be linked in a coalition to which self-government could not be denied. Such an approach naturally appealed to those parties that, unable to challenge the India-wide dominance of Congress, turned to audiences restricted by religion, language or region.

A choice between these approaches was offered at the historic August 1942 meeting of the All-India Central Committee of Congress. Communist participants urged self-determination as the basis for creating a powerful Indian federation to which the British could not deny independence. The CPI suggestion — voluntary federation of units marked by contiguous territory, historical tradition, language, culture, "psychological make-up," and common economic life — fell on deaf ears. At most 12 or 13 of the 250 delegates supported the Communists' stand. The committee instead ratified the "Quit India" resolution that, in a matter of hours, brought the arrest of leading Congress officers and widespread disturbances. For most of the remainder of World War II, Congress leaders were held incommunicado, leaving the political field open to their opponents.

Self-determination became official CPI policy at its September 1942 conference. The arousal of rural interest meant "national unity itself more and more assumes the form of multi-national unity"; self-determination "becomes the progressive lever by means of which alone the various nationalities can be rallied and mobilized shoulder to shoulder."[46] A United National Front, to which the British would have to transfer political power, would thus be based on "perfect equality between nationalities and communities that live together in India." And, in a notation particularly applicable to Andhra, the party resolved that "the territories which are the homelands of such nationalities and which today are split up by the artificial boundaries of the present British provinces and the so-called 'Indian states' would be reunited and restored to them in a free India."[47] For the remainder of World War II, extending from their foundation in Madras, the Communists pressed for unity among Telugu speakers.

Since Telugu speakers joined both the CPI and Congress, further information must be presented. The two parties drew from different castes. Rivalry between the Kammas and the Reddis — both "rising peasant proprietor caste groups"[48] — was carried over into competition between the parties. Kammas led the Andhra communists; Reddis assumed the chief positions in Congress, behind a screen of Brahmans. Harrison's detailed study of election returns[49] illustrates the high degree of caste solidarity each party could draw upon. Caste as a basis for collective action thereby abetted the spread of political parties, but also confined the major ones to preexisting social formations.

By 1947, the lines of political conflict had been drawn in Hyderabad. Congress pressed the Nizam to withdraw his ban on the Hyderabad State Congress, and emphasized the importance of his voluntarily granting responsible government and acceding to India. Its appeal, in other words, was mainly political, and based on the Reddis. The Communist party pressed more on cultural and economic lines, using the organizational foundation it established during World War II to spread the Andhra ideal, slogans for relieving peasant indebtedness, and Kamma support. Both parties sought to bring the princely state into India, but appealed to different audiences. Congress wanted change in Hyderabad State and was for the nonce willing to maintain its boundaries and the Nizam as titular head; the CPI wanted creation of Andhra and to this end encouraged peasant action.

What was the effect of the Congress-CPI debate on rural political awareness? A contrast seemed to exist between the encouragement of individual cadres and extensive support by the Communist party. It took several months of peasant activity in Telengana before the CPI officially took notice. Only in February 1948, at the second party congress, did the CPI seek to attach itself to, and to guide from above, the small-scale rural struggle that had flared up in Telengana.

The political thesis approved at the 1948 party congress stressed economic problems in rural areas:

> The economic crisis, which will smite the agrarian areas most ruthlessly, will set in motion colossal forces. These agrarian movements, uniting the entire mass of the poor peasants, will serve to bring about an alliance between

the workers and the peasants which is the crux of any successful democratic movement.[50]

Armed struggle mounted from below, would bring revolution throughout the Indian subcontinent. Events in Hyderabad provided an apt model:

> The heroic people of Telengana, the great example of the fight against autocracy, not only show what will happen inside the States, but also what will be the real future of India and Pakistan. That is the way the victorious people must march to freedom and real democracy....We must be proud to say that here at last there is the force that will achieve Indian liberation.[51]

Thus the Communists ironically found themselves, like the Nizam, struggling against the government of India. Realization that the rural revolt might be turned outward rather than inward may account for the seeming lack of enthusiasm with which the Nizam's regime prosecuted the battle against the Telengana insurgents, a point to which we shall return in the following chapter.

The change of line of February 1948 proclaimed mobilization against the Nehru government in New Delhi. Rebels in Telengana had been mobilized against more immediate targets: large landlords, the razakars. Congress—the movement of the Mahatma—was not an enemy to Hindu villagers. The problems to which CPI leaders referred, such as "irreconcilable" conflict beteween "Anglo-American imperialists" and the "democratic camp led by the Soviet Union," were far removed from village realities. India-wide class struggle may have been almost as distant. It would have required a profound transformation of a struggle ignited by local conditions, of which the Communist party was more the benefactor than the instigator, to extend the Telengana rebellion beyond its regional limits, despite the beliefs pressed by the CPI.

A final comment on the official ideology should be made. Resolutions espousing rural revolution, political militancy and unity among affected groups cannot bring any of these into being. Peasant revolution in India, I believe, would have required polarization far greater than that characterizing the country in 1948. The Congress government, having achieved independence, enjoyed a wide basis of popular support. The Telengana rebellion was an aberration, made possible by the idiosyncratic conditions of Hyderabad. The local successes of this uprising could not be transferred to the revolutionary objectives of the CPI. In a term to be hurled later at CPI leaders, "left sectarianism" had led them astray.

Telengana villagers nonetheless provided a solid foundation for an ideology of collective political violence. What the peasants had been denied, they were ready (with the weakening of restraints on their action) to take by force. The goals of greatest importance were material and personal: they involved property, safety, and livelihood. Land redistribution, cancellation of hereditary indebtedness, reduction of taxes, abolition of *vetti*, and protection against further landlord and razakar raids constituted the chief peasant needs—and the Communists were willing and able to encourage all. "Lands to the tiller" proved as potent a slogan for rural mobilization in Telengana as it had in many similar settings of landlord-peasant confrontation.

By formulating the issue thus, I am drastically simplifying a far more complex phenomenon. Landlord-peasant confrontation constituted only the first stage, the "easy and necessary"[52] confiscation of the lands of the extremely well-off. How much further the redistribution should extend was to become an important point in the eventual suffocation of the rebellion. Paradoxically, as its class content became sharpened with the landless taking a more prominent role, many "peasants" withdrew their support.[53] Peasant-peasant confrontation supplanted landlord-peasant confrontation, as will be noted in the following chapter. An ideology of struggle against the government in New Delhi could not bridge the gap that grew in the Telengana movement after the 1948 police action and implementation of some land reforms.

Mau Mau: Oaths and Basic Objectives

The most direct evidence of ideological themes in the Mau Mau rebellion can be found in the oaths, songs and prayers shared by participants. They set forth the goals of collective political violence, various does and don'ts of permitted behavior and Kikuyu solidarity. Moral precepts juxtaposed to group secrecy; obedience coupled with opposition to influences corrupting indigenous society; struggle against those who usurped land and their allies: these were major elements. Hopes for a better future required militancy. Death would be the price for backsliding, for transgressing the vows solemnly taken.

The basic pledge, the oath of unity, seems to have spread with the direct encouragement of Kikuyu leaders, including Kenyatta's close associate, Chief Koinange.[54] Building on a heritage of oaths, broadened and transformed by the Olenguruone experience, they sought to counter settler and administrative pressures with indisputable evidence of Kikuyu solidarity. The multifaceted nature of the appeal is evident in the oath itself, as reported by Karari Njama:

I swear before God and before all the people present here that...
   (1) I shall never reveal this secret of the KCA oath—which is of Gikuyu and Mumbi and which demands land and freedom—to any person who is not a member of our society. If I ever reveal it, may this oath kill me!

(2) I shall always help any member of our society who is in difficulty or need of help. If I ever reveal it, etc.

(3) If I am ever called, during the day or night, to do any work for this society, I shall obey....

(4) I shall on no account ever disobey the leaders of this society...

(5) If I am ever given firearms or ammunition to hide, I shall do so...

(6) I shall always give money or goods to this society whenever called upon to do so...

(7) I shall never sell land to Europeans or an Asian...

(8) I shall not permit intermarriage between Africans and the white community...

(9) I will never go with a prostitute...

(10) I shall never cause a girl to become pregnant and leave her unmarried...

(11) I will never marry and then seek a divorce...

(12) I shall never allow any daughter to remain uncircumcised...

(13) I shall never drink European manufactured beer or cigarettes...

(14) I shall never spy on or otherwise sell my people to Government...

(15) I shall never help the missionaries in their Christian faith to ruin our traditional and cultural customs...

(16) I will never accept the Beecher Report [a report published in 1949 urging government subsidies to independent schools if they accepted greater government control]...

(17) I shall never steal any property belonging to a member of our society...

(18) I shall obey any strike call, whenever notified...

(19) I will never retreat or abandon any of our mentioned demands but will daily increase more and stronger demands until we achieve our goals...

(20) I shall pay 62/50s. and a ram as assessed by this society as soon as I am able...

(21) I shall always follow the leadership of Jomo Kenyatta and Mbiyu Koinange....[55]

This was the oath, administered with slight variations to thousands of Kikuyu from early 1950 on. Two dominant themes — land and freedom — emerge; sub-themes of unity, leadership, and moral behavior defined in ethnic terms (e.g. female circumcision) appear as well. Each reflected problems of the past; each suggested avenues for future change.

I need not belabor further the acute discontent Kikuyu felt about land. The history of European settlement in Kenya had been one of perceived continuous abridgement of indigenous rights. No convention seemed sacrosanct to, no promise bonding on, the *mzungu* (white man). His apparently unquenchable thirst for land touched all Kikuyu. Although the largest proportion of Mau Mau fighters were drawn from the young and the landless, one should not assume that the unpropertied alone responded to the appeal. "Stolen lands" touched all Kikuyu. None could have escaped this concern; it had been the central theme for forty years. No sharper issue existed for an agricultural people whose social system focused on *mbari* holdings.

Freedom was an equally palpable issue. The colonial situation denied majority rights. Africans needed little reminder about color bar, the *kipande*, or European monopolization of economic and political control. All manner of ills could be ascribed to the colonial presence; the cure was simple to envision, albeit complicated to achieve. British rule was thus the target, *uhuru* (freedom) the portmanteau objective.

The sub-themes of unity and leadership drew their importance from the divisions that long had racked the Kikuyu. Effectively reversing the shared sense of exploitation required the backing of all members of the ethnic group, irrespective of *mbari* or ridge loyalties, irrespective equally of differences in power, wealth or status. The children of Gikuyu and Mumbi — legendary founders of the Kikuyu people — had to band together under Kenyatta's and Koinange's guidance. The most highly educated members of the society were thus invoked as the leaders of a movement whose ascriptive foundations became more pronounced with time. To what extent were they, in fact, the architects of the attempt to achieve unity through the oath of solidarity, continued emphasis on land adjustment, and increased attention to independence?

The key point is historic continuity. Kenyatta was chosen as fulltime secretary of the KCA (Kikuyu Central Association) in 1927; his prolonged sojourn in England started with his representing the KCA; his appearances and publications sounded the familiar refrain of land. What Kenyatta said to a Communist party newspaper in 1929 — "The present situation means that once again the natives of the colony are showing their determination not to submit to the outrageous tyranny which has been their lot since the British robbers stole their land"[56] — expressed in less temperate terms what early Kikuyu spokesmen had been saying. Koinange was the son of senior chief Mbiyu Koinange who (despite his association with the Kikuyu Association, an officially-encouraged "moderate" voice of African opinion) had often lent his prestige to claims for land. A graduate of Columbia and student at Cambridge, Peter Mbiyu Koinange combined detailed knowledge of the West with prestige through his educational accomplishments and family ties. Kenyatta and Koinange formed the nucleus of the Kiambu elite — the presumed "brains" of the Kikuyu, by whose efforts the oath of unity was strongly encouraged. Both gave voice to self-government, Kenyatta having expressed in 1933 the conviction that "all Kenya Africans must fight for their liberation . . . .Let none of our countrymen have any faith in these imperialist hypocritical 'promises' which mean nothing but the oppression and exploitation of the masses."[57]

If the issues were not new after World War II, the tactics represented a change. *Uhuru* might be approached in several ways. Cooperation with the colonial administration, trusting it to rectify grievances brought to its attention, provided one option. A gradualist approach of this sort required

British willingness to negotiate, concede, and reform, to deal in good faith with those using officially-recognized channels. Officially, this was the approach adopted by KAU (Kenya African Union), founded in 1944 with the encouragement of a former Chief Native Commissioner.[58] Independence did not appear among the objectives enumerated in its constitution; stress lay rather on preparing the majority for political rights. A second approach to *uhuru* lay in oiling the cogs of official machinery through pressure, within legal limits. KAU's increasing efforts to achieve a mass foundation reflected this desire to harness popular concern openly—and events such as the Olenguruone expulsion and compulsory terracing campaigns gave ample opportunity for organizing public discontent. The third path to freedom, obviously, came in insurrection. Officially and I believe temperamentally, Kenyatta and Koinange doubted the utility of this approach. Koinange, for example, left Kenya in late 1951 with a petition, signed by 37,000 people, intended to draw United Nations' attention to land issues. When requests and public pressures failed, and when the grievances remained blatant, militant leaders came to the fore. The veterans and urbanites in the Nairobi branch of KAU provided the spark, as indicated in the preceding chapter. Their 1951 demand for independence in three years, and their encouragement of mass oathing, contributed to the tensions of 1952. With the declaration of the state of emergency, the imprisonment of KAU leaders, and the expulsion of Kikuyu squatters, the militants' approach received powerful impetus indeed. Many responses of the British government thus played into the hands of those who saw collective political violence as the only suitable means for change.

Mau Mau ideology depicted the obvious and familiar shortcomings of the *ancien régime* in orthodox ways. The repetition of the land and freedom demands suggests the relatively unchanging nature of Kikuyu concerns; the objectives were not in question, only the means. No clear representation of institutions to be built or gains to be consolidated can be discerned in Mau Mau statements. The obvious nature of colonial shortcomings made their antitheses equally apparent. For most, I suspect, the desired objective remained restoration of land and personal rights, respect for customary social practices, and opportunity for advancement through education. Independence for all of Kenya was an abstraction of concern primarily to the leaders, of far less importance to most forest fighters. In the words of one Mau Mau militant, "For my part I was only hoping to be given a small piece of land somewhere and to be treated a little more decently by the Kenya Government and white settlers. It didn't seem too much to hope that the democracy we were supposed to be fighting for would be extended to cover the Africans of Kenya."[59]

The stamp of the militants emerged most clearly in the pledge potential forest fighters had to take. To maintain the discipline and spirit necessary for conflict, the *batuni* (platoon) oath was administered to men aged sixteen to thirty—the traditional ages for warriors. Surrounded by the paraphernalia of a solemn pledge, the initiate (on threat of death) swore:

(1) I have today become a soldier of Gikuyu and Mumbi and I will from now onwards fight the real fight for the land and freedom of our country till we get it or till my last drop of blood. Today I have set my first step [stepping over the first line of the goat's small intestine] as a warrior and I will never retreat. And if I ever retreat:
    May this soil and all its products be a curse upon me!
(2) If ever I am called to accompany a raid or bring in the head of an enemy, I shall obey and never give lame excuses. And if I ever refuse:
    May this soil and all its products curse upon me!
(3) I will never spy or inform on my people, and if ever sent to spy on our enemies I will always report the truth. And if I fail in this:
    May this soil and all its products curse upon me!
(4) I will never reveal a raid or crime committed to any person who has not taken the *Bgero Oath* [*Muma wa Ngero*, Oath of Violence or Crime] and will steal firearms wherever possible. And if I ever reveal our secrets or fail to use or turn over to our warriors any firearms I acquire:
    May this soil and all its products curse upon me!
(5) I will never leave a member in difficulty without trying to help him. And if I ever abandon a member in trouble:
    May this soil and all its products be a curse upon me!
(6) I will obey the orders of my leaders at all times without any argument or complaint and will never fail to give them any money or goods taken in a raid and will never hide any pillages or take them for myself. And if I fail in these things:
    May this soil and all its products curse upon me!
(7) I will never sell land to any white man. And if I sell:
    May this soil and all its products be a curse upon me![60]

Less known and publicized than the Mau Mau oaths, but of major importance in spreading awareness of its objectives and maintaining group morale, were hymns. For a society in which literacy remained unusual, familiar tunes joined to political verses proved highly efficacious. They could be readily learned, and sung in Europeans' presence generally without fear of reprisal.[61] Few whites realized that it was not "Onward Christian Soldiers" or "God Save the Queen" they were hearing! The standard themes—land, freedom, unity, Kenyatta, moral uprightness—appear in the texts, as evident in the following:

God created Gikuyu and Mumbi and placed them in Kikuyu land, but they were deceived by Europeans and their land was stolen from them.

I will never abandon Jomo, he has promised that our land will be returned to us.[62]

Tell the elders to shut up, they let our lands be taken. Tell the young men to rise up in arms so that our lands may be returned to us.

When the Europeans came they came with great cunning saying they came to make us wise, but really they came to deceive us.

The time has come to open our eyes and our ears. Our hearts, too, must be opened.

The whole land is nothing but darkness and the squatter system, when the young men want to rise up they are told 'The time is not yet.'[63]

You Europeans you are nothing but robbers, though you pretended to lead us. Go away, go away you Europeans, the years that are past have been more than enough for us.

You of Kikuyu and Mumbi fight hard, that we may be given self-government, that our land may be given back to us. The corn is ripe for harvest, if we are late the harvest will be lost.[64]

Who is he who will weep when Kenyatta is proclaimed King?[65]

Such reiteration of the undisputed popular view gave forest fighters and passive supporters alike a sense of unity in their struggle. The "Loyalists" and the cautious elders were warned not to press their views. The militants, by contrast, were praised.

Mau Mau ideology reiterated old goals. Its continuity with earlier expressions of discontent emerges clearly. Any "new ideas" came in tactics rather than objectives. Mau Mau fighters looked back to the historical travails of their people even as they looked forward to self-government and the elimination of land restrictions. The Kikuyu would at last be relieved of the inequities British rule had imposed on them, by the combination of militant ideology and military pressure.

There, of course, lay the rub. Each increase in Kikuyu solidarity strained interethnic solidarity. Though important for all Kenya, Mau Mau gained far greater support among the Kikuyu, because of the differential impact of colonialism, openness of social structure, continuity of protest, demographic pressures, and the like. Oathing ceremonies pregnant with Kikuyu symbolism had their costs, as well as their benefits. References to the house of Kikuyu and Mumbi, or to "the community," made sense in a context of intraethnic pluralism; they seemed counterproductive in enhancing interethnic unity. Mau Mau militancy became an almost exclusive Kikuyu endeavor, sanitized of involvement by other groups.

Open conflict, seemingly so necessary for the indigenous cause, affected Kikuyu solidarity as well. The oath of unity carried little risk and was close to universal among the Kikuyu: the *batuni* or warrior oath carried the risk of death. Not all were ready to take the fateful plunge. As we shall see in the following chapter, those who fought tended disproportionately to come from the young, the poor, and the north. The warrior oath was administered to men aged sixteen to thirty, traditional ages for fighters; the landless clearly had less to lose, more to gain, by combat; inhabitants of North Tetu in Nyeri Division formed by far the largest part of the Aberdares guerrillas.[66] The warriors, supposedly fighting for all Kenyans, could be presented as fighting for the Kikuyu alone. Divisions within the Kikuyu, papered over by oathing campaigns and reinforced by early British steps at repression, could be reopened. The unity thereby achieved proved fragile as "pacification" replaced repression, and as the political and economic changes Mau Mau spokesmen had demanded started to appear on the horizon.

A final note should be added. Were we to contrast the belief systems of the four rebellions along an indigenous-exogenous spectrum, we would find Mau Mau ideology very much toward the indigenous side, as shown by the use of ethnic symbols. The plight of the Kikuyu squatters could have been presented, for example, in class terms. Few groups in Africa seemed better suited to be deemed an agricultural proletariat. But struggle along economic lines (despite the efforts of some militant trade unionists) linking Kikuyu to other dispossessed groups never really got off the ground. In fact, the divisions that emerged among the Kikuyu impeded efforts at widening the struggle. Increasing effort had to be expended on maintaining support within an ethnic group fragmented by history, geography, clan, age, economic status, and genuine differences about the best means of bringing change. The increasingly strident protestations of unity indicated an increasingly divided base. Might Mau Mau leaders have reduced some of these cleavages by emphasizing (as did Kenyatta in the 1930s, and as did Pierre Mulele later in Kwilu) the class nature of struggle and non-African models for change? Would more "modern" and fewer "traditional" ideological elements have made a difference? It is conceivable that they might. I believe, however, that the political interests of the Kikuyu, similar to those of the Pende and Mbunda, meant the promise of economic and personal security ranked foremost as a goal, and clear limits existed to the extent to which such desires could be directed toward class struggle. The Kwilu rebellion, to which we now turn, substantiates this general point.

Kwilu: Mulele's Redefinition of Maoism

The ideology of Kwilu rebellion may be analyzed at several levels. It mixed—as did justifications for the other uprisings—a variety of issues, explanations, objectives, and appeals. Designed to touch a wide variety of audiences, the generalized beliefs thus incorporated what may seem to be contradictory elements. Concepts of class conflict contrasted with popular beliefs in magic; appeals for widespread and immediate personal affluence collided with emphasis on collective sacrifice; implicit appeals to ethnic solidarity jostled with explicit calls for class unity. It was a combination as wide-ranging as the beliefs of the Taipings. The outside observer may find ideology in Kwilu a pastiche barely credible in its range of concerns. Yet such a perspective could lead to serious misunderstanding. The seemingly divergent elements were in fact mutually reinforcing. Ideology cannot be isolated from the environment in which it flourishes. Mulelist beliefs struck a sympathetic chord. In rural areas of Kwilu, the result was a widely supported movement against the dominance of the central government, memories of which remained significant long after the main actors had passed from the scene.

The following major strands existed within the ideology of the Kwilu rebellion:

a Maoist element, learned by Mulele during his months of study in China;

a messianic element, focused on the personal attributes of Mulele himself;

a magical element, through which the incredible became credible and participants gained special powers;

a material element, compounded of popular expectations about gaining the fruits withheld at the first independence; and

a mass element, implicit rather than explicit, that encouraged ethnic solidarity behind a favorite son.

The Maoist element was introduced by Mulele himself after he and some close associates decided to continue their struggle by securing additional backing outside the Congo. As noted in the previous chapter, Mulele had served the Stanleyville government of Gizenga in its chief external post, ambassador to Cairo. Cairo housed the Front de Libération Nationale of Algeria. The Algerian revolution was then close to triumphing over the French (such, at least, was the view in the Egyptial capital) as a result of rural mobilization. What Frantz Fanon was soon to express in *The Wretched of the Earth* was very much the subject of discussion. Cairo provided homes for many other liberation movements and groups, such as the Afro-Asian Peoples Solidarity Organization. In such a setting, peasant warfare seemed to offer the surefire route to success. Contacts were made; Mulele accepted the invitation offered him, and departed for Peking around March 1962.

Obviously, the conditions the Chinese Community party faced in Yenan or the Chingkanshan mountains differed markedly from the conditions the Parti Solidaire Africain faced in Kwilu, or from those Marx observed in mid-nineteenth century Europe. To the extent that Maoist prescriptions reflected unique aspects, their employment in other settings could be questioned. The elaboration of "people's war" beliefs, however, suggested they could be employed in a variety of circumstances. Basic principles—class conflict, the necessity for rural mobilization, the utility of guerrilla struggle, the importance of the party commanding the gun, guerrillas as close to the people as fish to water—appeared as applicable to the Congo in 1962-3 as they had in China in 1936-8. Direct parallels existed between Mao's writings and the principles taught in forest camps. The "Order of Mission" for Mulelist fighters included twenty-seven points, many drawn directly from Mao's three great rules of discipline and eight recommendations for guerrilla conduct.[67] More important than similar wording was parallelism of thought. Mulele drew heavily on the concept of class struggle. This, I need not emphasize, is a central tenet in Marxist thought ("All history is the history of class struggle"). The adaptation of this concept to the Congo in the early 1960s posed problems. Prior to independence, a clear cleavage in power, status, and wealth had divided the Belgian masters from the Congolese subjects. Exploitation existed, and was resented. The highly successful popular mobilization that benefited the PSA in Kwilu testified to the popular wish for change. But with self-government formally achieved, and with the Force Publique mutiny having led to the hasty departure of most Belgian cadres, the racial/class dichotomy diminished in intensity. The concept of class struggle had to be fitted to Congolese realities. The following extracts give the flavor of Mulele's adaptation:

> In a country of this sort, all persons are divided into two classes:
> — — The rich have all the wealth of the country in their hands: these are the capitalists; they profit from the labors of all persons, in the same way a mosquito sucks people's blood.
> — — The peasants and workers suffer many pains in their heavy labor, but all the profit, it is the rich who take it, all their money, the rich or the capitalists take it.
> All the wealth of the country is thus in the hands of foreigners....
>
> Here is the way to survive (*manière de vivre*): the villagers have revolted and are combatting the rulers; the day they conquer the rulers, they will enact (*prendront*) the law which follows: all persons must have work; if someone doesn't work, he will not longer eat. Foreigners cannot come to take or steal the riches of our country....[68]

Class struggle, it should be noted, was delineated in social as well as economic terms. The people in the quotation above were divided into three categories: strangers or imperialists; the "reactionaries", members of the "bad government who aid the foreigners or the imperialists to steal the wealth of the country"; and all others who live in poverty, "like the dogs who encircle the game but who eat only the bones."[69] On other occasions, Mulele distinguished among *réactionnaires, retardaires* and *advancés*, between those who opposed and those who supported his movement. Those who were "young and progressive in spirit and belief"[70] were to combat those who lagged behind in their beliefs. They were to oppose the reactionaries, those who collaborated with the "bad government" — in other words, the new Congolese political class and also its local allies. Members of what we may deem the rural intelligentsia, teachers and clerks in particular, belonged to this group. Their advanced training gave them advantages relatively few Congolese enjoyed; their salaries (when they were paid) came from the government; they opposed the use of force for social or political ends. Many were suspect and, in the first phase of the uprising, were eliminated; others came to exercise significant responsibilities as *quipe* leaders when the importance of their skills became apparent. Class struggle was thus subject in Kwilu to several interpretations, some of them well removed from the formulations of Marx or Mao. Such adaptations led some observers of the Kwilu rebellion to deem the influence of Communist ideologies "an expedient, tactical response to the inherently Congolese social revolution already taking place."[71]

Mulele not only shaped ideology; he was one of its major parts. His marked personal qualities were extolled. To many followers, Mulele partook of messianic qualities. As had Simon Kimbangu, Pierre Mulele might be assailed by foreigners, perhaps even killed, but his spirit and contributions would long survive.

This element seems to differ somewhat from Weber's description of charismatic authority. Charisma (literally the "gift of grace") involves a relationship between persons in the throes of rapid social change and a trusted leader in whom all confidence would be vested. As noted previously, the early God-Worshippers put their confidence in Hung Hsiu-ch'üan in such a fashion. Charismatic authority differs markedly from both traditional authority and rational-legal authority. Charismatic authority might provide a bridge to a more stable or "routinized" system: only under unusual circumstances should it arise. Only the work of Feng Yün-shan established Hung's charisma in organizational form. The continuity among messianic sects in the western Congo suggests thus not the uniqueness of charisma, but the revival of messianism. The earlier political consequences of Kimbanguism and its offshoots seem organically linked to Mulelist ideology.

Fox and her colleagues point to similarities between Mulele and various leaders of religious movements; all were "reputed to have special magico-religious powers of invulnerability, invincibility and metamorphosis, with which they could protect their followers as well as themselves."[72] Mulele was indeed presumed to wield *dawa* (magic). On occasion, he would point a loaded revolver at his temple, pull the trigger, and walk away unscathed — the explosion of the blank cartridge having suitably impressed his gullible audience. Those who followed his precepts shared his invulnerability. Members of the *maquis* were subject to certain taboos, infraction of which might open them to injury. For example, the partisans could not use, or even touch, objects belonging to Europeans; they were neither to wash nor cut their hair until final victory; they entered battle barechested.[73] Such practices were psychologically important. They helped convince the Mulelist fighters of their power — and the ANC soldiers of their corresponding impotence. After all, could the national army claim to have a leader whose name sufficed to turn bullets into water? A brave show by the purportedly invulnerable, and the defenders would flee. This tactic, I should add, proved remarkably successful in the early stages of fighting. The Congolese version of the power of positive thinking served Mulele's fighters well. It meant most "battles" between ANC and Mulelist detachments were more displays than overt combat. Few bullets were fired by the Kwilu rebels, for, as we shall see in the following chapters, they collectively possessed fewer than 100 rifles. Death at the hands of the ANC could be explained as failure to obey all the taboos and injunctions; the presumed invulnerability of the leader and his convinced followers remained.

The fourth element in the composite ideology was material. Its roots lay in the preindependence expectations which the PSA both nurtured and responded to. Party slogans, I have already noted, stressed economic advancement. The dreams had not come true. Government revenues had been diverted to the interests of the few rather than to the needs of the many. Only a profound change in the governing class and its foreign supporters could rectify the situation.

Many direct appeals to the instinct for property figured in the Mulelist beliefs. Asphalted roads would connect hamlets; along these highways would run automobiles powered by free gasoline. "A beautiful house, complete with furniture, will be built for each person by the new government."[74] One can see in these wishes clear reflections of the unmet 1960 electoral promises. What elections could not achieve peacefully, the people must wrest by force. Light-fingered politicians seemingly had profited; now it was the public's turn.

Contributing finally to the appeal for collective action was a belief in the need for ethnic unity. The mass basis on which the Kwilu rebellion rested was primarily a Mbunda and Pende basis.[75] The Pende stood out among Congolese peoples with their heritage of revolt; Gizenga seems to have captured their support far more than the Pende chief minister of Kwilu, Norbert Leta.[76] The Mbunda stood solidly behind Mulele. Given the federative, multiethnic nature of the PSA, such tribal solidarity may appear surprising. It was not. The ethnic complexity of Kwilu as a whole, and the consequent ethnic complexity of the PSA, by no means precluded near-unanimous support for favorite sons.

It remains more fully to explore how these sources of collective action were translated into collective political violence. Calls to villagers to combat the incumbents' acts had to be translated into action. Here, Mulele's establishment of forest training camps represented the clearest step toward open insurgency.

The thick forests of parts of rural Kwilu provided suitable cover; the sympathy of the populace offered satisfactory protection. Since clear evidence of public support was essential to Muleist beliefs — "This must be a battle of all the people of the country — the popular masses — who must raise themselves out of their suffering"[77] — the training centers were located close to villages. Participants spent days in the villages, leading normal rural lives, evenings in the camps. This tie was to remain until ANC harassment forced villagers to flee further into the forests.

In the latter part of 1963, the blunders of the ANC contributed to politicization. Military probes into the area of Mulele's support were insufficient to bring victory, but succeeded "in exacerbating the discontent of villagers of the Mbunda region against ANC soldiers who plunged unreservedly (*se livrent sans plus aucune retenue*) into exactions of every sort."[78] The Mulelist groups responded in kind. Isolated incidents — capture and execution of some policemen, arson of administrative offices and petroleum storage tanks — became increasingly common. A general strike was launched with the ominous warning, "All those who work with the whites will leave with the whites." ANC and police pressure grew apace, a newspaper report suggesting both "kill without distinction and fire as if to amuse themselves."[79] A state of exception for the entire province of Kwilu was proclaimed by the central government 18 January 1964. A few days later, the full fury of the uprising was felt, with a series of attacks on missions and the rupture of communications with the outside world. The teachings of the forest camps were at last coming to fruition. The violence Mulele had prescribed as the remedy was now being dosed out.

Mulelist ideology, it should be clear, drew on multiple sources of inspiration. Its appeal came from its correspondence with Congolese realities. The seeming unresponsiveness of the central and provincial governments to villagers' concerns, combined with the indiscriminate repression of the armed forces and police, prepared the rural populace for collective political violence. The Maoist element on which contemporary reports focused represented but one of several elements in the justification for rebellion.

Without the initiatives taken by Mulele, would the Kwilu rural populace have remained passive spectators of the political game from which they had been excluded? Probably not, I believe: the heritage of revolt in Kwilu was deep; the other revolts of the "second independence" seem to have stirred the political cauldron without such an explicit effort at rural guerrilla preparation. But Mulele's efforts boosted the stakes, as it were. He wanted a revolution, initiated in the countryside. He encouraged collective political violence by leavening the Congolese situation with references to China and Mao Tse-tung. He sought to generalize the particular grievances of the residents of Kwilu by linking them to broad concepts of class struggle, not to self-limiting concepts of ethnic solidarity. He saw the uprising in his province as initial steps toward a national revolution. Kwilu to Mulele was the Yenan of the Congo, the base from which profound economic, political and social alteration would spread. As had CPI proponents of the Telengana uprising, the PSA leader sought to create a "base area" for wider change.

The overwhelming portion of the Mbunda and Pende supported collective political violence. The Mulelist partisans enjoyed a supportive milieu of discontented persons, to whom revolt seemed the best way, and perhaps the only way, to rectify detested conditions. The shortcoming of the existing channels left no other route. Collective political violence in some form was the likely outcome. The discontent that had been politicized needed outlet. Mulele crystallized and pointed; he did not cause what was inherent in the situation. The multiple elements of the Mulelist ideology accorded well with the profound and widespread grievances of early 1964. Though the "second independence" was not achieved, as the following chapter will illustrate, the extent of popular discontent came clearly to the fore.

With the development of ideological justifications, we reach the end of the longest section of this book. The politicization of discontent, it should be readily apparent, involved a variety of steps that affected the scope, magnitude and intensity of collective political violence. I have presented the steps in a rough chronological sequence: the intensification of relative deprivation as a result of generally unexpected, abrupt changes for the worse in living conditions; apparent deafness of those in power to pleas for local reform, worsened by violence on behalf of resented privileged groups; organizational and ideological adaptation by protestors, melding elements unique to each social milieu with aspects drawn from alien settings. The result, clearly, was a hardening of divisions. Polarization between ruler and ruled appeared in ever-sharper relief. Initiative on both sides passed to the militants, ready to defend their privileges, or to restructure society as they deemed fit. Collective political violence suggested, in effect, the lack of other avenues for resolving differences. Armed groups were ready to strike at each other, the privileged in the name of order, the downtrodden and aspirant in the name of justice. Beliefs justifying the use of violence—whether to retain or to alter the status quo—marked the contenders.

Our four case studies make apparent the importance of the rural dispossessed. Their militancy, desire for economic redistribution, and relative freedom to move made them chief supporters of the rebellions. Such persons were hampered, however, by the effects of years (perhaps centuries) of economic, political, and social subordination. As individuals of low status, limited in their education and outlook, they often hesitated before committing themselves to struggle. They suffered in silence until others pointed the way to struggle. When the initiative had been taken—by a disappointed degree candidate preaching an unorthodox religion; by sons of Reddi landlords concerned with cultural recognition; by rural artisans linked to dispossessed squatters; by an ambitious politician exiled for his leanings—the rural poor joined in great numbers. The goals they sought reflected their economic and social needs. The land system of the Taipings theoretically offered improvement to rural laborers and sharecroppers. The parcelling-out of *deshmukhs'* land in Telengana, and the centrality of land in Kikuyu claims, underlined the needs of many for land. Even in Kwilu, economic security for exploited rural groups figured prominently in Mulele's appeals to class solidarity.

Does this mean the rural poor constituted the social stratum most susceptible to ideological appeals for collective political violence?

Such is the message of perhaps the most-quoted ideologues of peasant revolution, with whom this chapter started. Mao Tse-tung and Frantz Fanon emphasized the central role of peasants in armed struggle. Poor peasants—the landless sharecroppers and tenants—had the greatest amount to gain, the least to lose, from land redistribution and political change. Both writers viewed the landless as the most violent, most revolutionary, group of all--perhaps at times too ready to turn to struggle. As Mao wrote in his 1927 Hunan report, he would award seven points on a scale of revolutionary fervor to peasants, only three to urban dwellers and the military.[80] The "colossal storm" he saw brewing in Chinese villages could be tapped to change the system in its entirety. Fanon viewed "the starving peasant, outside the class system" as the person who is "first among the exploited to discover that only violence pays...."[81]; "the proof of success lies in a whole structure being changed from the bottom up . . . .after a murderous and decisive struggle...."[82]

Both men idealized the struggles they observed. Mao (according to Alavi's trenchant critique)[83] considerably overplayed the actual role of poor peasants in his Hunan report when, in point of fact, the middle peasants were far more militant than poor peasants in resisting the extractions of landlords and warlords. Fanon generalized from the Algerian revolution — its shortcomings as well as its accomplishments — to suggest an initiating role for the rural dispossessed.[84] In his words, "...the masses...push the leaders on to prompt action. The armed struggle has begun . . .once the match is lit, the blaze spreads liked wildfire through the whole country."[85] I grant the central importance of the landless in the four uprisings we have examined. The evidence does not support the contention that they *initiated* violence, however, nor that they exercised significant leadership responsibilities. They followed where others had led.

Mao and Fanon concerned themselves with rural revolutions. They believed (as had Marx) peasant movements were consigned to impotence vis-a-vis "the system." Such movements could only palliate, not transform. Any revolution mounted from rural areas required alliances with more enlightened groups, leaders from outside the peasant setting. In Fanon's words,

> the leaders of the rising realize that the various groups must be enlightened; that they must be educated and indoctrinated; and that an army and a central authority must be created...The leaders of the rebellion come to see that even very large-scale peasant risings need to be controlled and directed into certain channels. These leaders are led to renounce the movement in so far as it can be termed a peasant revolt, and to transform it into a revolutionary war.[86]

It was necessary, in other words, to go well beyond what villagers initially desired. Their beliefs, practices and outlooks had to be broadened.

The ideological melanges we have considered in this chapter drew their inspirations from dramatically different sources. Indigenous sources held up an ideal rural social order, far more egalitarian and village centered than what existed. Peasant wisdom regarding the subsistence ethic and patron-client mutuality provided yardsticks by which to gauge landlords' performance. Exogenous sources (such as the syncretistic Christianity of Hung Hsiu-ch'üan or the Maoism of Pierre Mulele) emphasized bases for social organization broader than the usual models. But when pressures grew, the larger groupings fragmented. As we shall see in the following chapter, Hung turned increasingly to members of his own clan, Mulele to members of his own ethnic group. The expansion in following brought by success turned into a contraction to the closest and most trusted when defeat loomed. The leaders themselves were accordingly affected by the greater security that kinship ties seemed to offer. They were less successful in creating a broader sense of community than in criticizing the existing order; more capable of envisaging an alternative system that of ousting the existing one.

Ideology, in short, cannot in and of itself transform a host of peasant grievances into a broad-based revolutionary war. Systems of belief do hold up a model for change, stress group consciousness, and direct coordinated efforts. They contribute a great deal indeed to the politicization of discontent. But ideologies, like rare plants, may thrive only in their native environments; in different settings, they might shrivel without careful adaptation. Hung's adjustments of Christianity, Mulele's use of magic and messianism in addition to Maoism, were necessary adaptations. The Taiping rebellion and the Kwilu rebellion challenged the status quo by suggesting new bases for social, economic and political organizations; hence, they were repressed by the incumbents as akin to heresies. Hung and Mulele offered defense against harassment. Ultimately, however, the politicization of discontent ran up against limits. Possibly the most important of these limits were the resources (skills, commitment, funds) the incumbents possessed. A determined political elite, as we shall see in Part III, may use many stratagems to retain its control. Even intensely politicized discontent might batter itself unsuccessfully against a steadfast opponent.

PART III /

REPRESSION AND
RESURGENCE

We have now marched our potential rebels up the hill. Armed, albeit scantily, against the armies of the incumbents, our would-be insurgents are ready to embark on actions from which they cannot retreat. Elements of hope and desperation mingle in their outlooks. Encouraged on the one hand by popular support for their cause, they may be disheartened on the other hand by the power of the dominant minority. As they march down the hill, what fate will they meet? How might their objectives fare with military clashes in the offing?

Part III recounts events sad in some respects. The immediate fruits of rebellion were indeed bitter. Despite widespread public approbation, the insurgents lost the wars. Military defeat and often inglorious death were their fates. What had started with both distaste for relative deprivation and hope for relative restitution concluded with despair. Even when reforms were carried out, they frequently failed to alleviate the miseries of the most miserable.

The early days of rebel-incumbent confrontation marked the high points for the challengers, particularly in Kenya and the Congo. Mau Mau and Mulelist forces enjoyed milieus conducive to rebellion. Support for their causes was close to universal among some ethnic groups, whose geographic concentration encouraged a bandwagon effect. Strength born of unity buoyed the insurgents. Early successes in staking out areas of unquestioned control provided psychological inducement to extend and intensify the confrontation. For a while at least, euphoria characterized the societies; rebellion carried no risks; few could resist the psychological pressure resulting from the murder of overly vocal opponents of the insurgents; the despised government at last had been brought to its knees by united action. Each retreat by the incumbents fueled the strength of the insurgents—a fact observable as well in the Taiping and Telengana rebellions. Success encouraged further success.

Items of concern appeared early, nonetheless. Certainly on paper, the coercive strength of the incumbents far outweighed what the insurgents could muster. The deliberate demilitarization of the population clearly favored those in control. Armaments and military skills were in short supply, monopolized by the dominant minority. The government enjoyed greater fiscal resources; it could more readily request and receive external assistance. Still having various levers of control at their command, the governing regime could revive and intensify the old divide-and-rule policy, neutralizing potential allies of the insurgents.

The balance of forces—the separate strengths of the insurgents and incumbents—shifted over time. As we shall see, "victory" for those in power may have reflected more their staying power and judicious concessions than their initial military superiority. The disparities in manpower and material that benefited the incumbents were countered by differential levels of commitment and competence. The rebels fought among and for a sympathetic population ready to conceal and support them. They enjoyed (in Gurr's terms) strong institutional support, and wielded not insignificant coercive control. At some point in the rebellion, accordingly, one can speak of rough equality between the contending sides. The evidence presented in the following pages suggests this parity came early in the period of open struggle. The initially restricted scale of combat and the widespread popular support given the rebels gave them an advantage the dominant minority could not counter effectively without both mobilization and reconsideration of policy. By counter effectively, I mean something other than the standard recipe of punitive raids, collective fines, or similar reprisals. It seems that only when *suppression* was replaced as the incumbents' strategy by *pacification* that a semblance of the status quo ante bellum could be restored.

Of course, the status quo itself could never be fully restored. The heritage of rebellion is cumulative. Even seemingly unsuccessful attacks added to the stock of indigenous collective political violence. Incumbent attempts fully to revive the *ancien régime* risked reviving the ancient grievances. Modification was necessary—a lesson the governing group certainly should have learned. It seems as though the more significant the changes they would countenance, the more likely peace might prevail after order was restored. Reform after the fact was far better than reform denied. Each reform modified the status quo, however. Citizens could never step twice into the same political system. Post-rebellion Hyderabad and Kenya, for example, came to enjoy completely different systems of rule, based on majority rights.

Granted the continuities in collective political violence, what possibility existed for transforming a rebellious heritage into a revolutionary future?

We have seen the distinctive amalgams of belief and practice which characterized the four uprisings. Under somewhat different conditions, might they have given birth to rapid, profound changes in political institutions, dominant values, and social stratification? This—the question from which this book sprang—fittingly concludes this study. Having pursued a circuitous path, trudging through a multitude of details about disparate political systems, we may be ready to exchange academic caution for political prognostication. This is the task with which the book concludes. While Chapter 8 illustrates the causes of immediate failure, Chapter 9 notes the longer-range implications.

Repression + Concession = Termination?

Contrasts Between Repression and Pacification

The four rebellions failed, militarily and politically, to reach their goals. The central governments remained in control, though their authority had been tested and, in Hyderabad, the Nizam stripped of power. Insurgent leaders faced possible execution for treason or sedition. Even if they avoided this fate, they risked continued exclusion from political arenas. Perceived as leaders "to darkness and death," as the British governor asserted of Jomo Kenyatta, they could be reintegrated only were substantial changes made in the status quo. Rebel armies were disbanded, their arms collected. Military triumph represented only part of the victors' obligations, however. Tranquility had to be established in rural areas, the passions of conflict calmed. The shock of defeat might soon be outgrown; unless the rebellion pushed the incumbents into overdue reform, frustrations might again start to grow. Once again, the cycle of discontent-protest-coercion-rebellion might start to turn. Thus, coercive steps had to be followed by corrective steps, lest history seem to repeat itself. Rebels' failures constituted incumbents' opportunities.

How, in more precise, comparative terms, were the four uprisings suppressed? What common strategies were evolved? Would the requisite steps in effect mitigate the grievances that encouraged collective political violence, or reinforce existing inequalities through greater coercion? What combinations occurred, in other words, between "military" and "political" strategies? Would a cup of coercion leavened by a teaspoon of concession suffice, or should the proportions be reversed? Obviously, no single, simple answer can be given these questions; equally obviously, the termination of the four rebellions reflected differing mixtures of force and reform. It makes sense, accordingly, to sketch in general terms the "military" and "political" problems inherent in the varying approaches before considering the specific details of each rebellion.

Suppression represents a two-edged sword, potentially as dangerous to the wielder as to the would-be victim. Coercion may seem a necessary course of action to the incumbents, yet their use of force may further inflame popular resentment. Clumsy, heavy-handed, erratic repression compounds discontent. On the other hand, the dominant minority may turn *faute de mieux* to force: their options may be restricted, their experience limited, their fear of concession well-founded. What the majority would gain, the minority would have to surrender. Concession could seem a greater risk than repression.

For the incumbents, the simplest means of terminating rebellion, it would seem, is overwhelming might. What is easy in theory is not so in fact. Coercion is costly—particularly when directed against a domestic opponent tapping widespread popular support. Only substantial external assistance might have made suppression, in the absence of other steps, a feasible means of action. The Kenya government drew heavily on British assistance, with a direct cost of more than £55 million thrust on the shoulders of taxpayers. In the end, however, "political" measures may have layed a greater part than "military" measures in subduing Mau Mau rebels. As we shall see, the Ch'ing government profited from Western assistance in combatting Taiping rebels; the Tshombe government of the Congo employed foreign mercenaries and permitted an extensive degree of direct external involvement in quelling various "second independence" uprisings, though not that in Kwilu. Neither the Telengana rebels nor the razakars received extensive outside aid; yet the eventual solution came through Indian intervention. Geopolitical reality made it impossible for the Hyderabad government to obtain external military aid—and even the fabled wealth of the Nizam could not instantly create an army powerful enough to stand up to Indian forces. Simply expressed, the scope of the uprisings became so great that sheer repression became economically unfeasible—even if it were militarily possible. The rebellions could not be crushed without external aid and internal steps carrying lower price tags.

On the principle of "Use fire to fight fire," incumbents turned militarily to units drawn from backgrounds similar to those of the insurgents. The tasks of repression could be completed more efficiently by paramilitary units, especially raised to counter the rebellion, than by orthodox troops drawn from other settings. Lower cost was one obvious advantage, more intimate knowledge of local conditions another. Nuclei existed for those special units in the persons utilized by the administration as local subalterns. These persons had profited by their association with the powerful — and presumably would fight to maintain this association unless the rebels applied strong counterpressure. Assassination of local leaders by the insurgents may have given evidence of their strength and objectives; it also made clear the privileged should hang together lest they hang separately.

A further strategy used in the four rebellions was that of isolation. Containment of the rebels so the bacillus did not spread became far more complicated in execution than in imagination. A first step came in setting apart the actively disaffected from the potentially disaffectable. The geographically and socially limited bases from which the uprisings were launched provided one opportunity for isolation. The insurgents' claims of representing large sectors of the populace could be countered by stressing differences among subject peoples. The oathing useful in steeling Kikuyu for militant action could be depicted, for example, as a tribal plot directed against other Africans; the divide-and-rule strategy, useful in peace, served the incumbents equally well in war. Anger within known confines — a "contained rebellion" — was far preferable to more widely diffused resistance.

Separation between presumed and possible rebels on the basis of ethnic or regional differences was far simpler, to be certain, than distinguishing loyalties among individuals in the rebellious group. Successful repression ultimately required that the incumbents seek out and punish the rebels without unduly alienating innocent bystanders, a discrimination requiring intelligence sources of high reliability. Differentiating among active fighters, passive supporters, genuine neutrals, and government loyalists required considerable skill. A tendency to tar all presumptive rebels with the same brush, as suggested in Chapter 5, exacerbated discontent, and seemed to make real the claims of the insurgents to represent the entire disaffected group. Screening of the subject populace could not be mounted without significant skills, information and resources; the best-financed repression, that of Mau Mau, seemed to give closest attention to classifying on the basis of presumed loyalty.

Geographical or physical isolation became a strategy as well. Any popular uprising derives its chief support from the indigenous peoples. A successful insurgent, in the famous Maoist aphorism, is one who lives among the people as a fish in water. Were it possible to separate the active fighters from the passive supporters, the nexus that strengthened the fighters would be broken, and the uprising suppressed. As we shall see later in this chapter, the British government undertook a major relocation of Kikuyu to break this link — a step eased by the refuge Mau Mau fighters took in the forests of the Aberdares and Mount Kenya. To some extent the villagers of Kwilu fled into wooded areas when Congolese soldiers approached, thereby maintaining the popular-guerrilla tie; many Taiping supporters drifted with Hung's army, its movement more at times resembling a popular migration than a military advance. It would literally have been impossible for the Ch'ing government to regroup the population, so as to separate the Taiping "bandits" from their peasant milieu or for the Tshombe government to break Mulele's support by moving rural dwellers in affected areas. Villagization programs require economic resources, intelligence sources, and political will far beyond the capacity of most governments surveyed in this book. Their closest approach was a simpler one akin to siege: cut off the entire rebel group from supplies, thereby pushing its members eventually into surrender.

The steps noted thus far have shaded from the purely coercive to the more markedly political. Military steps to terminate rebellion constituted only part of the government's arsenal. Successful repression involved political concessions as well. In order to swing the balance of forces, inducements had to be offered collaborators, passive supporters had to be encouraged to give up their allegiance. In short, the incumbents needed to couple coercive steps with diversions and potentially significant concessions.

Political concession, like military repression, cuts two ways. Reforms extracted by pressure from the incumbents could increase the appetite for more. The "slippery slope" fear, to which attention was drawn earlier, no doubt justified the dominant group in opposition to concession. The fact remained, however, that timely changes in policy may accomplish, quickly, cheaply, and relatively painlessly, what hundreds of skilled troops could not effect.

The most effective political steps naturally are those sufficiently attractive to diminish insurgent support significantly, yet insuficiently threatening to dissolve incumbent unity. Concessions viewed as inadequate may steel the resolve of those seeking change; concessions viewed as overly abundant may slacken the resolve of those holding power. Finding the appropriate balance taxes the most ingenious of leaders, and certainly places strains on the unity of the incumbents. The inconsistent policies historians have often noted — sudden lurches from military repression to significant concession and back again — have their source in the undoubted complexity of finding the correct balance. What seems correct today proves wrong tomorrow. Faced with uprisings beyond the scope and intensity with which they had previously dealt, the governments understandably found it difficult to establish and maintain a consistent policy. The apparent military and political success of the British in Kenya rested in large measure on their prior success in Malaya; the other incumbents examined in this book lacked not only the economic resources HMG could bring to bear, but also the counterinsurgency finesse it had gained.

The ultimate carrot that could be offered rebels was a pledge of autonomy. Such a concession seemed to belie the goals for which the incumbents fought. If insurgents' pressure had resulted in an offer of self-government, had they not succeeded? Might military victory for the regime come only at the cost of political defeat?

Steps short of political autonomy, taken at an early point, might well have satisfied rebel claims. In the many pages that have preceded this, I have examined the grievances that led to collective political violence. The participants responded more to economic than to political grievances. Threats to their livelihood and safety, or the unexpected denial of presumed resources, crystallized in the form of relative deprivation. Popular participation rested on issues that touched a wide variety of people; the grievances most readily politicized were economic in nature. Thus, rectification of these frustrations might accomplish the basic objective of the government: restore as much of the status quo as possible at the minimum cost. Significant political steps might not be necessary; cancellation of rural debts, opening of lands for agriculture, or restoration of normal rural markets might suffice. Economic reform might better stem the effusion of resources brought by rebellion than political concession. Because of 1) the close link between control of land and control of government, and 2) the political nature of claims made by the rebels, however, political change was necessary. Only steps toward recognition of majority participation, coupled with land reform, objectively shifted the "balance of forces" to the incumbents. In thus seeming to deny that for which they fought, they might "win." But if the "victors" in effect "lose," who then is triumphant?

Conundrums of this sort probably did not bother government leaders. They had a struggle to carry out. They sought to make the costs of insurgency too onerous for the rebels to bear. Because the proponents of change suffered from low status, the incumbents avoided even minor concessions to these. Equally, however, government leaders had to ensure the costs of counterinsurgency did not overstrain their own resources. The complex calculus of endurance and esprit, of resources and rewards, shifted over time. A prolonged struggle could be decided by staying power, and any concession by the incumbents had to be weighed against the effects it might have on both parties. Military and political questions had answers that were inevitably intertwined. The "politics by other means" that constitutes war might require an explicitly political answer. Thus, I am tempted to assert that economic reforms ultimately constituted political concessions. The seeming weakening of the rulers' hegemony might alone maintain it in the long run. Successful termination required a combination of repression and concession. Only supplementing military steps by political changes achieved what was sought initially by coercion, unless those in control were prepared (as was the Ch'ing dynasty) to extirpate all resistance and to encourage arming of local groups. What we will see in this chapter, accordingly, is a shift by the incumbents from repression to pacification. The change is more than terminological; it is one of basic approach.

The pages that follow relate grim stories — grim especially for those whose sympathies lie with the rebels. As a rough equilibrium was established at the local level between the two contenders, the innocent bystanders may have suffered most. Guerrillas might defend themselves; villagers had few defenses. The civil war-like conditions introduced (especially in China and Kenya) fratricidal conflict. In the short run, no one "won." Rebellion remains an act of grim desperation when both parties are determined in their resolve — a lesson our four uprisings teaches clearly.

Taiping: Suppression without Accommodation

Expunging the Taiping rebels cost more lives than any civil war in world history. The Ch'ing dynasty and their gentry collaborators had no desire to leave behind any remaining trace of Hung Hsiu-ch'üan's combination of heresy and treason. After a decade and a half of combat, the government was fixed in its intention to repress. Concessions to the insurgents — such as repatriating Taiping soldiers to their home province following the surrender of the "Heavenly Capital" — were quickly rejected. Those who had proclaimed the passing of the Mandate were put to the sword.

In terms of elapsed time, suppression of the Taiping rebellion took more years than the three other uprisings combined. This reflects both the scope and scale of the conflict and the weaknesses of the Manchu rulers. Their inadequacies had provoked collective political violence; their ineptitude exacerbated and prolonged it. Unwilling either to make a few timely concessions, or to throw efficient troops into the fray at an early stage, the incumbents "won" only by rallying gentry, whose profitably symbiotic relationships with the court had been threatened by the rebels' ideology, and by letting time take its toll of rebel solidarity. The court's caution had good reason. The more it had to depend on quasi-independent troops under local control, the more readily the central administration itself might be challenged. Keeping power in the capital meant, in effect, not conceding too much autonomy to those supporting the dynasty — for who could tell the purposes to which such autonomy might be put?

A complete history of the fall of the "Heavenly Kingdom" lies beyond the scope of this work—and many able scholars have already plowed the historical academic furrow. The collapse may best be understood by four facets. The 1854-6 period stands as a clear turning point. Problems manifested at that time betokened internal weaknesses. The vaunted dedication and singularity of the Taipings seemed to wither in Nanking. That the rebellion did not collapse completely at that time points to the second facet, the shortcomings of the Ch'ing dynasty itself. When the court overcame some of its cautions and authorized a different form of military recruitment, the tide turned fully. The special contributions of Tseng Kuo-fan and his Hunan Army thus constitute the third facet. Finally, the rivalry and incompetence of Taiping leaders cost them their lives. Tseng Kuo-fan tightened his military noose around Nanking until the final slaughter and pursuit of escapees. The ideals for which the *T'ai-p'ing t'ien-kuo* stood had long since weakened, leaving few to press for revival.

The capture of Nanking in May 1853, a great triumph for the rebels, in fact cost the Taiping movement dear. As suggested in the preceding chapter, the rebels' organization and ideology were far better suited to mobility than to static administration. On the march, the Taipings could distribute to the poor what the fleeing wealthy and officials had abandoned. Once in place, however, Hung and his colleagues found they had to rely on local gentry. Taxes had to be collected, order maintained in rural areas. Compromise with what they had sworn to attack inevitably weakened the Taiping basis of support among the impecunious. The Sacred Treasury operated inadequately, the program for land distribution not at all. Admittedly, military operations absorbed the major attention of Taiping leaders. Had they been fully revolutionary, however, they might have built a very different sort of rural society on the basis of land distribution. They did not.

Numerical success took its toll in diluting the religious enthusiasm and charismatic qualities Hung and Feng had propagated. The largely Hakka community at Mount Thistle and Chin-t'ien had been stirred by deep conviction. Obviously, such intensity could not be maintained under the conditions of extraordinary expansion. As we have already seen, the religious messages of the Society of God-Worshippers were to a large extent overshadowed by racialist attacks on the Manchu rulers, and by the egalitarian promises of land distribution. The unusual Christian elements of early days became far less important as more traditional themes of rural rebellion surfaced.

Strategic weaknesses, especially effective marshalling of forces, plagued the rebels. Within a month of their occupation of Nanking, the Taipings mounted two major expeditions: one heading north toward Peking, the other west along the Yangtse valley. The Northern Expeditionary Force (itself divided into three corps) numbered only 70,000 to 80,000[1] — yet it was clear that the dynasty could mobilize many more banner troops to defend the capital. Further strategic errors followed, such as a two-month siege of the city of Huai-ch'ing (now known as Ch'in-yang), an unnecessary massacre of civilians in Ts'ang-chou, and failure to bring sufficient clothing for wintry conditions.[2] Taiping troops were stalled, then roundly defeated. Inability to seize the capital meant the Taipings could not claim fully the Mandate of Heaven. For the next dozen years, China was divided between imperial and rebel sectors. The momentum that had been lost took its toll in dissension within the Taiping movement itself.

Major internal disputes came to a head in Nanking after the failure to take Peking. By the time the Taipings occupied the city, power had largely flowed into the hands of Yang Hsiu-ch'ing. Official proclamations were issued in his name. Hung Hsiu-ch'üan became little more than a "figurehead"[3] manipulated by Yang. As chief of staff, leading ideologue, and recipient of all powers delegated by Hung, Yang established a clear hierarchy, with himself at the top; this contrasted sharply with the division of authority and power that initially characterized the movement. One indication of Yang's importance is provided by his staff—for in Imperial China as elsewhere, the size of an official's personal staff usually betokens his power. Yang enjoyed more than 7,200 persons as assistants, half of them of high rank.[4] This, added to his overweening pride and ambition, fostered dissension; Yang was assassinated by one of his fellow kings, and more than 20,000 others killed, in September 1856.[5] Adding to the picture of fratricidal dissension was the decision of the capable Taiping general Shih Ta-kai to pursue independent action; he took a substantial part of the remaining rebel troops with him. By early 1857, the movement was in difficult straits.

The sapped vitality of the rebels was paralleled by the decrepitude of the incumbents. The Ch'ing dynasty, it should be abundantly clear, suffered from numerous internal weaknesses. Its attention was divided. The conditions that spawned the Taiping uprising encouraged other insurrections. For example, the "Red Turbans" roamed through Kwangtung;[6] the Niens carved out their own zone of power between the Taipings and imperial control;[7] Muslim forces threatened provinces west of the capital. So many challenges to government authority suggested a systemic disorder. As the court seemed to spiral downwards, the burdens of defense fell more heavily, and the opportunities for excesses multiplied. Admittedly, a brief burst of reform came after the Taipings had been suppressed[8] but during the campaigns themselves, little evidence appeared of imperial willingness to put its own house in order.

Help came to the court from two quarters. The less important was the West. Foreign military advisers and even foreign troops joined the fray. Major Charles ("Chinese") Gordon—later to win greater fame as the ill-fated British commander in Khartoum during the Mahdist uprising—took command of the "Ever Victorious Army" in March 1863. It played a supplementary role in denying eastern Kiangsu to the Taipings. Foreign artillery helped defend the important ports of Ningpo and Shanghai from rebel attacks; walls of Taiping cities were breached by superior Western firepower.[9] All things considered, however, western involvement hammered another nail into an already closing coffin; external assistance hastened rather than made possible the defeat of the insurgents. This, we shall shortly see, contrasted markedly with the termination of the Telengana and Mau Mau uprisings.

Far more significant were indigenous Chinese steps to strengthen imperial defenses. The court was aided by Taiping attacks on the Confucian order. Rebel ideology suggested an alternative to the system under which China had long been governed. The Sacred Treasury and proposals on land undercut gentry economic control; Christian-style teachings eroded the legitimacy of the traditional social order; protonationalistic mobilization against the Manchus challenged the comfortable relationship officials had reached with their alien overlords. Thus, the privileged could be rallied in the name of order, just as the dispossessed had been rallied in the name of justice.

One step came in the mobilization of local militias. We have already glimpsed these in the shaping of the Taiping rebellion; recall the arming of rival groups that marked southern China in the wake of the Opium War. Such conflicts had then manifested the dynasty's inadequacies; now they were to represent its major gamble. The court had long opposed, with ample reason and precedent, the creation of defense groups outside its control. Such groups could be turned against the dynasty. In balancing the proven challenge of the Taipings against the potential challenge of gentry-led local units, however, the rulers had little choice: how else might the rebels be defeated? As Michael notes, the success of militia versus the failure of regular troops "taught a lesson which was instrumental in persuading the Manchu court to permit and encourage the establishment of local defense forces by the gentry."[10]

But the key figure was the Hunan leader Tseng Kuo-fan, member of one of the half dozen great families of China and recipient of the highest academic degree before his twenty-seventh birthday.[11] Tseng envisioned something far greater than village protection: he sought to build armies at the provincial level, whose size, discipline and equipment would enable him to defeat the insurgents. He believed local defense inadequate, since it could be manipulated or weakened by unscrupulous gentry.[12] To achieve his desired organizational goal, however, Tseng had to overcome the court's scruples. Evocation of provincial loyalties and leadership opened the way to fragmentation, a risk the dynasty was unwilling to take knowingly. He accordingly masked his intentions, exceeded his official mandate, and paid his soldiers nearly double what government troops were allegedly receiving.[13] In military terms, his strategy was one of denying the Taipings control over the Yangtse and fertile areas north and east of the "Heavenly Capital." The isolation of Hung Hsiu-ch'üan's forces, immured in Nanking and inadequately provisioned, followed inexorably.

More than military foresight abetted Tseng Kuo-fan's efforts. He tapped the concern many gentry and officials felt regarding their status, were the Taipings to succeed. A coalition of the privileged, in other words, would combat the challengers. Tseng emphasized the Confucian values the rebels were questioning. Taiping attacks constituted "not only a tragedy for our Ch'ing dynasty but a great tragedy for the whole Chinese tradition and causes Confucius and Mencius to weep bitterly in the underworld."[14] The strength, resilience, and deeply-seated nature of the traditional order were thus employed by Tseng and his associates. To them, the Manchu basis of the Ch'ing dynasty meant far less than its adherence to Confucian norms; to them, the radical claims of the rebels (including the Sacred Treasury and the modernizing steps suggested by Hung Jen-kan) threatened the order they knew and appreciated. Honest application of longstanding principles was to Tseng by far the best way to meet the rebel challenge. The order should not be overthrown, merely rid of its excesses and weaknesses.

The Hunan army Tseng created was financed from several sources: gentry contributions; sale of academic degrees, official titles, and appointment of offices; administration of internal customs taxes.[15] Freed thus of fiscal dependence on the court, Tseng enjoyed less imperial interference in other matters, such as recruitment and training.[16] Though numerically far smaller than the Taiping forces it opposed, the Hunan army more than overcame this disparity through efficiency, careful planning, and cautious advances. Victory was steady rather than rapid. Tseng built up pressure against the Taiping court, accentuating thereby its internal weaknesses.

Finally, the Taiping movement collapsed from within. We have already seen the problems manifest in 1854-6. If anything, they were magnified in following years. Hung Hsiu-ch'üan delivered himself increasingly to religious meditations. His writings are said to show evidence of mental disorder.[17] He surrounded himself with weak sycophants.[18] The reform/reinvigoration proposals of Hung Jen-kan, for example, came to naught, their protagonist being shuffled aside in power struggles. Hung

Hsiu-ch'üan had provided religious inspiration; others had to translate his visions into organizational reality. Thus, the successes of the Taiping movement rested far more on the accomplishments of Feng Yün-shan or Yang Hsiu-ch'ing than on the acts of Hung Hsiu-ch'üan. When the "heavenly King" deigned to involve himself in mundane matters, he more likely created confusion than commitment. He assigned power to his adolescent son, himself scarcely capable of understanding the basic responsibilities. Hung's death seven weeks before the fall of Nanking spared him the fate of traitors to the imperial cause.

Military errors compounded the decline shown in other aspects. Simplistically put, the Taiping commanders failed to ensure adequate supplies when Nanking was besieged. Earlier, they ineffectually resisted Tseng Kuo-fan's tightening encirclement.[19] The intensifying military threat accentuated the internal divisions at the Taiping court; equally, it fostered the further decline of rebel ideals and practices.

The social and political foundations of the "Heavenly Kingdom" shifted to a marked extent from what they had been. What attracted adherents in the early stages of dynamic expansion could not provide efficient local control in the later stages of static administration. To collect taxes and ensure village loyalty, the Taiping rulers had to rely (like the Manchu "imps" they castigated) on local gentry and landlords. No wonder, accordingly, that the promise of equal land distribution remained a mirage. The decline of the religious message (despite Hung Jen-kan's effort at spiritual revitalization) deprived the rebels of their major claim to distinctiveness. They came eventually to differ but slightly, or so it seemed, from the usual groups that lorded over Chinese rural society. Most bluntly, they failed to perform as promised in shifting peasants' status.

Telengana: Incorporation, Reform and the Ebbing of Rebellion

The so-called police action, by means of which the Indian army forcibly and fully incorporated Hyderabad into India, spelled the beginning of the end of the Telengana rebellion. It had been aimed at a government whose supporters had imposed burdens villagers no longer were willing to bear. The repressive features of the Nizam's regime were swept away; the razakars became the victims rather than the perpetrators of rural violence. A military administration, headed by General J. N. Chaudhuri, brought peace to the countryside.

The active Communist encouragement of the revolt, however, meant that fighting lingered until late 1951. The guerrilla squads never constituted a serious threat to the Indian government which created an atmosphere in which land reform was imposed and the communists were given the opportunity for open electoral competition. Of the four rebellions under review, that in Telengana best illustrated the connection between reform and the end of revolt. With the removal of feudal land privileges, and with the encouragement of means of local political expression, the primary concerns of many rural dwellers had been satisfied.

Incorporation of Hyderabad took a brief 108 hours.[20] Striking toward Hyderabad City along two major highways, Indian troops encountered little serious opposition. The Indians, it should be noted, held an immense advantage: a full combat division, with 150 tanks and armoured personnel carriers, slashed into the state.[21] Neither the razakars nor the Hyderabad army could sustain resistance against this force. Opposition would have been suicidal. Many prominent Muslims fled to Pakistan. The Nizam signed the agreement of accession he had earlier spurned, and cabled the United Nations Security Council to withdraw his complaint against India.[22] General Chaudhuri and his Indian colleagues turned to the immense task of reordering state administrative practices. To maintain institutional continuity and reassure the large Muslim population, the Nizam remained on the throne. Now, however, his privy purse depended on Indian good will; constitutional monarchy had been externally imposed, not internally granted as Muslim liberals had urged. Razakar leaders were rounded up, tried, imprisoned, and released in the 1950s. As an historical footnote, some revived the Ittehad in 1960 as a political party contesting elections in Hyderabad City and to the Lok Sabha (the Indian equivalent of the House of Representatives) and the Andhra State Assembly.[23] Communal concerns had been shifted from violent maintenance of privilege to open electoral competition.

Pacification of the rural areas took far longer. One reason was the prior collapse of the machinery of state government outside the Muslim-dominated cities. The Indian caretaker administration sought to operate as fully as possible through existing Hyderabad institutions. An obvious problem existed with the administrative institutions the Indians sought to resuscitate. Their overwhelmingly Muslim character has been emphasized frequently in this book. To expect a demoralized, fearful, 95 percent Muslim police force to cooperate effectively in the suppression of revolt was nonsensical. In fact, the new military governor of Hyderabad could do little to halt Hindu vengeances; 50,000 to 200,000 Muslims were killed in the immediate aftermath of incorporation.[24] The rural razakars thus reaped the murderous fruits of their attempt to reinforce minority domination. Violence continued to echo through Hyderabad for many months. A second reason for the slow pace of the pacification was the chain-reaction nature of rural unrest. Having found that action brought immediate benefit, villagers continued to take justice and local administration into their own hands. The petty tyranny of *patwaris* disappeared, as peasants burned land records. Having enjoyed the unusual pleasure of not paying taxes, the villagers were understandably reluctant to submit to anything smacking of their earlier economic subordination. Only the promise of permanent change might persuade them to give up rebellion. And, thirdly, the Communist party maintained its advocacy of guerrilla struggle. The unsettled conditions of late 1948 facilitated continued rebellion. A political response, not military repression, seemed to the Indian government the best long-term response.

Let us first take note of Communist means of fostering rebellion. Their village-based strategy rested on an alliance among rural classes.[25] In effect, only the very rich (in rural terms) came under attack. The relatively well-off upper and middle peasants felt no threat at first. Quite the contrary: petty landlords figured among the most prominent CPI members in the Andhra Mahasabha. They found easy targets in a handful of *deshmukhs* whose exactions had aroused extraordinary discontent. Since many lived far removed from their lands, such *deshmukhs'* fields could be readily occupied. A ceiling—of 500 acres!—was imposed in Communist-controlled areas. Reductions in this limit reflected the changing nature of leadership. The four-class arrangement could not be maintained as peasant militancy increased. The revolt lurched leftward in the villages. *Bhagelas*, tenants, and poor sharecroppers demanded more equitable divisions. As their enthusiasm for redistribution rose, the enthusiasm of the landed leadership fell. Communist leaders, in fact, showed little enthusiasm for widespread redistribution; "not without reluctance"[26] did the Party legitimize the seizure of land. The following of the rebellion was broadened considerably, as Dhanagare notes, at some cost to the broad alliance of support.[27] Not having developed a comprehensive program of rural transformation, the Communists were overtaken by a relatively spontaneous series of actions whose leftward surge could not be checked.

Serious logistical problems beset the rebels. Their weapons—their slingshots, for example—were ineffectual. As the Taiping rebels had earlier discovered, and as the Mau Mau fighters were soon to learn, arms captured from the forces of repression were insufficient to wage a prolonged struggle. Popular belief notwithstanding, sack cloth could not stop bullets.[28] The government of India was committed to containing, and ultimately to eliminating, the Communist rural threat; the base areas useful in the anti-razakar struggle could not be utilized against the Indians. Rebel leaders were practically devoid of military knowledge. In the words of Sundarayya:

...knowledge of use of fire-arms, its manufacture or its repair was so dismally poor that even great enthusiasm and sacrifice could not overcome it. Elementary lack of military tactics, for planning attacks or retreat, was so glaring that we failed to coordinate small guerrilla squads action against the enemy....Nor were we able to capture any worthwhile number of modern weapons from the enemy by destroying them, till the Indian military intervention.[29]

Zonal companies of 100-200 men proved too large for effective guerrilla combat — in other words, were too large to conceal or move quickly. Squads of ten — reduced after the "police action" to groups of three to five — were ineffectual against the more sophisticated Indian army.[30] Eventually Telengana rebels were hunted down in the forest, as Mau Mau fighters were to be, their utility slight and their ability to foment insurrection elsewhere nonexistent. Approximately 4,000 were killed.[31]

The Indian military administration, thirdly, took quick, relatively effective steps against the rebels. The Communist party, which had remained legal under the Nizam, was banned in the state. Once the razakar threat had been neutralized, Indian troops turned their full attention to Telengana. According to D. N. Pritt — the noted left wing Indian lawyer who defended Jomo Kenyatta against the charge of leading an illegal association — the Indian offensive brought the deaths of 2,000 peasants and Party workers. By mid-1950, 10,000 Communists and active participants had been detained.[32] An estimated 2,000 tribal hamlets in densely forested areas were destroyed and inhabitants relocated. The Indian intervention and the suppression of the razakars removed much of the impetus for rural revolt.[33] With the Muslims essentially eliminated, outside the cities, and with the *deshmukhs* previously neutralized by peasant action, the villagers had gained many of their goals.

What has been implied should be made explicit. Little had been done in Telengana to prolong the rebellion. The insurgents had responded to initiatives from below much more than they had planned for protracted struggle. Telengana was far from being a carefully prepared rural revolution. Little basis was created within the villages for sustaining, organizationally, the changes that had been wrought. Maoist precepts notwithstanding, siege conditions could not be sustained. Village committees had little real substance to them. The desire to maintain a multiclass alliance — more accurately, to retain the support of the upper layer — led to dissension. A fair amount of Communist support scarcely represented disinterested acts by rich peasants. They had much to gain from the elimination of the Nizam and the *deshmukhs*, but conversely had much to lose from major land redistribution. Let me quote at length from one critic:

There occurred, towards the end [of 1948] a number of what Sundarayya terms "mistakes" — i.e., actions against rich peasants, forcing them to return land which they had acquired through grain lending. Now actions like these can be termed "mistakes" only in the context of a multi-class front such as the one the CPI imagined it could build. Such actions would be rather less of a "mistake," (sic) if it was aimed to have a movement which was becoming increasingly dominated by the agricultural labourers, poor and middle peasants, and artisans. It was in any case these layers…who provided 80 percent of the CPI activists throughout the period. The "mistake" may then be seen to lie in the attempt to restrain the development of the struggle in the hope of retaining the support of the upper layer who were initially vacillating and latterly treacherous.[34]

One indication of the tussle for control between rich and poor peasants came from ceilings on land holdings. In areas of successful revolt against the *deshmukhs*, an initial limit of 500 acres was imposed. Given the minute size of average holdings, and the high percentage of the landless, pressure for reduction inevitably mounted. The success of the rebellion in stimulating participation by the poor had the effect of pushing out many of the initial leaders. The maximum holding permitted in rebel areas was cut to 200 acres, then to 100 acres; in densely settled irrigated regions, the limit was set at 10 acres. (It should be recalled that a minimally viable holding was considered to be fifteen dry or five irrigated acres.)[35] Those who came to the fore after the police action were often *bhagelas* with much to gain — but with little to offer in terms of experience or of commitment to CPI ideology. Internal struggles within the Communist party reflected lack of agreement about tactics based on rural class struggle. Telengana was not, for the CPI, a Yenan base in which a belief in a people's war could be formulated and implemented. Eventual and unavoidable exhaustion set in; the successes of 1948 could not be extended, as the Indian government imposed its own version of land reform. The rebellion dies of inanition.

The fifth and most important cause of the gradual extinction of the Telengana unrest was administrative reform after the police action. The land grievances that figured so prominently in the causes of unrest were substantially righted. The Nizam remained as constitutional monarch, but surrendered the *Sarf-e-Khas* lands from which he had drawn his immense personal fortune. (The Indian government granted him a lifetime privy purse of Rs. 25 lakhs.) Lands of the 1500 or so *jagidars* were expropriated — resulting in an immediate relief of 12 1/2 percent in land assessments for five million persons. (Compensation to *jagidars* ranged from 41 2/3 to 75 percent of their previous annual income.)[36] Despite these changes, shortcomings remained. An Agricultural Enquiry Commission, headed by Professor Iyengar, discovered once again that average holdings fell well below what was required for satisfactory life.[37] Tenants (of whom seven out of nine were tenants at will)[38] gained new rights in the 1950 Hyderabad Tenancy and Agricultural Lands Act, which was amended in

1954.[39] What had so long been denied by the Muslim-dominated regime came under the temporary Indian military administration. Its clear political plan undercut the economic and social base of the uprising. Support for the Communists ebbed. As already emphasized, more articulate peasant strata threw themselves behind the reform efforts. The uprising changed in character, in a manner analogous to the isolation of Mau Mau rebels in heavily wooded areas. I concur with Pavier's assessment:

> The net result of the CPI's policy was that, by the beginning of 1949, they were reduced to small squads being chased around the hills by the Indian army. The land distribution programme taken as a whole was finished, and the "defence" was almost entirely left to the peasants themselves. Only a few underground and passive cadres remained permanently in the plains areas. The struggle between 1949 and 1951 was of a distinctly different nature—in forest areas amongst a relatively undifferentiated tribal peasantry with a much lower cultural level....The campaign, by the end of 1951, had degenerated into a collection of *focos*, almost completely isolated from the elements in the plains who had been their principal support.[40]

A similar judgment was offered by the Communist party itself. The reforms pressed by the military administration vitiated the prime issue of the rebellion. The diminution of popular support made continuation impractical. According to M. B. Rao, the police action ushered in a new set of circumstances:

> But by then a political change had come over the entire area. The people hoped and believed that they would have a better deal at the hands of the India government. They were ready to fight the Nizam but not the India government headed by the national leaders.
> Telengana got isolated and from a broad agrarian movement became the armed force of the area organization. There was dwindling support in the villages, the earlier broad unity with the radical section of the State congress was disrupted, and the agrarian reforms promised by the new rulers broke the peasant unity. The fighting peasant squads were decimated until October 1951 when the glorious Telengana movement was finally withdrawn.[41]

Formal abandonment was not only a product of necessity; it was also a commitment to future good behavior. Elections were to be held March 1952; the Communists wished to participate. Formal withdrawal from antigovernment agitation in Telengana, announced late in October 1951, permitted the Indian government to remove its ban on the CPI. Face was saved on all sides: a hopeless struggle on the verge of extinction could be abandoned, the principles of competitive democracy introduced into the former princely state. Belated reform drew the fangs of the peasant uprising, from which the Communists had unsuccessfully attempted to develop an India-wide basis for agrarian revolution. Politics in Telengana returned to peaceful normalcy.

Mau Mau: Lessons from Malaya and the Loyalists' Role

Although the Emergency in Kenya was not terminated until 1960, the back of the Mau Mau uprising had been broken by late 1956. In duration, it was thus longer than all but the Taiping rebellion; in military terms, it witnessed the most complete battery of conventional and unconventional warfare; in political terms, the formal change in majority participation was the most striking. "Mau Mau" was defeated by superior force. Yet British coercive might was exercised to a substantial extent through indigenous units — and was ultimately sustained by political concessions. Fission among the Kikuyu, and between the Kikuyu and other major ethnic groups, provided an opening for recruitment of "Loyalists." It was by and through their "Loyalist" allies that effective counterinsurgency was mounted. It was on their support, further, that the colonial administration hoped to base a new Kenyan political system, in which paramountcy entailed majority rule sooner rather than later.

The role of the Loyalists was made possible by British concessions, special recognition, and pressure. Recruitment focused on those who, broadly speaking, profited from the colonial presence, or who held no truck for militant upheaval. Entrusted at first with little responsibility or weaponry, the Kikuyu Home Guard was expanded rapidly and given greater roles in village protection. Intelligence gathering was stressed. Extensive use of hooded informers in screening operations helped root out Mau Mau sympathizers in urban as well as rural areas. In the forests where the guerrillas had been forced to establish their camps, a military noose was gradually tightened. Isolated thus by a mixture of coercive pressure and inducements for "Loyalists," the Mau Mau fighters were pushed to surrender, capture, or death in the inhospitable surroundings of the high forest.

To clarify the mixture of military and political steps taken by the British government, the following areas merit closer attention: the example of early British counterinsurgency efforts, the inducements given Loyalists, the interruption of the urban-rural link through widespread arrests in Nairobi, the physical isolation of the insurgents in the forests, and agricultural improvement through land consolidation and cash crop farming.

The British were no strangers to counterinsurgency warfare. Doctrine evolved in several settings, especially Palestine and Malaya. Major lessons included the following:[12]

— physically isolate the insurgents, interrupting support provided by the "passive" wing;

—establish integrated military and political control at all feasible levels;

—stress intelligence-gathering, so as to reduce the number of fruitless, costly military engagements;

—recognize that political concessions must be offered to counter the rebels' claims.

The challenge to British rule in Malaya had been mounted by the Malayan Communist party (MCP). Heavily Chinese in composition, the Party launched attacks in June 1948 — reflecting in some measure the general lurch of Asian Communists to military confrontation following the Calcutta conference. Isolated British planters became the targets of MCP action; murders and damage to rubber plantations, the insurgents assumed, would (over several years) so sap the will and resources of the incumbents as to force them to withdraw. MCP guerrillas fought under the banner of the "Malayan Races Liberation Army," in an effort to counter the disadvantage of drawing almost exclusively from a single group in an emphatically plural sociaty. Abetted by the "Min Yuen" supply and intelligence unit, the rebels drew support from Chinese farmers — known ironically in Malaya as "squatters" — living on state land on the edge of the jungle. Their resettlement in protected areas involved substantial risks, for (as one official report noted) "Nobody likes to be compulsorily moved from the home he has built with the sweat of his brow."[43] No less than 740,000 rural Chinese were resettled, the British government having built 490 new villages at a cost of $41 million.[44] The military command in Kenya drew lessons of enforced villagization from this experience.

Integrated command ran counter to the usual British wisdom of subordinating military tactics to political strategies. The centralized power General Sir Gerald Templer enjoyed in Malaya had few parallels. According to one observer, "The British government had armed him with the most extensive powers ever invested in any chief executive and commander-in-chief of a British dependency or protected state. Indeed he had more power than the British prime minister had possessed during the Second World War."[45] At lower levels (individual states of the Malay Federation, and districts within these), Templer and his associates joined civil and military officials into war executive committees. These were not British preserves, but included indigenous participants. This concession — tied closely to the approach to self-government — blunted the insurgents' claim to be fighting on behalf of all citizens of the peninsula.

For information, the British relied on a reorganized, expanded Special Branch. What more than a decade later were to be called "search and destroy" missions in Vietnam had no parallel in Malaya, where large-scale engagements were kept to a minimum. Once the MCP guerrillas had been driven into the jungles, they would be harried by denial of food and medical supplies, perhaps tracked by surrendered enemy personnel willing to cooperate with the British, and eventually induced to surrender, tempted into betrayal, or polished off by a precise military strike, usually an ambush. The war was long, patience a paramount virtue. Again to quote a correspondent of the *Straits Times*, "Nothing better illustrated the demands on the [British and Commonwealth troops] and police jungle squads better than the fact that a man had to spend an average of one thousand hours on patrol or about three hundred hours waiting in ambush before he saw a Communist, even for fleeting seconds."[46]

Counter-insurgency in Malaya rested finally on the promise of political change. Military and political steps could not be separated. Although Templer stressed the "restoration of law and order" as the "immediate task of defeating the terrorists," he opened his first public statement with a reinforcement of imperial policy: "The policy of the British Government is that Malaya should in due course become a fully self-governing nation..."[47] Welcoming Malays and Indians into the war executive committees broadened the anti-MCP effort; taking major steps toward independence robbed the guerrillas of one of their major arguments.

Given the overlap in time between the emergencies in Malaya and Kenya, one was bound to affect the other. The success with which MCP guerrillas were separated from their rural bases, especially from the Min Yuen, spawned many imitations, as did the unification of the military and political commands. What Templer and his predecessor, General Sir Harold Briggs, brought to the war against the Malayan guerrilas, General Sir George Erskine was to bring to the war against the Mau Mau partisans after May 1953. Much of what worked on the slopes and in the forests of Mount Kenya had earlier been tried in the jungles of Malaya.

Not all lessons derived from Malaya were applied successfully in East Africa. Take, for example, the combination of civil and military, both in the commander-in-chief and at lower levels. Emergency Committees in Kenya were created at the district level, their membership including the District Commissioner, senior police and military officers, and perhaps one or two representatives of other departments. Who was to control committees became an item of contention, settlers wishing a prominent role. As Clayton notes, "The system as a whole tended to create friction between the military command and the local committees, particularly where these were under strong European political influence."[48] This integration was later paralleled at the provincial and divisional levels. At the national level, a "War Council" meeting twice per week operated from spring 1954 to 1956, the elected leaders of European members of Legco serving with the governor and the general officer commanding.[49] But the total subordination to unified command of both military and civilian hierarchies was precluded. General Erskine was given a letter authorizing him to proclaim martial law and assume control of the civil government, but kept this letter "neatly folded in his spectacle case" during the Emergency.[50]

The importance of physically isolating the insurgents had been clearly demonstrated in Malaya. Application was complicated in Kenya by several factors. The high population density made it well-nigh impossible to carve new areas for settlement out of the Reserves. The repatriation of Kikuyu from Nairobi and European farming areas both exacerbated crowding and spread discontent more rapidly. In fact, movement of Kikuyu from the Rift Valley and the Highlands "drove many men, in despair, to join the insurgents."[51] The expulsion of Kikuyu seemed more a reflex of beleaguered Europeans than a carefully considered policy; not until the 1954 emphasis on villagization, land reform and consolidation, was serious thought given to how former squatters could survive.

For obvious reasons, Mau Mau partisans sought concealment. There existed three obvious places: in the thronged African quarters of Nairobi; in the forests of Mount Kenya and the Aberdares, flanking the Kikuyu reserve respectively to the north and west; and in regular Kikuyu settlements, benefiting from the tacit support of the populace. The process of separating "fish" from "water" started in the reserve in 1952-3, focused on Nairobi in 1954, and was completed in the forests by late 1956.

Despite the population pressures in the reserve, Kikuyu preferred scattered rather than agglomerated settlement patterns. Compact villages were rare. Consonant with their egalitarian social structure based on clans, and consistent as well with minimizing home-to-field travel, Kikuyu established new households amidst the fields. Physical control of movement was impractical under these conditions. Settlements could not be defended against attack, impressment, or oathing. Regrouping seemed the answer.

Defensible villages involved fiscal and human costs. Kikuyu were ordered to destroy their homes and build new accommodations in approved areas. Thorn hedges surrounded the new villages, as did ditches filled with sharpened saplings. Access was restricted (at one point, a 23-hour per day curfew prevailed); those outside villages at night were deemed hostile, and were liable to immediate arrest or worse.

Physical separation, including the villagization program, found its clearest expression on the edge of the forest. There, all *shambas* (farm plots) and structures were destroyed within a mile of the forest. Ditches were dug by compulsory labor to preclude men taking refuge in the forest from obtaining food. The effects of this interdiction were profound. Forest gangs spent their time and energies on sheer survival. Their diet of honey and trapped wild animals was irregular and probably unsatisfying to Kikuyu used to a series of root crops. Memoirs penned by survivors note the physical travails of the forest and the corrosive effects on morale of such containment.[52]

As important as this enclosure of Mau Mau fighters may have been for the eventual British military triumph, of far greater significance was the interruption of the "Nairobi connection." Mau Mau, portrayed by many critics as an atavistic movement masterminded by a London-educated anthropologist/politician/educator, was in fact, a guerrilla movement in which urban trade unionists played a crucial role in the militant phase. The revolt took place in the countryside, and increasingly reflected rural grievances — but its initiation and political coherence reflected its city roots as well. Nairobi furnished resources, intelligence, a modicum of communication and coordination, and the opportunity of joining Kikuyu concerns to the grievances of other groups.

"Operation Anvil" represented the most complex military operation the British undertook, yet it involved no fighting. Its intention was to clear Nairobi of the thousands of supporters whose contributions were prolonging the conflict. In a joint police-military action, Nairobi was sealed off and, over a month, house-by-house searches were conducted. All Africans were paraded before hooded Loyalists, who commented on the supposed political reliability of each. Those deemed suspicious — some 16,500 of them — were bundled off to special detention camps, there to start through the rehabilitation process. The results were clear. Again to quote Clayton, Operation Anvil "certainly served to shatter the city's Mau Mau hierarchy and cells, and destroy the lines of communication between the forest groups and their city supporters."[53]

The flow of supplies, especially of armaments, was cut almost totally by Operation Anvil. Physical isolation went hand-in-hand with a drying up of sources of food and munitions. Surviving Mau Mau leaders, in their *apologiae pro vitas suas*, stressed their foresight in collecting arms before the declaration of the Emergency. Their efforts were more successful than those of the Algerian nationalists, whose armaments on 1 November 1954, reportedly consisted of less than fifty obsolete shotguns, and certainly greater than the Kwilu rebels.[54] Corfield, using official sources unavailable to scholars, estimated that Mau Mau partisans possessed at least 400, and potentially 800 precision weapons and 140,000 rounds of ammunition when the Emergency was imposed, and that 280 additional weapons were gained in the first year. Thereafter, losses far exceeded gains, forcing forest fighters to fabricate weapons far more dangerous to themselves than to their opponents; some 3600 homemade weapons had been captured by mid-1958.[55] I believe these figures to be on the generous side: rifles or shotguns stolen in Kenya were of great value for hunting or cattle raiding, and tended to drift northwards from the forest areas; hence, what Europeans lost ended up outside the affected areas of Central Province. Shortages of munitions and firearms made nearly impossible any raids on protected villages or police posts by mid-1954. Interdiction of supplies, the consequence of Operation Anvil and improved protection of munitions dumps, was a key part of the suppression of Mau Mau. It went hand-in-hand with the creation of the Kikuyu Home Guard, intended to function directly in the reserves, leaving to British troops (including the predominantly African King's African Rifles) the sweeps through forest areas.[56]

Cost played a part in the decision to raise the Home Guard, as did efficacy. The British might gain a military victory by sheer might, but would not achieve political victory without widespread collaboration. According to an official publication, "It had always been evident that final victory could not be achieved until the Kikuyu, Embu, and Meru population as a whole had been brought [sic] to realize the horror of *Mau Mau* and had risen in their strength to throw it out."[57] And, not incidentally, the exchequer and British public opinion might have found it equally difficult to thrust large numbers of white troops into what was presented to the world as a localized, atavistic tribal uprising of limited military importance.

Indigenous defenders had to be developed essentially from scratch. Rural Kenya prior to the emergency had few police, let alone members of the armed forces. In Kiambu, 44 African policemen were stationed in early 1952, a ratio of one per 6,000 inhabitants. The ratios in the two other Kikuyu divisions, Fort Hall and Nyeri, stood respectively at 1:7,000 and 1:11,500. As might be expected, expansion was rapid. Membership of the heavily white Kenya Police rose in Central Province during 1952 from 160 to 723; by the end of 1954, it had jumped to 2,775. The Kenya Police Reserve rose in the same period from 624 to 1,500 to 2,741.[58] The more important contribution came from the Kikuyu Home Guard, whose nuclei were furnished by informal bodyguards assembled by chiefs known for their pro-British sympathies, and by the Tribal Police, a small (240 men), lightly-armed group whose duties were primarily custodial.

What sources did the British government tap to create the Home Guard? According to an official publication, it included "members of practically every occupation and faith to be found among the tribe — traders, artisans, schoolteachers, chiefs and headmen — but the majority of its members are simple peasants."[59] They were not. Both in theory and in fact, the Kikuyu Loyalists came heavily from the older, more privileged sectors of society.

According to Rosberg and Nottingham, the British hoped to use "the few who could be trusted—the 'Loyalists'—as a nucleus for creating a new society."[60] This core would be composed of yeoman farmers, of cautious Christians, of constitutional moderates, of educated elements—in short, of the more conservative elements of Kikuyu society willing to accept the slow-paced, evolutionary approach from below the colonial administration favored, persons "who were for various reasons out of sympathy with militant and radical nationalism."[61]

Given the overwhelming portion of the Kikuyu who took the first oath, the cautious proto-gentry, proto-bourgeoisie the British sought were thus bound to come from restricted groups.

Ogot sees the Loyalists as comprised of five groups: those loyal to law and order, to traditions and customs, to Mammon, to Christianity, and to constitutionalism.[62] It seems to me that a simpler classification involves two categories: the privileged and the old. What few empirical details as have been published suggest that the Home Guard drew from men well over thirty years of age, with a substantial stake in the economic status quo. Take, for example, the following evidence. Of the twenty-five camp leaders in the Githunguri Home Guard, none was landless or poor: three were "very" rich, eighteen rich, and two above average in wealth. Among the rank-and-file, 44 were "very" rich, 265 rich, 77 above average in wealth, 79 below average, and 144 poor. Over 90 percent of the Loyalist leaders were over forty-five in a society of low life expectancy. Of the Loyalist followers, 387 had passed their 45th birthdays; 423 were under 45.[63] Such does not represent a typical distribution pattern. In the words of Sorrenson, active loyalists belonged to "the landed and wealthy classes" of the Kikuyu.[64] One might expect such persons to support law and order; to be faithful to ethnic traditions; to want to protect what they had accumulated. In other words, they embodied the qualities on which the British hoped to base a renewed development from below in the rebirth of Kikuyu society.

Rewards flowed to those who cast in their lot with the colonial administration, or whose sympathies changed as the incumbent-insurgent balance shifted. But the rewards were not immediate. For example, members of the Home Guard did not receive salaries. Concerned lest the Guards be branded as mercenaries, the British nonetheless developed incentives. As supposedly proven loyalists, Guards were excused from paying the twenty shilling tax levied late in 1952 on adult male Kikuyu, to pay for police and government action against Mau Mau; they were similarly excused from payment of school fees (a major boon to education-conscious parents), and were given free clothing. Having to live in Guard posts meant wives could not readily cultivate their plots, for fear of reprisal; on the other hand, opportunity existed, as already noted, for claiming *shambas* tilled by the spouses of forest fighters. No doubt other inducements existed, at which the British winked. Eventually, however, the winding down of the overt conflict and the growing rapaciousness of the Guard made reorganization essential. In August 1954, the British decided to release 20,000 Guards, absorbing some into an expanded Tribal Police, but returning most to peasant cultivation. The Guards had fulfilled their role. With modest (at best) military efficiency, they had achieved a political goal of making abundantly clear what groups and proclivities the British favored.

Guard duties were overwhelmingly local. Village protection constituted their chief responsibility. A far more daring military step came with the utilization of surrendered Mau Mau fighters against their former comrades. Grouped into "pseudo-gangs" after screening, these units (accompanied often by European officers in blackface) sought contact in the forest with the remaining *maquisards* — in order to exterminate them. The "pseudo-gangs" took on special importance in 1955-6, when the estimated number of active Mau Mau fighters had shrunk to 1500, scattered over an area of 6000 square miles.[65] It should be noted that a Malayan analog existed in the so-called Special Operational Volunteer Force, to which 300 surrendered enemy personnel had been recruited by June 1954.[66]

British troops were kept busy in Kenya, but saw little direct action. Their role was initially defensive, providing the screen behind which the Kikuyu Guard took shape. As "villagization" proceeded, however, they took a major role in patrolling — changing thereby from defense to attack — along the edges of the forests. Sweeps through the forest came next, with limited success, although contacts with guerrilla groups were made. "Operation Anvil" required several hundred British troops, but led to no military engagements. The "mopping up" of forest fighters took a small number of highly specialized soldiers. It should be clear, accordingly, that the chief defense burden fell on indigenous, specially recruited forces thrown into action in the crowded reserves.

As for the majority of the Kikuyu, their sympathies lay with the objectives of the Mau Mau rebels, their sense of survival with the activities of the Home Guard and British forces. They were in essence bystanders, flexible to some degree in their beliefs, but primarily concerned with survival in unpleasant circumstances. Once they recognized the one-sided nature of the military struggle, they sought to disengage themselves, while nonetheless maintaining their hopes for future improvements. Sorrenson's judgment bears quoting *in extenso*:

> for many allegiances were determined not so much by material or heroic circumstances but by the simple fact that those concerned wanted, above all, to

go on living. They may have been sympathetic to the rebels and their cause but in the last resort they accepted the facts of power. Even during the height of the Emergency the bulk of the Kikuyu population was loyal to government in the daytime — in such conditions a *panga* (sword) was useless against a sten gun — and loyal to the rebels at night.[67]

To sap the morale of Mau Mau fighters forest areas were regularly peppered with leaflets urging surrender. Through an operation entitled "Green Branch," amnesty was offered those who carried arms or consorted with the insurgents — an offer that attracted 800 by early 1955,[68] but whose terms excluded those involved in killing. Delicate negotiations involving captured Mau Mau leaders, paroled for the occasion, failed to produce a negotiated surrender. The point is not that efforts did not succeed; it is rather that British officials (including the minister for African Affairs and General Eskine's chief of staff) participated in face-to-face negotiations early in 1954.

Offers of anmesty indicated British willingness — once London had taken full control of the situation — to reconsider the pace of advance toward self-government. It became clear that the settlers could not expect to maintain their unquestioned superiority. Full implementation of at least multiracialism would be necessary, and might keep the infection of the Kikuyu virus from spreading to other African groups. Political concessions offered by the British in fact accounted for a substantial part of the successful containment of the Mau Mau rebellion. One step was taken early in 1954, with the announcement of the Lyttelton constitution. For the first time, an African member of Legco could assume ministerial responsibilities — although he would be precluded from introducing or supporting legislation affecting the land rights of any group.[69] More important, Africans gained the right to vote, with eight Legco members to be elected. Although the elections were not held until March 1957, they held out a promise that soon bore fruit: six of the eight nominated African members were defeated by candidates who rejected the multiracial precepts of the Lyttelton constitution and stood strongly for African rights.[70]

Finally, the British offensive against Mau Mau took to the land — the basis of the rebellion. A key document was published in 1954, the so-called Swynnerton plan.[71] It stressed agricultural change in the reserves, not in European areas. Cash cropping and improved pastoral techniques, it was held, would meet the needs of all Kikuyu — including most of the 100,000 or so repatriated from European farms. Villagization provided an unparalleled opportunity for changing traditional farming practices. Not only had Kikuyu homesteads been decentralized; families' tilled lands were usually divided among several plots. The cadastral surveys, registration of titles, and consolidation of holdings were "casually assumed," in Sorren-

son's words, to "pave the way for an agricultural revolution . . . . "[72] The
chief reason for land consolidation was political rather than humanitarian,
however. Loyalists could garner the fruits denied their fellow Kikuyu who
had taken to the forest. The process itself served as a considerable inducement to those arrested to confess their errors and profess loyalty to the
government, for only in this way might they gain release. According to Sorrenson,

> Once adjudication proceedings had started in any unit, it was essential for all
> who claimed land to be present or at least to be represented to ensure, if
> possible, that they got a fair hearing . . . the majority of detainees sought an
> early release so that they could look after their interests during consolidation.
> Thus consolidation provoked a great and final scramble on the part of all
> and sundry to secure claims to land. Those Kikuyu who may have harboured
> Mau Mau sympathies could not afford to be detained lest they lose the oppor-
> tunity to protect their interests. Because consolidation followed so closely on
> the heels of villagization it was to play an important part in bringing the
> Emergency to a rapid conclusion. By the end of 1956 peace reigned
> throughout the Kikuyu country . . . . [73]

It was a peace brought by a well-financed, carefully-executed plan that
owed much to British experience in Malaya, and that recognized the importance of political incentives combined with military deterrents. Rarely
have the two approaches been as effectively used — even if, as we shall see in
the following chapter, European primacy was soon to disappear while
many land grievances remained unresolved.

Kwilu: Ineffectual Repression, Inept Pacification

Wave the carrot or wield the stick? This time-honored dichotomy provides a useful means of examining incumbent action against the Kwilu
rebellion. By comparison with the British campaign against Mau Mau, the
Congolese campaign against Mulelist partisans appears singularly ineffectual. Formal termination of the state of exception in April 1966 ratified far
more a natural ebbing of support than a triumph by military or political
means. Congolese policy makers waffled, uncertain whether carrot or stick
would be satisfactory. The successive governments of Cyrille Adoula,
Moise Tshombe and Joseph-Desirée Mobutu offered few incentives for
peaceful reintegration of the rebels, despite some gestures and rhetoric;
the armed forces pursued neither a vigorous military campaign based on
clear punishment of resisters, nor a carefully considered pacification effort
based on clear incentives for peaceful reintegration. The ANC itself proved
as inept at peacekeeping as it was at warmaking. It appeared to develop

self-interest in keeping the rebellion alive. As a Belgian observer noted, "It seems in effect that the soldiers stationed in the so-called troubled areas have acquired the habit and taste for harassing (*ranconner*) the villages, and any efficacious intervention putting an end to the rebellion would have signified for them the end of a privileged situation."[74] Under these circumstances, the Kwilu rebellion went into a phase of dormancy, never completely subdued, never fully pacified.

In examining the winding-down of the rebellion, we should examine shortcomings within the movement itself, policies of the central government, and specific military-cum-pacification steps taken by the ANC.

One of the most surprising features of the Kwilu uprising was its volcanic eruption. Its borders were staked out essentially within forty-eight hours. On 21-22 January 1964, the insurgents literally cut off an area approximately 300 kilometers by 150 kilometers from the rest of Kwilu.[75] The districts of Gungu, Idiofa and Kikwit were the most affected. Communications with the outside world were interrupted: bridges destroyed, some telephone lines cut. The rapidity of its spread thus contrasted with the far slower course of rebellion in our other cases. From the formal proclamation of the Heavenly Kingdom of the Taiping rebels to its maximum spread, close to five years passed; Telengana seizure of village control from *deshmukhs* went on for more than two years before the "police action"; the origins of oathing among the Kikuyu are to be found in the immediate postwar condition of squatters. The development of territorial bases in these three instances was thus more gradual and organic—or, one might say, far less planned—than was the case in Kwilu. Mulele seems clearly to have decided that his version of a Congolese Yenan had to be isolated; the cloistered nature of the rebellion was a matter of conscious choice. It was also a matter of ethnic solidarity. All areas dominated by Mbunda and Pende supported the revolt. The combination of tribal unity with PSA organization, Mulele's personal appeal, and acute resentment of the shortcomings of the "first independence" facilitated insurrection. To the world outside, the uprising tended to be viewed either as a Communist insurgency or as an ethnic revolt. The far more complex nature of the uprising became apparent only later.

From its very beginnings, the Kwilu rebellion was defensive rather than offensive. Mulele preceded others in the Conseil National de Libération in overt action against the government. The uprising was "contained," to use Davies' adjective,[76] by the choice of its prime mover. The *jeunesse* remained close to their village and forest refuges. With the exception of unsuccessful assaults on Gungu in February and on Idiofa in June, the rebels avoided major engagements and open combat of the type the capture of a town would have required. This seemingly paradoxical situation of a ver-

bally aggressive ideology with military defensive tactics requires explanation.

One obvious factor was the absence of arms. The chief weapons for the
rebels remained bows and arrows. One insurgent commander gave the
following inventory of Mulele's equipment: 5 Fal rifles, one of which was in
poor repair; 6 revolvers; 6 Sten machine guns; 3 Mauser 52 and 4 Mauser
36; and 19 Mausers for each zone commander.[77] When one considers that,
at the start of 1965, there may have been 2000 partisans,[78] the severe
limitation on materiel becomes even more apparent. What was captured
from Congolese police, gendarmes, or soldiers was minimal, due in large
measure to the relative absence of direct combat. Supplies from outside remained interdicted. The Kwilu rebels enjoyed a base area, but not one
that could be readily provisioned. Unlike the insurgents of the eastern Congo, to whom arms could be delivered across the 600 kilometers of Lake
Tanganyika or the ill-defined and lightly-patrolled frontiers with the
Sudan and Uganda, Mulelist fighters had to become almost totally self-
reliant. Women traded sexual favors with Congolese soldiers for munitions; unspent cartridges were carefully retrieved after every engagement.
These were not enough to overcome the fundamental equipment shortage.

A second factor was the political as well as military nature of the struggle. Central to Mulele was political indoctrination and awareness. He
recognized Mao's caveat regarding the power that flows from the barrel of
a gun: the gun must always be subordinated to the party. Mulele thus
stressed politics far more than military operations. Once the rebels had
carved out their zone of control, they spent most of their days learning the
Maoist/Mulelist catechism quoted in the preceding chapter. Two captured
documents, both dating from January 1966, provide the flavor of camp
life. The Kipola-Gudi unit spent at most 12½ days in military activity,
only three of which involved potential combat, the others devoted to unsuccessful ambushes; 18 ½ days passed on political lessons and administrative work. The Kilembe unit reported what I calculate as five days
of militarily-related action, but no contact with ANC forces. (For example: "construct a ditch with female labor for an ambush"; "catch those
fleeing from Pinda"; "inspect ambushes and put guards in place.")[79] Of
course the low levels of armaments, the declining numbers of fighters, and
the growing uncertainty of the Mulelist cause all counselled caution at that
point—but the leader's caution and political concerns seem to have been
more important.

The ANC itself, it seems in retrospect, took scant interest in major campaigns against Mulele. This figures as a third reason for the low level of
combat. Civil wars are often said to be especially bloody. Such was not the
case in the Kwilu rebellion, at least in terms of government casualties.

These were incredibly low: a mere ten to twenty soldiers died (several in accidents), three were taken prisoner, and a few dozen were wounded. Two officers were killed, the Congolese chief of staff by a rebel arrow, and an ANC second lieutenant at the hands of one of his own men. Such was the official toll in the uprising, through early 1966.[80] A similarly small number of rebel troops seems to have perished. The chief cost in human lives thus came in January 1964 execution of *reactionnaires*, and in the tug of war for villagers' loyalties. Perhaps 150 persons (my estimate) were assassinated in the quick assertion of rebel control, most of them being *penepene* ("intellectuals") suspected of potential collusion with the government.[81] And, not to forget the innocent but unsung victims, a few hundred villagers were killed in the see-saw efforts by partisans and by government troops.

We should also recall that the ANC was engaged on other fronts during this period. In the summer of 1964, a series of rebel forces loosely coordinated through the Conseil National de Libération swept through the eastern Congo.[82] These uprisings posed a far more serious economic, military and political threat to the government in Leopoldville than did the Kwilu rebellion. The major mineral resources of the country — copper, diamonds, cobalt, gold, uranium — lay in the east; foreign investment was heavy; the country's economic health rested on a steady flow of mineral exports. Under such circumstances, the self-contained uprising in Kwilu could be — and essentially was — ignored. Mulele seems in retrospect to have made little impact on the ANC or the central government; his revolutionary rhetoric could not be matched by revolutionary deeds.

The personal qualitiers of Mulele should be considered as both a strength and a weakness of the insurgency. He has been called charismatic; Willame more acurately deems him chiliastic and messianic.[83] Mulele obviously enticed many into the *maquis* by his demonstrations of individual prowess and his reputation for superior magic. This renown stretched beyond the forest camps. The low casualty rate I have already noted resulted in part from the fact "battles" were rarely fought in the opening phase of the rebellion. *Dawa* — magic — played a greater part in so-called combat between the ANC and Mulelist partisans than did actual armaments. Striding into battle chanting *mai Mulele*, the forest fighters frightened Congolese troops into flight, rather than provoked them into resistance. The engagements were thus far more psychological than physical. Obviously, a reputation for superior magic can be sustained only as long as it is perceived as being efficacious. Proof that bullets did not automatically turn into water eventually reduced the rebels' enthusiasm — as had happened in many earlier African uprisings marked by the same belief.[84]

Mulele may have weakened the movement by his increasing tendency to surround himself with fellow Mbunda. Pende supporters came to see themselves as inferior partners, given little trust and responsibility. Signing himself "Revolutionary 100%," Pierre Damien Kandaka expressed various grievances against Mulele in ethnic terms: "Why do we march empty-handed. You give all the arms and munitions to Mbunda . . . . When Gizenga formed the PSA . . . for Pende affairs he chose no one although there were many diploma holders; he preached that he was nationalist and that he had killed no Mbunda. Now Mulele exterminates Pende whom he takes for enemies, why is that?"[85] The ebbing of Pende support obviously diminished rebel strength.

Static defense, as the Taiping and Mau Mau rebels had earlier learned, tended to intensify internal disputes. Disputes based on personality and "tribalism" burst into the open, further sapping insurgent strength and unity. Since only the Mbunda and Pende had rallied to the call for collective resistance, the disaffection of the latter represented a serious blow. Not having left their ethnic stronghold, the rebels were the stronger in resisting external pressure. But this could not eliminate ANC pressure, which continued to take its toll of inhabitants, nor could it avoid internecine conflict within the bottled-up rural group.

Rural support for the rebellion reflected in some degree the widespread fear of the armed forces. The notorious indiscipline of Congolese soldiers had contributed markedly to the politicization of discontent, discussed in Chapter 5, and made resistance more palatable than compliance. After a while, however, the cure proved worse than the disease. Faced by growing shortages of food and medicine, as had been Kikuyu passive supporters of Mau Mau, rural dwellers started to leave the forest where they had taken refuge to return to their villages. The process was by no means straightforward. Only when the risk of starvation in the bush seemed to outweigh the dangers of ANC repression did the trickle of returnees grow. As a CRISP report notes, "It was only after famine and sickness had decimated villages that [their inhabitants] began to leave the forest and return to their former areas, or enter the refugee camps created by the army."[86] One official report counted 275 anaemic persons among 458 who returned home.[87] Army doctors probably made more difference in the gradual erosion of rebel support than did all the military efforts combined.

I noted earlier the failure of the Congolese government to choose between carrot and stick. Both were used, the effects cancelling out. The ANC continued its harassment, making resettlement the less attractive. Meanwhile, civilian administrators tried to persuade persons to come home. Since military raids had accounted in the first place for this flight, discipline and disengagement of the army might have been the best remedy. This option was not chosen; civilians had continually to pressure soldiers to cease their repressive activities. Not that many ANC troops moved into the affected area; there was never more than a battalion on duty in Kwilu, and patrols of five to ten soldiers were the rule.[88] But those foisted on villagers for quarters and provisions had an impact deeper than numbers would suggest.

By now, it should be obvious that the relatively sophisticated arsenal of military, economic, and psychological weapons the British mobilized against Mau Mau had no parallel in Congolese steps against the Kwilu rebellion. The administration in Leopoldville could not satisfy the claims of many insurgents by promises of reform, as the Indian government did after the incorporation of Hyderabad. Nor did the Congolese government profit from the support of a socially powerful group, as Tseng Kuo-fan did in the suppression of the Taiping rebellion. The Kwilu rebellion gradually declined, its objectives unrealized, the rancors that provoked it unresolved.

By February 1965, hunger and disease had started to take their toll of popular support. Administrative officers tried to convince villagers of the government's wish for peaceful reintegration — a message often belied by soldiers' activities — leading by September 1965 to negotiations with some rebel leaders.[89] In this gradual way, Kwilu returned sullenly to the Congolese fold. The rebellion had never englobed the entire province; only the Mbunda and Pende had accorded Mulele their support. Other major groups, affiliated with the Kamitatu wing of the PSA, suffered few of the losses of war. The provincial administration had gained support from them.

There was only one problem. Kwilu lost its provincial status in April 1966. This was not a punishment for rebellion, but part of a national administrative reorganization designed to save money and reduce political tensions. What had been twenty-two provinces were cut to eight; their political accoutrements, such as provincial assemblies, were eliminated. Judging by what marked Kwilu, reorganization was essential. The situation was characterized "by near-total disorganization, anarchy, irresponsibility, politicization, and ineffectiveness." The public payroll had become abundantly padded. In the colonial period, Kwilu district had been served by thirty-eight administrative agents and fourteen orderlies; six years after independence, official salaries were being paid to 8459 persons in the Kwilu administration, this figure excluding the provincial assembly and associated staff![90] The public seems not to have been well served, since "the sole preoccupation of government employees is the payment of their salaries and their expense accounts (*déclarations de créance*)."[91] Each month, Kwilu derived three million francs from local sources to meet monthly salary costs of 86 million francs; unpaid bills of

247 million francs and salary arrears of 167 million francs had piled up; laborers had not been paid for a year or more.[92] The paring of the payroll, since it entailed no reduction in government taxes, and since it further diminished the limited influence and political contacts of rural dwellers, came as scant blessing. Villagers continued to feel a clear sense of disengagement from national politics. Their effort to pursue a "second independence" had been throttled, rather than resolved, by encirclement and military pressure.

Preceding pages have recounted how the four challenges to government authority were suppressed. One underlying question remained unanswered: why did the various incumbents respond as they did? What considerations entered into the varying combinations of "military" and "political" strategies? Do the suggestions made at the start of Chapter 5 accord with the evidence?

The historical experiences of the incumbents provide one basis for comparison. Where clear restraints have previously been placed on the use of coercion against domestic dissidents, reform might have seemed the wiser path. Take, for example, the heritage of British civil-military relations, clearly crucial in the termination of the Mau Mau rebellion and contributory to the police action in Hyderabad. Great Britain weathered many uprisings in colonial settings and, more often than not, muddled through successfully. On almost all occasions, military considerations were subordinated to political imperatives; save under extreme circumstances, formal control remained with civilians.[93] Coercive steps were viewed as necessary supplements, not ends in themselves. This tradition, of military "aid to the civil," characterized civil-military relations in post-independence India as well as in the Colony and Protectorate of Kenya. Definite limits on the use of force existed; coercion was to be controlled and directed in small doses under civilian auspices. Such a heritage seemed weaker in late Ch'ing China, in combatting the Taiping rebels, and in the post-independence Congo. Though the governments of both recognized the dangers posed by unruly troops, neither succeeded in fully disciplining or controlling them. Soldiers' exactions, as we observed previously, directly contributed to the support the rebels garnered, and may well have prolonged conflict. Minimal control over the agents of official coercion seems to accompany a tendency to take military steps; clear and understood subordination of the armed forces seems to accompany a willingness to make political changes.

To some extent, attention to potential international implications of how an uprising was quelled encouraged "political" solutions. A rebellion viewed in domestic terms—as a matter for the sole resolution of the government concerned—led by contrast toward military steps. Once again, Mau Mau serves as an example. Administrators in Kenya drew on the expertise developed in Malaya and other strife-ripped British Colonial possessions. Officials in London recognized that the manner in which collective political violence was reduced in East Africa could affect Britain's relationships with other colonial territories moving toward independence. Experience and foresight, within an international context, argued for cautious reform following and capping a strategy of military isolation. The government of India similarly was aware of the ramifications of the Hyderabad settlement. Wishing both to succeed in land reform and to reestablish communal harmony, Prime Minister Nehru followed quick, decisive military steps with an equally important series of rural changes. The implications of his actions spread well beyond the boundaries of the former princely state. By contrast, and despite the external military assistance that had some bearing on the success of the incumbents, the Taiping and Kwilu rebellions ended through siege and exhaustion, unaccompanied by major internal reform. The prolonged death throes of the Taiping rebellion—though followed by the brief T'ung-chih reform—basically brought no change for the better. External impact and internal erosion had advanced too far for the Ch'ing dynasty to excise its rotting core, as significant reforms would have required. Kwilu lost the provincial status it had briefly enjoyed, while the military coup d'etat of November 1965 wrote *finis* to party politics. Thus, not only were the British and Indian governments more aware of the international context; they started from a stronger position. Military steps, it seems, more likely constituted the approach of the weak; only the strong, aware and self-assured dared to deal with political changes that conceded the validity of some rebel criticisms.

Let us follow this line of reasoning further, by joining it to the composition and locus of the governing elite. Political strategies require the ability, when necessary, to alter policies and leaders; military strategies derive from the belief that existing policies and leaders can, indeed must, be maintained. In Imperial China and in the Congo, those atop the pyramid of power sought to reinforce their own control. In Hyderabad and Kenya, by contrast, those who tugged strongest on the reins of power were willing to scrap beliefs and individuals no longer suited to changed circumstances.

The Taiping rebellion challenged gentry and Manchu control alike; the "second independence" uprising sought to depose those who ruled in Leopoldville. Both uprisings were thus internal wars, a species of conflict notorious for bloodiness, in which compromise appeared difficult, given the exclusive claims of both sides. The incumbents fought to maintain themselves, and to restore the status quo ante bellum; the insurgents fought to bring a different order. National leaders were impelled by the recognition that the system they knew, probably admired, and certainly profited from, hung in the balance. Compromise was nearly impossible, given perspectives of this sort. I doubt, however, whether those who made the crucial decisions in the Telengana and Mau Mau rebellions saw the uprisings in such all-or-nothing terms. The uprisings did not challenge authority in Delhi and London; from the perspective of the capital, the Telengana and Mau Mau rebellions remained isolated, insignificant, and distant. Extensive military steps appeared unnecessary when political reforms sufficed. The police action in Hyderabad installed an administration fully capable, given the steps taken toward land reform, of meeting the aspirations of the important middle peasant stratum. Little connection existed between the administrations before and after September 1948; the Nizam's power and Muslim dominance were swept aside; new leaders, eventually with electoral mandate, came to the fore. In effect, the Hyderabad elite was replaced with both the active involvement of political superiors outside the local setting and the direct support of the indigenous majority. So too, though at a slower pace, did white domination of Kenyan politics end. Direction of counterinsurgency efforts was moved increasingly from Nairobi to London, the latter a setting where the liabilities of settler dominance and the effects on policy elsewhere stood out in bold relief. The wave of decolonization that was building up strength was not to be diverted by a relatively small group of European farmers, if an appropriate bargain could be arranged.[94] Thus, despite rhetorical flourishes such as "safeguarding civilization in Africa," Her Majesty's Government directed its efforts, from mid-1954 or so, toward grooming indigenous successors to white supremacy. African paramountcy would be realized through carefully cultivated Kenyans, willing to work within British presumptions regarding the peaceful transfer of power. Thus, political reform was linked inescapably with a willingness to transfer power; adamant opposition to political reform signaled a desire to reinforce the power of those already in control.

Somewhat more problematically, the choice of strategy was influenced by the incumbents' perceptions of the rebels' status. The harshest treatment appears to have been meted out to those usually allied to governing groups who threw their lot in with low-status rural dwellers. The potential combination of a disaffected village majority with ambitious potential leaders aroused great concern; movements limited to rural dwellers could be, and were, left without rectification. As Landsberger has aptly commented, Third World governments neglect peasant needs and demands; rarely are concessions made, although a few modest reforms might in fact preserve the status quo essentially intact.[95] Neglect stems from the fact members of the "awkward class" (in Shanin's phrase) find it difficult to remind distant, urbanized political leaders of their discontent. Yet those who govern, and wish to remain in power, cannot close their ears and eyes entirely to evidence of rural disgruntlement. They choose to ignore or palliate in minimal ways—unless discontent is stirred. Then it seems, repression comes far more readily than concession.

Chinese practice differentiated between those who incited rebellion, who were liable to often gruesome executions, and those pressured into participation, who were often pardoned. In the Taiping rebellion, however, the ideological claims of Hung's followers, and the limited discipline of many imperial troops, resulted in widespread slaughter. Although the most severe forms of death were reserved for the leaders, hundreds of thousands of followers were killed—for they had been infected by a virus of change. Despite the essentially coercive steps taken to subdue the Kwilu insurrection, however, the final toll was limited. A far greater human cost was exacted by the Mau Mau rebellion, which took on the character of a civil war. There, the battle was joined: the older, propertied and pro-British versus the younger, landless, and militant—with the superior arms furnished through the colonial connection and policies of isolation eventually giving the edge to the Loyalists. Finally, despite the claims of Communists to lead the Telengana insurrection, this would-be alliance among intellectuals, proletarians, and landless laborers was met by incarceration rather than execution. Perceptions of status, it thus seems, offer at best an uncertain guide to the incumbents' choice of strategy.

A final, and ultimately unanswerable, question concludes this chapter. Does the way in which a rebellion ends in fact make any difference? The theory of relative deprivation suggests that opportunities denied are not necessarily opportunities forgotten. Reinforcement of status differentials and of the status quo means the potential for politicized discontent remains. Frustration in the past thus foreshadows frustration in the future, even if expectations are revised downwards and other adjustments can be made. To be certain, a display of overwhelming disparity in power may help direct discontent into different channels. I would argue, however, that even though defeat may await most rebels, what has the greatest future relevance is not the fact of defeat as much as the experience of collective political violence. The first challenge to the incumbents may be the hardest to mount; thereafter, a heritage of resistance exists. Force met by counterforce will continue to give rise to militant challenge. Force met by counterforce and followed by reform may give rise to peaceful challenge. It might be, accordingly, that political strategies—where the incumbent elites feel capable of effecting these—may more readily raise the threshold of frustration that can be endured before violence results. Evidence with which to examine this idea appears in the following chapter.

CHAPTER 9 /

The Continuity of Protest and
the Significance of Politics

The value of history lies in its lessons for the future. What general points can we draw from the uprisings chronicled in this book?

Rural unrest will continue well into the foreseeable future, for the forces that affected the societies examined in this book remain powerful generators of political discontent. Despite the rapid pace of urbanization in developing countries, a majority of the world's population remain in rural settings. Few of them, however, continue to avoid involvement in market forces. Many have shifted fully into commercialized agriculture. By far the greatest portion remain subject to contending pressures: the unrestorable ideal of unfettered rural autonomy, the inexorable demands of the state, their continuing integration into cash economies. Equally complex is their integration into national political systems. Ideals of local political autonomy are often overridden in the process. The adjustments involved are complex, far-reaching, and unsettling, affecting all aspects of society. Transition brings troubled times.

The pattern I have been sketching is not unique to the contemporary Third World. Other societies have weathered the resultant changes — though they may have done so over an extended period. To assert they avoided violence in the process belies historic reality. According to a major expert, if there is a "universal ultimate cause" of peasant unrest, it rises from the sequence of economic integration of an agrarian society into a larger market, a consequent drive to commercialize agriculture, and subsequent encroachment on peasant lands and peasants' rights in general.[1] It was, and is, a profoundly upsetting set of events. This process marked Western societies in earlier centuries, and became manifest during the twentieth century in peasant wars. General similarities in this process make it possible to compare change in rural societies across centuries and across cultures — so long as the analyst ensures his or her interest in global similarities highlights rather than overshadows the relevant differences.

If the economic and social causes of rural unrest have received detailed attention, the same cannot be asserted confidently for the political causes of rural unrest. Attention to increased exploitation by landlords, to the breakdown of reciprocal obligations between tenants and proprietors, and to the continued survival of norms of collective action within ascriptively-defined rural groups, has at times directed attention away from governmental shortcomings. The uprisings we have surveyed were as important politically as they were economically and socially. Rebellion became, for lack of a more efficacious alternative, the means whereby the weak and exploited pressed their claims. Their efforts were inadvertently abetted by the misperceptions and ill-considered actions of the respective governments. Unrest was converted into large-scale collective political violence through the interplay between popular means of collective action and government steps toward military/political resolution. Those in control underestimated the potential for violence in their policies. They either ignored the obstacles over which previous leaders had stumbled, or believed themselves endowed with exceptional wisdom. Whether knowledgeable or ill-informed historically, it mattered little; the point is that the portents of discontent were misread, and the consequences intensified, by government action. The "universal ultimate cause" of widespread rebellion may thus be government ineptitude, a deferral of timely adjustments until too late, a proclivity to rebuff rural claims with a combination of studious neglect and direct attacks. *Anatomy of Rebellion*, as its overriding concern, has stressed the significance of political factors. Collective political violence is anchored in government actions. Economic deprivation encouraged unrest; political shortcomings brought widespread collective action.

One should not always expect similar government actions to produce similar results in different settings. Societies differ in their propensities for collective action, and hence for collective political violence. Supposedly universal models for violence find expression through culturally specific means of protest. Accordingly, in dealing with the prospects for future rebellions, we must note both the indigenous bases for collective action, and how they are supplemented by outside ideas of transformation. Would-be rebels can draw on traditions of violence propagated within their societies, as well as a varied corpus of revolutionary writings based on other situations. The contemporary world has many popularizers of peasant violence. The writings of Mao, Fanon, and scores of others can be cited as proof positive of the necessity for initiative from below. What cannot be assured is a clear fit between exogenous and indigenous elements — "new" and "old" justifications for collective political violence. Chapter 7 illustrated how the "elite" and "folk" justifications pointed toward steps against the incumbents, but differed on the nature and extent of the aggrieved community, on the precise alterations to be sought, and on the ways in which government initiatives should be answered. Such groping for definition took its toll. The subduing of dissent resulted as much from divisions among the insurgents as from the superior resources

316 / Repression and Resurgence

of the incumbents. The initiation of rebellion, it seems, bears witness to economic inequities and government inadequacies; the defeat of collective political violence, it then follows, testifies to rebel shortcomings and policy alterations.

To what extent did the seeming immediate failure of the uprisings reflect their peculiar mixtures of general and specific elements? Did the eruption of collective political violence represent shadows from the past, or harbingers of the future? These are the broad questions with which I shall deal in this conclusion. In order to do so, we should look at the post-rebellion repercussions, especially at the consequences of "political" and "military" steps in termination. The four cases suggest that the militancy and consciousness evoked by collective action did not disappear, though they might be considerably transformed. The heritage of revolt remained, and could be activated under conditions of renewed social stress.

Of the four rebellions, the most sweeping reforms came in Hyderabad and Kenya. The distant governments in Delhi and London transferred control to elected indigenous groups. Political reforms ensured what military steps had first gained—and answered some of the originating grievances. Let us look more closely at the manner in which the "police action" and the "Emergency" ended.

Indian troops succeeded in Hyderabad more speedily than their superiors had deemed probable. Three days of war sufficed for military victory. These were followed by three years of military administration, during which significant economic and political changes were made. The rebellion itself flickered out, a product of exhaustion and change of Communist tactics. The diminishing base of support made continuation next to impossible, as participants found reform allowed an alternative to struggle. Land reform was undertaken: the middle peasants in particular reaped benefits. The Untouchables—by 1949-50, the backbone of the uprising—were offered special access to education, employment, and land. Haughty Muslims were taken down several pegs, while communal hostilities diminished. The Nizam was transformed into a constitutional monarch, as noted in the previous chapter; the essentially Muslim police force was restaffed. Steady progress was made in re-establishing rural peace. By 1951, an Osmania University team reported that "cordiality" had returned to Hindu-Muslim relations in the village they studied intensively.[2]

The police action restored to Telengana villagers many elements of the semiautonomous, relatively undisturbed rural life they favored. Deposed were the Muslim *jagirdars* and large Hindu *deshmukhs*, although village *patwaris* and *pattidars* remained. Gone also were the razakars, although

Muslims continued to constitute a large part of the government. Untouchability was legally abolished. But were the changes effected in ways that touched all? The scheduled castes did not overnight alter their submissive behavior of centuries, for they were widely perceived as inferior despite their role in the rebellion, particularly its later stages. Local influentials retained their economic, political and social primacy. The elimination of glaring inequalities by no means entailed full leveling of resources. Change was still viewed with skepticism. Clear evidence for the relatively minor alterations in village life came from Dube and his associates, reporting their 1951 study of a Telengana village:

On the whole rigid adherence to traditional life-styles is regarded as the ideal and most satisfactory method of adjustment with the universe and its unseen forces. Activities of political parties, particularly of the Communist Party, have tried to awaken people to a more positive attitude, not without total lack of success, but the new ideas are still greeted with frank dismay and skepticism and so far there has been very little change in their basic attitude towards life and the principal goal of the community, which still remains peaceful adjustment and adaptation to the laws that control the universe.[3]

One family continued to control a quarter of the village's agricultural area, eight families another quarter; although 240 families had at least some land, 110 families remained landless.[4] Although some diminution of inequalities doubtless resulted from the 1954 land reform amendments, patterns of ownership persisted to a surprising degree.[5] Economic and social changes were thus relatively modest, by no means constituting a revolution in village-level relationships.

The apparent continuity in the local pattern contrasted with the political fate of Hyderabad as a whole. Its incorporation into India, and the dismantling of much of the Nizam's government, opened new opportunities for aspirant officeholders, especially Hindus. Major issues involved organizing elections, deciding whether to maintain the former princely state as an entity or divide it along linguistic lines, and filling government positions. These were matters that concerned the urban elite—and it is within this far smaller group that the sense of a distinct Telengana identity continued to echo in later years.

Military administration was a temporary expedient, the "aid to the civil" to be terminated as soon as feasible. Congress established branches in the state, to capitalize on support expected from the reforms introduced; the CPI pointed to its militancy on behalf of the poor. In the March 1952 elections, Congress won 93 of the 175 seats, the Communists 42 (under the name "People's Democratic Front," since the CPI was still formally banned in the state). All the Communist victors stood in Telengana constituencies, indication of the support the party had gained through its unstinting advocacy of Telengana and middle peasant rights.[6] This rural stronghold remained through later elections.

Far more perplexing was the future organization of Hyderabad as a whole. In the short run, administrative convenience was best served by maintaining the state's borders and governmental apparatus. In the long run, however, the multilingual basis of Hyderabad provided grounds for dispute. Congress leaders wrestled with concern that national unity might be undermined, were the principle of *cuius lingua, eius lingua* granted. Although theoretically in favor of linguistic self-determination,[7] they in fact acted cautiously when the time for choice came. The Communists, by contrast, did not waver in their support for language as a chief basis for political divisions. It should be recalled that creation of "Vishal Andhra," (Greater Andhra), based on the Telugu language, provided the CPI one of its initial bases for organizing in rural areas.[8] Prior to the police action about one-third of the Telugu-speaking populace had lived under the Nizam's jurisdiction, almost all the others in the sprawling, polyglot Madras Province. Communists portrayed this division as an imperialist plot: "The British keep up the Nizam, and his satellites...only to keep our people divided and to suppress our common freedom movement," Sundarayya wrote in 1946.[9] According to him, the "dream of generations of Andhra people" was "a free Vishala Andhra comprising the whole of Telugu land, in a free India...."[10] With the deposition of the Nizam, the way was open to redrawing the political map—were leaders of the government willing.

The skepticism of Prime Minister Nehru and his associates about splitting Hyderabad stemmed from the bloody consequences of communalism and partition in 1947. Linguistic bases for organizing states seemed liable to encourage disintegration. Rather than open Pandora's box wider, they hoped to slam it shut. A 1948 commission strongly recommended against immediate provincial reorganization on language lines, to which the government added the proviso such change could be effected but only after careful thought, and only were administrative dislocation and mutual conflicts avoided. A recipe, in other words, for keeping the status quo. It took the December 1952 fasting-unto-death of Andhra leader Potti Siramalu and riots in Telugu-speaking parts of Madras to convince those in Delhi. Nehru decreed the carving out of Andhra State from Madras; he did nothing, however, relative to Telugu-speaking parts of Hyderabad until the State Reorganization Commission reported in October 1955. It recognized that change was imperative, since the "superimposed and superficial unity [of Hyderabad] has already broken down in effect."[11] Yet there was no obvious best path to take. Public opinion in Andhra State favored the amalgamation of Telengana; public opinion in Telengana had yet to crystallize. Combination of the two seemed likely to create administrative problems, and might require safeguards regarding Telengana employment in government and special allocation of development funds; compared with Madras, Telengana was backwards. The Commission chose the cautious path. It suggested Telengana be constituted into a separate state, and merged with Andhra only if the second subsequently-elected legislature voted in favor by a two-thirds majority.[12] Nehru rejected this cautious suggestion and mandated the merger. Andhra Pradesh was created in 1956 from the former Andhra State and Telengana. Greater Andhra came into being, despite the increasing desire of many Telengana residents for a State unto themselves.

Suspicions about amalgamation came primarily from the urban aspirant elite, not from the rural poor to whom these debates had little direct or immediate relevance. The quest for government employment — for there, I believe, was the heart of the matter — occupied the attention of the educated. It was a debate which had started the moment Hyderabad was incorporated into India. Who should be hired: the indigenous? the historically underprivileged? the best-qualified, irrespective of background? The first round after the police action went to those wishing to retain the local character of administration. Only "mulkis" — those resident in Hyderabad for a minimum of fifteen years[13] — could be employed. The slogan, "Hyderabad for the Hyderabadis," united the would-be local elite in that most potent of political motivations, self-interest. But, since mulki certificates could be obtained through bribery, indigenes' claims were not always heeded. The merger changed the rules of the game. Round two went to the best-qualified who, too often for local taste, came from the former Andhra State, an area traditionally of greater educational opportunities that until 1953 had been part of Madras. Resentment increased. Competition for positions diminished the unity language purportedly brought.

In June 1969, collective political violence once again erupted in Hyderabad. The scene this time was Hyderabad City, not rural Telengana. Feelings of discrimination, and a sense promises had been shelved, lay behind this outburst. The action started with a student strike, which led to a chorus of protests from teachers and other professionals, concerned as well about corruption, caste differences, and the untrammeled power of the chief minister.[14] The objective was not radical alteration, but implementation of a gentleman's agreement made when Andhra Pradesh was created in 1956 that gave special recognition to Telengana.[15] The agreement had remained a rhetorical flourish; its clauses were not fully implemented. In the words of one manifesto, "For centuries under the

feudal rulers the people of Telengana lived in servitude. For the first time
in history they had elected a popular government of their own in 1952 to
govern themselves. Hardly did they breath [sic] the air of freedom, for four
years they were again subjected to economic and political colonization by
the Andhras, much against their wishes, and the recommendations of a expert Commission."[16] In the escalation of conflict, boycotts, marches and
hunger strikes were countered by police fusillades and lathi charges. Only
after seven months of urban turmoil did tensions abate.

These stirrings of Telengana political militancy bore witness to the fact
that a sense of collective identity, once aroused, can be revived under varying circumstances. Only time, patience and concessions might have recon-
ciled the Telengana urbanized to their perceived inferior position vis-a-vis
other urbanized Telugu-speakers. Feeling a sense of relative deprivation,
they turned to longstanding tactics of protest. The obvious ploy for resolution—creation of a separate Telengana state—was rejected by Prime
Minister Gandhi. Sharing her father's reluctance about further division of
the body politic, Mrs. Gandhi maintained Andhra Pradesh as an entity.
She recognized that the bark of disaffected city residents came from
politically toothless gums. Agitation in the capital did not seep into the
villages. The continuing calm in rural Telengana made clear that modest
land reform had succeeded at least to the extent of dampening enthusiasm
for further violence. Thus, though the 1969 riots testified to a continuing
sense of Telengana identification relative to other Telugu speakers, they
did not indicate that urban and rural dwellers shared a common sense of
what should be done. Political and economic reforms had removed the
major excesses of village life; indifference had returned; the self-interest of
the educated seemed far removed from hamlet concerns. The urban revolt
of Telengana changed far less than had the earlier rural uprising.

In turning to the aftermath of the Mau Mau rebellion, we find that
echoes of the struggle for land and freedom reverberated for many years.
The overall goals of the uprising were achieved by the mid-1960s, with the
grant of independence and opening of the areas reserved for Europeans to
African settlement. Incomplete translation of these general gains into individual improvement sustained flickers of resistance, however. Surviving
forest fighters, though publicly lionized, found themselves at a great
political disadvantage after independence. The Kenya government,
solicitous of their support, seemed nonetheless more concerned about accommodation with European capitalism, and economic improvement for
the Kikuyu governing elite. Loyalists and fence-sitters enjoyed the greatest
gains from the emergency. They profited from British steps during the
suppression, and solidified their advantage during land consolidation, as
indicated in Chapter 8. The British willingly transferred political control

and made capital grants to Kenyan constitutional moderates; these moderates, in their turn, lent their blessings to the internal land redistribution that occurred during the emergency to the benefit of loyalists and neutrals. The "extremists" gained little in fact relative to the risks they took.[17]

Kenyans gained materially from the achievement of independence, in the aggregate. As is usual, however, some gained far more than others; to paraphrase George Washington Plunkett, they had their opportunities, and they took 'em. A new "tribe" came into being, the WaBenzi — those who purchased costly Mercedes. Class differentiation accelerated, as income inequalities became more pronounced. Some Kenyans were drawn into lucrative partnerships with expatriate firms; others gained privileged access to lands vacated by Europeans. All were elated by *Uhuru*; only some gained direct and immediate benefits.

The novels of Ngugi Wa Thiong'o provide a sensitive barometer to the shifting currents. His 1965 novel, *The River Between*, epitomized the ridge loyalties that complicated collective action among the Kikuyu. In *A Grain of Wheat* (1967), Ngugi portrayed the fratricidal rivalries that ripped Kikuyu society during the emergency. The search for the betrayer of a Mau Mau leader formed the book's major plot; at its conclusion, Ngugi depicted the crushed hopes of villagers, who hoped to create a cooperative on former European land, only to discover the elected M.P. had grabbed the property for his personal benefit. In later writings, Ngugi became even more pointed in his criticism of the post-independence order. *The Trial of Dedan Kimathi* (a coauthored play published in 1977) included several ringing denunciations of Kenyan society as it existed after independence. For example, "There has never been and will never be justice for the people under imperialism. Justice is created through a revolutionary struggle against all the forces of imperialism. Our struggle must therefore continue. Don't walk into the mouth of guns unless you have yours organized!"[18] *Petals of Blood*, Ngugi's lengthy 1977 novel, assailed the increasing monopolization of power, status and wealth in Kenya. A few weeks after the book's publication, Ngugi was detained without trial. (In fairness to the Kenya government, let me quickly add that the book itself was not banned.)

The verbal barbs of a gifted writer bothered the Kenya government. Of greater concern to it than Ngugi's novels, however, were explicit efforts to rally the former Mau Mau fighters. For many years, members of the governing elite seemed determined to weaken any nucleus of resisters who might conceivably turn against the new incumbents. For example, registration was refused in 1964 for the Kenya Freedom Fighters' Union; in February 1969 the Kenya War Council, the ex-Freedom Fighters' Union,

and the Waliolete Uhuru Union ("Those who brought Freedom" Union)
were banned as "dangerous to the good government of the Republic."[19]
The strongest challenge of all came from Oginga Odinga, a Luo leader
who had counted among the strongest advocates of Kenyatta's assuming
official leadership before KANU would participate in parliamentary matters. By 1966, the two men had parted company. Odinga, joined by
Achieng Oneko (a Luo defendant at the Kapenguria trial) and Bildad
Kaggia, created the Kenya People's Union (KPU). All three were known
for their radical sympathies and their support for the claims of former Mau
Mau partisans. To them, the heroic actions of the forest fighters were being swept aside by unconscious indifference and conscious neglect. The
divisions of Kikuyu society, upon which British repression had been largely
based, continued to gape widely. Let me quote Odinga's rationale for
creating the KPU:

> The two sides of the Emergency persisted into later years; freedom-fighters
> were unemployed and landless; and loyalists had entrenched themselves and
> had become the dependable middle group that government had aimed to
> create. Those who had sacrificed most in the struggle had lost out to the peo-
> ple who had played safe. Political divisions had been given concrete
> economic shape, and so would persist into the post-Emergency period. This,
> as much as the toll of dead, injured, and detained, was the harvest that
> government policy reaped: the creation of a group that had vested interests
> to defend would, it was hoped, block the struggle rising again in open revolt
> and would capture not only the military but the political victory of the years
> to come.[20]

The threat to the new elite was real. Odinga commanded the support of
the Luo, second largest ethnic group in Kenya—while the assassination of
the Luo KANU leader Tom Mboya in July 1969 removed the obvious non-
Kikuyu sucessor to Kenyatta. Odinga offered a choice, not an echo to
Kenyatta; his seeming class basis for political organizing touched a sensitive nerve. The major losers, were the KPU to triumph, would be the
Kikuyu political elite who had soared to political power and economic affluence. The question was whether an anti-Kikuyu coalition, or a union of
the poor, would drive the elite from office; Odinga's KPU threatened both.
The antidote: ethnic solidarity, buttressed by legal harassment of the
KPU.

From early 1969 on, oathing ceremonies were revived among the
Kikuyu. What Mau Mau had once used to counteract the incumbents, the
elite now sought to turn to their own benefit. Ascriptive solidarity would
rebuff the threat. In the words of Kenyatta's biographer,

As might have been expected, the campaign got out of hand. Once again the ridges of Kikuyuland seethed with activity as lorry-load after lorry-load made its way to Gatundu to 'have tea with the President', the euphemism for oathing ceremonies. There they swore that 'the flag of Kenya shall not leave the House of Mumbi'....Intimidation grew, the local authorities being unwilling to intervene. Government servants themselves often took a lead in the oathing arrangements. Threats produced stiffer resistance which in turn led to increased violence.[21]

I do not intend to equate the anti-colonial struggle of Mau Mau with the 1969 resurgence of oathing. The prevailing circumstances, however, encouraged appeals to ethnic solidarity, calls for collective action based on a sense of what the Kikuyu required. In 1969, oathing was intended to maintain rather than to challenge a status quo. The Kikuyu had moved into control; like the British before them, they sought to minimize widening the elite. The threat from the left was countered by jailing (Odinga was incarcerated from late 1969 to 1972), by legal restrictions (the KPU was ordered dissolved in October 1969), and by blandishments to KPU members to rejoin KANU. But the chief weapon of defense remained the oath. The lessons of history were clear. The Mau Mau struggle had underscored the importance of unity. Although the guerrilla struggle of the 1950s had been suppressed by loosing the Kikuyu Home Guard against the Kikuyu forest fighters, the political struggle of the 1960s would be won by uniting the House of Mumbi against potential interlopers. Divided in achieving power, the Kikuyu would nonetheless join in maintaining it in Kikuyu hands. Other groups, lacking the searing experience of rebellion, did not have similar weapons of unity at hand. Collective action in the name of land and freedom provided a heritage that could be subsequently turned in other directions. The Kikuyu had gained a head start in the race for economic and political power, and were determined to maintain their advantage.

The oathing of 1969 represented an immediate response dictated by the political climate. In the long term, the solidarity born of ethnicity will be increasingly affected by economic differentiation. Its political consequences are uncertain. The would-be class appeals of the KPU may have been premature rather than incorrect. Contrasts in income had become manifest by 1969, but had not crystallized into political form. Such may come and affect Kikuyu solidarity. On the other hand, access to the fruits of power could consolidate Kikuyu unity, and at the same time encourage anti-Kikuyu alliances. In either event — economic differentiation cutting across ethnic lines; polarization between Kikuyu and non-Kikuyu strengthening perceptions of Kikuyu unity — the lessons of Mau Mau will be remembered. Collective action requires commitment and means of reinforcement. These the Kikuyu seem to enjoy. The contest for power in Kenya, as in India, had been largely though not fully, transferred to political rather than violent channels, since it seems possible to reach desired goals without goading rural supporters into militant resistance. The new leaders had a stake in the system they too had to maintain.

The Kwilu rebellion, it will be recalled, ended with nary a shred of political concession. By late 1966, most participants had returned as best they could to their previous pursuits, their economic position heavily dependent on the palm fruit harvest, their security affected by military incursions. Mulele went into exile in Brazzaville, a ferry ride from Kinshasa (as the capital, Leopoldville, had been rechristened). The political situation gave little cause for optimism about reform. There seemed to be no place for competitive, open politics. Power became increasingly concentrated in the hands of General Mobutu Sese Seko. The frenetic politics of the immediate pre- and post-independence periods evaporated. In its stead, the national government reverted to a centralized, authoritarian, bureaucratic style, with a substantial admixture of patrimonialism.[22] What political participation was officially recognized had to be channeled through the Mouvement Populaire Revolutionaire (MPR), headed by President Mobutu. Initiatives from below were distrusted. Those at the top gave the orders, "Le Guide" — Mobutu himself — brooking no opposition.

Even in exile, Mulele constituted a threat to the government of Zaire. In what soon proved to be a hollow gesture of reconciliation, the government extended an amnesty in 1968 to its former opponents. Mulele returned from his Brazzaville refuge. Within ten hours of his arrival, he had been executed. The promised safe conduct was a ruse. Although Mobutu was out of the country at the time, he was likely aware of the fate that awaited his opponent.

Given the marked personal imprint of Mulele on the 1964 uprising, his killing might have seemed to remove threats of further violence in Kwilu. It did not. Mulele, though dead, entered the pantheon of rural folk heroes who dared oppose the central government. His name could be invoked to justify steps against the government. The conditions of relative deprivation remained largely unchanged, with the suppression of the Kwilu rebellion. The sense of collective action shaped in the 1931 strike, in the mobilization of the PSA, and in the "second independence" insurrection, could be drawn upon — and indeed was. In January 1978, collective political violence once again broke out in Kwilu. Little press attention was given it; indeed, the government of Zaire tried to restrict information. A subsequent journalist's report merits citation:

Those involved in the revolt...were indigenous villagers sympathetic to the

teachings of Pierre Mulele, a populist leader who led a revolt in the former
Belgian Congo in 1964 and 1965 and has remained a powerful cult figure
since his death....
With the activity concentrated on the village of Mulembe, Mr. Mulele's
birthplace, bands of rebels soon roamed in the area, gathering supporters in
surrounding villages, looting and burning municipal offices and carrying off
records....
The troops that attacked Mulembe were met by a rain of arrows — the movement eschews non-African weapons — ravaged the village, killing perhaps 50
persons.......after local army units had effectively quelled the insurrection,
paratroopers were brought in and went on a rampage, burning villages and
killing as many as 500 persons.[23]

Pierre Mulele's heritage lived on. His name and memory could be invoked to mount collective political violence. More than ever, however, the
villagers of Kwilu appeared to be "primitive rebels," as Hobsbawm would
define them. The sharp distinction Mulele had drawn between exploiters
and exploited was expressed almost totally in ethnic rather than economic
terms. The villagers' quest for recognition in 1978 lacked the national
political outlook Mulele attempted to superimpose. What had been aimed
in 1964 toward rural political revolution had devolved a decade plus later
into endemic rural unrest, a sign of disaffection, but not in and of itself a
serious threat to the central government. As long as discontent remained
fragmented, outbursts such as that of January 1978 could be contained.
Kwilu would retain its mark of simmering discontent; the writ of the national government would carry little weight, but the inhabitants would
gain little from their unabated opposition.

The manner in which the 1978 uprising was subdued indicated the continuity of government policy in Zaire. Military steps predominated. The
initial deaths the army caused were multiplied tenfold by the actions of the
paratroopers. In the Kinshasa perspective, the misled followers of Mulele
had to be taught a lesson. Significant concessions would gain nothing. A
strong show of force would best serve national objectives. Mulelist partisans
could be isolated from other potentially disaffected groups, through emphasis on their narrow "tribalism."

The Zaire of President Mobutu was not a state in which opposition could
be readily expressed. The MPR monopolized legal party activity — though
it gave scant evidence of serving as a conduit for popular concerns, serving
rather as an instrument of control directed from the top.[24] Proclamation of
the party's "revolutionary" nature, Mobutu's posthumous rehabilitation of
Lumumba, or the wholesale changing of names to reflect "authenticity,"
could not alter the basic nature of the MPR. It was to guard against further rural effervescence, capturing it instead for officially-approved ends.
The people of Kwilu, peripheral to the interests of those in Kinshasa, could

be ignored rather than paid heed to. The short-lived revolt of January 1978 suggests that, where indigenous traditions of collective action exist, resented impositions by the elite may be resisted violently. Kwilu thus points in a direction contrary to Kenya. The leadership of Kenyatta meant Kikuyu solidarity might be invoked to support the government; by contrast, the martyrdom of Mulele meant Mbunda solidarity might be utilized to oppose the government. In either event, ethnic sentiments as reinforced by the searing experiences of rebellion provided the basis for collective action; the policies of the government determined whether support or opposition would occur.

What repercussions stemmed from the Taiping rebellion? Most distant in time, broadest in scope and magnitude of our four uprisings, it stood at a critical divide in Chinese history. Understanding the Chinese revolution of 1949 requires understanding the Taiping rebellion of 1851. For, as a major intellectual historian of China wrote, "Proto-revolutionary Taiping rebels took the Confucian-imperial order out of the path of rebellions, and set it up for the unmistakable revolutionaries who were still to come."[25]

The consequences of the 1850-1864 upheaval lie in both physical and intellectual realms. The Taipings undercut the Ch'ing dynasty, and the tenets of Confucianism, by sword and pen. Weakening the structure of the imperial state through military assault, the rebels eroded its basic values by asserting ideas drawn from outside the Confucian tradition. Though a century passed before the proclamation of the new political and ideological order, Hung Hsiu-ch'üan and his followers had sown some of the seeds of this major revision.

The direct physical consequences can be quickly expressed. No quarter was given in the struggle. Imperial troops tried to expunge all traces of the rebels—taking an immense human toll in the process. The paucity of statistics, the unreliability of what are available, and the collapse of the usual means for gathering figures complicate the analyst's task; I can only repeat Ho's suggestion that twenty to thirty million deaths represent too low a figure.[26] The immensity of the Chinese population notwithstanding, such destruction had immense costs. Perhaps most significantly, there was no major effort to revive sympathy for Taiping objectives until the time of Sun Yat-sen, himself a Hakka from Kwangtung province.

As already noted, not only the Taipings took up arms against the imperial government in the mid-nineenth century. The concurrent Red Turban, Nien and Moslem uprisings all confirmed the dynasty's weaknesses, and contributed to its further enervation. Each county or province taken by a rebel force diminished the resource base from which the government drew, while its need for funds and troops grew. Insurrection weakened even further the admittedly limited ability of Peking to control actions at the periphery. The extractions and exactions of local officials and gentry in areas still under Ch'ing control increased in the mid-nineteenth century.

Internal weakening was affected as well by growing foreign pressures. British incursions into South China encouraged the initial rise of the Taipings, as elaborated in previous chapters. The Opium War demonstrated Ch'ing weakness. In the words of a contemporary British observer of the Taiping rebellion, 'There can be no doubt whatever of the existing insurrection having been the result of our own war.'[27] But Western powers, particularly Great Britain, found advantage in propping up the tottering dynasty. The benefits were mutual. Faced with both external and internal enemies, Ch'ing rulers chose collaboration with the lesser of two evils. In Levenson's words,

> Since in 1860 the foreigners sought only the dynasty's capitulation, while the Taipings sought its extirpation, the dynasty's one recourse was to suffer the evil of foreign aggrandizement at China's expense, and to try to turn the loss to account; when it was hammered home to the Ch'ing that they had no hope of two victories, they became grudgingly reconciled to accepting the one defeat (and the lesser one) which could be put to use in staving off the other.[28]

In addition to western support, the court turned to its traditional stay, the gentry. I have already taken note of the major part Tseng Kuo-fan took in the suppression of the Taipings. Tseng appealed to local loyalties, thus raising (as the ruling house fully realized) the spectre of provincial autonomy. The special Hunan army served as a bulwark against the threat of Hung and his followers, but led to decentralization. Weakened central control was to have major consequences in later decades. Unable effectively to control troops ostensibly under its command, the government in Peking eventually became the victim of contending armies. Ho describes the consequences thus:

> Since these new armies had a strong sense of solidarity and local patriotism and looked exclusively to their leaders for orders, they were virtually 'personal' armies. It would not be an exaggeration to say that the origins of twentieth-century warlordism can be traced back to the Taiping period....[29]

Yet the brush Hung wielded may have been mightier than the swords his followers carried. Taiping beliefs, even with their many overlaps with various Chinese systems of thought, represented a significant alternative to the Confucian beliefs on which imperial rule had been based for centuries. Hung implied that not only the court had lost the Mandate of Heaven; the whole retinue of gentry supporters had also forfeited it. The Taipings did not seek to renew the Mandate of Heaven, for Hung claimed he had direct access to "God in Heaven."[30] Despite the use of the Taipings made of the educated, the rebels' values corroded the basic Confucian underpinnings of Chinese society. The symbiotic self-interest that bound the literati to the imperial court came in for strong criticism that could only weaken it.

The ideological pretensions of Hung Hsiu-ch'üan and Yang Hsiu-Ch'ing foreshadowed elements of the future, as well as reflected elements of the past. With a bit of historic license, one can see in Taiping ideology many elements highlighted in twentieth-century China. The proto-nationalist opposition to the Manchus bore fruit in the 1911 revolution, in which the dynasty collapsed. The Taipings' universalist claims for beliefs drawn from outside China later yielded to other imported ideologies, including western liberalism and Marxism. The concept of the sacred land system, shadowy as this aspect of Taiping practice may have been, went further in its potential application than had earlier attempts at redistribution by directly involving the state. Maldistribution of land had provided impetus to almost all earlier Chinese rural uprisings, but only local changes had occurred; the Taipings proposed but could not implement change on a national scale; the Communists carried out massive redistribution, then almost complete collectivization, in less than a decade. Given these varied parallels, one need not wonder why twentieth-century Chinese leaders have found justification in the Taiping rebellion for many of the steps they took.

Because Taiping claims appeared to represent such a profound break with the past, Ch'ing officials felt far more comfortable with destroying them than with reaching compromise. Basic values conflicted. No *modus vivendi* could have been achieved; both the Taipings and the Manchu dynasty (with its gentry supporters) claimed the right to rule all Chinese in very different ways. Their desires were mutually exclusive and incompatible. Hung would not have been content with local autonomy as were the supporters of a separate Telengana state or, for that matter, the revivers of Mulele's resistance. All-or-nothing claims, carried out militarily and ideologically, made the Taiping rebellion the most sweeping in its goals of the four examined in this book.

Yet each rebellion included elements basically antagonistic to the existing patterns. Telengana villagers challenged the *deshmukhs* and *jagirdars* whose feudal powers bore little evidence of reciprocity. Claims for land and freedom in colonial Kenya challenged the central tenets of "white man's country." The uprising in Kwilu was directed at changing the central government, given Mulele's interest in a broad coalition among insurgents. Accordingly, what the rebels sought should not be dismissed as totally parochial or backward-looking. True, self-interest motivated many, if not most, of the participants. They wanted a more secure life, freed from the economic and social pressures that initially drove them into collective action. Equally true, the "elite" ideology of profound transformation may have been less important in explaining individuals' adherence than the "folk" ideology of rectification. Equally likewise, many rebel claims remained dead letters, while particularistic bases of solidarity accounted more for popular support than did presumably nonascriptive bases such as class, religion, or nationality. These are undeniably facts. They do not override the fundamental contradictions between the goals of the rebels and the concerns of the incumbents, however. What the insurgents wanted involved profound changes in the government—its policies, composition, and basic rationale. The four insurrections with which we have been concerned partook of elements of revolution, even while drawing heavily on indigenous elements of rebellion.

In the final analysis, were these uprisings more akin to revolutions or to rebellions? I believe the Taiping rebellion was an aborted revolution, the others large scale but unsuccessful rebellions—unsuccessful, that is, in terms of the major protagonists' rapidly bettering their political and economic status.

Four conditions seem requisite for revolution as a form of collective political violence: clear social polarization; government ineptitude; a combination of rural and urban insurrection; and the assertion of goals fundamentally incompatible with the existing means of justification. Let us give brief attention to each.

A diffuse sense of differentiation may long exist in a society without there being a whisper of revolution. Intense, focused resentment—"us" versus "them"—necessarily precedes major outbursts of collective political violence. What happens should deeply based resentment be local in nature? I see no necessary contradiction between grievances that are confined in their immediate spread and widespread collective action—as long as the aggrieved unite their actions. A revolution does not burst full-grown onto the scene; it likely develops from alliances of discontented, who find a common, political cause in their grievances. Should a sense of commonality not emerge, resentment remains contained. A government (assuming reasonable efficiency in administration) might thus weather widespread but low-level antipathy; it might equally ride out intense, geographically restricted resentment. Any widening of the latter, or intensification of the former, opens the way to revolutionary change.

The uneven nature of discontent, and the similarly uneven extent of politicization described in Chapter 4, obviously affect the course of political awareness. Perhaps the greatest allies of the incumbents in the four rebellions were social pluralism and conflicting economic goals of many participants. Coordinated action proved difficult. The intense resentment some experienced was moderated by the ignorance of others, and the approbation of still others. For example, the deep-rooted relative deprivation among Kikuyu squatters had no real parallel among the pastoral Masai, or among the agricultural Luo who escaped the weight of European settlement. Kenya experienced a bloody but confined insurrection. Though black-white polarization and anti-colonial sentiment were on the rise, the British disengaged in time to keep more of the colony from potentially being engulfed in violence. The Telengana rebels were even more isolated than their Mau Mau counterparts; other Hindu groups in Hyderabad, despite landlord exploitation and Muslim dominance, were not liable to such intense land hunger, nor to comparable expressions of cultural pride. Telugu speakers felt a sense of linguistic pride sharply at variance with their economic and political subordination; this sense of disparity, reinforced by concentration of land holdings and political organizing, gave the Telengana uprising a parochial rather than an expandable foundation. In the Congo and late Ch'ing China, by contrast, local grievances flared more readily into widespread revolt. The most obvious difference appeared in the competence of the government, a second condition for the transformation of rebellion into revolution.

The government of Kenya may have been oblivious to signs of rural unrest prior to mid-1952, but its members were assuredly neither stupid nor incompetent. Heirs of a long tradition of colonial administration, they recognized — eventually — the advantage of strategic retreat. The economic resources of Great Britain made possible sophisticated military steps by Nairobi-based administrators; at the same time, however, the funds available were not so great as to permit them to neglect political steps. Determined but also supple, the British suppressors of Mau Mau corraled dissidence effectively. By confirming its Kikuyu basis, and then by exploiting divisions within this basis, the British kept Kenya from becoming a major battleground for African nationalism. In a similar fashion, the government of India embarked on political steps immediately after the swift police action. The collapse of the rural coalition limited both the spread of collective political violence to other groups, and the effectiveness of such violence within the group itself.

Earlier pages depicted what I consider to have been widespread political ineptitude in late Ch'ing China and the post-independence Congo. The self-serving nature of many government members, and the shameful breakdowns of military discipline, intensified the popular grievances that existed. Lack of political finesse pushed the government to punitive policies, carried out by ill-disciplined troops. Resentment became directed all the more easily against members of the privileged elite. Discontent was expressed as collective political violence, since no other channels for rapid rectification existed. Resentment, nascent in the contrasts between rulers and ruled, matured with the government's imposition of violence.

Government intransigence has often been identified as a major cause of revolution. I suggest minor modification. Persistence in seeking military victory—a form of intransigence—spurs the polarization and competitive mobilization that mark revolution. Nothing may better drive persons into opposition than the realization that life and livelihood may be at stake. Escalation of violence by the government forcing an all-or-nothing choice can confirm rather than break the will to resist. A mark of political ineptness thus comes in unstinted military repression, contrasted with political reform and "pacification." I realize the Vietnam war surrounded this latter term with negative connotations. But a policy of making peaceful adjustment—as distinct from a policy of crushing resistance—betokens government awareness, flexibility, and willingness to attempt to act upon what the rebels are claiming. What happens should incumbents' needs and insurgents' desires prove totally incompatible? There, the lines are drawn for an all-or-nothing confrontation. To have reached such a level of division indicates that sharp polarization has occurred. A bifurcation of society into antagonistic groups lends itself to bloody coercive steps, to an internal war that might lead to profound change. Total confrontation precedes revolution. Repression can further internal war, pacification might avoid it.

A third condition for revolution comes in uniting rural and urban forms of collective political violence. Rebellion flourishes in the countryside, turmoil in the cities. Either poses problems for a government; neither necessarily poses a final choice. Unless village rebels fight their way into the capital, they may have little direct impact on national policy. The shift from rebellion to revolution requires a concerted, coordinated attempt to seize power centrally, and, accordingly, requires a linking of dissent by groups unaccustomed to working with each other. Trotsky, with his "law of combined development" and his assertions about the dual roots of the Russian revolution, headed along the correct path.[31]

The four rebellions were, in essence, wars of numerous inhabitants of the countryside against the numerically limited rulers of the countryside. City dwellers supported the unrest that developed from rural causes only in indirect ways. Urban areas were avoided, by-passed, or neglected in the rebels' combat. The Taiping armies, for example, by-passed Kweilin and Changsha; only late in 1852, more than a year after breaking through encirclements by imperial troops, was any major town taken. The Telengana, Mau Mau and Mulelist partisans never fought in Hyderabad City, Nairobi, or even Idiofa. Provisions and information forwarded by the "passive wing" made, I believe, only trivial impact, compared to what the rebels could have gained (and also risked) by urban insurrection. They might have seized full power centrally; they certainly would have encountered far more severe opposition. The capital had to be guarded lest the *ancien régime* collapse totally. For successful rebel assault, far greater military resources and planning coordination would have been required. Only the Taipings came close to success, a mistaken division of their forces prior to the northern Expedition probably costing them a chance of victory. Even so, with the exception of Mau Mau, the insurgents left urban areas unorganized, evidence equally of their insufficient understanding of the dynamics of power.

The rebellions were confined to rural areas for four reasons. First, the grievances that spurred collective political violence concerned villagers far more than the urban lumpen-proletariat. What was denied locally could be restored locally. Rectification could be sought in the rural areas, at least to satisfy most claims for better treatment. As a result, secondly, few links were forged between the wretched of the earth and the miserable of the pavements. Organizations bridging the urban and rural interests did not emerge. Thirdly, guerrilla weakness took its toll. The rebels encountered increasingly strong resistance as they moved from the political periphery toward the political heart. Their limited military resources (with the exception of the Taipings) could not be turned simultaneously to defense of territory already staked out in rural areas, and to attack on urban areas. And, in addition to this weakness in armaments, the rebels were bounded, fourthly, by the cultural specificity of their participants. Only the Taiping revolutionary movement (to use Jen's title) moved to a significant degree beyond an ethnic identification of the disaffected. The three other uprisings were confined by particularism.

As a final condition for revolution, those seeking change should offer a set of values incompatible in significant respects with the prevailing, or at least the officially-espoused, set of values. Taiping beliefs appear historically to have met this criterion — and the sharp attack of those influenced by Confucianism clinches the point. Hung Hsiu-ch'üan and his followers sought goals that could not be co-opted or conceded in minor respects. Having mounted a frontal assault on Confucian values as exercised by the governing elite, they followed its implications to its sanguinary conclusion.

The claims of Telengana and Mau Mau fighters might appear, at first blush, to be equally antagonistic toward the old order. In fact, however, the claims might have been resolved by compassion and responsibility without resort to collective political violence. They were not met voluntarily, as we know. The landless—Kikuyu squatters; *bhagela* tenants—needed security that only the landed could provide, and would provide only under pressure. Growing demands for unrecompensed labor, unmitigated by any (or little) sense of obligation toward the poor, created the mass basis for rural protest. A degree of satisfaction of their needs drew the fangs of collective political violence. Compared with (for example) the post-1949 redistribution of land in China, the reforms in Telengana and Kikuyuland were limited—yet they proved sufficient to allay the needs many had expressed. The old adage about a stitch in time seems appropriate.

We may thus conclude that collective political violence bounded by ethnic or regional exclusivity, confined to rural areas, asserting values potentially attainable within the existing system, and confronting a government willing to leaven military repression with political pacification, will remain rebellion. Change these parameters, and the way opens to revolution. The two phenomena are closely linked, in drawing from similar sources of discontent. They differ, however, in the scope of the group involved, the claims advanced, and the policies of the governments involved. Broadly speaking, the economic and social conditions are similar, while the ideological and political conditions differ, between rebellion and revolution.

Rebellion, admittedly, remains a term fraught with ambiguities. It shades at one extreme into petty, confined, small-scale revolts, at the other extreme into large-scale, widely heralded revolutions. Rebellions uneasily graft elements of traditional insurrection onto planned revolt. They vary enormously in scope, magnitude, and intensity. They reflect conditions of change, the attractions of the past vying with the promises of the future. Forward- as well as backward-looking, rebellions at times constitute last gasps of an old order, at other times first breaths of a new. As complex social phenomena, to which a myriad of economic, political, and social causes contribute, rebellions deserve more study than they are usually given. This book hopefully fills some of this need.

Having looked at the past of rebellion, we should briefly ponder its future. Will rural insurgencies of the type examined in previous pages become the most common form of changing governments through collective political violence in developing countries? The answer, I believe, must be a qualified No. Military coups d'etat doubtless will remain the quickest, simplest means of replacing government personnel in states lacking more peaceful or constitutional means. Weaknesses in civilian control of the military, and obstacles to military regimes' working themselves out of power, provide continuing opportunities and incentives to coup-makers.

The ferment manifested in rural rebellions may also be overshadowed by urban terrorism. Planned and executed by small, essentially self-contained groups, acts of violence can create an atmosphere of endemic vulnerability to which major cities seem peculiarly susceptible. The anonymity that urban life offers; the vulnerability of technologically complex systems to sabotage at a few vital nodes; perhaps the belief that a blow against "the system" comes from shooting businessmen in the knees or threatening to down aircraft landing at a popularly resented terminal: these are the ingredients that could lead to a Hobbesian state of anarchy, or to its antithesis, the leviathan of a 1984-style society, englobing its citizens in a net of tight surveillance to snare a small number of plotters. Either prospect is unpalatable, to say the least. Some societies have attempted to live with urban terrorism, Northern Ireland being a case in point. Other states may face significant likelihood of such violence, Israel and South Africa being possible centers in the near future.

The ubiquity of military intervention, and the dramatic impact of urban terrorism, must not overshadow the political significance of rural rebellion. The majority of humanity live in rural settings. They may be touched only episodically by government pressures and policies. The traditions of the past remain; yet they no longer accurately limn the conditions of life. Increasing challenges come through agricultural commercialization, direct taxation, greater educational opportunities, and the like. "Traditional" societies in rural Africa, Asia and Latin America are being transformed—and the results can be profound. Whenever major changes are introduced, political consequences should be expected. The potential for collective political violence is inherent in the dynamics of "modernization," as these are imposed upon, and partially adopted by, societies that have operated according to different values and rhythms of life. Thus, in addition to the elite political violence manifested in coups d'etat and in urban terrorism, one should expect mass political violence in the form of rebellion in the "Third World."

Finally, ours is not a peaceful age. Ideologies of violence come from many quarters, and rationalize all sorts of acts taken in the name of justice. As we have seen, such steps interact with violence taken in the name of order—while fear is the fate of most. Coercive pressure may indeed be the sole stimulus to which some political systems respond. Should they persist in a knee-jerk reflex, failing to temper their military actions with political reforms, they may only postpone rather than preclude an even bloodier confrontation.

The ultimate lesson of this book—its moral, if you will—is that collective political violence is facilitated by changes increasingly characteristic of developing countries today. The scope, magnitude and nature of such violence remain significantly, and directly, affected by government actions. Blind economic determinism cannot explain why men rebel, nor can a mechanically applied calculus of aspirations and frustrations. Political acts such as rebellion require political explanations. It is in the weakness of governments that rebellion arises; it is in the absence of reform that minor discontents become magnified into widespread challenge. Violence should remind those who rule of their ultimate responsibility to the hopes, fears, and basic concerns of those they govern.

Notes

Preface

1. Claude E. Welch, Jr., ed., *Soldier and State in Africa: A Comparative Analysis of Military Intervention and Political Change* (Evanston: Northwestern University Press, 1970); *Military Role and Rule: Perspectives on Civil-Military Relations* (North Scituate: Duxbury, 1974), with Arthur K. Smith; *Civilian Control of the Military: Theory and Cases from Developing Countries* (Albany: State University of New York Press, 1976).
2. Edward C. Banfield, *The Moral Basis of a Backward Society* (Glencoe: Free Press, 1958).
3. Claude E. Welch, Jr. and Mavis Bunker Taintor, eds., *Revolution and Political Change* (North Scituate: Duxbury Press, 1972).
4. Claude E. Welch, Jr., "Obstacles to Peasant Warfare in Africa," *African Studies Review* 20, 3 (December 1977), pp. 121-30. Also see I. William Zartman, "Revolution and Development: Form and Substance," *Civilisations* 20 (1970), 181-97.

1/The Four Rebellions and Their Physical Settings

1. Jean Chesneaux, *Peasant Revolts in China, 1840-1949* (London: Thames & Hudson, 1973), p. 7.
2. Ibid., pp. 9-10.
3. Franz Michael, *The Taiping Rebellion, History and Documents* (Seattle: University of Washington Press, 1966), Vol. 1, p. 19.
4. Ibid., p. 20.
5. Frederick Wakeman, Jr., *Strangers at the Gate: Social Disorder in South China, 1839-1861* (Berkeley: University of California Press, 1966), p. 32.
6. Jen Yu-wen, *The Taiping Revolutionary Movement* (New Haven: Yale University Press, 1973), p. 53.
7. Wakeman, *Strangers at the Gate*, p. 126.
8. Jen, *Taiping Revolutionary Movement*, p. 53. Jen uses the noun "gangs."
9. Kung-chuan Hsiao, *Rural China: Imperial Control in the Nineteenth Century* (Seattle: University of Washington Press, 1960), pp. 498-9.
10. Wakeman, *Strangers at the Gate*, pp. 67-8.
11. See below, Chapter 7. The most thorough examination is provided by Vincent Y. C. Shih, *The Taiping Ideology: Its Sources, Interpretations, and Influences* (Seattle: University of Washington Press, 1967). Also see Eugene P. Boardman, *Christian Influences upon the Ideology of the Taiping Rebellion* (Madison: University of Wisconsin Press, 1952).

12. Jen *Taiping Revolutionary Movement*, p. 161.

13. Ibid., p. 170.

14. Barrington Moore, Jr., *Social Origins of Dictatorship and Democracy: Lord and Peasant in the Making of the Modern World* (Boston: Beacon Press, 1966), pp. 203, 459.

15. Kathleen Gough, "Indian Peasant Uprisings," *Economic and Political Weekly* 9, 32-4 (August 1974), p. 1391.

16. Ibid., p. 1402. Also see Conrad Wood, "Peasant Revolt: An Interpretation of Moplah Violence in the Nineteenth and Twentieth Centuries," in Clive Dewey and A. G. Hopkins, eds., *The Imperial Impact: Studies in the Economic History of Africa and India* (London: Athlone Press, 1978), pp. 132-51.

17. Calculated from figures presented in Gough, "Indian Peasant Uprisings," pp. 1396-1402. She distinguishes among five types of violence: restorative rebellions to drive out the British and restore earlier rulers and social relations; religious movements for the liberation of a region or an ethnic group under a new form of government; social banditry; terrorist vengeance, with ideas of meting out collective justice; and mass insurrections for redress of particular grievances.

18. Donald Zagoria, "The Ecology of Peasant Comunism in India," *American Political Science Review* 65, 1 (March 1971), 144-60.

19. Ian Bedford, *The Telengana Insurrection: A Study in the Causes and Development of a Communist Insurrection in Rural India, 1946-51* (Ph.D. thesis, Australian National University, 1967), p. 106.

20. Ibid., p. 45.

21. Ibid., p. 26.

22. Ibid., p. 162.

23. See, in particular, S. Keseva Iyengar, *Economic Investigations in the Hyderabad State 1929-30* (Hyderabad: Government Central Press, 1931).

24. M.P.K. Sorrenson, *Origins of European Settlement in Kenya* (Nairobi: Oxford University Press, 1968), p. 180.

25. Ibid., p. 184.

26. Ibid., p. 224. Also see Robert L. Tignor, *The Colonial Transformation of Kenya: The Kamba, Kikuyu, and Maasai from 1900 to 1939* (Princeton: Princeton University Press,) 1976, pp. 25-32, and Raymond Leslie Buell, *The Native Problem in Africa* (New York: Macmillan, 1928), Vol. 1, pp. 298-310.

27. Henri Nicolai, *Le Kwilu: Etude géographique d'une région congolaise* (Brussels: Centre scientifique et medical de l'Université Libre de Bruxelles en Afrique Centrale, 1963), p. 5.

28. Robert Buijtenhuijs, *Le mouvement "mau-mau": Une révolte paysanne et anti-coloniale en Afrique noire* (Paris: Mouton, 1971), p. 96.

29. Nicolai, *Le Kwilu*, p. 93.

30. Ibid., p. 310. It should be noted that the area of the concession was reduced in 1938 to 350,000 hectares.

31. Ibid., p. 332.

32. Loc. cit.

33. Crawford Young, *Politics in the Congo: Decolonization and Independence* (Princeton: Princeton University Press, 1965), p. 222.

34. Mao Tse-tung, *Selected Works* (Peking: Foreign Languages Press, 1969), Vol. IV, pp. 155-6.

35. Edward Mitchell, "Inequality and Insurgency: A Statistical Study of South Vietnam," *World Politics* 20, 3 (April 1968), 421-38. For a stinging rebuttal, see Robert L. Sansom, *The Economics of Insurgency in the Mekong Delta of Vietnam* (Cambridge: M.I.T. Press, 1970), pp. 230-3.

36. Michael Barkun, *Disaster and the Millennium* (New Haven: Yale University Press, 1974).

37. Norman Cohn, *The Pursuit of the Millennium: Revolutionary Millenarians and Mystical Anarchists of the Middle Ages* (New York: Oxford University Press, 1970, revised and enlarged edition), p. 13.

38. Barkun, *Disaster and the Millennium*, p. 77.

39. Jack Shepherd, *The Politics of Starvation* (New York: Carnegie Endowment for International Peace, 1975).

40. Charles L. Taylor and Michael C. Hudson, *The World Handbook of Political Indicators* (New Haven: Yale University Press, 1972, second edition), p. 268.

41. Donald C. Hindley, "Thailand: The Politics of Passivity," *Pacific Affairs* 41, 3 (Fall 1968), pp. 362, 369.

42. Moore, *Social Origins of Dictatorship and Democracy*, p. 8.

43. Eric R. Wolf, *Peasant Wars of the Twentieth Century* (New York: Harper & Row, 1969), pp. 278-9.

44. James C. Scott, *The Moral Economy of the Peasant: Rebellion and Subsistence in Southeast Asia* (New Haven: Yale University Press, 1976).

2/The Bases for Collective Political Violence

1. Max Gluckman, *Order and Rebellion in Tropical Africa* (London: Cohen & West, 1963), pp. 110-36.

2. Aristotle, *Politics* (translated by John Warrington) (New York: Dutton, 1959), p. 134.

3. Lester W. Milbrath, *Political Participation* (Chicago: Rand McNally, 1965).

4. Robert Dahl, *Modern Political Analysis* (Englewood Cliffs: Prentice-Hall, 1970, second edition), pp. 15-17.

5. For the Taiping rebellion: James P. Harrison, *The Communists and Chinese Peasant Rebellions: A Study in the Rewriting of Chinese History* (New York: Atheneum, 1969); Ssu-yu Teng, *Historiography of the Taiping Rebellion* (Cambridge: Harvard University Press, 1962), pp. 59-81 passim.

For the Telengana rebellion: Hamza Alavi, "Peasants and Revolution," in Kathleen Gough and Hari P. Sharma, eds., *Imperialism and Revolution in South Asia* (New York: Monthly Review Press), pp. 291-337; Mohan Ram, "The Telengana Peasant Armed Struggle, 1946-51," *Economic and Political Weekly* 8, 23, (9 June 1973), 1025-32; P. Sundarayya, *Telengana People's Struggle and its Lessons* (Calcutta: Desraj Chadha for CPI(M), 1972); and the sources cited in Barry Pavier, "The Telengana Armed Struggle," *Economic and Political Weekly* 9, 32-4 (August 1974), 1420 n. 2.

For the Mau Mau rebellion: three autobiographical booklets prepared by Don Barnett, *The Hard Core: The Story of Karigo Muchai*; *Man in the Middle: Ngugi Kabiro*; and *The Urban Guerrilla: Mohamed Mathu* (Richmond, B.C.: Liberation Support Movement Information Center, 1973 and 1974). A useful guide to literature to early 1975 appears in Marshall S. Clough and Kennell A. Jackson, "A Bibliography on Mau Mau" (Stanford: 1975).

For the Kwilu rebellion: Paul Demunter, *Masses rurales et luttes politiques au Zaire* (Paris: Editions Anthropos, 1975). (This study, though focused on the Bakongo, has a wider interest.)

6. Karl Marx, *The Eighteenth Brumaire of Louis Bonaparte* (New York: International Publishers, 1957), p. 109.

7. Quoted in Michael Duggett, "Marx on Peasants," *Journal of Peasant Studies* 2, 2 (January 1975), p. 171.

8. Ibid., p. 176.

9. Teodor Shanin, ed., *Peasants and Peasant Societies* (Harmondsworth: Penguin, 1971), pp. 253-54.

10. Quoted in Renée C. Fox, Willy de Craemer and Jean-Marie Ribeaucourt, "The 'Second Independence': A Case Study of the Kwilu Rebellion in the Congo," *Comparative Studies in Society and History* 8, 1 (October 1965), p. 96.

11. James S. Coleman, "Nationalism in Tropical Africa," *American Political Science Review* 48, 2 (June 1954), 404-26; Thomas L. Hodgkin, *Nationalism in Colonial Africa* (New York: New York University Press, 1957).

12. Historians customarily date Chinese unification from 221 B.C., when the King of Ch'in assumed the title of "First Emperor."

13. Ping-ti Ho, *The Ladder of Success in Imperial China* (New York: Wiley, 1964), p. 4.

14. Barrington Moore, Jr., *Social Origins of Dictatorship and Democracy: Lord and Peasant in the Making of the Modern World* (Boston: Beacon Press, 1966), p. 174.

15. Kung-chuan Hsiao, *Rural China: Imperial Control in the Nineteenth Century* (Seattle: University of Washington Press, 1960), p. 380.

16. Ho, *Ladder of Success*, p. 51.

17. Ibid., p. 18.

18. Ibid., p. 17; also quoted in Joseph R. Levenson, *Confucian China and its Modern Fate: A Trilogy* (Berkeley: University of California Press, 1968), II, 82.

19. Ho, *Ladder of Success*, p. 34.

20. Hsiao, *Rural China*, p. 415-6.

21. Franz Michael, "State and Society in Nineteenth Century China," in Albert Feuerwerker, ed., *Modern China* (Englewood Cliffs: Prentice-Hall; 1960), p. 60.

22. Eric R. Wolf, *Peasant Wars of the Twentieth Century* (New York: Harper & Row, 1970), p. 105.

23. Ho, *Ladder of Success*, pp. 15-6.

24. Hsiao, *Rural China*, p. 416.

25. "Sacred Edict of K'ang-hsi" (1670), quoted in Ibid., pp. 187-8.

26. Ibid., p. 199.

27. Quoted in Ibid., p. 186.

28. Ibid., p. 249.

29. Ibid., p. 142.

30. Ibid., p. 257.

31. Jen Yu-wen, *The Taiping Revolutionary Movement* (New Haven: Yale University Press, 1973), p. 11.

32. Ibid., pp. 37-8.

33. J.H. Hutton, *Caste in India: Its Nature, Function and Origins* (Bombay: Oxford University Press, 1963, fourth edition), pp. 121-2.

34. Ian Bedford, *The Telengana Insurrection: A Study in the Causes and Development of a Communist Insurrection in Rural India, 1946-51* [Ph.D. thesis, Australian National University, 1967], p. 62.

35. Quoted in Carolyn M. Elliott, "Decline of a Patrimonial Regime: The

Telengana Rebellion in India, 1946-51," *Journal of Asian Studies* 34, 1 (November 1974), p. 29.

36. Bedford, *Telengana Insurrection*, p. 106.

37. J. H. Tawney, *Land and Labour in China* (London: George Allen & Unwin, 1932), p. 77.

38. Bedford, *Telengana Insurrection*, pp. 122-3.

39. S. Kesava Iyengar, *Economic Investigations in the Hyderabad State 1929-30*, Vol. 1 (Hyderabad: Government Central Press, 1931), pp. 20-2, 112-35. Iyengar called the district "almost a bottled up specimen of life lived centuries ago" (p. 112) but said sufficient land existed for a good standard of life "provided land is not monopolized." (p. 114). About three-quarters of the Warangal farmers lacked sufficient land (p. 15).

40. To be specific, of 489 tenancies surveyed, 117 were paid in kind, 343 in cash, and 29 in both. Ibid., p. 123.

41. *Census of India, 1931*. Vol. XXIII, H.E.H. the Nizam's Dominions (Hyderabad: Government Central Press, 1933, Part I), p. 209.

42. V.P. Menon, *The Story of the Integration of the Indian States* (London: Longmans, 1955), p. 382; Hugh Gray, "Andhra Pradesh," in Myron Weiner, ed., *State Politics in India* (Princeton: Princeton University Press, 1968), p. 402.

43. Hutton, *Caste in India*, p. 11. The 1931 Census, last to give figures by caste, gave a population of 164,372 Reddis in Hyderabad plus 778,548 Kapu. *Census of India 1931*, Vol. XXIII, Part II, p. 244.

44. See, for example, John Markakis, *Ethiopia: Anatomy of a Traditional Polity* (Oxford: Clarendon Press, 1974).

45. A.G. Hopkins, *Economic History of West Africa* (London: Longman, 1973), pp. 32-9.

46. L.A. Fallers, "Are African Cultivators to be called 'Peasants'?", reprinted in Jack M. Potter, May N. Diaz, and George M. Foster, *Peasant Society: A Reader* (Boston: Little, Brown, 1967), p. 40. For a contrasting view, see Lionel Cliffe, "Rural Class Formation in East Africa," *Journal of Peasant Studies* 4, 2 (1976-7), 195-224.

47. For general discussions of the nature of such systems, see M. Fortes and E.E. Evans-Pritchard, *African Political Systems* (London: Oxford University Press, 1970), pp. 5-23, and John Middleton and David Tate, eds., *Tribes Without Rulers: Studies in African Segmentary Systems* (London: Routledge and Kegan Paul, 1958), pp. 1-31.

48. Godfrey Muriuki, *A History of the Kikuyu 1500-1900* (Nairobi: Oxford University Press, 1974), p. 56.

49. Ibid., p. 63.

50. Ibid., p. 75.

51. Jomo Kenyatta, *Facing Mount Kenya: The Tribal Life of the Gikuyu* (London: Secker and Warburg, 1961), pp. 26, 30.

52. For a novelist's approach, see James Ngugi, *The River Between* (London: Heinemann, 1965).

53. Muriuki, *History of the Kikuyu*, pp. 74-5.

54. Ibid., p. 75.

55. Ibid., p. 119.

56. Ibid., p. 131.

57. Ibid., p. 113.

58. Kenyatta, *Facing Mount Kenya*, p. 115.

59. T. O. Ranger, *Revolt in Southern Rhodesia; 1896-7: A Study in African Resistance* (London: Heinemann, 1967): Robert I. Rotberg and Ali A. Mazrui, eds., *Protest and Power in Black Africa* (New York: Oxford University Press, 1970), esp. pp. 377-568.

60. One example should suffice. Bildad Kaggia declared himself "very interested" in religious studies while in school (p. 12), joined the King's African Rifles so he could visit Jerusalem (p. 22), but had his belief shaken when he became aware that Biblical scholarship indicated not all the Bible was God's inspired words (p. 39). While in England during World War II, he spoke in Assemblies of God—but came to feel missionaries were part of the European effort to maintain African subordination. "In my enthusiasm I felt charged by God to liberate Kenya, just as Moses was commanded to liberate the Israelites from Egyptian bondage." (p. 55). Bildad Kaggia, *Roots of Freedom 1921-1963* (Nairobi: East African Publishing House, 1975).

61. Herbert F. Weiss, *Political Protest in the Congo: The Parti Solidaire Africain During the Independence Struggle* (Princeton: Princeton University Press, 1967), pp. 293-5.

62. Henri Nicolai, *Le Kwilu: Etude géographique d'une région congolaise* (Brussels: Centre scientifique et medical de l'Université Libre de Bruxelles en Afrique Centrale, 1963), p. 350.

63. Ibid, pp. 323, 426.

64. Ibid., pp. 323-4.

65. *Report of the Commission of Inquiry into Disturbances in the Gold Coast, 1948* (London: H.M.S.O., Col. No. 231); Dennis Austin, *Politics in Ghana 1948-1960* (London: Oxford University Press, 1964), pp. 11-28.

66. Nicolai, *Le Kwilu*, p. 338.

67. Ibid., p. 365.

68. Rene Lemarchand, *Political Awakening in the Belgian Congo* (Berkeley: University of California Press, 1964), p. 80.

69. Such a map appears in Weiss, *Political Protest*, p. 163.

70. Lemarchand, *Political Awakening*, pp. 29, 62-5.

71. Nicolai, *Le Kwilu*, p. 212.

72. Ibid., p. 325.

73. Fox et al., "The Second Independence," p. 85; Vittorio Lanternari, *The Religions of the Oppressed: A Study of Modern Messianic Cults* (New York: Mentor, 1965), p. 10.

74. Fox et al., "The Second Independence," p. 86; Ephraim Andersson, *Messianic Movements in the Lower Congo* (Uppsala: Almquist & Wiksells, 1958), pp. 48-116.

75. Lemarchand, *Political Awakening*, p. 42.

76. Ibid., p. 37.

77. Aristide R. Zolberg, "The Structure of Political Conflict in the New States of Tropical Africa," *American Political Science Review* 62, 1 (March, 1968), pp. 73-4.

3/Alien Rule and the Potential for Discontent

1. Howard Wriggins, *The Ruler's Imperative: Strategies for Political Survival in Asia and Africa* (New York: Columbia University Press, 1969).

2. Michael Wolf, "Jean Bodin on Taxes," *Political Science Quarterly* 83,2 (June 1968), 268-84.

3. Mark N. Hagopian, *The Phenomenon of Revolution* (New York: Dodd Mead, 1974), p. 17; Shula Marks, *Reluctant Rebellion: The 1906-1908 Disturbances in Natal* (Oxford: Clarendon Press, 1970), pp. 140-3; T. O. Ranger, *Revolt in Southern Rhodesia 1896-7: A Study in African Resistance* (London: Heinemann, 1967) pp. 77-8.

4. Robert A. Dahl and Charles E. Lindblom, *Politics, Economics, and Welfare* (New York: Harper, 1953), p. 106.

5. Crawford Young, *Politics in the Congo: Decolonization and Independence* (Princeton: Princeton University Press, 1965), p. 88.

6. Rene Lemarchand, *Political Awakening in the Belgian Congo* (Berkeley: University of California Press, 1964), p. 75.

7. Lawrence D. Kessler, *K'ang-hsi and the Consolidation of Ch'ing Rule 1661-1684* (Chicago: University of Chicago Press, 1976), esp. pp. 154-68.

8. Kung-chuan Hsiao, *Rural China: Imperial Control in the Nineteenth Century* (Seattle: University of Washington Press, 1960), pp. 506-7.

9. Ibid., p. 185.

10. Ibid., pp. 187-8.

11. Ibid., p. 240.

12. Ibid., pp. 253-4.

13. Ibid., p. 86.

14. Ibid., pp. 105-6.

15. Ibid., p. 152.

16. Ibid., p. 504.

17. Ibid., p. 248.

18. Ibid., pp. 256-7.

19. Ibid., p. 43.

20. Kessler, *K'ang-hsi*, p. 5.

21. Hsiao, *Rural China,* p. 45.

22. Ibid., p. 55.

23. Ibid., p. 294: Philip A. Kuhn, *Rebellion and Its Enemies in Late Imperial China: Militarization and Social Structure, 1796-1864* (Cambridge: Harvard University Press, 1970).

24. According to an 1853 treaty, the Hyderabad contingent "shall be commanded by British officers, fully equipped and disciplined, and controlled by the British Government through its representative the Resident at Hyderabad"; the force "shall be employed when required to execute services of importance, such as protecting the person of His Highness, his heirs and successors, and reducing to obedience all rebels and exciters of disturbance in His Highness's dominions...." William Lee-Warner, *The Native States of India* (London: Macmillan, 1910), pp. 231, 225-26.

25. William Barton, *The Princes of India* (London: Nisbet, 1934), p. 190.

26. H.H. Dodwell, "The Relations of the Government of India with the Indian States, 1858-1918," in H.H. Dodwell, ed., *The Cambridge History of India*, Vol. 6, *The Indian Empire 1858-1918* (Cambridge: Cambridge University Press, 1932), p. 490. The difficulties of applying formal analysis were aptly expressed by Lee-Warner: extraordinary jurisdiction by the British over internal matters in the states "does not pretend to be based on right of delegation; it rests upon an act of state and defies jural analysis. In such cases the Government of India interferes with authority by virtue of its paramount powers, and it does not cloak its intervention, or weaken its authority by straining legal ties, or misapplying legal phrases which

were devised for a totally different set of conditions." *Native States of India*, p. 343.

27. Dodwell, "Relations of the Government of India," p. 493.

28. *Report of the Indian States Committee 1928-1929* (London: HMSO, 1929; Cmd. 3302), pp. 56-8.

29. It should be noted that the Iyengar study omitted the *jagir* and *Sarf-e-Khas* lands. Since the jagirdars could, in effect, write their own tickets, the extractions documented by Iyengar for *diwani* lands were likely higher in the *jagir* grants. S. Kesava Iyengar, *Economic Investigations in the Hyderabad State 1929-30*, Vol. 1 (Hyderabad: Government Central Press, 1931).

30. Barry Pavier, "The Telengana Armed Struggle", *Economic and Political Weekly* 9, 32-4 (August 1974), p. 1413; P. Sundarayya, *Telengana People's Struggle and its Lessons* (Calcutta: CPI(M), 1971), p. 10.

31. *Census of India, 1931*, Vol. XXIII, H.E.H. The Nizam's Dominions (Hyderabad: Government Central Press, 1933), Part I, pp. 2, 57.

32. Ibid., p. 232.

33. Ibid., pp. 162-3.

34. Ibid., p. 48.

35. Ibid., p. 207.

36. Ibid., p. 196.

37. Ibid., p. 222.

38. Ibid., p. 45.

39. *Census of India, 1941*, Vol. XXI, H.E.H. The Nizam's Dominions (Hyderabad State) (Hyderabad: Government Press, 1945), p. 61.

40. Kathleen Gough, "Indian Peasant Uprisings," *Economic and Political Weekly* 9, 32-4 (August 1974), p. 1397.

41. Iyengar, *Economic Investigations ... 1929-30*, p. 133.

42. *Census of India, 1931*, p. 160.

43. "Primarily Kenya is an African territory, and His Majesty's Government think it necessary to record their considered opinion that the interests of the African natives must be paramount, and that if, and when, those interests and the interests of the immigrant races should conflict, the former should prevail." "Indians in Kenya" (London: HMSO, 1923, Cmd. 1922), p. 9.

44. Robert Buijtenhuijs, *Le Mouvement "Mau-Mau": Une revolte paysanne et anti-coloniale en Afrique noire* (Paris: Mouton, 1971), p. 95.

45. M.P.K. Sorrenson, *Origins of European Settlement in Kenya* (Nairobi: Oxford University Press, 1968), p. 27.

46. E. A. Brett, *Colonialism and Underdevelopment in East Africa: The Politics of Economic Change, 1919-39* (London: Heinemann, 1973), pp. 40-1.

47. F.D. Corfield, *Historical Survey of the Origins and Growth of Mau Mau* (London: HMSO, 1960, Cmd. 1030), p. 316. Some idea of the treatment meted out can be gleaned from the contrast between the 11,503 "terrorists" killed versus the 1,035 wounded and captured. The 63 European police and soldiers, and the 32 European civilians who died in the battles, constituted a negligible share of the deaths (just over eight-tenths of one percent).

48. Sir Philip Mitchell, *African Afterthoughts* (London: Hutchinson, 1954), p. 221.

39. Ursula K. Hicks, *Development from Below: Local Government and Finance in Developing Countries of the Commonwealth* (Oxford: Clarendon Press, 1961).

50. Despatch by the Secretary of State for the Colonies to the Governors of the

344 / Anatomy of Rebellion

African Territories, 25 February 1947, reprinted in A.H.M. Kirk-Greene, ed., *The Principles of Native Administration in Nigeria: Selected Documents 1900-1947* (London: Oxford University Press, 1965), pp. 239-40.

51. J.C. Carothers, "The Psychology of Mau Mau" (Nairobi: Government Printer, 1954). Similar conclusions are reached by L.S.B. Leakey, *Defeating Mau Mau* (London: Methuen, 1954).

52. Lord Lugard's memorandum on native administration, reprinted in Kirk-Greene, *Principles of Native Administration*, p. 71.

53. Sorrenson, *Origins of European Settlement*, p. 37.

54. Carl G. Rosberg, Jr. and John Nottingham, *The Myth of "Mau Mau": Nationalism in Kenya* (New York: Praeger, 1966), p. 25.

55. M.P.K. Sorrenson, *Land Reform in the Kikuyu Country: A Study in Government Policy* (Nairobi: Oxford University Press, 1967), pp. 34-5.

56. Electors Union of Kenya, "An Outline of Policy for the Colony and Protectorate of Kenya" (Nairobi: W. Boyd, 1946), pp. 18, 22.

57. Sorrenson, *Land Reform*, p. 44.

58. Electors Union, "Outline of Policy," p. 20.

59. Brett, *Colonialism and Underdevelopment*, pp. 165-216.

60. Ibid., p. 169.

61. Corfield, *Historical Survey*, pp. 236-240.

62. Ibid., p. 229.

63. Ibid., p. 240.

64. Anthony Clayton, *Counter-Insurgency in Kenya: A Study of Military Operations against Mau Mau* (Nairobi: Transafrica, 1976), p. 22.

65. Historically, Kamba had dominated African positions in the Kenyan KAR battalion. President Kenyatta announced shortly after independence that the ethnic composition of the armed forces should be roughly equivalent to the ethnic composition of the entire Kenya population. By 1966, this goal had been substantially achieved. J.M. Lee, *African Armies and Civil Order* (London: Chatto & Windus, 1969), pp. 71, 110.

66. Young, *Politics in the Congo*, pp. 33-58.

67. Quoted in ibid., p. 39.

68. Ibid., p. 12.

69. Ibid., p. 11.

70. Lemarchand, *Political Awakening*, pp. 31-2.

71. Ibid., p. 75.

72. Ibid., p. 35.

73. Young, *Politics in the Congo*, p. 60.

74. Ibid., p. 95.

75. Lemarchand, *Political Awakening*, p. 70.

76. Young, *Politics in the Congo*, p. 13.

77. Lemarchand, *Political Awakening*, p. 75.

Part II/The Politicization of Discontent

1. Irwin Scheiner, "The Mindful Peasant: Sketches for a Study of Rebellion," *Journal of Asian Studies* 32, 4 (August 1973), 579-91.

4/The Sense of Relative Deprivation

1. Alexis de Tocqueville, *The Old Regime and the French Revolution* (Garden City: Doubleday, 1955), p. 177.

2. Several valuable examples of quantitative approaches to political violence are reprinted in Ivor Feierabend, Rosalind L. Feierabend, and Ted Robert Gurr, eds., *Anger, Violence, and Politics* (Englewood Cliffs: Prentice Hall, 1972), and in James Chowning Davies, *When Men Revolt and Why: A Reader in Political Violence and Revolution* (New York: Free Press, 1971), pp. 206-313. Also see Douglas A. Hibbs, Jr., *Mass Political Violence: A Cross-National Causal Analysis* (New York: Wiley, 1973).

3. Renée C. Fox, Willy de Craemer and Jean-Marie Ribeaucourt, "The 'Second Independence': A Case Study of the Kwilu Rebellion in the Congo," *Comparative Studies in Society and History* 8, 1 (October 1965), 78-109; Herbert F. Weiss, *Political Protest in the Congo: The Parti Solidaire Africain During the Independence Struggle* (Princeton: Princeton University Press, 1967), esp. pp. 198-215, 251-99.

4. Neil J. Smelser, *Theory of Collective Behavior* (London: Routledge & Kegan Paul, 1962).

5. Hadley Cantril, *The Pattern of Human Concerns* (New Brunswick: Rutgers University Press, 1965), pp. 279-80.

6. More specifically, Cantril asked those in the various national samples which were their greatest hopes and wishes for the future, and their greatest fears and worries for the future. The open minded responses were coded as follows:

Perceptions of Personal Hopes and Fears

	Average of hopes and fears	Average of hopes	Average of fears
Personal economic	60	71	48
Family	35	46	24
Health	45	27	41
Values and Character	34	20	7
Job or work situation	13	19	6

Ibid., p. 162

7. Ibid., p. 303.

8. Ted Robert Gurr, *Why Men Rebel* (Princeton: Princeton University Press, 1970), p. 179.

9. Two examples from Africa illustrate the precipitating role of taxation: Shula Marks, *Reluctant Rebellion: The 1906-1908 Disturbances in Natal* (Oxford: Clarendon Press, 1970), p. 143; T.O. Ranger, *Revolt in Southern Rhodesia 1896-7: A Study in African Resistance* (London: Heinemann, 1967), p. 87.

10. James C. Scott, *Moral Economy of the Peasant: Rebellion and Subsistence in Southeast Asia* (New Haven: Yale University Press, 1976), pp. 187.

11. A full list appears in Gurr, *Why Men Rebel*, pp. 360-7.

12. Ibid., p. 48.

13. James C. Davies, "Toward a Theory of Revolution," *American Sociological Review* 6, 1 (February 1962), 5-19; James C. Davies, "The J-Curve of Rising and Declining Satisfactions as a Cause of Some Great Revolutions and a Contained Rebellion," in Hugh David Graham and Ted Robert Gurr, eds., *Violence in America: Historical and Comparative Perspectives, A Report Submitted to the National Commission on the Causes and Prevention of Violence* (New York: Praeger, 1969), pp. 690-730.

14. Gurr, *Why Men Rebel*, pp. 182-3.

15. Ibid., pp. 125-6.

16. Ssu-Yu Teng, *Historiography of the Taiping Rebellion* (Cambridge: East Asian Research Center, 1962), p. 44; Vincent Yu-chung Shih, "Interpretations of the Taiping Tienkuo by Noncommunist Chinese Writers," *Far Eastern Quarterly* 10 (1951), 248-57; James P. Harrison, *The Communists and Chinese Peasant Rebellions: A Study in the Rewriting of Chinese History* (New York: Atheneum, 1969).

17. Franz Michael, *The Taiping Rebellion: History and Documents*, Vol. 1 (Seattle: University of Washington Press, 1966), p. 15. The figures should be used with some caution. Regular land tax was assessed on cultivated land owned by the people, using registers carried over from the Ming. Actual demarcation and measurement were probably not carried out during the Ch'ing dynasty. Kung-chuan Hsiao, *Rural China: Imperial Control in the Nineteenth Century* (Seattle: University of Washington Press, 1960), p. 85. Nonetheless, the direction of change was clear: the amount of cultivated land per person fell by close to 50 percent from 1766 to 1833.

18. Jen Yu-wen, *The Taiping Revolutionary Movement* (New Haven: Yale University Press, 1973), p. 11.

19. Michael, *Taiping Rebellion*, I, p. 20.

20. Jen, *Taiping Revolutionary Movement*, p. 45.

21. Loc. cit. Professor Jen qualifies this assertion a few pages later, in pointing to the need for defense: effective action by the God Worshippers gradually won "the respect and allegiance of the terrorized people." Ibid., p. 53.

22. Philip A. Kuhn, *Rebellion and its Enemies in Late Imperial China: Militarization and Social Structure, 1796-1864* (Cambridge: Harvard University Press, 1970); Frederic Wakeman, Jr., *Strangers at the Gate: Social Disorder in South China, 1839-1861* (Berkeley: University of California Press, 1966). See below, Chapter 5, note 1 for information on the Ch'ing dynasty's military strength.

23. Jen, *Taiping Revolutionary Movement*, p. 53.

24. Ibid., pp. 54-5; Wakeman, *Strangers at the Gate*, p. 127.

25. Evelyn S. Rawski, *Agricultural Change and the Peasant Economy of South China* (Cambridge: Harvard University Press, 1972).

26. Anwar Iqbal Qureshi, *The Economic Development of Hyderabad*, Volume I

Rural Economy (Bombay: Orient Longmans, 1947), pp. 154, 149. The simile, of course, is Lenin's.

27. Ibid., p. 158.

28. Ibid., pp. 149-50.

29. Ibid., p. 275.

30. Ibid., pp. 166, 167, and 193.

31. Ibid., p. 159.

32. Ibid., pp. 169-70.

33. Ibid., p. 251.

34. Ibid., p. 291.

35. S. Kesava Iyengar, *Economic Investigations in the Hyderabad State, 1929-30*, Vol. 1 (Hyderabad: Government Central Press, 1931), p. 21.

36. Barry Pavier, "The Telengana Armed Struggle," *Economic and Political Weekly* 9, 32-4 (August 1974), 1417.

37. His title alone made the Nizam distinctive — Lieutenant General His Exalted Highness Asaf Jah Muzaffar-ul-Mulk Wal Mamalik, Nizam-ul-Mulk Nizam-ud-Dowla, Nawab Sir Mir Osman Ali Khan Bahadur, Fathe Jung, Faithful Ally of the British Government, G.C.S.I., G.B.E., Nizam of Hyderabad and Berar. He could not readily transform himself into a constitutional monarch, as post-war events were to prove. To the Muslims of the state, the Nizam was the chief symbol of their political preeminence. Although no divinity hedged his brow, the Nizam clearly occupied an exalted position. For details, see the report from the 1937-8 Constitutional Reform Committee, quoted in Chapter 6.

38. *Census of India 1941*, Vol. XXI, H.E.H. the Nizam's Dominions (Hyderabad State) (Hyderabad: Government Press, 1945), pp. 29-30.

39. Ibid., p. 30.

40. Ibid., p. 211.

41. Ibid., pp. 207-8.

42. Ibid., pp. 237, 27.

43. Ibid,, pp. 254-5.

44. Penderel Moon, *Divide and Quit* (London: Chatto & Windus, 1961). An entertaining, well-informed journalists' account appears in Larry Collins and Dominique Lapierre, *Freedom at Midnight* (London: Collins, 1975).

45. According to Sir Philip Mitchell, "...there cannot be said to be any form of title, in our sense, to land of this kind....To people of this kind, land was something akin to water or air; it had no owner, as cattle, hoes, spears and the like could have an owner; if no one else was in the way, a man entered on it as readily as he embarked by canoe on lake or river. It was a part of the country in which his tribe lived and tribes in that kind of country can never have known a state of affairs when there was not vastly more land than anyone could use." *African Afterthoughts* (London: Hutchinson, 1954), p. 159.

46. Donald L. Barnett and Karari Njama, *Mau Mau From Within: Autobiography and Analysis of Kenya's Peasant Revolt* (London: Macgibbon and Kee, 1966), pp. 49-51.

47. "In studying the Gikuyu tribal organisation it is necessary to take into consideration land tenure as the most important factor in the social, political, religious, and economic life of the tribe . . . . According to the Gikuyu customary law of land tenure every family unit had a land right of one form or another. While the whole tribe defended collectively the boundary of their territory, every inch of land within

it had its owner." Jomo Kenyatta, *Facing Mount Kenya: The Tribal Life of the Gikuyu* (London: Secker & Warburg, 1961), p. 21.

48. Ibid., p. 44.

49. Carl G. Rosberg Jr., and John Nottingham, *The Myth of "Mau Mau": Nationalism in Kenya* (New York: Praeger for the Hoover Institution), 1966, pp. 25-6; M.P.K. Sorrenson, *Origins of European Settlement in Kenya* (Nairobi: Oxford University Press, 1968), p. 272.

50. Fenner Brockway, *African Journeys* (London 1955), pp. 87-8; quoted in Rosberg and Nottingham, *Myth of "Mau Mau"*, p. 74.

51. Sorrenson, *Origins of European Settlement*, pp. 282-3.

52. See text of Chief Koinange's letter in ibid., pp. 285-6.

53. As a British District Officer wrote in May 1914, the Kikuyu "as a race are hostile, negatively hostile to the Government. This hostility arises from many causes, the chief of which is the loss of what they consider much of their land." Quoted in ibid., p. 283.

54. M.P.K. Sorrenson, *Land Reform in the Kikuyu Country: A Study in Government Policy* (Nairobi: Oxford University Press, 1967), p. 21.

55. For details, see Jeremy Murray-Brown, *Kenyatta* (London: George Allen & Unwin, 1972), pp. 114-33, 159-60.

56. See table in E.A. Brett, *Colonialism and Underdevelopment in East Africa: The Politics of Economic Change 1919-39* (London: Heinemann, 1973), p. 175.

57. Frank Furedi, "Kikuyu Squatters and the Changing Political Economy of the White Highlands," unpublished paper.

58. Ibid., p. 6; Anthony Clayton and Donald C. Savage, *Government and Labour in Kenya 1895-1963* (London: Cass, 1974), pp. 307-8; Rosberg and Nottingham, *Myth of "Mau Mau"*, p. 252.

59. Clayton and Savage, *Government and Labour*, p. 246. Given the size of squatter families, it is likely that 200,000 dependents accompanied the heads of household. Their increasing awareness of deprivation meant group action was possible: "Squatters as individuals may have continued to accept paternalism, but they had reached a stage at which they thought of themselves as an exploited and deprived class." Loc. cit.

60. Michael Blundell, *So Rough a Wind* (London: Weidenfeld & Nicolson, 1964), p. 81; cf. Clayton and Savage, *Government and Labour*, p. 291.

61. George Bennett and Alison Smith, "Kenya: From 'White Man's Country' to Kenyatta's State 1945-1963," in D.A. Low and Alison Smith, eds., *History of East Africa*, Vol. III (Oxford: Clarendon Press, 1978), p. 112.

62. Ibid., pp. 112-3.

63. Bruce J. Berman, "Bureaucracy and Incumbent Violence: Colonial Administration and the Origins of the 'Mau Mau' Emergency in Kenya," *British Journal of Political Science* 6, 2 (April 1976), 152.

64. Ibid., p. 156.

65. Clayton and Savage, *Government and Labour*, p. 247.

66. Ibid., p. 294.

67. *The Hardcore: The Story of Karigo Muchai* (Richmond, B.C.: LSM Information Center, 1973), p. 40.

68. Electors Union of Kenya, "An Outline of Policy for the Colony and Protectorate of Kenya" (Nairobi: W. Boyd, 1946), p. 20.

69. Ibid., p. 9.

70. Clayton and Savage, *Government and Labour*, pp. 295-6.

71. De Tocqueville, *The Old Regime*, pp. 176-7.
72. Crawford Young, *Politics in the Congo: Decolonization and Independence* (Princeton: Princeton University Press, 1965), p. 152.
73. J.S. La Fontaine, *City Politics: A Study of Leopoldville, 1962-63* (Cambridge: Cambridge University Press, 1970), p. 28.
74. Ibid., p. 31.
75. Ibid., p. 45.
76. Centre de Recherche et d'Information Socio-Politiques, *A.B.A.K.O. 1950-1960* (Brussels: CRISP, 1962), p. 11.
77. This demand, first published in September 1958, is reprinted in ibid., pp. 144-5.
78. Young, *Politics in the Congo*, p. 118.
79. Ibid., p. 290; La Fontaine gives a figure of 42 (*City Politics*, p. 14).
80. Centre de Recherche et d'Information Socio-Politiques, *Congo 1959* (Brussels: CRISP, 1959), p. 10. Author's translations.
81. See the report of Acting Governor-General Schoeller, cited in Young, *Politics in the Congo*, p. 153.
82. Michel Merlier, *Le Congo de la colonisation belge à l'indépendance* (Paris: Maspero, 1962), p. 305.
83. La Fontaine, *City Politics*, p. 64.
64. M. Crawford Young, "Rebellion and the Congo," in Robert I. Rotberg, ed., *Rebellion in Black Africa* (London: Oxford University Press, 1971), p. 218.
85. La Fontaine, *City Politics*, Table 2 (facing page 30).
86. Ibid., p. 50; Young, *Politics in the Congo*, p. 354.
87. Weiss, *Political Protest*, p. 24.
88. Gurr, *Why Men Rebel*, p. 339.
89. Scott, *Moral Economy of the Peasant*, pp. 187-88.
90. Ibid., pp. 188-89.
91. Ibid., p. 203.
92. Ibid., p. 229.
93. Smelser, *Theory of Collective Behavior*.

5/Incumbent Response and the Actualization of Violence

1. The primary burden for local pacification rested on "Green Standard" troops, Chinese in the rank-and-file, mixed Chinese and Manchu in the officer corps. Garrisons were dotted throughout the countryside, usually within fifty miles of each other. They could not suppress large-scale uprisings, having been deliberately limited to a few hundred soldiers. The 1202 garrisons of the early nineteenth century included 640,000 Green Standard troops. The 350,000 "Banner" troops—the official rather than the actual figure—were Manchu in composition. Such banner groups guarded major cities, the Imperial court, the Great Wall, and Manchuria (in which ethnic Chinese were not ordinarily permitted to reside). For brief details on these forces, see Susan Naquin, *Millenarian Rebellion in China: The Eight Trigrams Uprising of 1813* (New Haven: Yale University Press, 1976), p. 238, and John K. Fairbank, Edwin O. Reischauer, and Albert Craig, *East Asia: Tradition and Transformation* (Boston: Houghton Mifflin, 1978), pp. 222-3.

350 / Anatomy of Rebellion

2. Jen Yu-wen, *The Taiping Revolutionary Movement* (New Haven: Yale University Press, 1973), p. 52.

3. Talcott Parsons, "Some Reflections on the Place of Force in Social Process," in Harry Eckstein, ed., *Internal War: Problems and Approaches* (New York: Free Press, 1964), pp. 65-6.

4. Frederic Wakeman, Jr., *Strangers at the Gate: Social Disorder in South China 1839-1861* (Berkeley: University of California Press, 1966), p. 36.

5. Ibid., p. 127. In the words of a Taiping general:

[in 1847, 1848] there were rebel and bandit risings all over Kwangsi, which disturbed the towns. Most communities had militia bands. There was a distinction between the militia and the God-worshippers; the God-worshippers stuck together as one group and the militia as another group. They vied with each other, and thus forced a rising.

C.A. Curwen, *Taiping Rebel: The Depositon of Li Hsiu-ch'eng* (Cambridge: Cambridge University Press, 1977), p. 81.

6. Jen, *Taiping Revolutionary Movement*, p. 52.

7. Ibid., p. 49. Imperial law forbade possession of offensive weapons. Pruning hooks and ploughshares could be beaten into swords, however, and other agricultural instruments turned to violence. Blacksmiths able to carry out such work were obviously essential to the initiation and support of rural insurrections.

8. Ibid., pp. 33-4.

9. Wakeman, *Strangers at the Gate*, pp. 131, 100.

10. Jen, *Taiping Revolutionary Movement*, pp. 78, 109.

11. P. Sundarayya, *Telengana People's Struggle and its Lessons* (Calcutta: Desjar Chadha for CPI(M), 1972), p. 38.

12. Tara Zinkin, *Reporting India* (London: Chatto & Windus, 1962), p. 62.

13. Negotiation of the agreement provided the Indian government clear evidence of the influence Muslim diehards could exert on the Nizam. Despite the insistence of S.V. Patel that the Hyderabad Government sign an instrument of accession rather than a treaty of association, the Nizam remained firm on his desire for autonomy. Less than a week before India's independence, Lord Mountbatten agreed to a two-month period for negotiations, the result of which was a draft standstill agreement essentially leaving unchanged the relations between the princely state and the Indian government. The Hyderabad Executive Council debated the draft for three days (October 23-5, 1947), finally advising the Nizam to sign it. The Nizam formally approved — but delayed signing the document. Early in the morning of 27 October a crowd organized by the Ittehad and estimated at twenty-five to thirty thousand surrounded the houses of the prime minister and various British advisers; Hyderabad police were conspicuously absent. The Nizam consulted with Kasim Razvi, head of the Ittehad, who pointed to India's preoccupation on other fronts. (Indian troops had entered Kashmir the preceding day.) His courage thus steeled, the Nizam refused to sign the standstill agreement. Lord Mountbatten, in turn, refused to accept any changes. More than a month passed. What the Nizam finally signed 29 November 1947, was unchanged in wording. However, the Muslims of Hyderabad City had clearly manifested their ability to bring pressure on the ruler. For details, see V.P. Menon, *The Story of the Integration of the Indian States* (London: Longmans, 1956), pp. 317-35.

14. Sir Mirza, a friend of Gandhi and prominent administrator who had served in several parts of India, was brought in as prime minister in 1946 as a token of the Nizam's desire for reform. His term was short, as he soon collided with the Ittehad.

In the words of his letter of resignation, "I have had the misfortune to find myself opposed at every turn by a certain section of the local Mussalmans, who, in my opinion, are set on a course that is suicidal to the State." Sir Mirza Ismail, *My Public Life: Recollections and Reflections* (London: George Allen & Unwin, 1954), p. 106. Sir Mirza continued to remain in touch with many prominent Indians following his resignation as prime minister, and continued to urge that Hyderabad peacefully accede to India. Take, as examples, the following quotations from letters Sir Mirza sent:

(to Lord Mountbatten, about mid-May 1948)

The Nizam has to be told firmly and in unequivocal terms — and this is best done by one of your personal prestige and official position — that he must turn over a new leaf, cease to be an autocrat and become a constitutional ruler, and get out of the clutches of the Ittehad and its razakars in his own interestes. I have tried to put this to him in plain terms and as tactfully as possible, but that is not sufficient. (Ibid., p. 112)

(to Prime Minister Nehru, 30 August 1948)

If Hyderabad goes on insisting on its own terms, no peaceful settlement is possible....Hyderabad must realize the weakness of its own position. (Ibid., p. 121)

15. Menon, *Integration of the Indian States*, p. 371. Dhanagare gives lower and I believe more acurate figures: 30,000 razakars in January 1948, about 100,000 in August. D.N. Dhanagare, "Social Origins of the Peasant Insurrection in Telengana (1946-51)," *Contributions to Indian Sociology* 8 (1974), 122.

16. Sundarayya, *Telengana People's Struggle*, p. 54. Italics added.

17. Menon, *Integration of the Indian States*, p. 370.

18. F.D. Corfield, *Historical Survey of the Origins and Growth of Mau Mau* (London: HMSO, 1960, Cmd. 1030), p. 7.

19. Ibid., p. 28.

20. Bruce J. Berman, "Bureaucracy and Incumbent Violence: Colonial Administration and the Origins of the 'Mau Mau' Emergency in Kenya," *British Journal of Political Science* 6, 2 (April 1976), p. 170; italics deleted.

21. E. A. Brett, *Colonialism and Underdevelopment in East Africa: The Politics of Economic Change, 1919-39* (London: Heinemann, 1973), p. 175. The number of settler farmers reached a pre-war height of 2035 in 1929.

22. Ibid., p. 176.

23. Carl G. Rosberg, Jr. and John Nottingham, *The Myth of "Mau Mau": Nationalism in Kenya* (New York: Frederick A. Praeger for the Hoover Institution, 1966), pp. 251-2.

24. Anthony Clayton and Donald C. Savage, *Government and Labour in Kenya 1895-1963* (London: Frank Cass, 1974), p. 246.

25. Frank Furedi, "The Social Composition of the Mau Mau Movement in the White Highlands," *Journal of Peasant Studies*, 1, 4 (1974), p. 492.

26. D. H. Rawcliffe, *The Struggle for Kenya* (London: Gollancz, 1954), p. 158.

27. Furedi, "Social Composition of Mau Mau," p. 495.

28. Rosberg and Nottingham, *Myth of "Mau Mau"*, pp. 248-59.

29. Ibid., p. 225.

30. Ibid., p. 258.

31. Sir Philip Mitchell, *African Afterthoughts* (London: Hutchinson, 1954), pp. 25-6.

32. Mitchell claims, disingenuously I believe, not to have been aware of the ban, since his diary made no reference to the event. Ibid., p. 255.

33. Quoted in Corfield, *Historical Survey*, p. 90.

34. One of the most noteworthy instances came in Kenyatta's speech to a heavily-attended meeting at Nyeri 26 July 1952. According to the report of assistant superintendent of police Ian Henderson (born in Kenya and fluent in Kikuyu), "He who calls us the *Mau Mau* is not truthful. We do not know this thing *Mau Mau*. (Jeers and applause.)" Reprinted in ibid., p. 302; for comments on the meeting, see Jeremy Murray-Brown, *Kenyatta* (London: George Allen & Unwin, 1972), pp. 244-5.

35. Ibid., p. 233.

36. Corfield, *Historical Survey*, p. 119.

37. Sir Michael Blundell, *So Rough a Wind* (London: Weidenfeld & Nicolson, 1964), p. 91.

38. Ibid., p. 95.

39. Corfield, *Historical Survey*, p. 144.

40. Ibid., p. 157.

41. Ibid., p. 159.

42. Bildad Kaggia, *Roots of Freedom 1921-1963* (Nairobi: East African Publishing House, 1975), p. 117.

43. Rosberg and Nottingham, *Myth of "Mau Mau,"* p. 277.

44. Crawford Young, *Politics in the Congo: Decolonization and Independence* (Princeton: Princeton University Press, 1965), pp. 444-5.

45. Ibid., p. 316; Centre de Recherche et d'Information Socio-Politiques, *Congo 1960*, Vol. I (Brussels: CRISP, 1961), p. 372; Catherine Hoskyns, *The Congo Since Independence July 1960 - December 1961* (London: Oxford University Press, 1963), p. 88.

46. Young, *Politics in the Congo*, p. 316.

47. Jules Gerard-Libois, *Katanga Secession* (Madison: University of Wisconsin Press, 1966); originally published in French by CRISP in 1963.

48. Jean-Claude Willame, *Patrimonialism and Political Change in the Congo* (Stanford: Stanford University Press, 1972), pp. 64-72.

49. CRISP, *Congo 1960*, Vol. II, pp. 869-953.

50. Pierre L. van den Berghe, "The Military and Political Change in Africa," in Claude E. Welch, Jr., ed., *Soldier and State in Africa* (Evanston: Northwestern University Press, 1970), p. 259.

51. Benoit Verhaegen, *Rebellions au Congo*, Vol. I (Brussels: CRISP, 1966), p. 63.

52. For details, see Young, *Politics in the Congo*, pp. 447-63.

53. Ibid., p. 472.

54. Jacques Tronchon, *L'insurrection malgache de 1947: Essai d'interpretation historique* (Paris: Maspero, 1974), pp. 120-2.

6/ Leaders, Organizations, and the Coordination of Dissent

1. Quoted in Samuel P. Huntington, "Political Development and Political Decay," *World Politics* 17, 3 (April 1965), p. 421.

2. Donald L. Barnett and Karari Njama, *Mau Mau From Within: Autobiography and Analysis of Kenya's Peasant Revolt* (London: Macgibbon & Kee, 1966), p. 133.

3. Zebulon C. Taintor, "Assessing the Revolutionary Personality," in Claude E. Welch, Jr. and Mavis Bunker Taintor, eds., *Revolution and Political Change* (North Scituate: Duxbury, 1972), p. 245.

4. Erik Erikson, *Gandhi's Truth: On the Origins of Militant Nonviolence* (New York: Norton, 1969) and *Young Man Luther: A Study in Psychoanalysis and History* (New York: Norton, 1958); E. Victor Wolfenstein, *The Revolutionary Personality: Lenin, Trotsky and Gandhi* (Princeton: Princeton University Press, 1967).

5. James David Barber, *The Presidential Character: Predicting Performance in the White House* (Englewood Cliffs: Prentice-Hall, 1977, second edition).

6. Useful and occasionally controversial contributions include Lowell Dittmer, *Liu Shao-ch'i and the Chinese Cultural Revolution: The Politics of Mass Criticism* (Berkeley: University of California Press, 1974), Lucian W. Pye, *Politics, Personality and Nation-Building: Burma's Search for Identity* (New Haven: Yale University Press, 1962), and Richard H. Solomon, *Mao's Revolution and the Chinese Political Culture* (Berkeley: University of California Press, 1971).

7. Kung-chuan Hsiao, *Rural China: Imperial Control in the Nineteenth Century* (Seattle: University of Washington Press, 1960), p. 323.

8. Ibid., p. 330.

9. Ibid., p. 338.

10. See the bibliography in Jean Chesneaux, Fei-ling Davis and Nguyen Nguyet Ho, *Mouvements populaires et sociétés secrètes en Chine aux xixe et xxe siècles* (Paris: Maspero, 1970), p. 485-8.

11. Susan Naquin, *Millenarian Rebellion in China: The Eight Trigrams Uprising of 1813* (New Haven: Yale University Press, 1976), p. 268.

12. Hsiao, *Rural China*, p. 460.

13. Franz Michael, *The Taiping Rebellion: History and Documents*, Vol. I (Seattle: University of Washington Press, 1966), pp. 12-13.

14. Chesneaux, *Mouvements populaires*, p. 37.

15. Ibid., p. 30.

16. Charles A. Curwen, "Les relations des Taiping avec les sociétés secrètes et les autres rebelles," in Chesneaux, *Mouvements populaires*, p. 154.

17. In South China, such entities fitted within the general rubric of Triad societies, in North China within the White Lotus. The former are often argued to be "lodges": more politicized, more linked to urban declassé elements; the latter are depicted as "sects": more religious, more linked to poor peasants. For a brief review, see Chesneaux, *Mouvements populaires*, p. 17.

18. Naquin, *Millenarian Rebellion*, pp. 7, 13.

19. Edward Friedman, *Backward Toward Revolution: The Chinese Revolutionary Party* (Berkeley: University of California Press, 1974), pp. 146-7.

20. Naquin, *Millenarian Rebellion*, p. 203. Cf. the statements of Taiping leader Li Hsiu-ch'eng, explaining how he and his family joined the movement:

Apart from these six men [early close associates of Hung Hsiu-ch'üan] no one else knew about the T'ien Wang [Hung Hsiu-ch'üan] wanting to establish his rule over the country. The others did not know and really followed for the sake of food.

The Hsi Wang stayed in a village near my home and he gave out that the God-worshippers need not be afraid and flee. They could eat together as one family, so why should they flee? My family was very poor, so because there was food to eat did not flee. When the army marched, the houses of all those who had joined the God-worshippers were set alight and burned.

C.A. Curwen, *Taiping Rebel: The Deposition of Li Hsiu-ch'eng* (Cambridge: Cambridge University press, 1977), pp. 80, 83. The Hsi Wang came from a poor peasant family and owed his claim to a high position in the Taiping hierarchy to his claim he spoke with the voice of Jesus. Ibid., pp. 181-2, n. 24.

21. Ibid., p. 100.

22. Jen Yu-wen, *The Taiping Revolutionary Movement* (New Haven: Yale University Press, 1973), p. 22.

23. Ibid., p. 32.

24. Ibid., p. 36. Li offers the following information regarding Hung's teaching:

> He often hid in the depths of the mountains, where he secretly taught people to worship God. He taught people about being eaten by serpents and tigers and about avoiding disasters and sickness. Each person passed on the word to ten others, ten to a hundred others, a hundred to a thousand, a thousand to ten thousand....But there were educated and intelligent scholars who did not join. Those who did were all peasants and poor people, and they assembled together and made a host.

Curwen, *Taiping Rebel*, p. 80.

25. Again in Li's deposition:

> ...everything was strictly regulated... In the city of Chiang-nan [Nanking, the Taiping capital] men and women were separated, the men into the men's quarters and the women into the women's quarters... Men and women were not allowed to speak to each other; mothers and children were not allowed to talk together. It was very strict and won the people's respect.

Ibid., p. 86. Separation of the sexes was abandoned in 1855.

26. The following proclamation illustrates how (by 1852) proto-nationalist elements had become highlighted in Taiping beliefs:

> Can the Chinese still deem themselves men? Ever since the Manchus spread their poisonous influences through China, the flames of oppression have risen up to heaven, the vapors of corruption have defiled the celestial throne, the filthy odors have spread over the four seas, and their devilishness exceeds that of the Five Barbarians. Yet the Chinese with bowed heads and dejected spirits willingly became their servants. Alas! there are no men in China....The Chinese have Chinese characteristics; but now the Manchus have ordered us to shave the hair around the head, leaving a long tail behind, thus making the Chinese appear to be brute animals. The Chinese have Chinese dress; but now the Manchus have adopted buttons on the hat, introduced barbarian clothes and monkey caps, and discarded the robes and headdresses of former dynasties, in order to make the Chinese forget their origins...The Chinese have Chinese spouses; but now the Manchu demons have taken all of China's beautiful girls to be their slaves and concubines. Thus three thousand beautiful women have been ravished by the barbarian dogs, one million pretty girls have slept with the odorous foxes; to speak of it distresses the heart, to talk of it pollutes the tongue.

Michael, *Taiping Rebellion*, Vol. II, pp. 145-6.

27. Reprinted in ibid., Vol. II, pp. 131-9.

28. Ibid., Vol. II, pp. 140-1. To cite a typical three of the ten strictures:

> 7. Let no one during the march enter the shops, light his lamps and go to sleep, and thus impede and delay the march; but let all, front or rear ranks, maintain their contacts, and do not attempt to run away.

8. Let no one set fire to the dwellings of the people, or urinate in the roads or in private houses.

9. Let no one unjustly put to death the aged, infirm, and those unable to bear their burdens.

29. Ibid., Vol. I, p. 190.

30. As we shall see in the following chapter, however, the CPI was far more willing than Congress to accept cultural pluralism and self-determination, including the creation of Pakistan.

31. *Census of India 1941*, Vol. XXI, H.E.H. the Nizam's Dominions (Hyderabad State) (Hyderabad: Government Press, 1945), pp. 30-31.

32. N. Ramesan, ed., *The Freedom Struggle in Hyderabad*, Vol. IV (1921-1947) (Andhra State Committee Appointed for the Compilation of a History of the Freedom Struggle in Andhra Pradesh, 1966), p. 43.

33. Ibid., p. 50.

34. Ibid., p. 133.

35. Ibid., p. 136.

36. Ibid., pp. 158, 199.

37. Ibid., p. 195.

38. Mohan Ram, "The Communist Movement in Andhra Pradesh," in Paul R. Brass and Marcus F. Franda, eds., *Radical Politics in South Asia* (Cambridge: M.I.T. Press, 1973), p. 284.

39. Technically speaking, the CPI was illegal at this point, having been banned by the British administration following its involvement in the Meerut conspiracy. Individual Communists joined the Congress effort until 1938 through the Congress Socialist party, a Marxist/Fabian ginger group within Congress. In June 1942, following Hitler's attack on the USSR the ban on the CPI was lifted.

40. Osmania University was founded in 1918, to a large extent intended as a training ground for the Muslim administrative elite. Inasmuch as most teaching was conducted in Urdu, few Hindus enjoyed access to the opportunities Osmania offered.

41. Carolyn M. Elliott, "Decline of a Patrimonial Regime: The Telengana Rebellion in India, 1946-51," *Journal of Asian Studies* 34, 1 (November 1974), p. 40.

42. P. Sundarayya, *Telengana People's Struggle and its Lessons* (Calcutta: Desraj Chadha for CPI(M), 1972), p. 21.

43. Elliott, "Decline of a Patrimonial Regime," p. 44.

44. Ibid., p. 36.

45. Ramesan, *Freedom Struggle*, p. 196.

46. Elliott, "Decline of a Patrimonial Regime," p. 37.

47. The *mulkis* included both Hindu, urbanized, Urdu-speaking Hyderabadis and local Muslims who opposed the North Indian Muslims brought into the state in the late nineteenth century by Sir Salar Jung. Most found government employment—and understandably had little taste for actively opposing the Nizam. For further information about their post-incorporation fate, see Chapter 9.

48. Elliott, "Decline of a Patrimonial Regime," p. 43.

49. V.P. Menon, *The Story of the Integration of the Indian States* (London: Longmans, 1955), pp. 351-2.

50. Ian Bedford, *The Telengana Insurrection: A Study in the Causes and Development of a Communist Insurrection in Rural India, 1946-51* (Ph.D. thesis, Australian National University, December 1967), p. 270.

51. Menon, *Integration of the Indian States*, p. 371.

52. As Sir Charles Eliot wrote in 1905, "The interior of the Protectorate is a white man's country....It is mere hypocrisy not to admit that white interests must be paramount, and that the main object of our policy and legislation should be to found a white colony." Quoted in M.P.K. Sorrenson, *Origins of European Settlement in Kenya* (Nairobi: Oxford University Press, 1968), p. 61. Despite the shock of the 1923 Devonshire Commission report, encouragement of settler farming continued to characterize British policy until well after World War II.

53. "Indians in Kenya" (London: HMSO, 1923, Cmd. 1922), p. 9.

54. Margery F. Perham, *Native Administration in Nigeria* (London: Oxford University Press, 1937), p. 361. Dame Margery opposed Africans' entering the Administrative Service: "...to build them into the scaffolding would be to create a vested interest which would make its demolition at the appropriate time very difficult." *Loc. cit.*

55. "Indians in Kenya," pp. 9, 10.

56. R.J. Martin Wight, *Development of the Legislative Council 1606-1945* (London: Faber, 1946).

57. E.S. Grogan, quoted in Jeremy Murray-Brown, *Kenyatta* (London: George Allen & Unwin, 1972), p. 77.

58. Ibid., p. 70.

59. The text of the telegram appears in Harry Thuku, *An Autobiography* (Nairobi: Oxford University Press, 1970), pp. 83-4.

60. Carl G. Rosberg, Jr., and John Nottingham, *The Myth of "Mau Mau": Nationalism in Kenya* (New York: Frederick A. Praeger for the Hoover Institution, 1966), p. 54.

61. Europeans considered the proposed abolition of the *kipande* "an assault on their privileged position, and they could not accept legislation which implied the equality of all citizens." Anthony Clayton and Donald C. Savage, *Government and Labour in Kenya 1895-1963* (London: Frank Cass, 1974), pp. 295-6.

62. E.P. Thompson, *The Making of the English Working Class 1790-1830* (Harmondsworth: Penguin, 1968), pp. 557-61.

63. Frank Furedi, "The Social Composition of the Mau Mau Movement in the White Highlands," *Journal of Peasant Studies*, 1, 4 (1974), p. 495.

64. Rosberg and Nottingham, *Myth of "Mau Mau,"* pp. 86-7.

65. John Spencer, "KAU and 'Mau Mau': Some Connections," unpublished paper presented to the conference on the Political Economy of Colonial Kenya, Cambridge, 26-29 June 1975, p. 5.

66. Rosberg and Nottingham point to the post-1925 oath of loyalty to the Kikuyu Central Association, "the earliest use of an oath in a modern political context...." *Myth of "Mau Mau,"* p. 245.

67. Ibid., p. 247.

68. Bildad Kaggia, *Roots of Freedom 1921-1963* (Nairobi: East African Publishing House, 1975), p. 80.

69. Ibid., p. 108. "Far from being a Kikuyu primitive organisation, as portrayed by our enemies, 'Mau Mau' was an organisation formed by KAU militants who had lost faith in constitutional methods of fighting for independence." Ibid., p. 112.

70. This did not preclude some from using trade unions as vehicles for political

agitation, in the absence of other means. Leaders of the East African Trade Unions Congress regarded it

> as a ginger group to prod the Kenya African Union into more dynamic political action. In practice this meant that the Congress in the first four months of 1950 issued a stream of press releases and sponsored some twenty-five to thirty meetings, the tenor of which became more and more radical.

Clayton and Savage, *Government and Labour*, p. 328; cf. Kaggia, *Roots of Freedom*, p. 66.

71. Rosberg and Nottingham, *Myth of "Mau Mau,"* p. 271; Kaggia, *Roots of Freedom*, pp. 79-82.

72. Murray-Brown, *Kenyatta*, p. 243.

73. Barnett and Njama, *Mau Mau from Within*, p. 174.

74. Kathy Santilli, "Kikuyu Women in the Mau-Mau Revolt: A Closer Look." *Ufahamu* 8, 1 (1977), 143-59.

75. L.S.B. Leakey, *Defeating Mau Mau* (London: Methuen, 1954), p. 61.

76. Robert Buijtenhuijs, *Le Mouvement "Mau-Mau": Une revolte paysanne et anti-coloniale en Afrique noire* (Paris: Mouton, 1971), pp. 349-55.

77. Furedi, "Social Composition," pp. 449-501.

78. Barnett and Njama, *Mau Mau from Within*, p. 299.

79. Herbert Weiss and Benoit Verhaegen, eds. *Parti Solidaire Africain (P.S.A.): Documents 1959-1960* (Brussels: CRISP, 1963), p. 15.

80. Ibid., p. 17.

81. Herbert F. Weiss, *Political Protest in the Congo: The Parti Solidaire Africain During the Independence Struggle* (Princeton: Princeton University Press, 1967), p. 98.

82. Weiss and Verhaegen, *Parti Solidaire Africain*, p. 9; author's translation.

83. Ibid., p. 274.

84. Weiss, *Political Protest*, pp. 279 ff.

85. Ibid., p. 162.

86. A useful summary of these confused events appears in Young, *Politics in the Congo*, pp. 330-6. Also see Catherine Hoskyns, *The Congo Since Independence July 1960 - December 1961* (London: Oxford University Press, 1963), pp. 289-92, and Centre de Recherche et d'Information Socio-Politiques, *Congo 1961* (Brussels: CRISP, 1962), pp. 151-212.

87. Young, *Politics in the Congo*, p. 393.

88. Immanuel Wallerstein, "The Decline of the Party in Single-Party African States," in Joseph LaPalombara and Myron Weiner, eds., *Political Parties and Political Development* (Princeton: Princeton University Press, 1966), pp. 207-11.

89. Young, *Politics in the Congo*, p. 377.

90. Renée C. Fox, Willy de Craemer and Jean-Marie Ribeaucourt, "The 'Second Independence': A Case Study of the Kwilu Rebellion in the Congo," *Comparative Studies in Society and History* 8, 1 (October 1965), 84.

91. Benoit Verhaegen, *Rebellions au Congo*, Vol. 1 (Brussels: CRISP, 1966), p. 178.

92. Frederic Wakeman Jr., "Les sociétés secrètes du Guandgong (1800-1856)," in Chesneaux, *Mouvements populaires*, p. 90.

358 / Anatomy of Rebellion

93. Barnett and Njama, *Mau Mau from Within*, p. 131.

94. Michael, *Taiping Rebellion*, Vol II, p. 140.

95. As Naquin notes, Ch'ing bureaucrats were aware of plans for the Eight Trigrams uprising—so much so that its initiation was moved up several days. Not a single member of the sect was arrested until noon September 15, 1813, at which time a handful of men was attempting to capture the palace of Peking—from which, by the way, the emperor was absent. Cold feet at the last moment made their unlikely attack even more hopeless: 30 to 40 of those supposed to join in the assault remained at home; of the 90 to 100 who left the safety of their houses, only 61 reached the immediate area of the palace gate. Naquin, *Millenarian Rebellion*, p. 165, 176.

7/ Ideology and the Justification and Direction of Rebellion

1. Leon Trotsky, *History of the Russian Revolution*, quoted in Ted Robert Gurr, *Why Men Rebel* (Princeton: Princeton University Press, 1970), p. 104.

2. Norman Cohn, *The Pursuit of the Millennium: Revolutionary Millenarians and Mystical Anarchists of the Middle Ages* (New York: Oxford University Press, 1970, revised edition), p. 13.

3. Ibid., pp. 281-3; cf. Michael Barkun, *Disaster and the Millenium* (New Haven: Yale University Press, 1974).

4. Gurr, *Why Men Rebel*, pp. 201-2. The scope of normative justifications, Gurr aptly notes, varies with the scope of the relative deprivation experienced.

5. Mark Hagopian, *The Phenomenon of Revolution* (New York: Dodd Mead, 1974), p. 258.

6. B. Marie Perinbam, "Fanon and the Myth of the Revolutionary Peasantry: The Algerian Case," *Journal of Modern African Studies*, 11, 3 (September 1973), 427-45.

7. Chalmers Johnson, *Peasant Nationalism and Communist Power* (Stanford: Stanford University Press, 1962); however, also see Mark Selden, *The Yenan Way in Revolutionary China* (Cambridge: Harvard University Press, 1972) and Tetsuya Kataoka, *Resistance and Revolution in China: The Communists and the Second United Front* (Berkeley: University of California Press, 1974).

8. Vincent Y.C. Shih, *The Taiping Ideology: Its Sources, Interpretations, and Influences* (Seattle: University of Washington Press, 1967), pp. xiii, xvi.

9. C.A. Curwen, *Taiping Rebel: The Deposition of Li Hsiu-ch'eng* (Cambridge: Cambridge University Press, 1977), p. 1.

10. Jen Yu-wen, *The Taiping Revolutionary Movement* (New Haven: Yale University Press, 1973).

11. Franz Michael, *The Taiping Rebellion*, Vol I (Seattle: University of Washington Press, 1966), p. 4.

12. Ibid., Vol. I, pp. 44; the document is reprinted in Vol. II, pp. 131-9.

13. Shih, *Taiping Ideology*, p. 17.

14. Yuji Muramatsu, "Some Themes in Chinese Rebel Ideologies," in Arthur F. Wright, ed., *The Confucian Persuasion* (Stanford: Stanford University Press, 1960), p. 249.

15. Shih, *Taiping Ideology*, p. 43.

16. Jen, *Taiping Revolutionary Movement*, p. 81.

17. Reprinted in Michael, *Taiping Rebellion*, Vol. II, p. 54.

18. Ibid., p. 56.

19. Ibid., p. 62.

20. Max Weber, *Theory of Economic and Political Organization*, ed. Talcott Parsons (New York: Free Press, 1964), pp. 363-73.

21. Jen, *Taiping Revolutionary Movement*, p. 32.

22. Michael, *Taiping Rebellion*, Vol. II, p. 143.

23. Ibid., p. 149.

24. Ibid., p. 151.

25. Jen, *Taiping Revolutionary Movement*, pp. 354-5.

26. Ibid., p. 357.

27. Reprinted in Michael, *Taiping Rebellion*, Vol. III, pp. 751-76.

28. Ibid., p. 753.

29. Ibid., p. 755.

30. The Founding Fathers would have some difficulty in recognizing their handiwork in Hung Jen-kan's paraphrase: "The president's term is five years and his salary and emoluments are defined. At the end of his term he retires to live in comfort, and the various states then again elect a president. All state affairs are discussed publicly by the heads of the various states, whose decisions are then submitted to the president for final approval." Ibid., p. 759.

31. Muramatsu, "Some Themes," p. 241.

32. Ibid., p. 264.

33. Michael, *Taiping Rebellion*, Vol. II, p. 28. Hung's renditions of the other Ten Commandments also mingle Biblical and typically Chinese elements.

34. Ibid., p. 30.

35. Ibid., p. 33

36. Ibid., p. 57.

37. Muramatsu, "Some Themes," p. 259.

38. Reprinted in Michael, *Taiping Rebellion*, Vol. II, pp. 309-20.

39. Jen, *Taiping Revolutionary Movement*, p. 143.

40. Michael, *Taiping Rebellion*, Vol. II, p. 314.

41. Ibid., p. 246.

42. Ibid., p. 77.

43. Selig S. Harrison, *India: The Most Dangerous Decades* (Princeton: Princeton University Press, 1960), p. 221.

44. Taya Zinkin, *Reporting India* (London: Chatto & Windus, 1962), p. 60.

45. P. Sundarayya, "Vishala Andhra" (Bombay: People's Publishing House, 1946), p. 7.

46. G. Adhikari, "Pakistan and Indian National Unity" (London: Labour Monthly, 1943), pp. 13, 15

47. Ibid., p. 31.

48. Harrison, *India*, p. 205.

49. Ibid., pp. 226-45.

50. "Political Thesis of the Communist Party of India," reprinted in M.B. Rao, ed., *Documents of the History of the Communist Party of India*, Vol VII (New Delhi: People's Publishing House, 1976), p. 61.

51. "Political Thesis," pp. 99-100.

52. P. Sundarayya, *Telengana People's Struggle and its Lessons* (Calcutta: Desraj Chadha for CPI(M), 1972), p. 117.

53. Hamza Alavi, "Peasants and Revolutions," in Kathleen Gough and Hari P. Sharma, eds., *Imperialism and Revolution in South Asia* (New York: Monthly Review Press, 1973), p. 327. Alavi terms the Telengana movement "the most revolutionary movement that has yet arisen in India." Op. cit., p. 325.

54. Jeremy Murray-Brown, *Kenyatta* (London: George Allen & Unwin, 1972), p. 2.

55. Donald L. Barnett and Karari Njama, *Mau Mau from Within: Autobiography and Analysis of Kenya's Peasant Revolt* (London: Macgibbon & Kee, 1966), pp. 118-9.

56. *Sunday Worker*, 27 October 1929, quoted in Murray-Brown, *Kenyatta*, pp. 119-20.

57. Jomo Kenyatta, "The Gold Rush in Kenya," *Labour Monthly*, November 1933, quoted in ibid., p. 178.

58. Carl G. Rosberg, Jr. and John Nottingham, *The Myth of "Mau Mau': Nationalism in Kenya* (New York: Frederick A. Praeger for the Hoover Institution, 1966), p. 214.

59. *The Hardcore: The Story of Karigo Muchai* (Richmodn, B.C.: LSM Press, 1973), p. 14.

60. Barnett and Njama, *Mau Mau from Within*, pp. 131-2.

61. L.S.B. Leakey, *Defeating Mau Mau* (London: Methuen, 1954), pp. 53-4.

62. Ibid., p. 59.

63. Ibid., p. 61.

64. Ibid., p. 63.

65. Ibid., p. 68.

66. Clearest evidence comes from the February 1954 "elections" to the "Kenya Parliament," the coordinating group for Mau Mau fighters formed in the Aberdare forests. Six of its thirteen members came from North Tetu Division of Nyeri District. Barnett and Njama, *Mau Mau from Within*, p. 329. Njama expressed his concern about the limited participation from southern Kikuyu thus: "The Kiambu people are the originators of the oath and all the ideas behind the Movement; why should they surrender when it is red hot? Wouldn't they like to harvest the fruit they planted?" Ibid., p. 298.

67. These appear as the "Three Main Rules of Discipline and the Eight Points for Attention," reissued October 10, 1947. They appear in Mao Tse-tung, *Selected Works*, Vol. 4 (Peking: Foreign Language Press, 1969), p. 155. A textual comparison of these with Mulele's instructions appears in Benoit Verhaegen, *Rebellions au Congo*, Vol. 1 (Brussels: CRISP, 1966), pp. 122-3.

68. Ibid., pp. 167-9, author's translation. Cf. Renée C. Fox, Willy De Craemer, and Jean-Marie Ribeaucourt, "The 'Second Independence': A Case Study of the Kwilu Rebellion in the Congo," *Comparative Studies in Society and History* 8, 1 (October 1965), pp. 95-6.

69. Verhaegen, *Rebellions au Congo*, p. 167; cf. Fox et al., "Second Independence," p. 94.

70. Fox et al., "Second Independence," p. 101.

71. Ibid., pp. 78-9.

72. Ibid., p. 99.

73. Ibid., p. 100; Verhaegen, *Rebellions au Congo*, p. 125.

74. Fox et al., "Second Independence," p. 125.

75. Primarily does not mean exclusively. Fox and her colleagues make note of participants from other ethnic backgrounds. Ibid., p. 101.

76. Kwilu was constituted as a province separate from Leopoldville in April 1962. Pende and Mbunda disappointment was profound, for the Kamitatu wing of the PSA controlled the province; of the twelve ministers selected, only three came from the two groups, who nonetheless constituted half the province's population. The

creation of a prefecture at Kamtsha-Loange (dividing Idiofa) was interpreted in May 1963 by both groups as a means of weakening them. For details, see Verhaegen, *Rebellions au Congo*, pp. 53-6.

77. Fox et al., "Second Independence," p. 96.

78. Verhaegen, *Rebellions au Congo*, p. 73.

79. Ibid., pp. 79-80.

80. Stuart R. Schram, *The Political Thought of Mao Tse-tung* (New York: Praeger, 1963), pp. 181-2. The sentence cited, it should be noted, was deleted in Volume I of Mao's selected works. Also deleted from the Hunan report, when published in English in 1951, were significant portions giving leadership credit to peasants. Note how the italicized words—all edited out—indicate shifts in Mao's thinking and CCP doctrine.

> The peasants have accomplished a revolutionary task for many years left unaccomplished, and done *the most* important work in the national revolution. But have all the peasants taken part in accomplishing such a great revolutionary task and doing this most important work? No. The peasantry consists of three sections—the rich peasants, the middle peasants, and the poor peasants....
>
> The *only group* in the countryside that has always put up the bitterest fight is the poor peasants. Throughout the period of underground organization and that of open organization, *it was they who fought, who organized, and who did the revolutionary work. They alone* are the deadliest enemies of the local bullies and evil gentry and attack their strongholds without the slightest hesitation; *they alone are able to carry out the work of destruction.*

Ibid., pp. 183-4. In place of the expunged words, Mao inserted a sentence totally changing the meaning: "They [poor peasants] accept leadership of the Communist party most willingly." The truth seems to be that the CCP in Hunan (like the CPI in Telengana just over forty years later) attached their efforts to an ongoing, indigenous process of rural mobilization.

81. Frantz Fanon, *The Wretched of the Earth*, translated by Constance Farringdon (Harmondsworth: Penguin, 1967), p. 47.

82. Ibid., pp. 26-7.

83. Alavi, "Peasants and Revolution," pp. 304-16.

84. Perinbam, "Fanon and the Myth of the Revolutionary Peasantry."

85. Fanon, *Wretched of the Earth*, p. 101.

86. Ibid., p. 108.

8/ *Repression* + *Concession* = *Termination?*

1. Jen Yu-wen, *The Taiping Revolutionary Movement* (New Haven: Yale University Press, 1973), p. 170.

2. Ibid., pp. 176-9.

3. Franz Michael, *The Taiping Rebellion*, Vol. I (Seattle: University of Washington Press, 1966), p. 79.

4. Ibid., p. 90.

5. Ibid., p. 113. The deposition of Li Hsiu-ch'eng also stresses the demoralizing effect of fratricidal strife. Feeling himself threatened and isolated, Hung Hsiu-ch'üan increasingly put his trust in incompetent persons largely because they were members of his own clan. C.A. Curwen, *Taiping Rebel: The Deposition of Li*

Hsiu-ch'eng (Cambridge: Cambridge University Press, 1977), p. 52.

6. Frederic Wakeman, Jr., *Strangers at the Gate: Social Disorder in South China, 1839-1861* (Berkeley: University of California Press, 1966), p. 151; Ella S. Laffey, "In the Wake of the Taipings: Some Patterns of Local Revolt in Kwangsi Province, 1850-1875," *Modern Asian Studies* 10, 1 (January 1975), 65-81.

7. Ssu-yü Teng, *The Nien Army and their Guerilla Warfare* (The Hague: Mouton, 1961); Jen, *Taiping Revolutionary Movement*, p. 173 fn. 7.

8. Mary C. Wright, *The Last Stand of Chinese Conservatism: The T'ung-Chih Restoration, 1862-1874* (Stanford: Stanford University Press, 1957).

9. Curwen, *Taiping Rebel*, pp. 142-3; J.S. Gregory, *Great Britain and the Taipings* (London: Routledge & Kegan Paul, 1969), pp. 111-31; Jen, *Taiping Revolutionary Movement*, pp. 443-54.

10. Michael, *Taiping Rebellion*, Vol. I, p. 67.

11. Wiliam James Hale, *Tseng Kuo-fan and the Taiping Rebellion* (New York: Paragon Books, 1964, reprint of 1927 edition), pp. 141-3. In Chinese terms, Tseng was already in his 27th *sui*.

12. To quote Tseng's own views: "*Hsiang-t'uan* [local militia] really cannot stand against large bandit hordes. It is particularly difficult to select suitable directors of the *t'uan* from among the gentry-managers. Those of them that are upright cannot keep the bandits in check after having tasted every drudgery and difficulty...; those among them that are unrighteous use the *t'uan* as a pretext to extort money, harass the people and arrogate the control of public affairs." Cited in Kung-chuan Hsiao, *Rural China: Imperial Control in the Nineteenth Century* (Seattle: University of Washington Press, 1966), p. 656, fn. 157.

13. Michael, *Taiping Rebellion*, Vol. I, pp. 97-101.

14. Ibid., p. 101.

15. Ibid., p. 102.

16. When he first opposed the Taipings, Tseng had only 20,000 men, and never exceeded 120,000 soldiers. Ibid., p. 103.

17. Ibid., p. 152.

18. Curwen, *Taiping Rebel*, pp. 103, 160.

19. Michael, *Taiping Rebellion*, Vol. I, p. 155.

20. V.P. Menon, *The Story of the Integration of the Indian States* (London: Longmans, 1955), p. 376.

21. Sir Mirza Ismail, *My Public Life: Recollections and Reflections* (London: George Allen & Unwin, 1954), p. 128.

22. On August 21, 1948, Hyderabad requested Security Council attention to the state's complaint against India (*The Complaint of Hyderabad Against the Dominion of India Under Article 35(2) of the Charter of the United Nations*, London: Waterlow, 1948). By the time the Security Council started its discussion, the die had been cast, Indian troops having invaded Hyderabad. India requested and received a five day adjournment to present its documents, by the end of which the occupation was complete and the Nizam had withdrawn the complaint. Still moving slowly, the Security Council listened to interested parties 19 May and 24 May, 1949, considered a request from Pakistan that the International Court of Justice hear the complaint, and adjourned without discussion. Smith, "Hyderabad: Muslim Tragedy," pp. 48-9 fn.

23. Theodore P. Wright, Jr., "Revival of the Majlis Ittihad-ul-Muslimin of Hyderabad," *The Muslim World* 53 (1963), 238-41. Of the nine candidates for the latter two assemblies, only one was victorious.

24. Wilfred Cantwell Smith, "Hyderabad: Muslim Tragedy," *Middle East Journal* 4, 1 (January 1950), 46. The lowest estimates of Muslim deaths, Smith notes, were at least ten times the number of murders of which razakars were officially accused.

25. Mao Tse-tung, "On New Democracy," *Selected Works*, Vol. II (Peking: Foreign Languages Press, 1965), p. 253: "The republic will take certain necessary steps to confiscate the land of the landlords and distribute it to the peasants having little or no land....A rich peasant economy will be allowed in the rural areas..."

26. P. Sundarayya, *Telengana People's Struggle and its Lessons* (Calcutta: Desraj Chadha for CPI(M), 1972), p. 118.

27. D.N. Dhanagare, "Social Origins of the Peasant Insurrection in Telengana (1946-51)," *Contributions to Indian Sociology* 8 (1974), 128.

28. Sundarayya, *Telengana People's Struggle*, p. 43.

29. Ibid., pp. 134-5.

30. Ibid., p. 66.

31. Moham Ram, "The Telengana Peasant Armed Struggle, 1946-51," *Economic and Political Weekly* 8, 23 (June 9, 1973), 1031.

32. D. N. Pritt, "Oppression in India," *The Labour Monthly* 32, 7 (1950), 319-20, cited in Dhanagare, "Social Origins of the Peasant Insurrection," 125.

33. Ram, "Telengana Peasant Armed Struggle," 1027.

34. Barry Pavier, "The Telengana Armed Struggle," *Economic and Political Weekly* 9, 32-4 (August 1974), 1418.

35. S. Kesava Iyengar, *Economic Investigations in the Hyderabad State 1929-30*, Vol. I (Hyderabad: Government Central Press, 1931), p. 15.

36. Menon, *Integration of the Indian States*, pp. 385-6.

37. S. Kesava Iyengar, *Rural Economic Enquiries in the Hyderabad State 1949-51* (Hyderabad: Government Press, 1951), p. 31.

38. Ibid., p. 58.

39. For details of the legislation, see B.K. Narayan, *Agricultural Development in Hyderabad State 1900-1956: A Study in Economic History* (Secunderabad: Keshav Prakashan, n.d.) pp. 74-9.

40. Pavier, "Telengana Armed Struggle," p. 1419.

41. M.B. Rao, ed., *Documents of the History of the Communist Party of India*, Vol. VII 1948-50 (New Delhi: People's Publishing House, 1976), p. xiii.

42. Among numerous sources, the following are particularly useful: Richard Clutterbuck, *The Long Long War: The Emergency in Malaya, 1948-1960* (London: Cassell, 1967), and *Riot and Revolution in Singapore and Malaya 1945-1963* (London: Faber and Faber, 1973); Harry Miller, *Jungle War in Malaya: The Campaign Against Communism 1948-60* (London: Arthur Barker, 1972); Edgar O'Balance, *Malaya—The Communist Insurgent War 1948-60* (London: Faber, 1966); Lucian W. Pye, *Guerrilla Communism in Malaya* (Princeton: Princeton University Press, 1956); and Robert Thompson, *Defeating Communist Insurgency: Experiences from Malaya and Vietnam* (London: Chatto and Windus, 1966).

43. Miller, *Jungle War in Malaya*, pp. 63-4.

44. Clutterbuck, *Riot and Revolution*, pp. 176-7.

45. Miller, *Jungle War*, p. 83.

46. Ibid., p. 23.

47. Ibid., p. 84.

48. Anthony Clayton, "Counter-Insurgency in Kenya: A Study of Military Operations against Mau Mau" (Nairobi: Transafrica Publishers, 1976), p. 9.

49. Ibid., p. 10; Sir Michael Blundell, *So Rough a Wind* (London: Weidenfeld & Nicolson, 1964), pp. 153-7.

50. Ibid., p. 163.

51. Clayton, "Counter-Insurgency in Kenya," p. 23.

52. Donald L. Barnett and Karari Njama, *Mau Mau from Within* (London: Macgibbon & Kee, 1966, p. 491.

53. Clayton, "Counter-Insurgency in Kenya," p. 25.

54. Arslan Humbaraci, *Algeria: A Revolution that Failed* (London: Pall Mall, 1966), p. 34.

55. F.C. Corfield, *Historical Survey of the Origins and Growth of Mau Mau* (London: HMSO, 1960; Cmd. 1040), p. 233.

56. Kikuyu recruitment into the King's African Rifles had never been great, the Kamba having furnished the largest portion of recruits through World War II. For example, Waruhiu Itote—"General China"—noted there were only nine Kikuyu in his entire battalion in 1942. Waruhiu Itote, *"Mau Mau" General* (Nairobi: East Africa Publishing House, 1967), p. 23.

57. "History of the Loyalists" (Nairobi: Government Printer, 1961), p. 12.

58. Corfield, *Historical Survey*, p. 240.

59. "The Kikuyu Who Fight Mau Mau" (Nairobi: Eagle Press, 1955), p. 2.

60. Carl G. Rosberg, Jr. and John Nottingham, *"The Myth of Mau Mau"*: Nationalism in Kenya (New York: Frederick A. Praeger for the Hoover Institution, 1966), p. 292.

61. Ibid., p. 294.

62. Bethwell A. Ogot, "Revolt of the Elders: An Anatomy of the Loyalist Crowd in the Mau Mau Uprising 1952-1956," in Ogot, *Politics and Nationalism in Colonial Kenya* (Hadith 4) (Nairobi: East African Publishing House, 1972), pp. 134-48.

63. M.P.K. Sorrenson, *Land Reform in the Kikuyu Country* (Nairobi: Oxford University Press, 1967), p. 108.

64. Ibid., p. 107.

65. Ian Henderson with Philip Goodhart, *The Hunt for Kimathi* (London: Hamish Hamilton, 1958). It should be noted that General Erskine estimated he confronted 12,000 Mau Mau partisans when he arrived in April 1953. Clayton, "Counter-Insurgency in Kenya," p. 21.

66. Miller, *Jungle War*, p. 107.

67. Sorrenson, *Land Reform*, p. 109.

68. Clayton, "Counter-Insurgency in Kenya," p. 25.

69. Rosberg and Nottingham, *Myth of "Mau Mau*," p. 311.

70. Ibid., p. 315.

71. R.J.M. Swynnerton, *A Plan to Intensify the Development of African Agriculture in Kenya* (Nairobi: Government Publishers, 1954).

72. Sorrenson, *Land Reform*, p. 221.

73. Ibid., p. 243.

74. Centre de Recherche et d'Information Socio-Politiques, *Congo 1966* (Brussels: CRISP, 1967), p. 329.

75. Benoit Verhaegen, *Rebellions au Congo*, Vol. I (Brussels: CRISP, 1966), p. 105.

76. James C. Davies, "The J-Curve of Rising and Declining Satisfactions as a Cause of Some Great Revolutions and a Contained Rebellion," in Hugh David

Graham and Ted Robert Gurr, eds., *Violence in American: Historical and Comparative Perspectives* (New York: Praeger, 1969) pp. 690-730.

77. Centre de Recherche et d'Information Socio-Politiques, *Congo 1965* (Brussels: CRISP, 1966), p. 117.

78. Ibid., p. 91.

79. Ibid., pp. 111-2.

80. Ibid., p. 105.

81. In Lingala, the foremost common language in Kwilu, "penepene" means "be near" and was often applied to educated Africans who adopted European characteristics. It was also used as a term of opprobrium against members of the PNP (Parti National du Progrès), known for its favorable attitude toward Belgian rule. On occasion, the PNP was deemed the "Parti des Negres Payés" ("Party of Hired Niggers").

82. M. Crawford Young, "Rebellion and the Congo," in Robert I. Rotberg, ed., *Rebellion in Black Africa* (London: Oxford University Press, 1971), pp. 208-45; Verhaegen, *Rebellions au Congo*, Vols. I and II.

83. Jean-Claude Willame, *Patrimonialism and Political Change in the Congo* (Stanford: Stanford University Press, 1972), p. 123.

84. Historically, the most famous African example comes from the "Maji-Maji" revolt of Tanganyika in 1907, "maji" being the Swahili word for water.

85. CRISP, *Congo 1965*, pp. 97, 99.

86. Ibid., p. 129.

87. Ibid., p. 132.

88. Ibid., p. 105.

89. Ibid., p. 130.

90. Centre de Recherche et d'Information Socio-Politiques, *Congo 1966* (Brussels: 1967), p. 297.

91. Ibid., p. 299.

92. Ibid., pp. 300-01.

93. A lesson in point here comes from Malaya. Among the five aims Sir Robert Thompson believed a government should follow for successful counterinsurgency, four were political rather than military in nature. Thompson advised governments to 1) establish and maintain a free, independent and united country, 2) function in accordance with law, 3) follow an overall plan, and 4) give first priority to defeating political subversion rather than the guerrillas themselves. Only in his final recommendation—secure government base areas first—did Thompson stress military steps. *Defeating Communist Insurgency*, pp. 51-7. He should have added a further proviso: be ready to spend a great deal of money and time. The emergency in Malaya cost the British and Malayan governments £600 per guerrilla killed, captured, or surrendered; seven years, eighty-five days of combat occurred before an amnesty for MCP guerrillas was proclaimed. Miller, *Jungle War in Malaya*, pp. 17, 181, and 161.

94. Donald Rothchild, *Racial Bargaining in Independent Kenya: A Study of Minorities and Decolonization* (London: Oxford University Press, 1973); Gary Wasserman, *Politics of Decolonization: Kenya Europeans and the Land Issue 1960-1965* (Cambridge: Cambridge University Press, 1976); Colin Leys, *Underdevelopment in Kenya: The Political Economy of Neo-Colonialism 1964-1971* (London: Heinemann, 1975), esp. pp. 63-117.

95. Henry A. Landsberger, "Peasant Unrest: Themes and Variations," in Lands-

berger, ed., *Rural Protest: Peasant Movements and Social Change* (London: Macmillan for the International Institute for Labour Studies, 1974), p. 63.

9/ The Continuity of Protest and the Significance of Politics

1. Henry A. Landsberger, "Peasant Unrest: Themes and Variations," in Landsberger, ed., *Rural Protest: Peasant Movements and Social Change* (London: Macmillan for the International Institute for Labour Studies, 1974), p. 29. Landsberger points to four "crucial" additional factors among the societal changes preceding the establishment of peasant movements: the conversion of landowners into pure rent, tax and service collectors not engaging in farming or performing any other useful function; failure to perform compensatory services for the peasantry, such as protection; the landowners' being generally weak, ineffectual, and functionless relative to the growing central government; and the partial survival of peasant communities, though damaged by the impact of outside forces. (Ibid., pp. 29-30). Landsberger's overall framework — in my view, the most suitable of those extant for comparative research — is weakened only by insufficient attention to political factors, and consequent overemphasis on social and societal factors. (Just the sort of comment, I suspect, that a political scientist would be expected to make about a sociologist.) Landsberger notes that peasant success in achieving substantial change usually required very powerful allies that courted the peasantry, and was due "as much" to the weakness of established elites as to the strength of the revolutionary forces. (Ibid., pp. 60-1) Why were these elites weak? What similarities might be discerned? Were alliances requisite for success of any sort, or contributory to the extent of change? The value of Landsberger's schema would be further heightened by consideration of these questions.

2. S.C. Dube, *Indian Village* (New York: Harper & Row, 1967), p. 223.

3. Ibid., p. 233.

4. Ibid., pp. 72, 74.

5. For further evidence of the ways in which *deshmukh* families retained local leadership and exercised substantial landed power, see Hugh Gray, "The Landed Gentry of the Telengana, Andhra Pradesh," in Edmund Leach and S.N. Mukherjee, eds., *Elites in South Asia* (Cambridge: Cambridge University Press, 1970), pp. 119-35. In Gray's view, ruling village families combine functions as landlord, moneylender, village official representative to government, and politician.

6. Obviously, had the CPI not called a halt to armed struggle in late 1951, it could not have presented candidates for election.

7. In its early days, Congress found support for linguistic provinces a means to curry popular favor and harry the British *raj*. The 1920 Nagpur conference accepted the principle of organizing political jurisdictions on language lines; the 1927 and 1937 party conferences made specific reference to Andhra. One must note, however, that these resolutions were aimed at the Madras presidency of British India, not to the state of Hyderabad then outside Congress's influence.

8. Mohan Ram, "The Communist Movement in Andhra Pradesh," in Paul R. Brass and Marcus E. Franda, eds., *Radical Politics in South Asia* (Cambridge: M.I.T. Press, 1973), pp. 284-92.

9. P. Sundarayya, "Vishala Andhra" (Bombay: People's Publishing House 1946), p. 7.

10. Ibid., p. 9.

11. Government of India, *Report of the States Reorganization Committee* (Delhi: Government Printer, 1955), p. 102.

12. Ibid., p. 107.

13. K. Seshadri, "The Telengana Agitation and the Politics of Andhra Pradesh," *Indian Journal of Political Science* 31, 1 (January-March 1970), p. 72n.

14. For details, see ibid., pp. 67-80, and Romesh Thapar, "Lessons from Telengana," *Economic and Political Weekly*, 4, 25 (21 June 1969). pp. 991-2.

15. According to this agreement, were the chief minister of Andhra Pradesh drawn from the former Andhra State, a deputy chief minister would be selected from Telengana; a Telengana Regional Council would be formed; development funds would be allocated so as to diminish existing disparities; and Telengana residents would have equal access to government employment. *The Telengana Movement: An Investigative Focus* (Hyderabad: Telengana University College and Teachers' Convention, 1969), pp. 143-5.

16. Ibid., p. 17.

17. The transfer of power was complicated by refusal of members of KANU (Kenya African National Union) to participate until Kenyatta was freed from detention. The governor, Sir Patrick Renison, had no desire to deal with the man he castigated as "the recognized leader of the non-co-operation movement which organized Mau Mau...the African leader to darkness and death." Renison turned, for lack of any other alternative, to the minority party KADU (Kenya African Democratic Union), itself a loose coalition of non-Kikuyu, non-Luo groups. The "solution" did not work. The resultant stalemate was resolved only by British retreat: Kenyatta was released from internment in August 1961, chosen president of KANU in October, elected to the Legislative Council in January 1962 and named prime minister in June 1963. By this time, the British more fully sensed that Kenyatta had been able to exercise little control over those who created Mau Mau into an organization of massive, often coerced oathing.

Even more striking evidence comes from Buijtenhuijs. In the first three years after independence, 436 plots of land were given to former Mau Mau fighters. Overall, more than 35,000 families were included in settlement schemes, a figure dwarfed by the 85,000 persons (mostly heads of household) detained during the emergency. For these and other details of seeming neglect, see Robert Buijtenhuijs, *Mau Mau Twenty Years After: The Myth and the Survivors* (The Hague: Mouton, 1973) pp. 122-7.

18. Ngugi Wa Thiong'o and Micere Githae Mugo, *The Trial of Dedan Kimathi* (London: Heinemann, 1977), p. 82.

19. Buijtenhuijs, *Mau Mau Twenty Years After*, p. 131.

20. Oginga Odinga, *Not Yet Uhuru* (London: Heinemann, 1967), pp. 126-7.

21. Jeremy Murray-Brown, *Kenyatta* (London: George Allen & Unwin, 1972), pp. 317-8.

22. Jean-Claude Willame, *Patrimonialism and Political Change in the Congo* (Stanford: Stanford University Press, 1972).

23. *International Herald-Tribune*, 5 May 1978.

24. The MPR followed an approach aptly described by Samuel P. Huntington, *Political Order in Changing Societies* (New Haven: Yale University Press, 1968), pp. 237-63, regarding military leaders' problems in creating mass-based movements from above.

25. Joseph R. Levenson, *Confucian China and its Modern Fate: A Trilogy* (Berkeley: University of California Press, 1968), Vol. II, p. 86.

26. Ping-ti Ho, *Studies on the Population of China, 1368-1953* (Cambridge: Harvard University Press, 1959), p. 275.

27. Quoted in Kung-chuan Hsiao, *Rural China: Imperial Control in the Nineteenth Century* (Seattle: University of Washington Press, 1960), p. 499.

28. Levenson, *Confucian China*, Vol. I, p. 148.

29. Ho, *Studies on the Population of China*, p. 67.

30. Levenson, *Confucian China*, Vol. II, p. 102.

31. Leon Trotsky, *History of the Russian Revolution*, edited by F.W. Dupee (Garden City: Doubleday, 1959), p. 4.

Bibliography

I. Rural Revolt: comparative analyses and case studies

AlRoy, Gil Carl. *The Involvement of Peasants in Internal Wars.* Princeton: Center of International Studies, Princeton University, 1966.

Barkun, Michael. *Disaster and the Millennium.* New Haven: Yale University Press, 1974.

Bequiraj, Mahmet. *Peasantry in Revolution.* Ithaca: Center for International Studies, Cornell University, 1967.

Brinton, Crane. *The Anatomy of Revolution.* New York: Vintage Books, 1965. Revised and Expanded Edition.

Buell, Raymond Leslie. *The Native Problem in Africa.* New York: Macmillan, 1928.

Cantril, Hadley. *The Pattern of Human Concerns.* New Brunswick: Rutgers University Press, 1965.

Cliffe, Lionel. "Rural Class Formation in East Africa." *Journal of Peasant Studies* 4 (1976-77), 195-224.

Clutterbuck, Richard. *Riot and Revolution in Singapore and Malaya 1945-1963.* London: Faber and Faber, 1973.

Cohn, Norman. *The Pursuit of the Milennium: Revolutionary Millenarians and Mystical Anarchists of the Middle Ages.* New York: Oxford University Press, 1970. Revised and Enlarged Edition.

Davidson, Basil. "African Peasants and Revolution." *Journal of Peasant Studies* 1, 3 (April, 1974), 269-90.

Davies, James Chowning, ed. *When Men Revolt and Why: A Reader in Political Violence and Revolution.* New York: The Free Press, 1971.

Deal, Douglas. "Peasant Revolts and Resistance in the Modern World." *Journal of Contemporary Asia* 5, 4, (1975), 414-45.

Duggett, Michael. "Marx on Peasants." *Journal of Peasant Studies* 2, 2 (January 1975), 159-82.

Eisenstadt, S. N. *Revolution and the Transformation of Societies: A Comparative Study of Civilizations.* New York: Free Press, 1978.

Gann, Lewis. *Guerrillas in History,* Stanford: Hoover Institution Press, 1971.

Geneletti, Carlo. "The Political Orientation of Agrarian Classes: A Theory." *Archives Europeennes de Sociologie* 17, 1 (1976), 55-73.

Gluckman, Max. "Rituals of Rebellion in South-East Africa." Manchester: Manchester University Press, 1954.

Gurr, Ted Robert. *Why Men Rebel.* Princeton: Princeton University Press, 1970.

Hagopian, Mark N. *The Phenomenon of Revolution.* New York: Dodd, Mead and Company, 1974.

Heggoy, Alf Andrew. *Insurgency and Counterinsurgency in Algeria.* Bloomington: Indiana University Press, 1972.

Hilton, Rodney. *Bond Men Made Free: Medieval Peasant Movements and the English Rising of 1381.* London: Temple Smith, 1973.

Hobsbawm, E. J. "Peasants and Politics." *Journal of Peasant Studies* 1, 1 (October 1973), 3-22.

— — "Peasant Land Occupations" *Past and Present* 62 (February 1974), 120-52.

— — *Primitive Rebels: Studies in Archaic Forms of Social Movement in the 19th and 20th Centuries.* New York: W. W. Norton and Company, Inc., 1959.

Horne, Alistair. *A Savage War of Peace: Algeria 1954-1962.* London: Macmillan, 1977.

Humbaraci, Arslan. *Algeria: A Revolution that Failed.* London: Pall Mall, 1966.

Hunter, Guy. *Modernizing Peasant Societies: A Comparative Study in Asia and Africa.* London: Oxford University Press, 1969.

Huntington, Samuel P. *Political Order in Changing Societies.* New Haven: Yale University Press, 1968.

Joseph, Richard A. *Radical Nationalism in Cameroun: Social Origins of the U.P.C. Rebellion.* Oxford: Clarendon Press, 1977.

Kerkvliet, Benedict J. *The Huk Rebellion: A Study of Peasant Revolt in the Philippines.* Berkeley: University of California Press, 1977.

Kielstra, Nico. "Was the Algerian Revolution a Peasant War?" *Peasant Studies* 7, 3 (Summer 1978), 172-86.

Landsberger, Harry S., ed. *Latin American Peasant Movements.* Ithaca: Cornell University Press, 1969.

— —, ed. *Rural Protest: Peasant Movements and Social Change.* London: International Institute for Labour Studies, 1974.

Lanternari, Vittorio. *The Religions of the Oppressed: A Study of Modern Messianic Cults.* New York: Mentor, 1965.

Leites, Nathan and Wolfe, Charles, Jr., *Rebellion and Authority: An Analytic Essay on Insurgent Conflicts* (Chicago: Markham, 1970).

Lewy, Gunther. *Religion and Revolution.* New York: Oxford University Press, 1974.

Longworth, Philip, "Peasant Leadership and the Pugachev Revolt." *Journal of Peasant Studies* 2, 2 (January 1975), 183-205.

Marks, Shula. *Reluctant Rebellion: The 1906-1908 Disturbances in Natal.* Oxford: Clarendon Press, 1970.

Migdal, Joel S. *Peasants, Politics, and Revolution: Pressures Toward Political and Social Change in the Third World.* Princeton: Princeton University Press, 1974.

Miller, Harry. *Jungle War in Malaya: The Campaign Against Communism 1948-1960.* London: Arthur Barker, 1972.

Mitchell, Edward J. "The Econometrics of the Huk Rebellion." *American Political Science Review* 63, 4 (December 1969), 1159-71.

— — "Inequality and Insurgency: A Statistical Study of South Vietnam." *World Politics* 20, 3 (April 1968), 421-38.

Moore, Barrington, Jr. *Social Origins of Dictatorship and Democracy: Lord and Peasant in the Making of the Modern World*. Boston: Beacon Press, 1966.

Nieburg, H. L. *Political Violence: The Behavioral Process*. New York: St. Martin's, 1969.

O'Ballance, Edgar. *The Algerian Insurrection, 1954-62*. London: Faber, 1967.

Paige, Jeffrey M. *Agrarian Revolution: Social Movements and Export Agriculture in the Underdeveloped World*. New York: The Free Press, 1975.

Perinbam, B. Marie. "Fanon and the Myth of the Revolutionary Peasantry—the Algerian Case." *Journal of Modern African Studies* 11, 3 (September 1973), 427-45.

Potter, Jack M., Diaz, May N., and Foster, George M., eds. *Peasant Society: A Reader*. Boston: Little, Brown and Company, 1967.

Powell, John Duncan. "The Adequacy of Social Science Models for the Study of Peasant Movements." *Comparative Politics* 8, 3 (April 1976), 327-37.

Prosterman, Roy L. " 'IRI': A Simplified Predictive Index of Rural Instability." *Comparative Politics* 8, 3 (April 1976), 339-53.

Ranger, T. O. *Revolt in Southern Rhodesia, 1896-7: A Study in African Resistance*. London: Heinemann, 1967.

Rotberg, Robert I., ed. *Rebellion in Black Africa*. London: Oxford University Press, 1971.

Rudé, George. *The Crowd in History: A Study of Popular Disturbances in France and England, 1730-1845*. New York: Wiley, 1964.

— — *Paris and London in the Eighteenth Century: Studies in Popular Protest*. New York: Viking, 1973.

Sansom, Robert L. *The Economics of Insurgency in the Mekong Delta of Vietnam*. Cambridge: M.I.T. Press, 1970.

Saul, J. S. "African Peasants and Revolution." *Review of African Political Economy* 1, 1 (October-December 1974), 41-68.

Scheiner, Irwin. "The Mindful Peasant: Sketches for a Study of Rebellion." *Journal of Asian Studies* 32, 4 (August 1973), 579-91.

Scott, James C. *The Moral Economy of the Peasant: Rebellion and Subsistence in Southeast Asia*. New Haven: Yale University Press, 1976.

Short, James F., Jr. and Marvin E. Wolfgang. *Collective Violence*. Chicago: Aldine-Atherton, 1972.

Smelser, Neil J. *Theory of Collective Behavior*. London: Routledge & Kegan Paul, 1962.

Thompson, Sir Robert. *Defeating Communist Insurgency: Experiences from Malaya and Vietnam*. London: Chatto and Windus, 1966.

Tilly, Charles. *The Vendee: A Sociological Analysis of the Counter-revolution of 1793*. New York: John Wiley and Sons, Inc., 1967.

Tronchon, Jacques. *L'Insurrection malgache de 1947*. Paris: Maspero, 1974.

Venturi, Franco. *Roots of Revolution: A History of the Populist and Socialist Movements in Nineteenth Century Russia*, translated by Francis Haskell. New York: Grosset and Dunlap, 1966.

Walter, Eugene Victor. *Terror and Resistance: A Study of Political Violence*. New York: Oxford University Press, 1969.

Welch, Claude E., Jr. "Obstacles to Peasant Warfare in Africa." *African Studies Review* 20, 3 (December 1977), 121-30.

—— "Warrior, Rebel, Guerrilla, and Putschist: Four Aspects of Political Violence." In *The Warrior Tradition in Africa*, edited by Ali A. Mazrui. Leiden: Brill, 1977.

Wolf, Eric R. *Peasants*. Englewood Cliffs: Prentice-Hall, Inc., 1966.

—— *Peasant Wars of the Twentieth Century* New York: Harper and Row, 1969.

II. Rural Revolts in China

Chang, Chung-Li. *The Income of the Chinese Gentry*. Seattle: University of Washington Press, 1962.

Cheng, J. C. *Chinese Sources for the Taiping Rebellion 1850-1864*. Hong Kong: Hong Kong University Press, 1963.

Chesneaux, Jean, Fei-ling Davis and Nguyen Nguyet Ho. *Mouvements populaires et sociétés secrètes en Chine aux xixe et xxe siecles*. Paris: Maspero, 1970. Also published in English as Jean Chesneaux, ed., *Popular Movements and Secret Societies in China, 1840-1950*. Stanford: Stanford University Press, 1972.

—— *Secret Societies in China*, trans. Gillian Nettle. London: Heinemann, 1971.

Curwen, C. A. *Taiping Rebel: The Deposition of Li Hsiu-ch'eng*. Cambridge: Cambridge University Press, 1977.

Davis, Fei-ling. *Primitive Revolutionaries of China: A Study of Secret Societies in the Late Nineteenth Century*. London: Routledge & Kegan Paul, 1977.

Elvin, Mark. *The Pattern of the Chinese Past*. London: Eyre Methuen, 1973.

Feuerwerker, Albert. "China's History in Marxian Dress." *American Historical Review* 66, 2 (January 1961), 323-53.

——. "Rebellion in Nineteenth-Century China." Ann Arbor: Center for Chinese Studies, University of Michigan, 1975.

Friedman, Edward. *Backward Toward Revolution: The Chinese Revolutionary Party*. Berkeley: University of California Press, 1974.

Gregory, J. S. *Great Britain and the Taipings*. London: Routledge & Kegan Paul, 1969.

Hall, William James. *Tseng Kuo-fan and the Taiping Rebellion*. New York: Paragon, 1964 (reprint of the 1927 edition of Yale University Press).

Harrison, James P. *The Communists and Chinese Peasant Rebellions: A Study in the Rewriting of Chinese History*. New York: Atheneum, 1969.

Ho, Ping-Ti. *The Ladder of Success in Imperial China: Aspects of Social Mobility, 1368-1911*. New York: John Wiley & Sons, Inc., 1964.

—— *Studies on the Population of China, 1368-1953*. Cambridge: Harvard University Press, 1959.

Hsiao, Kung-chuan. *Rural China: Imperial Control in the Nineteenth Century*. Seattle: University of Washington Press, 1960.

Jen Yu-Wen. *The Taiping Revolutionary Movement*. New Haven: Yale University Press, 1973.

Jones, Susan Mann and Philip A. Kuhn. "Dynastic Decline and the Roots of Rebellion." In *The Cambridge History of China*, Vol. 10, Part I, edited by John K. Fairbank. Cambridge: Cambridge University Press, 1978.

Kuhn, Philip A. *Rebellion and its Enemies in Late Imperial China: Militarization and Social Structure, 1796-1864*. Cambridge: Harvard University Press, 1970.

—— "The Taiping Rebellion." In *The Cambridge History of China*, Vol. 10, Part I, edited by John K. Fairbank. Cambridge: Cambridge University Press, 1978.

Laffey, Ella S. "In the Wake of the Taipings: Some Patterns of Local Revolt in Kwangsi Province, 1850-1875." *Modern Asian Studies* 10, 1 (January 1976), 65-81.

Levenson, Joseph R. *Confucian China and its Modern Fate: A Trilogy*. Berkeley: University of California Press, 1968.

Michael, Franz. *The Taiping Rebellion: History and Documents*. 3 vols. Seattle: University of Washington Press, 1966, 1971

Muramatsu, Yuji. "Some Themes in Chinese Rebel Ideologies." In *The Confucian Persuasion*, edited by Arthur F. Wright. Stanford: Stanford University Press, 1960.

Naquin, Susan. *Millenarian Rebellion in China: The Eight Trigrams Uprising of 1813*. New Haven: Yale University Press, 1976.

Selden, Mark. *The Yenan Way in Revolutionary China*. Cambridge: Harvard University Press, 1971.

Shih, Vincent Y. C. *The Taiping Ideology: Its Sources, Interpretations, and Influences*. Seattle: University of Washington Press, 1967.

Tawney, R. H. *Land and Labour in China*. London: George Allen & Unwin, 1932.

Teng, Ssu-Yu. *Historiography of the Taiping Rebellion*. Cambridge: East Asian Research Center, 1962.

—— *The Nien Army and their Guerilla Warfare*. The Hague: Mouton, 1961.

—— *The Taiping Rebellion and the Western Powers: A Comprehensive Survey*. Oxford: Oxford University Press, 1971.

Thaxton, Ralph, "Some Critical Comments on Peasant Revolts and Revolutions in China." *Journal of Asian Studies* 33, 2 (February 1974), 279-88.

—— "Tenants in Revolution: The Tenacity of Traditional Morality." *Modern China* 1, 3 (July 1975), 323-58.

Wakeman, Frederick Jr. "Rebellion and Revolution: The Study of Popular Movements in Chinese History," *Journal of Asian Studies* 36, 2 (February 1977), 201-37.

—— *Strangers at the Gate: Social Disorder in South China, 1839-1861*. Berkeley: University of California Press, 1966.

Weems, Benjamin B. *Reform, Rebellion, and the Heavenly Way*. Tucson: University of Arizona Press, 1964.

Wright, Mary C. *The Last Stand of Chinese Conservatism: The T'ung-chih Restoration, 1862-1914*. Stanford: Stanford University Press, 1957.

III. Hyderabad and the Telengana Uprising

Ahmed, Zahir. *Dusk and Dawn in Village India*. New York: Praeger, 1965.

Alavi, Hamza. "Peasants and Revolution." In *Imperialism and Revolution in South Asia*, edited by Kathleen Gough and Hari P. Sharma. New York: Monthly Review Press, 1973.

Ali, Mir Laik. *Tragedy of Hyderabad.* Karachi: Pakistan Cooperative Book Society, n.d.

Barton, William. *The Princes of India.* London: Nisbet, 1934.

Bedford, Ian. *The Telengana Insurrection: A Study in the Causes and Development of a Communist Insurrection in Rural India, 1946-51.* Unpublished Ph.D. thesis. Australian National University, December 1967.

Bhargava, G. S. "A Study of the Communist Movement in Andhra." Delhi: Siddhartha Publications, 1955.

Brass, Paul R. and Franda, Marcus E., eds. *Radical Politics in South Asia.* Cambridge: M.I.T. Press, 1973.

The Complaint of Hyderabad Against the Dominion of India Under Article 35(2) of the Charter of the United Nations. London: Waterlow, 1948.

Dhanagare, D. N. "Agrarian Conflict, Religion and Politics: The Moplah Rebellions in Malabar in the Nineteenth and Early Twentieth Centuries. *Past and Present* 74 (February 1977) 112-41.

— — "Peasant Protest and Politics—the Tebhaga Movement in Bengal (India), 1943-47." *Journal of Peasant Studies* 3, 3 (April 1976) 360-78.

— — "Social Origins of the Peasant Insurrection in Telengana (1946-51)." *Contributions to Indian Sociology* 8 (1974), 109-34.

Donaldson, Robert H. *Soviet Policy Toward India: Ideology and Strategy.* Cambridge: Harvard University Press, 1974.

Druhe, David N. *Soviet Russia and Indian Communism.* New York: Bookman Associates, 1959.

Dube, S. C. *Indian Village.* New York: Harper & Row, 1967.

Elliott, Carolyn M. "Decline of a Patrimonial Regime: The Telengana Rebellion in India 1946-51." *Journal of Asian Studies* 34, 1 (November 1974), 27-47.

— — *Participation in an Expanding Polity: A Study of Andhra Pradesh, India.* Unpublished Ph.D. Thesis, Harvard University, September 1962.

Frykenberg, Robert Eric, ed. *Land Control and Social Structure in Indian History.* Madison: University of Wisconsin Press, 1969.

Gough, Kathleen. "Indian Peasant Uprisings." *Economic and Political Weekly* 9, 32-34 (August 1974), 1391-1412.

— — "Peasant Resistance and Revolt in South India." *Pacific Affairs* 41, 4 (Winter 1968-69), 526-44.

Gray, Hugh. "The Demand for a Separate Telengana State in India." *Asian Survey* 11, 5 (May 1971), 463-74.

— — "The Failure of the Demand for a Separate Andhra State." *Asian Survey* 14, 4 (April 1974), 338-49.

— — "The Landed Gentry of the Telengana, Andhra Pradesh." In *Elites in South Asia*, edited by Edmund Leach and S. N. Mukherjee. Cambridge: Cambridge University Press, 1970.

— — "The 1962 Indian General Election in a Communist Stronghold in Andhra Pradesh." *Journal of Commonwealth Political Studies*, I, 4 (1963), 296-311.

Harrison, Selig. "Caste and the Andhra Communists," *American Political Science Review* 50, 2 (June 1956), 378-404.

— — *India: The Most Dangerous Decades.* Princeton: Princeton University Press, 1960.

Hutton, J. H. *Caste in India: Its Nature, Function, and Origins*. Bombay: Oxford University Press, 1963, Fourth edition.

Ismail, Sir Mirza. *My Public Life: Recollections and Reflections*. London: George Allen and Unwin, 1954.

Iyengar, S. Kesava. *Economic Investigations in the Hyderabad State, 1929-30*. Vol. I. Hyderabad: Government Central Press, 1931.

— — *Rural Economic Enquiries in the Hyderabad State, 1949-51*. Hyderabad: Government Press, 1951.

Joshi, P. C. "The Indian Communist Party: Its Policy and Work in the War of Liberation." London: Communist Party of Great Britain, 1942.

Kautsky, John H. *Moscow and the Communist Party of India: A Study in the Postwar Evolution of International Communist Strategy*. New York: Technology Press of the Massachusetts Institute of Technology and John Wiley & Sons, 1956.

Lee-Warner, William. *The Native States of India*. London: Macmillan, 1910.

Menon, V. P. *The Story of the Integration of the Indian States*. London: Longmans, 1956.

Moon, Penderel. *Divide and Quit*. London: Chatto & Windus, 1961.

Munshi, K. N. *The End of an Era: Hyderabad Memories*. Bombay: Bharatiya Vidya Bhavan, 1957.

Nair, Kusum. *Blossoms in the Dust: The Human Element in Indian Development*. London: Duckworth, 1961.

Namboodripad, E.M.S. "On the Agrarian Question in India." Bombay: People's Publishing House, 1952.

Narayan, B. K. *Agricultural Development in Hyderabad State 1900-1956: A Study in Economic History*. Secunderabad: Keshav Prakashan, n.d.

Natarajan, L. "Peasant Uprisings in India 1850-1900." Bombay: People's Publishing House, 1953.

Overstreet, Gene D. and Windmiller, Marshall. *Communism in India*. Berkeley: University of California Press, 1960.

Pavier, Barry. "The Telengana Armed Struggle." *Economic and Political Weekly* 9, 32-34 (August 1974), 1413-20.

Qureshi, Anwar Iqbal. *The Economic Development of Hyderabad*, Vol. I Rural Economy. Bombay: Orient Longmans, 1947.

Ram, Mohan. "The Communist Movement in Andhra Pradesh." In *Radical Politics in South Asia*, edited by Paul R. Brass and Marcus E. Franda. Cambridge: M.I.T. Press, 1973.

— — *Maoism in India*. New York: Barnes and Noble, 1971.

— — "The Telengana Peasant Armed Struggle, 1946-51." *Economic and Political Weekly* 8, 23 (9 June 1973), 1025-32.

Ramesan, N., ed. *The Freedom Struggle in Hyderabad* (four volumes). Andhra State Committee Appointed for the Compilation of a History of the Freedom Struggle in Andhra Pradesh, n.d.

Ranga, N. G. *Fight for Freedom*. Delhi: S. Chand, 1968.

Rao, M. B., ed. *Documents of the History of the Communist Party of India*, Vol. VII, 1948-50. New Delhi: People's Publishing House, 1976.

Report of the Indian States Committee 1928-1929. London: HMSO, 1929. Cmd. 3302.

Report of the States Reorganization Committee. Delhi: Government Printer, 1955.

Seal, Anil. "Imperialism and Nationalism in India." *Modern Asian Studies*

7, 3 (July 1973), 321-47.

Seshadri, K. "The Telengana Agitation and the Politics of Andhra Pradesh." *Indian Journal of Political Science* 31, 1 (January-March 1970), 60-81.

Singh, Gurmukh Nihal. *Indian States and British India: Their Future Relations.* Benares: Nand Kishore, n.d.

Smith, Wilfred Cantwell. "Hyderabad: Muslim Tragedy." *Middle East Journal* 4, 1 (January 1950), 27-51.

Stokes, Eric. *The Peasant and the Raj: Studies in Agrarian Society and Peasant Rebellion.* Cambridge: Cambridge University Press, 1978.

— — "Traditional Resistance Movements and Afro-Asian Nationalism: The Context of the 1857 Mutiny in India." *Past and Present* 45 (August 1970), 100-18.

Sundarayya, P. *Telengana People's Struggle and its Lessons.* Calcutta: Desraj Chadha for CPI (M), 1972.

— — "Vishala Andhra," Bombay: People's Publishing House, 1946.

Thapar, Romesh. *Storm over Hyderabad.* Bombay: Kutub, 1948.

Wiser, William H. and Charlotte V. *Behind Mud Walls, 1930-1960: With a Sequel, The Village in 1970.* Berkeley: University of California Press, 1971.

Wood, Conrad. "The First Moplah Rebellion against British Rule in Malabar." *Modern Asian Studies* 10, 4 (1976), 543-56.

— — "Peasant Revolt: An Interpretation of Moplah Violence in the Nineteenth and Twentieth Centuries." In *The Imperial Impact: Studies in the Economic History of Africa and India,* edited by Clive Dewey and A. G. Hopkins. London: Athlone Press, 1978.

Zagoria, Donald S. "The Ecology of Peasant Communism in India." *American Political Science Review* 65, 1 (March 1971), 144-60.

— — "The Social Bases of Indian Communism." In *Issues in the Future of Asia,* edited by Richard Lowenthal. New York: Praeger, 1969.

IV. The Kikuyu and the Mau Mau Uprising

Atieno-Odhiambo, E. S. "The Rise and Decline of the Kenya Peasant, 1888-1922." *East Africa Journal,* 9, 5 (May 1972), 11-15.

Barnett, Donald L. and Karari, Njama. *Mau Mau from Within: Autobiography and Analysis of Kenya's Peasant Revolt.* London: Macgibbon & Kee, 1966.

Bennett, George and Smith, Alison. "Kenya: From 'White Man's Country' to Kenyatta's State 1945-1963." In *History of East Africa,* Vol. III, edited by D. A. Low and Alison Smith. Oxford: Clarendon Press, 1976.

Berman, Bruce J. "Bureaucracy and Incumbent Violence: Colonial Administration and the Origins of the 'Mau Mau' Emergency in Kenya." *British Journal of Political Science* 6, 2 (April 1976), 143-75.

Blundell, Sir Michael. *So Rough a Wind.* London: Weidenfeld & Nicolson, 1964.

Brett, E. A. *Colonialism and Underdevelopment in East Africa: The Politics of Economic Change, 1919-39.* London: Heinemann, 1973.

Buijtenhuijs, Robert. *Mau Mau Twenty Years After: The Myth and the Survivors.* The Hague: Mouton, 1973.

— — *Le Mouvement "Mau-Mau": Une révolte paysanne et anti-coloniale en Afrique noire.* Paris: Mouton, 1971.

Carothers, J. C. "The Psychology of Mau Mau." Nairobi: Government Printer, 1954.

Clayton, Anthony. *Counter-insurgency in Kenya: A Study of Military Operations against Mau Mau.* Nairobi: Transafrica Publishers Ltd., 1976.

Clayton, Anthony and Savage, Donald C. *Government and Labour in Kenya 1895-1963.* London: Frank Cass, 1974.

Clough, Marshall Sander and Jackson, Kennell Ardoway. *A Bibliography on Mau Mau.* Stanford: 1975.

Corfield, F. C. *Historical Survey of the Origins and Growth of Mau Mau.* London: HMSO, 1960.

Douglas-Home, Charles. *Evelyn Baring: The Last Pro-Consul.* London: Collins, 1978.

Electors Union of Kenya. *An Outline of Policy for the Colony and Protectorate of Kenya.* Nairobi: W. Boyd, 1946.

Foran, W. Robert. *The Kenya Police 1887-1960.* London: Hale, 1962.

Furedi, Frank. "The African Crowd in Nairobi: Popular Movements and Elite Politics." *Journal of African History* 14, 2 (1973), 275-90.

— — "The Kikuyu Squatters in the Rift Valley: 1918-1929." In *Economic and Social History of East Africa,* edited by Bethwell A. Ogot. Nairobi: East African Literature Bureau, 1975.

— — "The Social Composition of the Mau Mau Movement in the White Highlands." *Journal of Peasant Studies,* I, 4 (1974), 486-505.

Furley, O. W. "The Historiography of Mau Mau." In *Politics and Nationalism in Colonial Kenya,* edited by Bethwell A. Ogot. Nairobi: East Africa Publishing House, 1972.

Henderson, Ian (with Goodhart, Philip), *The Hunt for Kimathi.* London: Hamish Hamilton, 1958.

History of the Loyalists. Nairobi: Government Printer, 1961.

"Indians in Kenya." London: HMSO, 1923. Cmd. 1922.

Itote, Waruhiu. *"Mau Mau" General.* Nairobi: East Africa Publishing House, 1967.

Kabiro, Ngugi. *Man in the Middle: The Story of Ngugi Kabiro.* Richmond, B.C., Canada: LSM Press, 1973.

Kaggia, Bildad. *Roots of Freedom 1921-1963.* Nairobi: East Africa Publishing House, 1975.

Kariuki, Josiah Mwangi. *'Mau Mau' Detainee: The Account by a Kenya African of his Experiences in Detention Camps 1953-1960.* London: Oxford University Press, 1963.

Kenyatta, Jomo. *Facing Mount Kenya: The Tribal Life of the Gikuyu.* London: Secker & Warburg, 1961.

"The Kikuyu Who Fight Mau Mau." Nairobi: Eagle Press, 1955.

Lamb, Geoff. *Peasant Politics: Conflict and Development in Murang'a.* Lewes: Friedman, 1974.

Leakey, L. S. B. *Defeating Mau Mau.* London: Methuen, 1954.

Leys, Colin. *Underdevelopment in Kenya: The Political Economy of Neo-Colonialism 1964-1971.* London: Heinemann, 1975.

Lonsdale, J. M. "European Attitudes and African Pressures: Missions and Government in Kenya between the Wars." *Race*, 10, 2 (1968), 141-51.

Low, D. A. and Smith, Alison eds. *History of East Africa*, Vol. III. Oxford: Clarendon Press, 1976.

Majdalany, Fred. *State of Emergency: The Full Story of Mau Mau*. London: Longmans, 1962.

Mathu, Mohamed. *The Urban Guerrilla: The Story of Mohamed Mathu*. Richmond, B. C., Canada: LSM Press, 1974.

Mitchell, Sir Philip. *African Afterthoughts*. London: Hutchinson, 1954.

Muchai, Karigo. *The Hard Core: The Story of Karigo Muchai*. Richmond: B.C., Canada: LSM Press, 1973.

Munro, J. Forbes. *Colonial Rule and the Kamba: Social Change in the Kenya Highlands 1889-1939*. Oxford: Clarendon Press, 1975.

Muriithi, J. Koboi (with Ndoria, Peter). *War in the Forest: The Autobiography of a Mau Mau Leader*. Nairobi: East Africa Publishing House, 1971.

Muriuki, Godfrey. *A History of the Kikuyu, 1500-1900*. Nairobi: Oxford University Press, 1974.

Murray-Brown, Jeremy. *Kenyatta*. London: George Allen and Unwin Ltd., 1972.

Mwangi, Meja. *Carcase for Hounds*. London: Heinemann, 1974.

Ngugi Wa Thiong'o. *Petals of Blood*. London: Heinemann, 1977.

Odinga, Oginga. *Not Yet Uhuru*. London: Heinemann, 1967.

Ogot, Bethwell A. "Revolt of the Elders: An Anatomy of the Loyalist Crowd in the Mau Mau Uprising 1952-1956." In *Politics and Nationalism in Colonial Kenya*, edited by Ogot. Nairobi: East Africa Publishing House, 1972.

Pirouet, Louise. "Armed Resistance and Counter-Insurgency: Reflections on the Anya Nya and Mau Mau Experiences." *Journal of Asian and African Studies* 12, 1-4 (January & October 1977), 197-214.

"Policy of the European Elected Members Organization," mimeographed, 4 November 1953.

Rawcliffe, D. H. *The Struggle for Kenya*. London: Victor Gollancz, 1954.

Report to the Secretary of State for the Colonies, by Parliamentary Delegation to Kenya, January 1954. London: HMSO, 1954. Cmd. 9801.

Rosberg, Carl G., Jr., and Nottingham, John. *The Myth of "Mau Mau": Nationalism in Kenya*. New York: Frederick A. Praeger for the Hoover Institution on War, Revolution, and Peace, 1966.

Rothchild, Donald. *Racial Bargaining in Independent Kenya: A Story of Minorities and Decolonization*. London: Oxford University Press, 1973.

Santilli, Kathy. "Kikuyu Women in the Mau Mau Revolt: A Closer Look." *Ufahamu*, 8, 1 (1977), 143-59.

Singh, Makhan. *History of Kenya's Trade Union Movement to 1952*. Nairobi: East Africa Publishing House, 1969.

Slater, Montagu. *The Trial of Jomo Kenyatta*. London: Secker & Warburg, 1955.

Sorrenson, M. P. K. *Land Reform in the Kikuyu Country: A Study in Government Policy*. Nairobi: Oxford University Press, 1967.

— — *Origins of European Settlement in Kenya*. Nairobi: Oxford University Press, 1968.

Spencer, John. "KAU anad Mau Mau," unpublished paper presented to conference on Political Economy of Colonial Kenya, Cambridge (U.K.), 26-29. June 1975.

Stichter, S. "The Formation of a Working Class in Kenya." In *The Development of an African Working Class: Studies in Class Formation and Action*, edited by Richard Sandbrook and Robin Cohen. London: Longmans, 1975.

— — "Workers, Trade Unions, and the Mau Mau Rebellion." *Canadian Journal of African Studies* 9, 2 (1975), 259-75.

Tignor, Robert L. *The Colonial Transformation of Kenya: The Kamba, Kikuyu, and Maasai from 1900 to 1939*. Princeton: Princeton University Press, 1976.

Wasserman, Gary. *Politics of Decolonization: Kenya Europeans and the Land Issue 1960-1965*. Cambridge: Cambridge University Press, 1976.

Welbourn, F. B. *East African Rebels: A Study of Some Independent Churches*. London: SCM Press, 1961.

Wipper, Audrey. *Rural Rebels: A Study of Two Protest Movements in Kenya*. Nairobi: Oxford University Press, 1977.

Wylie, Diane. "Confrontation over Kenya: The Colonial Office and its Critics, 1918-1940." *Journal of African History* 18, 3 (1977), 427-77.

V. The Kwilu Rebellion

Andersson, Efram. *Messianic Popular Movements in the Lower Congo*. Uppsala: Almquist & Wiksells, 1958.

Centre de Recherche et d'Information Socio-Politiques. *Congo 1959*. Brussels: CRISP, 1960.

— — *Congo 1960*, 2 vols. Brussels: CRISP, 1961.

— — *Congo 1961*. Brussels: CRISP, 1962.

— — *Congo 1962*. Brussels: CRISP, 1963.

— — *Congo 1963*. Brussels: CRISP, 1964.

— — *Congo 1964*. Brussels: CRISP, 1965.

— — *Congo 1965*. Brussels: CRISP, 1966.

— — *Congo 1966*. Brussels: CRISP, 1967.

— — *Congo 1967*. Brussels: CRISP, 1969.

— — *A.B.A.K.O.* 1950-60. Brussels: 1962.

Chome, Jules. *L'ascension de Mobutu*. Brussels: Editions Complexe, 1974.

Fox, Renée C., De Craemer, Willy and Ribeaucourt, Jean-Marie. "The 'Second Independence': A Case Study of the Kwilu Rebellion in the Congo." *Comparative Studies in Society and History* 8, 1 (October 1965), 78-109.

Hoskyns, Catherine. *The Congo Since Independence June 1960 - December 1961*. London: Oxford University Press, 1963.

Jeffries, Richard. "Political Radicalism in Africa: 'The Second Independence.' " *African Affairs* 77 (July 1978), 335-46.

La Fontaine, J. S. *City Politics: A Study of Leopoldville, 1962-63*. Cambridge: Cambridge University Press, 1970.

Lemarchand, Rene. *Political Awakening in the Belgian Congo*. Berkeley: University of California Press, 1964.

Nkemdirim, Bernard A. "Reflections on Political Conflict, Rebellion and Revolution in Africa." *Journal of Modern African Studies* 15, 1 (March 1977), 75-90.

Nicolai, Henri. *Le Kwilu: Etude géographique d'une region congolaise*. Brussels: Centre scientifique et medical de l'Université Libre de Bruselles en Afrique Centrale, 1963.

Ryckmans, Pierre. *Dominer pour servir*. Brussels: Edition Universelle, 1948.

Sinda, Martial. *Le Messianisme Congolais*. Paris: Payot, 1972.

Verhaegen, Benoit. *Rebellions au Congo*, Tome I. Brussels: Centre de Recherche et d'Information Socio-Politiques, 1966.

Weiss, Herbert F. *Political Protest in the Congo: The Parti Solidaire Africain During the Independence Struggle*. Princeton: Princeton University Press, 1967.

Weiss, Herbert and Verhaegen, Benoit. *Parti Solidaire Africain (P.S.A.): Documents 1959-1960*. Brussels: Centre de Recherche et d'Information Socio-Politiques, 1963.

Welch, Claude E., Jr. "Ideological Foundations of Revolution in Kwilu." *African Studies Review*, 18, 2 (September 1975), 116-28.

Willame, J. C. *Les Provinces de Congo, Structure et Fonctionnement*. Leopoldville: Institut de Recherches Economiques et Sociales, Cahiers Economiques et Sociaux, 1964.

— — *Patrimonialism and Political Change in the Congo*. Stanford: Stanford University Press, 1972.

Young, Crawford. *Politics in the Congo: Decolonization and Independence*. Princeton: Princeton University Press, 1965.

— — "Rebellion and the Congo." In *Rebellion in Black Africa*, edited by Robert I. Rotberg. London: Oxford University Press, 1971.

Index